A

HISTORY

OF THE

VALLEY OF VIRGINIA.

By Samuel Kercheval.

SECOND EDITION:

REVISED AND EXTENDED BY THE AUTHOR.

WOODSTOCK, VA.

JOHN GATEWOOD, PRINTER.

1850.

Entered according to act of Congress, in the year 1833, in the Clerk's Office of the Western District of Virginia.

DEDICATION.

TO GENERAL JOHN SMITH.

LIKE Nestor of old, you have lived to see "two generations pass away, and now remain the example of the third." You saw Dunmore's war with the Indians in 1774; you witnessed the war of the Revolution and the war of 1812, with the haughty Briton. In all these great struggles of our country, you have given the most conclusive evidence of unbending virtue and uncompromising patriotism. The author has had the gratification of knowing you for a full half century.— When a small boy he frequently saw you, though he was then too young to attract your notice, and it was not until he entered upon the active duties of life that he had the high satisfaction of a personal acquaintance.

The author disclaims every thing like insincere flattery, and feels assured that your candor will readily pardon him for the freedom he uses in his dedication of his History of the Valley to you. To you, sir, is he indebted for much of the valuable information detailed in the following pages.— In you, sir, he has witnessed the calm, dignified statesman and philosopher, the uniform and consistent republican, the active and zealous officer, whether in the field or councils of the country. He has witnessed more: he has seen you in high pecuniary prosperity; he has seen you in later years struggling with adverse fortune; and in all, has discovered the calm, dignified resignation to misfortune, which always characterises the great and the good man. Yes, sir, you have spent at least fifty years of your valuable life in the service of your country; and when you go hence, that you may enter into the joy of your Lord, is the fervent prayer of

THE AUTHOR.

INTRODUCTION.

ORIGIN OF THE INDIANS IN AMERICA.

From what particular part of the old world the aboriginals found their way to this continent, is a question which has given rise to much philosophical and learned disquisition among historians. It however appears now to be the settled opinion that America first received its inhabitants from Asia. Mr. Snowden, in his History of America, advances many able and ingenious arguments in support of this opinion. After citing many great revolutions which have from time to time taken place in various parts of our globe, Mr. Snowden states:

"In the strait which separates America from Asia, many islands are found, which are supposed to be the mountainous parts of land, formerly swallowed up by earthquakes: which appears the more probable, by the multitude of volcanoes, now known in the peninsula of Kamtschatka.—It is imagined, however, that the sinking of that land and the separation of the new continents, has been occasioned by those great earthquakes, mentioned in the history of the Americans; which formed an era almost as memorable as that of the deluge. We can form no conjecture of the time mentioned in the histories of the Taltecas, or of the year 1, (Tecpatl,) when that great calamity happened.

"If a great earthquake should overwhelm the isthmus of Suez, and there should be at the same time as great a scarcity of historians as there was in the first age of the deluge, it would be doubted in three or four hundred years after, whether Asia had ever been united by that part of Africa; and many would finally deny it.

"Whether that great event, the separation of the continents, took place before or after the population of America, it is impossible to determine; but we are indebted to the above-mentioned navigators, [Cook and others,] for settling the long dispute about the point from which it was effected. Their observations prove, that in one place the distance between continent and continent is only thirty-nine miles; and in the middle of this narrow strait, there are two islands, which would greatly facilitate the passage of the Asiatics into the new world, supposing it took place in canoes, after the convulsion which rent the two continents asunder.

"It may also be added, that these straits are, even in the summer, often filled with ice; in winter frozen over, so as to admit a passage for mankind, and by which quadrupeds might easily cross, and stock the continent. But where, from the vast expanse of the north-eastern world, to fix on the first tribes who contributed to people the new continent, now inhabited from end to end, is a matter that has baffled human reason. The learneed may make bold and ingenious conjectures, but plain good sense cannot always accede to them.

"As mankind increased in numbers, they naturally protruded one another forward. Wars might be another cause of migrations. No reason appears why the Asiatic north might not be an *officina virorum* as well as the European. The overteeming country to the east of the Riphean mountains, must have found it necessary to discharge its inhabitants : the first great increase of people were forced forwards by the next to it : at length reaching the utmost limits of the old world, found a new, with ample space to occupy unmolested for ages; till Columbus, in an evil hour for them, discovered their country; which brought again new sins and new deaths to both worlds. It is impossible, with the lights which we have so recently received, to admit that America could have received its inhabitants (that is, the bulk of them,) from any other place than Eastern Asia. A few proofs may be added, taken from the customs or dresses, common to the inhabitants of both worlds. Some have been long extinct in the old, others remain in full force in both.

" The custom of scalping was a barbarism in use among the Scythians, who carried about them at all times this savage mark of triumph. A little image found among the Kalmucs,* of a Tartarian deity, mounted on a horse, and sitting on a human skin, with scalps pendant from the breast, fully illustrates the custom of the ancient Scythians, as described by the Greek historian. This usage, we well know by horrid experience, is continued to this day in America. The ferocity of the Scythians to their prisoners, extended to the remotest part of Asia. The Kamtskatkans, even at the time of their discovery by the Russians, put their prisoners to death by the most lingering and excruciating torments; a practice now in full force among the aboriginal Americans. A race of the Scythians were named Anthropophagi, from their feeding on human flesh : the people of Nootka sound still make a repast on their fellow creatures.

"The savages of North America have been known to throw the mangled limbs of their prisoners into the horrible cauldron, and devour them with the same relish as those of a quadruped. The Kamtskatkans in their marches never went abreast, but followed one another in the same track: the same custom is still observed by the uncultivated natives of North America. The Tungusi, the most numerous nation resident in Siberia, prick their skins with small punctures, in various shapes, with a needle; then rub them with charcoal, so that the marks become indellible: this custom is still observed in several parts of South America. The Tungusi use canoes made of birch bark, distended over ribs of wood, and nicely put together: the Canadian, and many other primitive American nations, use no other sort of boats. In fine, the conjectures of the learned, respecting the vicinity of the old and new world, are now, by the discoveries of late navigators, lost in conviction ; and in the place of an imaginary hypothesis, the place of migration is almost incontrovertibly pointed out."

* The Kalmuc Tartars are now subjects of Russia.

SKETCH OF THE FIRST SETTLEMENT OF VIRGINIA.

Having given the foregoing brief sketch of the probable origin of the Indians in America, the author will now turn his attention to the first settlement of Virginia, a brief history of which he considers will not be unacceptable to the general reader, and as a preliminary introduction to his main object, i. e., the history of the early settlement of the Valley of Shenandoah in Virginia.

On the 10th of April, 1606, James I. King of England, granted charters to two separate companies, called the "London and Plymouth companies," for settling colonies in Virginia.* The London company sent Capt. Christopher Newport to Virginia, December 20, 1606, with a colony of one hundred and five persons, to commence a settlement on the island of Roanoke, now in North Carolina. By stress of weather, however, they were driven north of their place of destination, and entered the Chesapeake Bay. Here, up a river which the called James river, on a beautiful peninsula, they commenced, in May, 1607, the settlement of Jamestown. This was the first permanent settlement in the country.

Several subsequent charters were granted by King James to the company for the better ordering and government of the colony, for the particulars of which the reader is referred to Hening's Statutes at Large.— And in the year 1619, the first legislative council was convened at Jamestown, then called 'James citty.'" This council was called the General Assembly. "It was to assist the Governor in the administration of justice, to advance christianity among Indians, to erect the colony in obedience to his majesty, and in maintaining the people in justice and christian conversation, and strengthening them against enemies. The said governor, council, and two burgesses out of every town, hundred or plantation, to be chosen by the inhabitants to make up a General Assembly, who are to decide all matters by the greatest number of voices; but the governor is to have a negative voice, to have power to make orders and acts necessary, wherein they are to imitate the policy of the form of government, laws, customs, manner of tryal, and other administration of justice used in England, as the company are required by their letters patents. No law to continue or to be of force till ratified by a quarter court to be held in England, and returned under seal. After the colony is well framed and settled, no order of quarter court in England shall bind till ratified by the General Assembly." *—Dated 24th July, 1621.

"INSTRUCTIONS TO GOVERNOR WYATT.

"To keep up religion of the church of England as near as may be;— to be obedient to the king and to do justice after the form of the laws of England; and not to injure the natives; and to forget old quarrels now buried:†

---

*Hening's Statutes at Large, vol. i., p. 113, 114.

†It appears that at a very early period of the colony, they were desirous of cultivating a friendly understanding with the natives of the country. Unfortunately, however, for our ancestors, and for the Indians themselves, this friendly disposition was never of long duration.

"To be industrious, and suppress drunkenness, gaming, and excess in cloaths; not to permit any but the council and heads of hundreds to wear gold in their cloaths, or to wear silk till they make it themselves:

"Not to offend any foreign princes; to punish piracies; to build fortresses and block-houses at the mouths of the rivers:

"To use means to convert the heathens, viz.: to converse with some; each town to teach som children fit for the college intended to be built:

"After Sir George Yeardly has gathered the present year's crop, he is to deliver to Sir Francis Wyatt, the hundred tenants belonging to the governor's place: Yeardley's government to expire the 18th November next, and then Wyatt to be published governor; to swear the council:

"George Sandis appointed treasurer, and he is to put in execution all orders of court about staple commodities; to whom is allotted fifteen hundred acres and fifty tenants. To the marshall, sir William Newce, the same. To the physician five hundred acres and twenty tenants; and the same to the secretary:

"To review the commissions to Sir George Yeardley, governor, and the council, dated 18th November, 1618, for dividing the colony into cities, boroughs, &c., and to observe all former instructions (a copy whereof was sent) if they did not contradict the present; and all orders of court (made in England):

"To make a catalogue of the people in every plantation, and their conditions; and of deaths, marriages and christenings:

"To take care of dead persons' estates for the right owners; to keep a list of all cattle and cause the secretary to return copies of the premises once a year:

"To take care of every plantation upon the death of their chief; not to plant above one hundred pounds of tobacco per head;* to sow great quantities of corn for their own use, and to support the multitudes to be sent yearly; to inclose lands; to keep cows, swine, poultry, &c., and particularly kyne, which are not to be killed yet:

"Next to corn, plant mulbury trees, and make silk, and take care of the French men and others sent about that work; to try silk grass; to plant abundance of vines, and take care of the vignerors sent:

"To put prentices to trades, and not let them forsake their trades for planting tobacco or any such useless commodity:

"To take care of the Dutch sent to build saw-mills, and seat them at the falls, that they may bring their timber by the current of the water:

"To build water-mills and block-houses in every plantation:

"That all contracts in England or Virginia be performed, and the breaches punished according to justice:

"The tenants not to be enticed away; to take care of those sent about an iron work, and especially Mr. John Berkeley, that they dont miscarry again, this being the greatest hope and expectation of the colonies:

"To make salt, pitch, tar, soap, ashes, &c., so often recommended,

---

*This order strikes the author as one of a singular character. It certainly requires great judgment and experience of the planter to decide what number of plants would make his 100 lbs. of tobacco, considering the casualties to which his crop was liable.

and for which materials had been sent; to make oyl of walnuts, and employ apothecaries in distilling lees of beer, and searching after minerals, dyes, gums, and drugs, &c., and send small quantities home:*

"To make small quantity of tobacco, and that very good; that the houses appointed for the reception of new comers and public storehouses be built, kept clean, &c.; to send the state of affairs quarterly, and a duplicate next shipping :

"To take care of Captain William Norton, and certain Italians sent to set up a glass house:

"A copy of a treatise of the plantation business and excellent observances made by a gentleman of capacity is sent to lie among the records, and recommended to the councillors to study :

"Mr. William Clayborne, a surveyor, sent to survey the planters-lands, and make a map of the country:

"To make discoveries along the coast, and find a fishery between James river and Cape Cod:

"As to raising staple commodities, the chief officers ought to set examples, and to aim at the establishment of the colony:

"Chief officers that have tenants reprimanded for taking fees; but require that the clerks have fees set for passes, warrants, copies of orders, &c.:

"Governor and council to appoint proper times for administration of justice, and provide for the entertainment of the council during their session; to be together one whole month about state affairs, and law suits ; to record plaints of consequence; to keep a register of the acts of quarter sessions, and send home copies :

"If a governor dies, the major part of the council to choose one of themselves within fourteen days; but if voices be divided, the lieutenant governor shall have the place; and next the marshall ; next the treasurer; and one of the two deputies next :

"Governor and chief officers not to let out their tenants as usual:

"The governor only to summon the council, and sign warrants, and execute or give authority to execute council orders, except in cases that do belong to the marshall, treasurer, deputies, &c. :

"The governor to have absolute authority to determine and punish all neglects, and contempts of authority, except the councils, who are to be tried at the quarter sessions and censured. Governor to have but the casting voice in council or court, but in the assembly a negative voice:

"That care be taken that there be no engrossing commodity, or forestalling of the market :

"All servants to fare alike in the colony, and their punishment for any offences is to serve the colony, in public works:

"To see that the earl of Pembroke's thirty thousand acres be very good :

"And lastly, not to let ships stay long, and to freight them with walnut and any leas valuable commodity:

"The governor administered the following oath to the council:

*Sending things to England, was, in the phrase of the times, termed sending things home. This mode of expression, "going home or sending home," was in use within the recollection of the author. In truth, the term "going or sending home," was never abandoned till after the war of the revolution.

" You shall swear to be a true and faithful servant unto the king's ma-
" jesty, as one of his council for Virginia : You shall in all things to be
" moved, treated, and debated in that council concerning Virginia or any
" the territories of America, between the degrees of thirty-four and forty-
" five from the equinoctial line northward, or the trade thereof, faithfully
" and truly declare your mind and opinion, according to your heart and
" conscience; and shall keep secret all matters committed and revealed
" to you concerning the same, and that shall be treated secretly in that
" council, or this council of Virginia, or the more part of them, publication
" shall not be made thereof; And of all matters of great importance, 'or
" difficulty, before you resolve thereupon, you shall make his majesty's
" privy council acquainted therewith, and follow their directions therein :
" You shall to your uttermost bear faith and allegiance to the king's ma-
" jesty, his heirs, and lawful successors, and shall assist and defend all
" jurisdictions, preheminences, and authorities, granted unto his majesty
" and annext unto the crown, against all foreign princes, persons, prelates
" or potentates whatsoever, be it by act of parliament or otherwise: and
" generally, in all things, you shall do as a faithful and true servant and
" subject ought to do. So help you God and the holy contents of this
" book."—Hening's Stat. at Large, vol. i. p. 114–118.

It appears the foregoing instructions were drawn up by the council,
and intended as the general principles for the government of the colony.

The recommendation "not to injure the natives and forget old quarrels
now buried," goes far to prove that hopes were entertained that the Indians were disposed to be at peace. " To use means to convert the heath-
en," is another evidence of this amicable state of feeling towards the natives. But lo! this state of peace and tranquility, in less than one year
after, was changed into one of devastation, blood and mourning. On the
22d of March, 1622, the Indians committed the most bloody massacre
on the colonists, recorded in the annals of our country.*

In the following year, to wit, March, 1623, the colonial general assembly, by statute, directed, "that the 22d March be yearly solemnized as
holliday."† This was done to commemorate the escape of the colony
from entire extirpation. This bloody massacre produced, on the part of
the whites, a most deadly and irreconcilable hatred towards the natives.
Accordingly, we find that a long continued and unabating state of hostility was kept up, and in about one hundred years the Indians were driven
from the country east of the Blue Ridge. At the same session, to wit,
1623, the legislature enacted several laws in relation to defending themselves against the savages. In the series are the following :

" That every dwelling house shall be pallizaded in for defence against
the Indians :

" That no man go or send abroad without a sufficient partie well armed :

---

*This year, (1622), says Mr. Gordon in his history of the American revolution, (vol.
i. p. 43,) "was remarkable for a massacre of the colonists by the *Indians*, which was executed with the utmost subtilty, and without any regard to age, sect, or dignity. A well
concerted attack on all the settlements destroyed in one hour, and almost at the same instant, 347 persons who were defenceless and incapable of making resistance."

†Hening's Statutes at Large, vol. i. p. 123.

"That people go not to work in the ground without their arms (and a centinell upon them :)

" That the inhabitants go not aboard ships or upon any other occasions, in such numbers as thereby to weaken and endanger the plantations :

" That the commander of every plantation take care that there be sufficient of powder and ammunition within the plantation under his command and their pieces fixt and their arms compleate :

" That there be dew watch kept by night :

" That no commander of any plantation do either himselfe or suffer others to spend powder unnecessarily, in drinking or entertainment, &c.:

" That at the beginning of July next the inhabitants of every corporation shall go upon their adjoining salvages, as we did the last year."— Hen. Stat. at Large, vol. i. p. 127, 128.

In the year 1629, the legislature again "ordered that every commander of the several plantations appointed by commission from the governor, shall have power and authoritie to levy a partie of men out of the inhabitants of that place soe many as may well be spared without too much weakening of the plantations, and to employ those men against the Indians," &c.—Idem, p. 140.

" It was the opinion of the whole bodie of the assembly that we should go three several marches upon the Indians, at three several times of the year, viz : first in November, secondly in March, thirdly in July," &c.— Idem, p. 141.

In 1631–32, "it is ordered that no person or persons shall dare to speak or to parlie with any Indians, either in the woods or in any plantation, yf he can possibly avoid it by any means," &c.—Idem, p. 167.

The author considers the foregoing extracts sufficient to enable the reader to form some opinion of the spirit and character of the early settlers of our state, particularly as it relates to their sufferings and difficulties with the Indian tribes. It is not deemed expedient or necessary to go into a detailed history of the first settlement of our country, as there are several general histories of Virginia now to be obtained, written by authors, whose abilities and means of information the author could not expect to equal.

The author will close this brief sketch of the first settlement of Virginia, with a few general remarks in relation to the first introduction of slavery. It appears from our early historians, that negroes were first introduced into our state from "a Dutch ship in the year 1620." O woful day for our country ! To use the language of Mr. Snowden, this was "an evil hour" for our country—It truly brought "*new sins* and *new deaths*" to the new world. The present generation have abundant cause to deplore the unhallowed cupidity and want of all the finer feelings of our nature, manifested in this baleful and unrighteous traffic. It has entailed upon us a heavy calamity, which will perhaps require the wisdom of ages yet to come to remove. That it must and will be removed, there can be but little doubt. History furnishes no example of any part of the human race being kept in perpetual slavery. Whether the scheme of sending them to Africa will ultimately produce the desired effect, can only be tested by time : it is however most "devoutly" to be desired.

BACON'S REBELLION IN VIRGINIA IN 1675-76.

The document which follows relates to one of the most singular events which ever occurred in Virginia, and its interest is a sufficient inducement for its insertion in this work. It was published in the Richmond Evangelical Magazine many years ago, but is now out of print. The editor of that work, (the late revered and highly esteemed Dr. Rice,) in introducing it into his pages, says: "It was taken verbatim from a copy in the library now belonging to congress, but formerly the property of Mr. Jefferson. Who the author is we cannot discover. He was certainly a man of much cleverness, and wrote well, But our readers will judge for themselves. The name of Bacon is very little known to our citizens in general: and this part of our history has been veiled in great obscurity.— There are two remembrances of this extraordinary man in the neighborhood of Richmond. A brook on the north-west of the city, which bears the name of "Bacon-quarter branch," is said to have received its name from the fact, that on that brook Bacon had his quarter. Buck says that he owned a plantation on Shockoe creek, of which the stream just mentioned is a branch. One of the finest springs in Richmond, or its vicinity, is on the east of the city, and is called Bloody-run spring. Its name is said to be derived from a sanguinary conflict which Bacon had with the Indians, on the margin of the streamlet which flows from this spring."

The following account of the original from which this document was taken, is given by Mr. Jefferson, in his own words:

"The original manuscript, of which the following is a copy, was communicated to me by Mr. King, our late minister plenipotentiary at the court of London, in a letter of Dec. 20, 1803. The transaction which it records, although of little extent or consequence, is yet marked on the history of Va. as having been the only rebellion or insurrection which took place in the colony during the 168 years of its existence preceding the American revolution, and one hundred years exactly before that event: in the contest with the house of Stuart, it only accompanied the steps of the mother country. The rebellion of Bacon has been little understood, its cause and course being imperfectly explained by any authentic materials hitherto possessed; this renders the present narrative of real value. It appears to have been written by a person intimately acquainted with its origin, progress and conclusion, thirty years after it took place, and when the passions of the day had subsided, and reason might take a cool and deliberate review of the transaction. It was written, too, not for the public eye, but to satisfy the desire of minister Lord Oxford; and the candor and simplicity of the narration cannot fail to command belief. On the outside of the cover of the manuscript is the No. 3947 in one place, and 5781 in another. Very possibly the one may indicate the place it held in Lord Oxford's library, and the other its number in the catalogue of the bookseller to whose hands it came afterwards; for it was at the sale of the stock of a bookseller that Mr. King purchased it.

"To bring the authenticity of this copy as near to that of the original as I could, I have most carefully copied it with my own hand. The pages and lines of the copy correspond exactly with those of the original ; the orthography, abbreviations, punctuations, interlineations and incorrectnesses, are preserved, so that it is a *fac simile* except as to the form of the letter. The orthography and abbreviations are evidences of the age of the writing.

"The author says of himself that he was a *planter;* that he lived in Northumberland, but was elected a member of the assembly of 1676 for the county of Stafford, Colonel Mason being his colleague, of which assembly *Col. Warner was speaker ;* that it was the first and should be the last time of his meddling with public affairs ; and he subscrbes the initials of his name T. M. Whether the records of the time (if they still exist,) with the aid of these circumstances, will shew what his name was, remains for farther inquiry."

THE MANUSCRIPT.

To the right hono'ble Robert Harley esq'r. her Mag'ties Principal Secretary of State, and one of her most Hono'ble Privy Council.
S'R.

The great honor of your command obliging my pen to step aside from its habitual element of ffigures into this little treatise of history; which having never before experienced, I am like *Sutor ultra crepidam*, and therefore dare pretend no more than (nakedly) recount matters of ffact.

Beseeching yo'r hono'r will vouch safe to allow, that in 30 years, divers occurrences are laps'd out of mind, and others imperfectly retained.

So as the most solemn obedience can be now paid, is to pursue the track of barefac'd truths, as close as my memory can recollect, to have seen, or believed, from credible ffriends with concurring circumstances :

And whatsoever yo'r celebrated wisdom shall finde amise in the composure, my entire dependence is upon yo'r candor favorably to accept these most sincere endeavors of Yo'r Hon'rs
Most devoted humble serv't.

The 13th July, 1705. T. M.

The beginning progress and conclusion of Bacons rebellion in Virginia in the year 1675 & 1676.

About the year 1675, appear'd three prodigies in that country, which from th' attending disasters were look'd upon as ominous presages.

The one was a large comet every evening for a week, or more at Southwest; thirty five degrees high streaming like a horse taile westwards, untill it reach'd (almost) the horison, and setting towards the North-west.

Another was, fflights of pigieons in breadth nigh a quarter of the midhemisphere, and of their length was no visible end ; whose weights brake down the limbs of large trees whereon these rested at nights, of which the ffowlers shot abundance and eat 'em; this sight put the old planters under the more portentous apprehensions, because the like was seen (as they said,)in the year 1640 when th' Indians committed the last massacre, but not after, until that present year 1675.

The third strange appearance was swarms of fflyes about an inch long, and big as the top of a man's little finger, rising out of spigot holes in the earth, which eat the new sprouted leaves from the tops of the trees without doing other harm, and in a month left us.

My dwelling was in Northumberland, the lowest county on Potomack river, Stafford being the upmost, where having also a plantation, servants, cattle &c. my overseer had agreed with one Rob't. Hen to come thither, and be my herdsman, who then lived ten miles above it; but on a sabbath day morning in the sumer anno 1675, people in their way to church, saw this Hen lying thwart his threshold, and an Indian without the door, both chopt on their heads, arms & other parts, as if done with Indian hatchetts, th' Indian was dead, but Hen when asked who did that? answered Doegs Doegs, and soon died, then a boy came out from under a bed where he had hid himself, and told them, Indians had come at break of day & done those murders.

ffrom this Englishman's bloud did (by decrees) arise Bacons rebellion with the following mischiefs which overspread all Virginia & twice endangered Maryland, as by the ensueing account is evident.

Of this horrid action Coll: Mason who commanded the militia regiment of ffoot & Capt. Brent the troop of horse in that county, (both dwelling six or eight miles downwards) having speedy notice raised 30, or more men, & and pursu'd those Indians 20 miles up & 4 miles over that river into Maryland, where landing at dawn of day, they found two small paths each leader with his party took a separate path and in less than a furlong either found a cabin, which they (silently) surrounded. Capt. Brent went to the Doegs cabin (as it proved to be) who speaking the Indian tongue called to have a "Machacomicha woewhio" i. e. a council called presently such being the usuall manner with Indians (the king came trembling forth, and wou'd have fled, when Capt. Brent, catching hold of his twisted lock (which was all the hair he wore) told him he was come for the murderer of Rob't Hen, the king pleaded ignorance and slipt loos, whom Brent shot dead with his pistoll, th' Indians shot two or three guns out of the cabin, th' English shot into it, th' Indians throng'd out at the door and fled, the English shot as many as they cou'd, so that they killed ten, as Capt. Brent told me, and brought away the kings son of about 8 years old, concerning whom is an observable passage, at the end of this expedition; the noise of this shooting awaken'd the Indians in the cabin, which Coll: Mason had encompassed, who likewise rush'd out & fled, of whom his company (supposing from that noise of shooting Brent's party to be engaged) shot (as the Coll: informed me) ffourteen before an Indian came, who with both hands shook him (friendly) by one arm saying Susquehanoughs netoughs i. e. Susquehanaugh friends and fled, whereupon he ran amongst his men, crying out "ffor the Lords sake shoot no more, these are our friends the Susquehanoughs.

This unhappy scene ended;—Collo. Mason took the king of the Doegs son home with him, who lay ten dayes in bed, as one dead, with eyes and mouth shutt, no breath discern'd, but his body continuing warm, they believed him yett alive; th' aforenamed Capt. Brent (a papist) coming thither on a visit, and seeing his little prisoner thus languishing said "perhaps he is pawewawd i. e. bewitch'd, and that he had heard baptism was an effectual remedy against witchcraft wherefore advis'd to baptise him Collo. Mason answered, no minister cou'd be had in many miles; Brent replied yo'r clerk Mr. Dobson may do that office, which was done by the church of England liturgy; Col: Mason with Capt. Brent godfathers and Mrs. Mason godmother, my overseer Mr. Pimet being present, from whom I first heard it, and which all th' other persons (afterwards) affirm'd to me; the ffour men returned to drinking punch, but Mrs. Mason stayed & looking on the child, it open'd the eyes, and breath'd whereat she ran for a cordial, which he took from a spoon, gaping for more and so (by degrees) recovered, tho' before his baptism, they had often tryed the same meanes but cou'd not by no endeavours wrench open his teeth.

This was taken for a convincing proofe against infidelity.

But to return from this digression, the Susquehanoughs were newly driven from their habitations, at the head of Chesepiack bay, by the Cinela-Indians, down to the head of Potomack, where they sought protection under the Pascataway Indians, who had a fort near the head of that river, and also were our ffriends.

After this unfortunate exploit of Mason & Brent, one or two being kill'd in Stafford, boats of war were equipt to prevent excursions over the river, and at the same time murders being likewise committed in Maryland, by whom not known, on either side the river, both countrys raised their quota's of a thousand men, upon whose coming before the ffort, the Indians sent out 4 of their great men, who ask'd the reason of that hostile appearance, what they said more or offered I do not remember to have heard; but our two commanders caused them to be (instantly) slaine, after which the Indians made an obstinate resistance shooting many of our men, and making frequent, fierce and bloody sallyes; and when they were call'd to, or offered parley, gave no other answer, than "where are our four Cockarouses, i. e. great men?

At the end of six weeks, march'd out seventy five Indians with their women children &c. who by moon light passed our guards hollowing & firing att them without opposition having 3 or 4 decrepits in the ffort.

The next morning th' English followed, but could not, or (for fear of ambuscades) would not overtake these desperate fugitives the number we lost in that siege I did not hear was published.

The walls of this fort were high banks of earth, with flankers having many loop-holes, and a ditch round all, and without this a row of tall trees fastened 3. feet deep in the earth, their bodies from 5. to 8. inches diameter, watled 6. inches apart to shoot through with the tops twisted together, and also artificially wrought, as our men could make no breach to storm it, nor (being low land) could they undermine it by reason of water neither had they cannon to batter itt, so that 'twas not taken, untill fflamine drove the Indians out of it.

These escap'd Indians (forsaking Maryland(took their rout over the head of that river, and thence over the heads of Rappahonnock & York rivers, killing whom they found of the upmost plantations untill they came to the head of James river, where (with Bacon and others) they slew Mr. Bacon's overseer whom he much loved, and one of his servants, whose bloud hee vowed to revenge if possible.

In these frightful times the most exposed small families withdrew into our houses of better numbers, which we fortified with palisadoes and redoubts, neighbours in bodys joined their labours from each plantation to others alternately, taking their arms into the ffields, and setting centinels; no man stirrd out of door unarm'd, Indians were (ever & anon) espied, three 4. 5. or 6. in a party lurking throughout the whole land, yet [what was remarkable] I rarely heard of any houses burnt, tho' abundance was forsaken, nor ever, of any corn or tobacco cut up, or other injury done, besides murders, except the killing of a very few cattle and swine.

Frequent complaints of bloudsheds were sent to Sr. Wm. Berkeley (then Govern'r) from the heads of the rivers, which were as often answered with promises of assistance.

These at the heads of James and York rivers (having now most people destoyed by the Indians flight thither from Potomack) grew impatient at the many slaughters of their neighbours and rose for their own defence, who chusing Mr. Bacon for their leader, sent oftentimes to the Govern'r, humbly beseeching a commission to go against those Indians at their own charge which his hono'r as often promised but did not send; the misteryes of these delays, were wondered at and which I ne'er heard coud penetrate into, other than the effects of his passion, and a new (not to be mentioned) occasion of avarice, to both which he was (by the common vogue) more than a little addicted; whatever were the popular surmizes & murmurins viz't.

"that no bullets would pierce bever skins.

"rebells forfeitures would be loyall inheritances &c.

During these protractions and people often slaine, most or all of the officers, civil & military with as many dwellers next the heads of the rivers as made up 300. men taking Mr. Bacon for their command'r met, and concerted together, the danger of going without a commiss'n on the one part, and the continuall murders of their neighbors on the other part (not knowing whose or how many of their own turns might be next) and came to this resolution viz't to prepare themselves with necessaries for a march, but interim to send again for a commission, which if could or could not be obtayned by a certaine day, they would proceed commission or no commission.

This day lapsing & no com'n come, they marched into the wilderness in quest of these Indians after whom the Govern'r sent his proclamation, denouncing all rebells, who should not return within a limited day, whereupon those of estates obey'd; but Mr. Bacon with 57. men proceeded until their provisions were near spent, without finding enemy's when coming nigh a ffort of ffriend Indians, on th' other side a branch of James river, they desired reliefe offering paym't. which these Indians kindly promised to help them with on the morrow, but put them off with promises untill the third day, so as then having eaten their last morsells they could not return, but must have starved in the way homeward and now 'twas suspected, these Indians had received private messages from the Govern'r & those to be the causes of these delusive procrastinations;

whereupon the English waded shoulder deep thro' that branch of the ffort palisado's still intreating and tendering pay, for victuals; but that evening a shot from the place they left on th' other side of that branch kill'd one of Mr. Bacon's men, which made them believe, those in the ffort had sent for other Indians to come behind 'em & cut 'em off.

Hereupon they fired the polisado's, storm'd & burnt the ffort and cabins, and (with the losse of three English) slew 150 Indians. The circumstances of this expedic'n Mr. Bacon entertain'd me with, at his own chamber, on a visit I made him, the occasion whereof is hereafter mentioned.

ffrom hence they returned home where writts were come up to elect members for an assembly, when Mr. Bacon was unanimously chosen for one, who coming down the river was commanded by a ship with guns to come on board, where waited Major Houe the high sheriff of James town ready to seize him, by whom he was carried down to the Govern'r & by him receiv'd with a surprizing civility in the following words "Mr. Bacon you had for got to be a gentleman." No, may it please yo'r hono'r answer'd Mr. Bacon; then replyed the Govern'r I'll take yo'r parol, and gave him his liberty: in March 1675-6 writts came up to Stafford to choose their two members for an assembly to meet in May; when Collo. Mason Capt. Brent and other gentlemen of that county, invited me to stand a candidate; a matter I little dreamt of, having never had inclinac'ons to tamper in the precarious intrigues of Govern't. and my hands being full of my own business: they press't severall cogent argum'ts. and I having considerable debts in that county, besides my plantation concerns, where (in one & th' other, I had much more severely suffered, than any of themselves by th' Indian disturbances in the summer and winter foregoing. I held it not [then] discreet to disoblige the rulers of it, so Collo: Mason with myself were elected without objection, he at time convenient went on horse back; I took my sloop & the morning I arriv'd to James town after a weeks voyage, was welcom'd with the strange acclamations of *All's Over* Bacon is taken, having not heard at home of these Southern com'otions, other than rumours like idle tales, of one Bacon risen up in rebellion, no body knew for what, concerning the Indians.

The next forenoon, th' Assembly being met in a chamber over the General court & our Speaker chosen, the Govern'r sent for us down, where his hono'r with a pathetic emphasis made a short abrupt speech wherein were these words.

"If they had killed my grandfather and my grandmother, my father
" and mother and all my friends, yet if they had come to treat of peace,
" they ought to have gone in peace, and sat down.

The two chief commanders at the forementioned seize, who slew the ffour Indian great men, being present and part of our assembly,

The Govern'r stood up againe and said "if there be joy in the presence
" of the Angels over one sinner that repententh, there is joy now, for we
" have a penitent sinner come before us, call Mr. Bacon; then did Mr. Bacon upon one knee at the bar deliver a sheet of paper confessing his crimes, and begging pardon of god the king and the Govern'r whereto

C

[after a short pause] he answered "God forgive you, I forgive you, thrice repeating the same words; when Collo. Cole [one of council] said, "and all that were with him, Yea, said the Governor & all that were with him, twenty or more persons being then in irons who were taken coming down in the same & other vessels with Mr. Bacon.

About a minute after this the Govern'r starting up from his chair a third time said "Mr. Bacon! if you will live civilly but till next Quarter court [doubling the words] but till next Quarter court, Ile promise to restore you againe to yo'r place, there pointing with his hand to Mr. Bacons seat, he having been of the Councill before these troubles, tho' he had been a very short time in Virginia but was deposed by the foresaid proclamoc'on, and in the afternoon passing by the court door, in my way up to our chamber, I saw Mr. Bacon on his quondam seat the Govern'r & councill which seemed a marveilous indulgence to one whom he had so lately proscribed as a rebell.

The Govern'r had directed us to consider of means for security from th' Indian insults and to defray the charge &c. advising us to beware of two rogues amongst us, naming Laurence and Drummond both dwelling at James town and who were not at the Pascataway siege.

But at our entrance upon businesse, some gentlemen took this opportunity to endeavour the redressing severall grievances the country then labor'd under, motions were made for inspecting the publick revenues, the Collectors accompts &c. and so far was proceeded as to name part of a committee whereof Mr. Bristol [now in London] was and myself another, when we were interrupted by pressing messages from the Govern'r to to meddle with nothing until the Indian business was dispatch't.

This debate rose high, but was overruled and I have not heard that these inspections have since then been insisted upon, tho such of that indigent people as had no benefits from the taxes groaned undr our being thus overborn.

The next thing was a Co'mittee for the Indian affaires, whereof in appointing members, myself was unwillingly nominated having no knowledge in martiall preparations, and after our names were taken, some of the house moved for sending 2. of our members to intreat the Govern'r wou'd please to assign two of his councill to sit with, and assist us in our debates, as had been usuall.

When seeing all silent looking at each other with many discontented faces, I adventur'd to offer my humble opinion to the Speaker "for the " co'mittee to form methods as agreeable to the sense of the house as we " could, and report 'em whereby they would more clearly see, on what " points to give the Govern'r and Councill that trouble if perhaps it might " be needfull."

These few words raised an uproar; one party urging hard "it had been customary and ought not to be omitted;" whereto Mr. Presley my neighbor an old assembly man, sitting next me, rose up, and [in a blundering manner replied] "tis true, it has been customary, but if we have any bad " customes amonst us, we are come here to mend 'em" which set the house in a laughter.

This was huddl'd off without coming to a vote, and so the co'mittee must submit to be overaw'd, and have every carpt at expression carried streight to the Govern'r.

Our co'mittee being sat, the Queen of Pakunky [descended from Op-pechankenough a former Emperor of Virginia] was introduced, who entered the chamber with a comportment graceful to admiration, bringing on her right had an Englishman interpreter and on the left her son a stripling twenty years of age, she having round her head a plat of black & white wampam peague three inches broad in imitation of a crown, and was cloathed in a mantle of dress't deerskins with the hair outwards & the edge cut round 6 inches deep which made strings resembling twisted fringè from the shoulders to the feet; thus with grave courtlike gestures and a majestick air in her face, she walk'd up our long room to the lower end of the table, where after a few intreaties she sat down; th' interpreter and her son standing by her on either side as they had walk'd up, our chairman asked her what men she would lend us for guides in the wilderness and to assist us against our enemy Indians, she spake to th' interpreter to inform her what the chairman said, [tho we believe she understood him] he told us she bid him ask her son to whom the English tongue was familiar, & who was reputed the son of an English colonel, yet neither wou'd he speak to or seem to understand the Chairmain but th' interpreter told us he referred all to his mother, who being againe urged she after a little musing with an earnest passionate countenance as if tears were ready to gush out and a fervent sort of expression made a harangue about a quarter of an hour, often interlacing [with a high shrill voice and vehement passion] these words "Tatapatomoi Chepiack, i. e. Tatapatomoi dead: Coll: Hill being next me, shook his head, I ask'd what was the matter, he told me all she said was too true to our shame, and that his father was generall in that battle, where diverse years before Tatapatamoi her husband had led a hundred of his Indians in help to th' English against our former enemy Indians, and was there slaine with most of his men; for which no compensation [at all] had been to that day rendered to her wherewith she now upbraided us.

Her discourse ending and our morose Chairman not advancing one cold word towards asswaging the anger and grief of her speech and demeanour manifested under her oppression, nor taking any notice of all she had said, neither considering that we (then) were in our great exigency, supplicants to her for a favour of the same kind as the former, for which we did not deny the having been so ingrate he rudely push'd againe the same question "what Indians will you now contribute &c? of this disregard she signified her resentment by a disdainful aspect, and turning her head half aside, sate mute till that same question being press't a third time, she not returning her face to the board, answered with a low slighting voice in her own language "six, but being further importun'd she sitting a little while sullen, without uttering a word between said "twelve, tho she then had a hundred and fifty Indian men, in her town, and so rose up and gravely walked away, as not pleased with her treatment.

Whilst some dais past in settling the Quota's of men arms and ammunié'on provisions &c. each county was to furnish one morning early a bruit ran about the town Bacon is fled Bacon is fled, whereupon I went straight to Mr. Laurence, who (formerly) was of Oxford university, and for wit learning and sobriety was equall'd there by few, and who some years before [as Col: Lee tho one of the councill and a friend of the Govern'rs inform'd me] had been partially treated at law, for a considerable estate on behalf of a corrupt favourite; which Laurence complaining loudly of, the Govern'r bore him a grudge and now shaking his head, said "old treacherous villain, and that his house was searcht that morn-"ing, at day break, but Bacon was escaped into the country, having in-"timation that the Govern'rs generosity in pardoning him and his follow-" ers and restoring him to his seat in the councill, were no other than " previous wheadles to amuse him & his adherents & to circumvent them " by stratagem, forasmuch as the taking Mr. Bacon again into the councill "was first to keep him out of the assembly, and in the next place the " Govern'r knew the country people were hastning down with dreadful " threatnings to double revenge all wrongs shou'd be done to Mr. " Bacon or his men; or whoever shou'd have had the least hand in 'em.'

And so much was true that this Mr. young Nathaniel Bacon [not yet arrived to 30 years] had a nigh relation namely Colo. Nathaniel Bacon of long standing in the council a very rich politick man, and childless, de-signing this kinsman for his heir, who [not without much paines] had prevailed with his uneasy cousin to deliver the forementioned written recan-tation at the Bar; having compiled it ready to his hand & by whose meanes 'twas supposed that timely intimation was convey'd to the young gentle-man to flee for his life, and also in 3: or four dais after Mr. Bacon was first seiz'd I saw abundance of men in town come thither from the heads of the rivers, who finding him restored & his men at liberty, return'd home satisfied; a few dais after which, the Govern'r seeing all quiet, gave out private warrants to take him againe, intending as was thought to raise the militia and so to dispose things as to prevent his friends from gather-ing any more into a like numerous body and coming down a second time to save him.

In three or ffour dais after this escape, upon news that Mr. Bacon was 30 miles up the river, at the head of four hundred men, the Govern'r sent to the parts adjacent, on both sides James river for the militia and all the men that could be gotten to come and defend the town, expres's came al-most hourly of th' army's approaches, whom in less than four dais after the first account of 'em att 2. of the clock entered the town, without be-ing withstood, and form*d a body upon a green, not a flight shot from the end of the State house of horse and ffoot; as well regular as veteran troops, who forthwith possesst themselves of all the avenues, disarming all in the town and coming thither in boats or by land.

In half an hour after this the drum beat for the house to meet, and in less than an hour more Mr. Bacon came with a file of ffusileers on either hand near the corner of the State-house where the Govern'r. and councill went forth to him; we saw from the window the Govern'r. open his breast, and Bacon strutting betwixt his two files of men with his left arm on Kenbow fligning his right arm every way both like men distracted; and if in this moment of fury, that enraged multitude had faln upon the Govern'r & councill we of the assembly expected the same imediate tate ;

I stept down and amongst the crown of Spectators found the seamon of my sloop, who pray'd me not to stir from them, when in two minutes, the Govern'r walk'd towards his private apartm't. a Coits cast distant at the other end of the Statehouse, the gentlemen of the councill following him, and after them walked Mr. Bacon with outragious postures of his head arms body & legs, often tossing his hands from his sword to his hat and after him came a detachment of ffusileers (musketts not being then in use) who with their cocks bent presented their ffusils at a window of the assembly chamber filled with faces, repeating with menacing voices "we will have it, we will have it," half a minute when as one of our house a person known to many of them, shook his handkercher out at the window, "saying you shall have it, you shall have it," 3 or 4 times; at these words they sate down their fusils unbent their locks and stood still untill Bacon coming back, they followed him to their main body; in this hubub a servant of mine got so nigh as to hear the Govern'rs words, and also followed Mr. Bacon, and heard what he said, who came & told me, that when the Govern'r opened his breast he said, "here! shoot me, foregod fair mark, shoot; often rehearsing the same, without any other words; whereto Mr. Bacon answered "No may it please yo'r hono'r we will not " hurt a hair of yo'r head, nor of any other mans, we are come for a " Co'mission to save our lives from th' Indians, which you have so often " promised, and now we will have it before we go."

But when Mr. Bacon followed the Govern'r & Councill with the fore-mentioned impetuous (like delirious) actions whil'st that party presented their ffusils at the window full of ffaces, he said " Dam my bloud I'le kill " Govern'r Councill assembly & all, and then I'le sheath my sword in my " own hearts bloud;" and afterwards 'twas said Bacon had given a sig-nal to his men who presented their fusils at those gasing out at the win-dow that if he should draw his sword, they were on sight of it to fire, and slay us, so near was the massacre of us all that very minute, had Bacon in that paroxism of phrentick fury but drawn his sword, before the pacifick handkercher was shaken out at window.

In an hour or more after these violent concussions Mr. Bacon came up to our chamber and desired a co'mission from us to go against the Indians; our Speaker sat silent, when one Mr. Blayton a neighbor to Mr. Bacon & elected with him a member of assembly for the same county (who there-fore durst speak to him) made answer, " 'twas not in our province, or " power, nor of any other, save the king's viceregent our Govern'r, he press'd hard nigh half an hours harangue on the preserving our lives from the Indians, inspecting the publick revenues, th' exorbitant taxes and re-dressing the grievances and calamities of that deplorable country, whereto having no other answer he went away dissatisfied.

Next day there was a rumour the Govern'r & councill had agreed Mr. Bacon shou'd have a co'mission to go Generall of the fforces, we then were raising, whereupon I being a member of Stafford, the most northern frontier, and where the war begun, considering that Mr. Bacon dwelling in the most Southern ffrontier, county, might the less regard the parts I represented, I went to Coll: Cole (an active member of the councill) desi-ring his advice, if applicac'ons to Mr. Bacon on that subject were then seasonable and safe, which he approving and earnestly advising, I went to Mr. Laurence who was esteemed Mr. Bacon's principal consultant, to whom he took me with him, and there left me where I was entertained 2 or 3 hours with the particular relac'ons of diverse before recited transactions; and as to the matter I spake of, he told me, the Govern'r had indeed promised him the command of the forces, and if his hono'r shou'd keep his word (which he doubted) he assured me "the like care should be " taken of the remotest corners in the land, as of his own dwelling-house, " and pray'd me to advise him what persons in those parts were most fit to " bear commands." I frankly gave him my opinion that the most satisfactory gentlemen to govern'r & people, wou'd be co'manders of the militia, wherewith he was well pleased, and himself wrote a list of those nominated.

That evening I made known what had passed with Mr. Bacon to my colleague Coll: Mason [whose bottle attendance doubted my task] the matter he liked well, but questioned the Govern'rs approbation of it.

I confess'd the case required sedate thoughts, reasoning, that he and such like gentlemen must either co'mand or be co'manded, and if on their denials Mr. Bacon should take distaste, and be constrained to appoint co'manders out of the rabble, the Govern'r himself with the persons & estates of all in the land woud be at their dispose, whereby their own ruine might be owing to themselves; in this he agreed & said "If " the Govern'r woud give his own co'mission he would be content " to serve under General Bacon [as now he began to be intituled] but " first would consult other gentlemen in the same circumstances; who all concurr'd 'twas the most safe barrier in view against pernicious designes, if such should be put in practice; with this I acquainted Mr. Laurence who went [rejoicing] to Mr. Bacon with the good tidings, that the militia co'manders were inclined to serve under him, as their Generall, in case the Governor would please to give them his own co'missions.

Wee of the house proceeded to finish the bill for the war, which by the assent of the Govern'r and councill being past into an act, the Govern'r sent us a letter directed to his majesty, wherein were these words "I have " above 30 years governed the most flourishing conntry the sun ever shone " over, but am now encompassed with rebellion like waters in every re- " spect like to that of Massanello except their leader, and of like import was the substance of that letter, But we did not believe his hono'r sent us all he wrote his majesty.

Some judicious gentlemen of our house likewise penn'd a letter or remonstrance to be sent his Maj'tie, setting forth the gradations of those erupc'ons, and two or three of them with Mr. Minge our clerk brought it me to compile a few lines for the conclusion of it, which I did [tho not without regret in those watchfull times, when every man had eyes on him, but what I wrote was with all possible deferrence to the Govern'r and in the most soft terms my pen cou'd find the case to admit.

Col. Spencer being my neighbor & intimate friend, and a prevalent member in the councill I pray'd him to intreat the Govern'r we might be dissolved, for that was my first and should be my last going astray from my wonted sphere of merchandize & other my private concernments into the dark and slippery meanders of court embarrasments, he told me the Govern'r had not [then] determined his intention, but he wou'd move his hono'r about itt, and in 2 or 3 days we were dissolved, which I was most heartily glad of, because of my getting loose againe from being hampered amongst those pernicious entanglem'ts in the labyrinths & snares of state ambiguities, & which untill then I had not seen the practice nor the dangers of, for it was observ'd that severall of the members had secret badges of distinction fixt upon 'em, as not docill enough to gallop the future races, that court seem'd disposed to lead 'em, whose maxims I had oft times heard whisper'd before, and then found confirm'd by diverse considerate gentlem'n viz't. "that the wise and the rich were prone to ffaction & se- " dition but the fools & poor were easy to be governed."

Many members being met one evening nigh sunsett, to take our leave of each other, in order next day to return homewards, came Gen'll. Bacon with his handfull of unfolded papers & overlooking us round, walking in the room said "which of these Gentlem'n shall I interest to write a few words for me, where every one looking aside as not willing to meddle; Mr. Lawrence pointed at me saying "that gentleman writes very well which I endeavoring to excuse Mr. Bacon came stooping to the ground and said "pray S'r Do me the ho'r to write a line for me."

This surprising accostm't shockt me into a melancholy consternation, dreading upon one hand, that Stafford county would feel the smart of his resentment, if I should refuse him whose favour I had so lately sought and been generously promis'd on their behalf; and on th' other hand fearing the Govern'rs displeasure who I knew would soon hear of it; what seem'd most prudent at this hazardous dilemma was to obviate the present impending peril; So Mr. Bacon made me sit the whole night by him filling up those papers, which I then saw were blank co'missions sign'd by the Govern'r incerting such names & writing other matters as he dictated, which I took to be the happy effects of the consult before mentioned, with the com'anders of the militia because he gave me the names of very few others to put into these com'issions, and in the morning he left me with an hours worke or more to finish, when came to me Capt. Carver, and said he had been to wait on the Generall for a com'ission, and that he was resolved to adventure his old bones against the Indian rogues with other the like discourse, and at length told me that I was in mighty favour —— and he was bid to tell me, that whatever I desired in the Generals power, was at my service, I pray'd him humbly to thank his hon'r and to acquaint him I had no other boon to crave, than his pro- mis'd kindness to Stafford county, for beside the not being worthy, I never had been conversant in military matters, and also having lived tenderly, my service cou'd be of no benefit because the hardships and fatigues of a wilderness campaigne would put a speedy period to my dais: little ex- pecting to hear of more intestine broiles, I went home to Potomack, where reports were afterwards various; we had account that Generall Bacon was march'd with a thousand men into the fforest to seek the enemy Indians, and in a few dais after our next news was, that the Govern'r had sum'on- ed together the militia of Gloucester & Middlesex counties to the number of twelve hundred men, and proposed to them to follow & and suppress that rebell Bacon, whereupon arose a murmuring before his face "Bacon Bacon Bocon, and all walked out of the field, muttering as they went "Bacon Bacon Bacon, leaving the Governor and those that came with him to themselves, who being thus abandon'd wafted over Chesepiacke. bay 30 miles to Accomack where are two counties of Virginia.

Mr. Bacon hearing of this came back part of the way, and sent out parties of horse patrolling through every county, carrying away prisoners all whom he distrusted might any more molest his Indian prosecuc'on yet giving liberty to such as pledg'd him their oaths to return home and live quiet; the copies or contents of which oaths I never saw, but heard were very strict, tho' little observed.

About this time was a spie detected pretending himself a deserter who had twice or thrice come and gone from party to party and was by councill of war sentenced to death. after which Bacon declared openly to him, "that if any one in the army wou'd speak a word to save him, he shou'd "not suffer," which no man appearing to do, he was executed, upon this manifestation of clemency Bacon was applauded for a mercifull man, not willing to spill Christian bloud, nor indeed was it said, that he put any other man to death in cold bloud, or plunder any house; nigh the same time came Maj'r Langston with his troop of horse and quartered two nights at my house who [after high compliments from the Generall] told me I was desired "to accept the Lieutenancy for preserving the peace in the 5 Northern counties betwixt Potomack and Rappahannock rivers, I humbly thank'd his hon'r excusing myself, as I had done before on that invitation of the like nature at James town, but did hear he was mightily offended at my evasions and threatened to remember me.

The Govern'r made 2d, attempt coming over from Accomack with what men he could procure in sloops and boats, forty miles up the river to James town, which Bacon hearing of, came againe down from his fforest pursuit, and finding a bank not a flight shot long, cast up thwart the neck of the peninsula there in James town, he stormed it, and took the town, in which attack were 12. men slaine & wounded but the Govern'r with most of his followers fled back, down the river in their vessells.

Here resting a few dais they concerted the burning of the town, wherein Mr. Lawrence and Mr. Drumond owning the two best houses save one, sat fire each to his own house, which example the souldiers following laid the whole town with church and State house in ashes, saying, the rogues should harbour no more there.

On these reiterated molestac'ons Bacon calls a convention at Midle plantation 15. miles from James town in the month of August 1676, where an oath with one or more proclamations were formed, and writts by him issued for an Assembly; the oaths or writts I never saw, but one proclamation com'anded all men in the land on pain of death to joine him, and retire into the wildernesse upon arrival of the forces expected from England, and oppose them untill they should propose to accept to treat of an accom'odntion, which we who lived comfortably coud not have undergone, so as the whole land must have become an Aceldama if gods exceeding mercy had not timely removed him.

During these tumults in Virginia a 2d. danger menaced Maryland by an insurrection in that province, complaining of their heavy taxes &c. where 2 or 3 of the leading malcontents [men otherwise of laudable characters] were put to death, which stifled the farther spreading of that flame. Mr. Bacon, [at this time] press't the best ship in James river, carrying 20 guns and putting into her his Lieutenant Generall Mr. Bland [a gentleman newly come thither from England to possesse the estate of his deceased uncle late of the council] and under him the forementioned Capt. Carver, formerly a com'ander of Merch'ts ships with men & all necessaries, he sent her to ride before Accomack to curb and intercept all small vessels of war com'ission'd by the Govern'r com'ing often over and making depredations on the Western shoar, as if we had been fforeign enemies, which gives occasion in this place to digress a few words.

Att first assembly after the peace came a message to them from the Govern'r for some marks of distinction to be set on his loyal friends of Accomack, who received him in his adversity which when came to be consider'd Col: Warner [then Speaker] told the house " Ye know that " what mark of distinction his hono'r coud have sett on those of Acco- " mack unlesse to give them ear marks or burnt marks for robbing and " ravaging honest people, who stay'd at home and preserv'd the estates " of those who ran away, when none intended to hurt 'em."

Now returning to Capt Carver the Govern'r sent for him to come on shoar, promising his peaceable return, who answer'd, he could not trust his word, but if he wou'd send his hand & seal, he wou'd adventure to wait upon his hono'r which was done, and Carver went in his sloop well arm'd & man'd with the most trusty of his men where he was caress'd with wine &c. and large promises, if he would forsake Bacon, resigne his ship or joine with him, to all which he answer'd that "if he served the " Devill he would be true to his trust, but that he was resolved to go " home and live quiet.

In the mean time of this recepc'on and parley, an armed boat was prepared with many oars in a creek not far off, but out of sight, which when Carver sail'd, row'd out of the creek, and it being almost calm the boat out went the sloop whilst all on board the ship were upon the deck staring at both, thinking the boats company coming on board by Carvers invitation to be civilly entertained in requitall for the kindness they supposed he had received on shoar, untill coming under the stern, those in the boat slipt nimbly in at the gun room ports with pistolls &c. when one courageous gentleman ran up to the deck, & clapt a pistoll to Blands breast, saying you are my prisorner, the boats company suddainly following with pistolls swords &c. and after Capt. Larimore (the com'ander of the ship before she was presst) having from the highest and hindmost part of the stern interchang'd a signal from the shoar, by flirting his handkercher about his nose, his own former crew had laid handspikes ready, which they [at that instant] caught up &c. so as Bland & Carvers men were amazed and yielded.

Carver seeing a hurly burly on the ships deck, woud have gone away with his sloop, but having little wind & the ship threat'ning to sink him, he tamely came on board, where Bland & he with their party were laid in irons,

and in 3, or 4 dais Carver was hang'd on shoar, which S'r Henry Chi-
chelly the first of the councill then a prisoner, [with diverse other gentle-
men] to Mr. Bacon, did afterwards exclaime against as a most rash and
wicked act of the Govern'r he in particular expecting to have been treated
by way of reprizall, as Bacons friend Carver had been by the Govern'r.
Mr. Bacon now returns from his last expedic'on sick of fflux; without
finding any enemy Indians, having not gone far by reason of the vexations
behind him, nor had he one dry day in all his marches to and fro in the
fforest whilst the plantations [not 50. miles distant] had a sum'er so dry
as stinted the Indian corn and tobacco &c. which the people ascribed to
the Pawawings i. e. the sorceries of the Indians, in a while Bacon dyes
& was succeeded by his Lieuten't Gen'll Ingram, who had one Wakelet
next in com'and under him, whereupon hasten'd over the Govern'r to
York river, and with whom they articled for themselves, and whom else
they could, and so all submitted and were pardoned exempting those
nominated and otherwise proscribed, in a proclamac'on of indemnity, the
principall of whom were Laurence and Drum'ond.

Mr. Bland was then a prisoner having been taken with Carver, as before noted, and in a few dais Mr. Drumond was brought in, when the
Govern'r being on board a ship came im'ediately on shore and complimented him with the ironicall sarcasm of a low bend, saying "Mr.
"Drummond! you are very unwelcome, I am more glad to see you,
"than any man in Virginia, Mr. Drumond you shall be hang'd in half
"an hour; who answered What yo'r hono'r pleases, and as soon as a
council of war cou'd meet, his sentence be dispatchat & a gibbet erected
[which took up near two houres] he was executed.

This Mr. Drumond was a sober Scotch gentleman of good repute with
whome I had not a particular acquaintance, nor do I know the cause of
that rancour his hono'r had against him other than his pretentions in
com'n for the publick but meeting him by accident the morning I left the
town, I advis'd him to be very wary, for he saw the Govern'r had put a
brand upon him, he [gravely expressing my name] answered "I am in
over shoes, I will be over boots," which I was sorry to heare & left him.

The last account of Mr. Laurence was from an uppermost plantation,
where he and ffour others desperado's with horses pistolls &c. march'd
away in a snow ancle deep, who were thought to have cast themselves
into a branch of some river, rather than to be treated like Drum'ond.

Bacons body was so made away, as his bones were never found to be
exposed on a gibbet as was purpos'd, stones being laid on his coffin,
supposed to be done by Laurence.

Near this time arrived a small ffleet with a regiment from England S'r
John Berry admirall, Col: Herbert Jefferies com'ander of the land forces and
Collo: Morrison who had one year been a former Govern'r there, all three
joined in a com'ission with or to S'r William Barclay, soon after when a
generall court, and also an assembly were held, where some of our former
assembly [with so many others] were put to death, diverse whereof were
persons of honest reputations and handsome estates, as that the Assembly
petitioned the Govern'r to spill no more bloud, and Mr. Presly at his coming
home told me, he believed the Govern'r would have hang'd half the

country, if they had let him alone, the first was Mr. Bland whose friends in England had procured his pardon to be sent over with the ffleet, which he pleaded at his tryall, was in the Govern'rs pocket [tho' whether 'twas so, or how it came there, I know not, yet did not hear 'twas openly contradicted] but he was answered by Collo. Morrison that he pleaded his pardon at swords point, which was look'd upon an odd sort of reply, and he was executed; [as was talked] by private instructions from England the Duke of York having sworn "by god Bacon & Bland shoud dye.

The Govern'r went in the ffleet to London [whether by com'and from his Majesty or spontaneous I did not hear] leaving Col. Jefferyes in his place, and by next shipping came back a person who waited on his hono'r in his voyage, and untill his death, from whom a report was whisper'd about, that the king did say "that old fool had hang'd more men in that " naked country, than he had done for the murther of his father, whereof the Govern'r hearing dyed soon after without having seen his majesty ; which shuts up this tragedy.

APPENDIX.

To avoid incumbering the body of the foregoing little discourse, I have not therein mentioned the received opinion in Virginia, which very much attributed the promoting these perturbac'ons to Mr. Laurence, & Mr. Bacon with his other adherents, were esteemed, as but wheels agitated by the weight of his former & present resentments, after their choler was raised up to a very high pitch, at having been [so long & often] trifled with on their humble supplications to the Govern'r for his im'ediate taking in hand the most speedy meanes towards stopping the continued effusions of so much English bloud, from time to time by the Indians; which com'on sentim'ts I have the more reason to believe were not altogether groundless, because my self have heard him [in his familiar discourse] insinuate as if his fancy gave him prospect of finding (at one time or other) some expedient not only to repair his great losse, but therewith to see those abuses rectified that the country was oppressed with through (as he said) the forwardness avarice & french despotick methods of the Govern'r & likewise I know him to be a thinking man, and tho' nicely honest, affable, & without blemish; in his conversation and dealings, yet did he manifest abundance of uneasiness in the sense of his hard usages, which might prompt him to improve that Indian quarrel to the service of his animosities, and for this the more fair & frequent opportunities offered themselves to him by his dwelling at James town, where was the concourse from all parts to the Govern'r and besides that he had married a welathy widow who kept a large house of public entertainm't unto which resorted those of the best quality and such others as businesse called to that town, and his parts with his even temper made his converse coveted by persons of all ranks ; so that being subtile, and having these advantages he might with lesse difficulty discover mens inclinations, and instill his notions where he found those woud be imbib'd with greatest satisfaction.

As for Mr. Bacon fame did lay to his charge the having run out his patrimony in England except what he brought to Virginia, and for that the most part to be exhausted, which together made him suspecting of casting an eye to search for retrievment in the troubled waters of popular discontents, wanting patience to wait the death of his opulent cousin, old Collo. Bacon, whose estate he expected to inherit.

But he was too young, too much a stranger there, and of a disposition too precipitate, to manage things to that length those were carried, had not thoughtfull Mr. Laurence been at the bottom.

HISTORY

OF

THE VALLEY.

————— ⁕•••⁕ —————

CHAPTER I.

INDIAN WARS.

FROM the best evidence the author has been able to obtain, and to this end he has devoted much time and research, the settlement of our fine and beautiful valley commenced in the year 1732, about one hundred and twenty-five years from the first settlement in Virginia. Before going into a detail of the first immigration to and improvement of the Valley, the author believes it will not be uninteresting to the general reader, to have a brief history of the long and bloody wars carried an between contending tribes of Indians. Tradition relates that the Delaware and Catawba tribes were engaged in war at the time the Valley was first known by the white people, and that that war was continued for many years after our section of country became pretty numerously inhabited by the white settlers.

I shall commence with a narrative of Indian battles fought on the Cohongoruton.* At the mouth of Antietam, a small creek on the Maryland

---

*Cohongoruton is the ancient Indian name of the Potomac, from its junction with the Shenandoah to the Allegany mountain. Lord Fairfax, in his grants for land on this water course, designated it Potomac; by which means it gradually lost its ancient name, and now is generally known by no other name. Maj. H. Bedinger writes the name of this river Cohongoluta. It is, however, written in the act laying off the county of Frederick in 1738, Cohongoruton.

side of the river, a most bloody affair took place between parties of the Catawba and Delaware tribes. This was probably about the year 1736. The Delawares had penetrated pretty far to the south, committed some acts of outrage on the Catawbas, and on their retreat were overtaken at the mouth of this creek, when a desperate conflict ensured. Every man of the Delaware party was put to death, with the exception of one who escaped after the battle was over, and every Catawba held up a scalp but one. This was a disgrace not to be borne; and he instantly gave chase to the fugitive, overtook him at the Susquehanna river, (a distance little short of one hundred miles,) killed and scalped him, and returning, showed his scalp to several white people, and exulted in what he had done.*

Another most bloody battle was fought at the mouth of Conococheague,† on Friend's land, in which but one Delaware escaped death, and he ran in to Friend's house, when the family shut the door, and kept the Catawbas out, by which means the poor fugitive was saved.‡

There is also a tradition, and there are evident signs of the fact, of another furious battle fought at what is called the Slim Bottom on Wappatomaka,§ (the ancient Indian name of the Great South Branch of the Potomac,) about one and a half miles from its mouth. At this place there are several large Indian graves, near what is called the Painted Rock. On this rock is exhibited the shape of a man with a large blotch, intended, probably, to represent a man bleeding to death. The stain, it appeared to the author, was made with human blood. The top of the rock projects over the painted part so as to protect it from the washings of the rains, and is on the east side of the rock. How long the stain of human blood would remain visible in a position like this, the author cannot pretend to express an opinion; but he well recollects the late Gen. Isaac Zane informed him that the Indians beat out the brains of an infant (near his old iron works) against a rock, and the stain of the blood was plainly to be seen about forty years afterwards. In this battle it is said but one Delaware escaped, and he did so by leaping into the river, diving under the water, and continuing to swim until he crossed the Cohongoruton.||

A great battle between these hostile tribes, it is said, was fought at what is called the Hanging Rocks, on the Wappatomaka, in the county

---

*This tradition was related to the author by Capt. James Glenn, of Jefferson county, now upwards of 73 years of age, and confirmed by the venerable John Tomlinson, near Cumberland, Maryland, now 92 years old.

†Mr. Tomlinson is of opinion this affair took place at the mouth of the Opequon.

‡Capt. James Glenn, confirmed by Mr. Tomlinson, except as to the place of battle.

§The name of this water course in Lord Fairfax's ancient grants is written Wappatomac; but Mr. Heath and Mr. Blue both stated that the proper name was Wappatomaka.

||Capt. James Glenn, confirmed by Mr. Garret Blue, of Hampshire.— Indeed, this tradition is familiar to most of the elderly citizens on the South Branch, as also the battle of the Hanging Rocks.

of Hampshire, where the river passes through the mountain.* A pretty large party of the Delawares had invaded the territory of the Catawbas, taken several prisoners, and commenced their retreat homewards. When they reached this place, they made a halt, and a number of them commenced fishing. Their Catawba enemies, close in pursuit, discovered them, and threw a party of men across the river, with another in their front. Thus enclosed, with the rock on one side, a party on the opposite side of the river, another in their front, and another in their rear, a most furious and bloody onset was made, and it is believed that several hundred of the Delawares were slaughtered. Indeed, the signs now to be seen at this place exhibit striking evidences of the fact. There is a row of Indian graves between the rock and public road, along the margin of the river, from sixty to seventy yards in length. It is believed that but very few of the Delawares escaped.

There are also signs of a bloody battle having been fought at the forks of the Wappatomaka; but of this battle, if it ever occurred, the author could obtain no traditional account.

Tradition also relates that the Southern Indians exterminated a tribe, called the Senedos, on the North fork of the Shenandoah river, at present the residence of William Steenbergen, Esq., in the county of Shenandoah. About the year 1734, Benjamin Allen, Riley Moore, and William White, settled in this neighborhood. Benjamin Allen settled on the beautiful estate called Allen's bottom. An aged Indian frequently visited him, and on one occasion informed him that the " Southern Indians killed his whole nation with the exception of himself and one other youth; that this bloody slaughter took place when he, the Indian, was a small boy."*— From this tradition, it is probable this horrid affair took place some time shortly after the middle of the seventeenth century. Maj. Andrew Keyser also informed the author that an Indian once called at his grandfather's, in Lancaster county, Pennsylvania, appeared to be much agitated, and asked for something to eat. After refreshing himself, he was asked what disturbed him. He replied, " The Southern Indians have killed my whole nation."

There are also evident signs of the truth of this tradition yet to be seen. On Mr. Steenbergen's land are the remains of an Indian mound, though it is now plowed down. The ancient settlers in the neighborhood differ in their opinion as to its original height. When they first saw it, some say it was eighteen or twenty feet high, others that it did not exceed twelve or fourteen, and that it was from fifty to sixty yards in circumference at the base. This mound was literally filled with human skeletons; and it is highly probably that this was the depository of the dead after the great massacre which took place as just related.

This brief account of Indian battles contains all the traditionary infor-

---

*As the author expects to give a detailed description of this extraordinary place, in his chapter of natural curiosities, he will barely mention the fact, that this rock, on one side of the river, is a perpendicular wall of several hundred feet high, and several hundred yards in length.

†Mr. Israel Allen related this tradition to the author.

mation the author has been able to collect, with one exception, which will
be noticed in the next chapter.   There is, however, a tradition, that on
one particular occasion, a party of thirty Delaware Indians, having penetrated far to the south, surprised a party of Catawbas, killed several, and
took a prisoner.   The party of Delawares, on their return, called at Mr.
Joseph Perrill's near Winchester, and exulted much at their success.—
The next day a party of ten Catawbas called at Mr. Perrill's in pursuit.—
They enquired when their enemy had passed.   Being informed, they
pushed off at a brisk step, overtook the thirty Delawares at the Cohongoruton, (Potomac,) killed every man, recovered their prisoner, called at
Mr. Perrill's on their return, and told what they had done.*   But it is
probable this is the same affair which took place at the mouth of the
Antietam, though it is possible that it may be a different one.   Mr. Tomlinson is under the impression that there was an Indian battle fought at
the mouth of Opequon.

The author has seen and conversed with several aged and respectable
individuals, who well recollect seeing numerous war parties of the Northern and Southern Indians passing and repassing through the Valley.—
Several warrior paths have been pointed out to him.   One of them led
from the Cohongoruton, (Potomac,) and passed a little west of Winchester southwardly.   This path forked a few miles north of Winchester, and
one branch of it diverged more to the east, crossed the Opequon, very
near Mr. Carter's paper mill, on the creek, and led on toward the forks
of the Shenandoah river.   Another crossed the North mountain and the
Valley a few miles above the Narrow Passage, thence over the Fort
mountain to the South river valley.   Another crossed from Cumberland,
in Maryland, and proceeded up the Wappatomaka or Great South Branch
valley, in the counties of Hampshire and Hardy.

An aged and respectable old lady, on Apple-pie ridge, informed the
author that she had frequently heard her mother speak of a party of Delaware Indians once stopping at her father's, where they stayed all night.—
They had in custody a young female Catawba prisoner, who was one of
the most beautiful females she had ever seen.   Maj. R. D. Glass also
informed the author that his father, who resided at the head of the Opequon, stated the same fact.   It was remarkable to see with what resignation this unfortunate young prisoner submitted to her fate.   Her unfeeling tormentors would tie her, and compel her at night to lay on her back,
with the cords distended from her hands and feet, and tied to branches
or what else they could get at to make her secure, while a man laid on
each side of her with the cords passing under their bodies.

Mr. John Tomlinson also informed the author, that when about seven
or eight years of age, he saw a party of Delawares pass his father's house,
with a female Catawba prisoner, who had an infant child in her arms;—
and that it was said they intended to sacrifice her when they reached
their towns.†

---

*Gen. John Smith communicated this tradition to the author.

†Mr. Tomlinson's father then resided about 7 miles below the mouth of
Conococheague on or near the Potomac, on the Maryland side.

Tradition also relates a very remarkable instance of the sacrifice of a female Catawba prisoner by the Delawares. A party of Delawares crossed the Potomac, near Oldtown, in Maryland, a short distance from which they cruelly murdered their prisoner: they then moved on. The next day several of them returned, and cut off the soles of her feet, in order to prevent her from pursuing and haunting them in their march.*

Capt. Glenn informed the author that a Mrs. Mary Friend, who resided on or near the Potomac, stated to him that she once saw a body of four or five hundred Catawba Indians on their march to invade the Delawares ; but from some cause they became alarmed, and returned without success.

The same gentleman stated to the author that a Mr. James Hendricks informed him that the last sacrifice made by the Delawares, of their Catawba prisoners, was at the first run or stream of water on the south side of Lancaster, Pennsylvania. Here several prisoners were tortured to death with all the wonted barbarity and cruelty peculiar to the savage character. Mr. Hendricks was an eye witness to this scene of horror. During the protracted and cruel sufferings of these unhappy victims, they tantalized and used the most insulting language to their tormentors, threatening them with the terrible vengeance of their nation as long as they could speak.

This bloody tragedy soon reached the ears of the Governor of Pennsylvania, and he forthwith issued his proclamation, commanding and requiring all the authorities, both civil and military, to interpose, and prohibit a repetition of such acts of barbarity and cruelty.

The author will now conclude this narrative of Indian wars, with a few general reflections.

It is the opinion of some philosophers, that it is inherent in the nature of man to fight. The correctness of this opinion Mr. Jefferson seems to doubt, and suggests that "it grows out of the abusive and not the natural state of man." But it really appears there are strong reasons to believe that there does exist "a natural state of hostility of man against man."— Upon what other principle can we account for the long and furious wars which have been carried on, at different periods, among the aboriginals of our country?

At an immense distance apart,† probably little less than six or seven hundred miles, without trade, commerce, or clashing of interests—without those causes of irritation common among civilized states,—we find these two nations for a long series of years engaged in the most implacable and destructive wars. Upon what other principle to account for this state of things, than that laid down, is a subject which the author cannot pretend to explain. It, however, affords matter of curious speculation

---

*Mr. G. Blue, of Hampshire, stated this tradition to the author.

†The Catawba tribes reside on the river of that name in South Carolina. They were a powerful and warlike nation, but are now reduced to less than two hundred souls. The Delawares resided at that period on the Susquehanna river, in Pennsylvania, and are now far west of the Allegany mountains.

E

and interesting reflection to the inquiring mind.   That nations are frequently urged to war and devastation by the restless and turbulent dis--
position so common to mankind, particularly among their leaders, is a
question of little doubt.   The glory and renown (falsely so termed) of
great achievements in war, is probably one principal cause of the wars.
frequently carried on by people in a state of nature.

—:0:—

CHAPTER II.

INDIAN SETTLEMENTS.

THE author deems it unnecessary to give a detailed account of all the
particular places which exhibit signs of the ancient residences of Indians,
but considers it sufficient to say that on all our water courses, evidences
of their dwellings are yet to be seen.   The two great branches of the
Shenandoah, and the south branch of the Potomac, appear to have been
their favorite places of residence.   There are numerous signs of
their villages to be seen on these water courses, than in any other part of
our Valley.

On the banks of the Cohongoruton, (Potomac,) there has doubtless
been a pretty considerable settlement.   The late Col. Joseph Swearengen's dwelling house stands within a circular wall or moat.*   When first
known by the white inhabitants, the wall was about eighteen inches
high, and the ditch about two feet deep.   This circular wall was made
of earth—is now considerably reduced, but yet plainly to be seen.   It is
not more than half a mile from Shepherdstown.

For what particular purpose this wall was thrown up, whether for ornament or defense, the author cannot pretend to form an opinion.   If it
was intended for defense, it appears to have been too low to answer any
valuable purpose in that way.

On the Wappatomaka, a few miles below the forks, tradition relates
that there was a very considerable Indian settlement.   On the farm of
Isaac Vanmeter, Esq., on this water course, in the county of Hardy,
when the country was first discovered, there were considerable openings
of the land, or natural prairies, which are called "the Indian old fields"
to this day.   Numerous Indian graves are to be seen in the neighbor-

---

*Maj. Henry Bedinger informed the author that at his first recollection
of this place, the wall or moat was about eighteen inches high, and the
ditch around it about two feet deep.   The wall was raised on the outside of the ditch, and carefully thrown up.

hood. A little above the forks of this river a very large Indian grave is now to be seen.* In the bank of the river, a little below the forks, numerous human skeletons have been discovered, and several articles of curious workmanship. A highly finished pipe, representing a snake coiled round the bowl, with its head projected above the bowl, was among them. There was the under jaw bone of a human being of great size found at the same place, which contained eight jaw teeth in each side of enormous size; and what is more remarkable, the teeth stood transversely in the jaw bone. It would pass over any common man's face with entire ease.†

There are many other signs of Indian settlements all along this river, both above and below the one just described. Mr. Garret Blue, of the county of Hampshire, informed the author, that about two miles below the Hanging Rocks, in the bank of the river, a stratum of ashes, about one rod in length, was some years ago discovered. At this place are signs of an Indian village, and their old fields. The Rev. John J. Jacobs, of Hampshire, informed the author that on Mr. Daniel Cresap's land, on the North branch of the Potomac, a few miles above Cumberland, a human skeleton was discovered, which had been covered with a coat of wood ashes, about two feet below the surface of the ground. An entire decomposition of the skeleton had taken place, with the exception of the teeth: they were in a perfect state of preservation.

On the two great branches of the Shenandoah there are now to be seen numerous sites of their ancient villages, several of which are so remarkable that they deserve a passing notice. It has been noticed, in my preceding chapter, that on Mr. Steenbergen's land, on the North fork of the Shenandoah, the remains of a large Indian mound are plainly to be seen. It is also suggested that this was once the residence of the Senedo tribe, and that that tribe had been exterminated by the Southern Indians. Exclusive of this large mound,‡ there are several other Indian graves. About this place many of their implements and domestic utensils have been found. A short distance below the mouth of Stony Creek, (a branch of the Shenandoah,) within four or five miles of Woodstock, are the signs of an Indian village. At this place a gun barrel, with several iron tomahawks, were found long after the Indians left the country.§

On Mr. Anthony Kline's farm, within about three miles of Stephensburg, in the county of Frederick, in a glen near his mill, a rifle was found, which had laid in the ground forty or fifty years. Every part of this gun, (even the stock, which was made of black walnut,) was sound. Mr.

---

*William Seymour, Esq., related this fact to the author.

†William Heath, Esq., in the county of Hardy, stated this fact to the author, and that he had repeatedly seen the remarkable jaw bone.

‡Mr. Steenbergen informed the author, that upon looking into this mound, it was discovered that at the head of each skeleton a stone was deposited: that these stones are of various sizes, supposed to indicate the size of the body buried.

§Mr. George Grandstaff stated this to the author. Mr. G. is an aged and respectable citizen of Shenandoah county.

Kline's father took the barrel from the stock, placed the britch on the fire, and it soon discharged with a loud explosion.*

In the county of Page, on the South fork of Shenandoah river, there are several Indian burying grounds and signs of their villages. These signs are also to be seen on the Hawksbill creek. A few miles above Luray, on the west side of the river, there are three large Indian graves, ranged nearly side by side, thirty or forty feet in length, twelve or fourteen feet wide, and five or six feet high. Around them, in circular form, are a number of single graves. The whole covers an area of little less than a quarter of an acre. They present to the eye a very ancient appearance, and are covered over with pine and other forest growth. The excavation of the ground around them is plainly to be seen. The three first mentioned graves are in oblong form, probably contain many hundred of human bodies, and were doubtless the work of ages.†

On the land of Mr. Noah Keyser, near the mouth of the Hawksbill creek, stand the remains of a large mound. This, like that at Mr. Steenbergen's, is considerably reduced by plowing, but is yet some twelve or fourteen feet high, and is upwards of sixty yards round at the base. It is found to be literally filled with human skeletons, and at every fresh plowing a fresh layer of bones are brought to the surface. The bones are found to be in a calcarious state, with the exception of the teeth, which are generally sound. Several unusually large skeletons have been discovered in this grave. On the lands now the residence of my venerable friend, John Gatewood, Esq. the signs of an Indian village are yet plainly to be seen. There are numerous fragments of their pots, cups, arrow points, and other implements for domestic use, found from time to time. Convenient to this village there are several pretty large graves.

There is also evidence of an Indian town in Powell's Fort, on the lands now owned by Mr. Daniel Munch. From appearances, this too was a pretty considerable village. A little above the forks of the Shenandoah, on the east side of the South fork, are the appearances of another settlement, exhibiting the remains of two considerable mounds now entirely reduced by plowing. About this place many pipes, tomahawks, axes, hommony pestles, &c. have been found. Some four or five miles below the forks of the river, on the south-east side, on the lands now owned by Capt. Daniel Oliver, is the site of another Indian village. At this place a considerable variety of articles have been plowed up. Among the number were several whole pots, cups, pipes, axes, tomahawks, hommony pestles, &c. A beautiful pipe of high finish, made of white flint stone, and several other articles of curious workmanship, all of very

*Mr. Anthony Kline related this occurrence to the author. No man who is acquainted with Mr. Kline, will for one moment doubt his assertions. This rifle was of a very large calibre, and was covered several feet below the surface of the ground, and doubtless left there by an Indian.

†These graves are on the lands now the residence of the widow Long, and appear never to have been disturbed.

hard stone, have been found. Their cups and pots were made of a mixture of clay and shells, of rude workmanship, but of firm texture.

There are many other places on all our water courses, to wit, Stony Creek, Cedar Creek, and Opequon, as well as the larger water courses, which exhibit evidences of ancient Indian settlements. The Shawnee tribe, it is well known, were settled about the neighborhood of Winchester. What are called the "Shawnee cabins," and "Shawnee springs," immediately adjoining the town, are well known. It is also equally certain, that this tribe had a considerable village on Babb's marsh, some three or four miles north-west of Winchester.*

The Tuscarora Indians resided in the neighborhood of Martinsburg, in the county of Berkeley,† on the Tuscarora creek. On the fine farm, now owned by and the residence of Matthew Ranson, Esq. (the former residence of Mr. Benjamin Beeson,) are the remains of several Indian graves. These, like several others, are now plowed down; but numerous fragments of human bones are to be found mixed with the clay on the surface. Mr. Ranson informed the author, that at this place the under jaw bone of a human being was plowed up, of enormous size; the teeth were found in a perfect state of preservation.

Near the Shannondale springs, on the lands of Mr. Fairfax, an Indian grave some years since was opened, in which a skeleton of unusual size was discovered.‡

Mr. E. Paget informed the author, that on Flint run, a small rivulet of the South river, in the county of Shenandoah, a skeleton was found by his father, the thigh bone of which measured three feet in length, and the under jaw bone of which would pass over any common man's face with ease.

Near the Indian village described on a preceding page, on Capt. Oliver's land, a few years ago, some hands in removing the stone covering an Indian grave, discovered a skeleton, whose great size attracted their attention. The stones were carefully taken off without disturbing the frame, when it was discovered, that the body had been laid at full length on the ground, and broad flat stones set round the corpse in the shape of a coffin. Capt. Oliver measured the skeleton as it lay, which was nearly seven feet long.‖

In the further progress of this work the author will occasionally advert

---

*Mr. Thomas Barrett, who was born in 1755, stated to the author, that within his recollection the signs of the Indian wigwams were to be seen on Babb's marsh.

†Mr. John Shobe, a very respectable old citizen of Martinsburg, stated to the author, that Mr. Benjamin Beeson, a highly respectable Quaker, informed him, that the Tuscarora Indians were living on the Tuscarora creek when he (Beeson) first knew the county.

‡Mr. George W. Fairfax gave the author this information.

‖Maximus, a Roman Emperor in the third century, "was the son of a Thracian shepherd, and is represented by historians as a man of gigantic stature and Herculean strength. He was fully eight feet in height, and perfectly symmetrical in form. Abridged U. History, vol. ii. p. 35.

to the subject of Indian antiquities and traits of the Indian character.—
This chapter will now be concluded with some general reflections on the
seemingly hard fate of this unfortunate race of people. It appears to the
author that no reflecting man can view so many burying places broken up
—their bones torn up with the plow—reduced to dust, and scattered to
the winds—without feeling some degree of melancholy regret. It is to
be lamented for another reason. If those mounds and places of burial
had been permittted to remain undisturbed, they would have stood as
lasting monuments in the history of our country. Many of them were
doubtless the work of ages, and future generations would have contem-
plated them with great interest and curiosity. But these memorials are
rapidly disappearing, and the time perhaps will come, when not a trace of
them will remain. The author has had the curiosity to open several Indian graves, in one of which he found a pipe, of different form from any
he has ever seen. It is made of a hard black stone, and glazed or rather
painted with a substance of a reddish cast. In all the graves he has examined, the bones are found in a great state of decay except the teeth,
which are generally in a perfect state of preservation.

It is no way wonderful that this unfortunate race of people reluctantly
yielded their rightful and just possession of this fine country. It is no
way wonderful that they resisted with all their force the intrusion of the
white people (who were strangers to them, from a foreign country,) upon
their rightful inheritance. But perhaps this was the fiat of Heaven.—
When God created this globe, he probably intended it should sustain the
greatest possible number of his creatures. And as the human family, in a
state of civil life, increases with vastly more rapidity than a people in a
state of nature or savage life, the law of force has been generally resorted
to, and the weaker compelled to give way to the stronger. That a part
of our country has been acquired by this law of force, is undeniable. It
is, however, matter of consoling reflection, that there are some honorable
exceptions to this arbitrary rule. The great and wise William Penn set
the example of purchasing the Indian lands. Several respectable individuals of the Quaker society thought it unjust to take possession of this
valley without making the Indians some compensation for their right.—
Measures were adopted to effect this great object. But upon inquiry, no
particular tribe could be found who pretended to have any prior claim to
the soil. It was considered the common hunting ground of various tribes,
and not claimed by any particular nation who had authority to sell.

This information was communicated to the author by two aged and highly respectable men of the Friends' society, Isaac Brown and Lewis Neill,
each of them upwards of eighty years of age, and both residents of the
county of Frederick.

In confirmation of this statement, a letter written by Thomas Chaukley
to the monthly meeting on Opequon, on the 21st of 5th month, 1738, is
strong circumstantial evidence; of which letter the following is a copy:

"VIRGINIA, at John Cheagle's, 21st 5th month, 1738.
" *To the friends of the monthly meeting at Opequon:*
"Dear friends who inhabit Shenandoah and Opequon:—Having a con-

cern for your welfare and prosperity, both now and hereafter, and also
the prosperity of your children, I had a desire to see you; but being in
years, and heavy, and much spent and fatigued with my long journeyings
in Virginia and Carolina, makes it seem too hard for me to perform a visit
in person to you, wherefore I take this way of writing to discharge my
mind of what lies weighty thereon; and

"First. I desire that you be very careful (being far and back inhabitants) to keep a friendly correspondence with the native Indians, giving
them no occasion of offense; they being a cruel and merciless enemy,
where they think they are wronged or defrauded of their rights; as woful
experience hath taught in Carolina, Virginia and Maryland, and especially in New England, &c.; and

"Secondly. As nature hath given them and their forefathers the possession of this continent of America (or this wilderness), they had a natural
right thereto in justice and equity; and no people, according to the law
of nature and justice and our own principle, which is according to the
glorious gospel of our dear and holy Jesus Christ, ought to take away or
settle on other men's lands or rights without consent, or purchasing the
same by agreement of parties concerned; which I suppose in your case
is not yet done.

"Thirdly. Therefore my counsel and christian advice to you is, my
dear friends, that the most reputable among you do with speed endeavor
to agree with and purchase your lands of the native Indians or inhabitants. Take example of our worthy and honorable late proprietor William Penn; who by the wise and religious care in that relation, hath settled a lasting peace and commerce with the natives, and through his prudent management therein hath been instrumental to plant in peace one of
the most flourishing provinces in the world.

"Fourthly. Who would run the risk of the lives of their wives and
children for the sparing a little cost and pains? I am concerned to lay
these things before you, under an uncommon exercise of mind, that your
new and flourishing little settlement may not be laid waste, and (if the
providence of the Almighty doth not intervene,) some of the blood of
yourselves, wives or children, be shed or spilt on the ground.

"Fifthly. Consider you are in the province of Virginia, holding what
rights you have under that government; and the Virginians have made an
agreement with the natives to go as far as the mountains and no farther;
and you are over and beyond the mountains, therefore out of that agreement; by which you lie open to the insults and incursions of the Southern
Indians, who have destroyed many of the inhabitants of Carolina and
Virginia, and even now destroyed more on the like occasion. The English going beyond the bounds of their agreement, eleven of them were
killed by the Indians while we were travelling in Virginia.

"Sixthly. If you believe yourselves to be within the bounds of William
Penn's patent from King Charles the second, which will be hard for you
to prove, you being far southward of his line, yet if done, that will be no
consideration with the Indians without a purchase from them, except you
will go about to convince them by fire and sword, contrary to our princi-

ples; and if that were done, they would ever be implacable enemies, and the land could never be enjoyed in peace.

"Seventhly. Please to note that in Pennsylvania no new settlements are made without an agreement with the natives; as witness Lancaster county, lately settled, though that is far within the grant of William Penn's patent from king Charles the second; wherefore you lie open to the insurrections of the Northern as well as Southern Indians; and

"Lastly. Thus having shewn my good will to you and to your new little settlement, that you might sit every one under your own shady tree, where none might make you afraid, and that you might prosper naturally and spiritually, you and your children; and having a little eased my mind of that weight and concern (in some measure) that lay upon me, I at present desist, and subscribe myself, in the love of our holy Lord Jesus Christ, your real friend,   T. C."

This excellent letter from this good man proves that the Quakers were among our earliest settlers, and that this class of people were early disposed to do justice to the natives of the country.

Had this humane and just policy of purchasing the Indian lands been first adopted and adhered to, it is highly probable the white people might have gradually obtained possession without the loss of so much blood and treasure.

The ancestors of the Neills, Walkers, Bransons, McKays, Hackneys, Beesons, Luptons, Barretts, Dillons, &c. were among the earliest Quaker immigrants to our valley.   Three Quakers by the name of Fawcett settled at an early period about 8 or 9 miles south of Winchester, near Zane's old iron works, from whom a pretty numerous progeny has descended.— They have, however, chiefly migrated to the west.

Mr. Jefferson, in his notes on Virginia, says, "That the lands of this country were taken from them (the Indians,) by conquest, is not so general a truth as is supposed.   I find in our historians and records, repeated proofs of purchase, which cover a considerable part of the lower country; and many more would doubtless be found on further search.   The upper country we know has been acquired altogether by purchase in the most unexceptionable form."

Tradition relates, that several tracts of land were purchased by Quakers from the Indians on Apple-pie ridge, and that the Indians never were known to disturb the people residing on the land so purchased.

CHAPTER III.

FIRST SETTLEMENT OF THE VALLEY.

In the year 1732, Joist Hite, with his family, and his sons-in-law, viz. George Bowman, Jacob Chrisman and Paul Froman, with their families, Robert McKay, Robert Green, William Duff, Peter Stephens, and several others, amounting in the whole to sixteen families, removed from Pennsylvania, cutting their road from York, and crossing the Cohongoruton about two miles above Harpers-Ferry. Hite settled on Opequon, about five miles south of Winchester, on the great highway from Winchester to Staunton, now the residence of the highly respectable widow of the late Richard Peters Barton, Esq. and also the residence of Richard W. Barton, Esq. Peter Stephens and several others settled at Stephensburg, and founded the town; Jacob Chrisman at what is now called Chrisman's spring, about two miles south of Stephensburg; Bowman on Cedar creek about six miles farther south; and Froman on the same creek, 8 or 9 miles north west of Bowman. Robert McKay settled on Crooked run, 8 or 9 miles south east of Stephensburg. The several other families settled in the same neighborhood, wherever they could find wood and water most convenient. From the most authentic information which the author has been able to obtain, Hite and his party were the first immigrants who settled west of the Blue ridge. They were, however, very soon followed by numerous others.

In 1734,[*] Benjamin Allen, Riley Moore, and William White, removed from Monoccacy, in Maryland, and settled on the North branch of the Shenandoah, now in the county of Shenandoah, about 12 miles south of Woodstock.

In 1733, Jacob Stover, an enterprising German, obtained from the then governor of Virginia, a grant for five thousand acres of land on the South fork of the Gerando[†] river, on what was called Mesinetto creek.[‡]

Tradition relates a singular and amusing account of Stover and his

---

[*] Mr. Steenbergen informed the author that the traditionary account of the first settlement of his farm, together with Allen's and Moore's, made it about 106 years; but Mr. Aaron Moore, grandson of Riley Moore, by referring to the family records, fixes the period pretty correctly. According to Mr. Moore's account, Moore, Allen and White, removed from Maryland in 1734.

[†] This water course was first written Gerando, then Sherandoah, now Shenandoah.

[‡] Mesinetto is now called Masinutton. There is a considerable settlement of highly improved farms, now called "the Masinutton settlement," in the new county of Page, on the west side of the South river, on Stover's ancient grant.   G

grant.* On his application to the executive for his grant, he was refused unless he could give satisfactory assurance that he would have the land settled with the requisite number of families within a given time. Being unable to do this, he forthwith passed over to England, petitioned the king to direct his grant to issue, and in order to insure success, had given human names to every horse, cow, hog and dog he owned, and which he represented as heads of families, ready to migrate and settle the land. By this disingenuous trick he succeeded in obtaining directions from the king and council for securing his grant; on obtaining which he immediately sold out his land in small divisions, at three pounds (equal to ten dollars) per hundred, and went off with the money.

Two men, John and Isaac Vanmeter, obtained a warrant from governor Gooch for locating forty thousand acres of land. This warrant was obtained in the year 1730. They sold or transferred part of their warrant to Joist Hite; and from this warrant emanated several of Hite's grants, which the author has seen. Of the titles to the land on which Hite settled, with several other tracts in the neighborhood of Stephensburg, the originals are founded on this warrant.

In the year 1734, Richard Morgan obtained a grant for a tract of land in the immediate neighborhood of Shepherdstown, on or near the Cohongoruton. Among the first settlers on this water course and its vicinity, were Robert Harper (Harpers-Ferry), William Stroop, Thomas and William Forester, Israel Friend, Thomas Shephard, Thomas Swearengen, Van Swearengen, James Forman, Edward Lucas, Jacob Hite,† John Lemon, Richard Mercer, Edward Mercer, Jacob Vanmeter and brothers, Robert Stockton, Robert Buckles, John Taylor, Samuel Taylor, Richard Morgan, John Wright, and others.

The first settlers on the Wappatomaka (South Branch) were Coburn, Howard, Walker and Rutledge. This settlement commenced about the year 1734 or 1735. It does not appear that the first immigrants to this fine section of country had the precaution to secure titles to their lands, until Lord Fairfax migrated to Virginia, and opened his office for granting warrants in the Northern Neck. The earliest grant which the author could find in this settlement bears date in 1747. The most of the grants are dated in 1749. This was a most unfortunate omission on the part of these people. It left Fairfax at the discretion of exercising his insatiable disposition for the monopoly of wealth ; and instead of granting these lands upon the usual terms allowed to other settlers, he availed himself of the opportunity of laying off in manors, fifty-five thousand acres, in what he called his South Branch manor, and nine thousand acres on Patterson's creek.

This was considered by the settlers an odious and oppressive act on the part of his lordship, and many of them left the country.‡ These two great

---

*Stover's grant is described as being in the county of Spottsylvania, St. Mark's Parish. Of course, Spottsylvania at that period, i. e. 1733, crossed the Blue Ridge.

†One of Joist Hite's sons.

‡William Heath, Esq. of Hardy, gave the author this information.

surveys were made in the year 1747. To such tenants as remained, his lordship granted leases for ninety-nine years, reserving an annual rent of twenty shillings sterling per hundred acres ; whereas to all other immigrants only two shillings sterling rent per hundred was reserved, with a fee simple title to the tenant. Some further notice of Lord Fairfax and his immense grant will be taken in a future chapter.

Tradition relates that a man by the name of John Howard, and his son, previous to the first settlement of our valley, explored the country, and discovered the charming valley of the South Branch, crossed the Allegany mountains, and on the Ohio killed a very large buffalo bull, skinned him, stretched his hide over ribs of wood, made a kind of boat, and in this frail bark descended the Ohio and Mississippi to New Orleans, where they were apprehended by the French as suspicious characters, and sent to France; but nothing criminal appearing against them, they were discharged. From hence they crossed over to England, where Fairfax by some means got to hear of Mr. Howard, sought an interview with him, and obtained from him a description of the fertility and immense value of the South Branch, which determined his lordship at once to secure it in manors.* Notwithstanding this selfish monopoly on the part of Fairfax, the great fertility and value of the country induced numerous tenants to take leases, settle, and improve the lands.

At an early period many immigrants settled on Capon, (anciently called Cacaphon, which is said to be the Indian name,) also on Lost river.—Along Back creek, Cedar creek, and Opequon, pretty numerous settlements were made. The two great branches of the Shenandoah, from its forks upwards, were among our earliest settlements.

An enterprising Quaker, by the name of Ross, obtained a warrant for surveying forty thousand acres of land. The surveys on this warrant were made along Opequon, north of Winchester, and up to Apple-pie ridge. Pretty numerous immigrants of the Quaker profession removed from Pennsylvania, and settled on Ross's surveys. The reader will have observed in my preceding chapter, that as early as 1738, this people had regular monthly meetings established on Opequon.†

The lands on the west side of the Shenandoah, from a little below the forks, were first settled by overseers and slaves, nearly down to the mouth of the Bullskin. A Col. Carter,‡ of the lower country, had obtained grants for about sixty-three thousand acres of land on this river. His surveys commenced a short distance below the forks of the river, and ran down a little below Snicker's ferry, upwards of 20 miles. This fine body of land is now subdivided into a great many most valuable farms, a considerable part of which are now owned by the highly respectable families of Burwells and Pages. But little of it now remains in the hands of Carter's heirs.

---

*Also related by Mr. Heath.

†See Chaukley's letter to the monthly meeting on Opequon, 21st May, 1738, page 39.

‡Col. Robert Carter obtained grants in September, 1730, for sixty-three thousand acres.

Another survey of thirteen thousand acres was granted to another person, and lies immediately below and adjoining Carter's line, running a considerable distance into the county of Jefferson. This fine tract of land, it is said, was sold under the hammer at Williamsburg, some time previous to the war of the revolution. The owner had been sporting, lost money, and sold the land to pay his debt of honor. General Washington happened to be present, knew the land, and advised the late Ralph Wormley, Esq.* to purchase it. Wormley bid five hundred guineas for it, and it was struck off to him. It is also said that Mr. Wormley, just before or at the time of the sale, had been regaling himself with a social glass, and that when he cooled off, he became extremely dissatisfied with his purchase, considering it as money thrown away. Washington hearing of his uneasiness, immediately waited on him, and told him he would take the purchase off his hands, and pay him his money again, but advised him by all means to hold it, assuring him that it would one day or other be the foundation of an independent fortune for his children; upon which Wormley became better reconciled, and consented to hold on. And truly, as Washington predicted, it would have become a splendid estate in the hands of two or three of his children, had they known how to preserve it. But it passed into other hands, and now constitutes the splendid farms of the late firm of Castleman & McCormick, Hierome L. Opie, Esq. the honorable judge Richard E. Parker, and several others. In truth, all the country about the larger water courses and mountains was settled before the fine country about Bullskin, Long marsh, Spot run, &c.

Much the greater part of the country between what is called the Little North mountain and the Shenandoah river, at the first settling of the valley was one vast prairie,† and like the rich prairies of the west, afforded the finest possible pasturage for wild animals. The country abounded in the larger kinds of game. The buffalo, elk, deer, bear, panther, wild-cat, wolf, fox, beaver, otter, and all other kinds of animals, wild fowl, &c., common to forest countries, were abundantly plenty. The country now the county of Shenandoah, between the Fort mountain and North mountain, was also settled at an early period. The counties of Rockingham and Augusta also were settled at an early time. The settlement of the upper part of our valley will be more particularly noticed, and form the subject of a second volume hereafter, should the public demand it.

From the best evidence the author has been able to collect, and for this purpose he has examined many ancient grants of lands, family records, &c., as well as the oral tradition of our ancient citizens, the settlement of our valley progressed without interruption from the native Indians for a period of about twenty-three years. In the year 1754, the Indians suddenly disappeared, and crossed the Allegany. The year preceding,

---

*Mr. Wormly, it is believed, resided at the time in the county of Middlesex.

†There are several aged individuals now living, who recollect when there were large bodies of land in the counties of Berkeley, Jefferson and Frederick, barren of timber. The barren land is now covered with the best of forest trees.

emissaries from the west of the Allegany came among the Valley Indians and invited them to move off.* This occurrence excited suspicion among the white people that a storm was brewing in the west, which it was essential to prepare to meet.

Tradition relates, that the Indians did not object to the Pennsylvanians settling the country. From the high character of William Penn, (the founder of Pennsylvania,) the poor simple natives believed that all Penn's men were honest, virtuous, humane and benevolent, and partook of the qualities of the illustrious founder of their government. But fatal experience soon taught them a very different lesson. They soon found to their cost that Pennsylvanians were not much better than others.

Tradition also informs us that the natives held in utter abhorence the Virginians, whom they designated "Long Knife," and were warmly opposed to their settling in the valley.

The author will conclude this chapter with some general remarks in relation to the circumstances under which the first settlement of the valley commenced. Tradition informs us, and the oral statements of several aged individuals of respectable character confirm the fact that the Indians and white people resided in the same neighborhood for several years after the first settlement commenced, and that the Indians were entirely peaceable and friendly. This statement must in the nature of things be true; because if it had been otherwise, the white people could not have succeeded in effecting the settlement. Had the natives resisted the first attempts to settle, the whites could not have succeeded without the aid of a pretty considerable army to awe the Indians into submission. It was truly fortunate for our ancestors that this quiescent spirit of the Indians afforded them the opportunity of acquiring considerable strength as to numbers, and the accumulation of considerable property and improvemants, before Indian hostilities commenced.

It has already been stated that it was twenty-three years from the first settlement, before the Indians committed any acts of outrage on the white people. During this period many pretty good dwelling houses were erected. Joist Hite had built a stone house on Opequon, which house is now standing, and has a very ancient appearance;† but there are no marks upon it by which to ascertain the time. In 1751, James Wilson erected a stone house which is still standing, and now the residence of Mr. Adam Kern, adjoining or near the village of Kernstown.

Jacob Chrisman also built a pretty large stone house in the year 1751, now the residence of Mr. Abraham Stickley, about two miles south of Stephensburg. Geo. Bowman and Paul Froman each of them built stone houses, about the same period. The late Col. John Hite, in the year 1753, built a stone house now the dwelling house of Mrs. Barton. This building was considered by far the finest dwelling house west of the Blue

---

*Mr. Thomas Barrett, an aged and respectable citizen of Frederick county, related this tradition to the author.

†On the wall plate of a framed barn built by Hite, the figures 1747 are plainly marked, and now to be seen.

ridge.* Lewis Stephens, in the year 1756, built a stone house, the ruins of which are now to be seen at the old iron works of the late Gen. Isaac Zane. It will hereafter be seen that these several stone buildings became of great importance to the people of the several neighborhoods, as places of protection and security against the attacks of the Indians.

The subject of the early settlement of the valley will be resumed in my next chapter.

——:o:——

CHAPTER IV.

FIRST SETTLEMENT OF THE VALLEY—Continued.

Tradition relates that a man by the name of John Vanmeter, from New York, some years previous to the first settlement of the valley, discovered the fine country on the Wappatomaka. This man was a kind of wandering Indian trader, became well acquainted with the Delawares, and once accompanied a war party who marched to the south for the purpose of invading the Catawbas. The Catawbas, however, anticipated them, met them very near the spot where Pendleton courthouse now stands, and encountered and defeated them with immense slaughter. Vanmeter was engaged on the side of the Deleware in this battle. When Vanmeter returned to New York, he advised his sons, that if they ever migrated to Virginia, by all means to secure a part of the South Branch bottom, and described the lands immediately above what is called "The Trough," as the finest body of land which he had ever discovered in all his travels.— One of his sons, Isaac Vanmeter, in conformity with his father's advice came to Virginia about the year 1736 or 1737, and made what was called a tomahawk improvement on the lands now owned by Isaac Vanmeter, Esq. immediately above the trough, where Fort Pleasant was afterwards erected. After this improvement, Mr. Vanmeter returned to New Jersey, came out again in 1740, and found a man by the name of Coburn settled on his land. Mr. Vanmeter bought out Coburn, and again returned to New Jersey; and in the year 1744 removed with his family and settled on the land.† Previous to Vanmeter's final removal to Virginia, several immigrants from Pennsylvania, chiefly Irish, had settled on the South branch.

---

*There is a tradition in this neighborhood that Col. Hite quarried every stone in this building with his own hands.

†Isaac Vanmeter, Esq., of Hardy, detailed this tradition to the author.

Howard, Coburn, Walker and Rutledge, were the first settlers on the Wappatomaka.*

William Miller and Abraham Hite were also among the early settlers. When the Indian wars broke out, Miller sold out his right to 500 acres of land, and all his stock of horses and cattle in the woods, for twenty-five pounds,† and removed to the South fork of the Shenandoah, a few miles above Front Royal. The 500 acres of land sold by Miller lie within about two miles of Moorefield, and one acre of it would now command more money than the whole tract, including his stock, was sold for.

Casey, Pancake, Forman, and a number of others, had settled on the Wappatomaka previous to Vanmeter's final removal.

In the year 1740, the late Isaac Hite, Esq. one of the sons of Joist Hite, settled on the North Branch of the Shenandoah, in the county of Frederick, on the beautiful farm called "Long meadows." This fine estate is now owned by Maj. Isaac Hite, the only son of Isaac Hite deceased.‡

About the same year, John Lindsey and James Lindsey, brothers, removed and settled on the Long marsh, between Bullskin and Berryville, in the county of Frederick; Isaac Larue removed from New-Jersey in 1743, and settled on the same marsh. About the same period, Christopher Beeler removed and settled within two or three miles from Larue; and about the year 1744, Joseph Hampton and two sons came from the eastern shore of Maryland, settled on Buck marsh, near Berryville, and lived the greater part of the year in a hollow sycamore tree. They enclosed a piece of land and made a crop preparatory to the removal of the family.§

In 1743 Joseph Carter removed from Bucks county, Pennsylvania, and settled on Opequon, about five miles east of Winchester. Very near Mr. Carter's residence, on the west side of the creek, was a beautiful grove of forest timber, immediately opposite which a fine limestone spring issued from the east bank of the creek. This grove was, at the time of Mr. Carter's first settlement, a favorite camping ground of the Indians, where numerous collections, sometimes two or three hundred at a time, would assemble, and remain for several weeks together. Mr. Carter was a shoemaker, and on one occasion two Indians called at his shop just as he had finished and hung up a pair of shoes, which one of the Indians seeing secretly slipped under his blanket, and attempted to make off. Carter detected him, and took the shoes from him. His companion manifested the utmost indignation at the theft, and gave Carter to understand that the culprit would be severely dealt with. As soon as the Indians returned to the encampment, information was given to the chiefs, and the unfortunate thief was so severely chastised, that Mr. Carter, from motives

---

*Communicated by William Heath, Esq.

†Isaac Vanmeter, Esq. stated this fact to the author.

‡Maj. Isaac Hite, of Frederick county, communicated this information to the author.

§Col. John B. Larue and William Castlemen, Esq. gave the author this information.

of humanity, interposed, and begged that the punishment might cease.*

Maj. Isaac Hite informed the author that numerous parties of Indians, in passing and repassing, frequently called at his grandfather's house, on Opequon, and that but one instance of theft was ever committed. On that occasion a pretty considerable party had called, and on their leaving the house some article of inconsiderable value was missing. A messenger was sent after them, and information of the theft given to the chiefs. Search was immediately made, the article found in the possession of one of them, and restored to its owner. These facts go far to show their high sense of honesty and summary justice. It has indeed been stated to the author, that their travelling parties would, if they needed provisions and could not otherwise procure them, kill fat hogs or fat cattle in the woods, in order to supply themselves with food. This they did not consider stealing. Every animal running at large they considered lawful game.

The Indians charge the white people with teaching them the knowledge of theft and several other vices. In the winter of 1815-16, the author spent some weeks in the state of Georgia, where he fell in with Col. Barnett, one of the commissioners for running the boundary line of Indian lands which had shortly before been ceded to the United States. Some conversation took place on the subject of the Indians and Indian character, in which Col. B. remarked, that in one of his excursions through the Indian country, he met with a very aged Cherokee chief, who spoke and understood the English language pretty well. The colonel had several conversations with this aged man, in one of which he congratulated him upon the prospect of his people having their condition greatly improved, there being every reason to believe that in the course of a few years they would become acquainted with the arts of civil life—would be better clothed, better fed, and erect better and more comfortable habitations— and what was of still greater importance, they would become acquainted with the doctrines and principles of the Christian religion. This venerable old man listened with the most profound and respectful attention until the colonel had concluded, and then with a significant shake of his head and much emphasis replied,—That he doubted the benefits to the red people pointed out by the colonel; that before their fathers were acquainted with the whites, the red people needed but little, and that little the Great Spirit gave them, the forest supplying them with food and raiment : that before their fathers were acquainted with the white people, the red people never got drunk, because they had nothing to make them drunk, and never committed theft, because they had no temptation to do so. It was true, that when parties were out hunting, and one party was unsuccessful and found the game of the more successful party hung up, if they needed provision they took it; and this was not stealing—it was the law and custom of the tribes. If they went to war they destroyed each other's property : this was done to weaken their enemy. Red people never swore,

---

*The late Mr. James Carter gave the author this tradition, which he received from his father, who was a boy of 12 or 13 years old at the time, and an eye-witness of the fact. Opposite to this camping ground, on a high hill east of the creek, is a large Indian grave.

because they had no words to express an oath.   Red people would not cheat, because they had no temptation to commit fraud : they never told falsehoods, because they had no temptation to tell lies.   And as to religion, you go to your churches, sing loud, pray loud, and make great noise. The red people meet once a year, at the feast of new corn, extinguish all their fires, and kindle up a new one, the smoke of which ascends to the Great Spirit as a grateful sacrifice.   Now what better is your religion than ours?   The white people have taught us to get drunk, to steal, to lie, to cheat, and to swear; and if the knowledge of these vices, as you profess to hold them, and punish by your laws, is beneficial to the red people, we are benefitted by our acquaintance with you; if not, we are greatly injured by that acquaintance.

To say the least of this untutored old man, his opinions, religion excepted, were but too well founded, and convey a severe rebuke upon the character of those who boast of the superior advantages of the lights of education and a knowledge of the religion of the Holy Redeemer.

From this digression the author will again turn his attention to the early history of our country.

About the year 1763, the first settlements were made at or near the head of Bullskin.   Two families, by the name of Riley and Allemong, first commenced the settlement of this immediate neighborhood.   At this period timber was so scarce that the settlers were compelled to cut small saplings to enclose their fields.*   The prairie produced grass five or six feet high;† and even our mountains and hills were covered with the sustenance of quadrupeds of every species.   The pea vine grew abundantly on the hilly and mountainous lands, than which no species of vegetable production afforded finer and richer pasturage.

From this state of the country, many of our first settlers turned their attention to rearing large herds of horses, cattle, hogs, &c.   Many of them became expert, hardy and adventurous hunters, and spent much of their time and depended chiefly for support and money-making on the sale of skins and furs.‡   Moses Russell, Esq. informed the author that the hilly lands about his residence, near the base of the North mountain, in the south west corner of Frederick, and which now present to the eye the appearance of great poverty of soil, within his recollection were cov-

---

*Messrs. Christian Allemong and George Riley both stated this fact to the author.

†Mr. George Riley, an aged and respectable citizen, stated to the author that the grass on the Bullskin barrens grew so tall, that he had frequently drawn it before him when on horseback, and tied it before him.

‡The late Henry Fry, one of the early settlers on Capon river, upwards of forty years ago informed the author, that he purchased the tract of land on which he first settled, on Capon river, for which he engaged to pay either £200 or £250; the author does not recollect which sum, and that he made every dollar of the money by the sale of skins and furs, the game being killed or caught with his own hands.

H

ered with a fine growth of pea vine, and that stock of every description grew abundantly fat in the summer season.

Isaac Larue, who settled on the Long marsh in 1743, as has been stated, soon became celebrated for his numerous herds of horses and cattle. The author was told by Col. J. B. Larue, who is the owner of part of his grandfather's fine landed estate, that his grandfather frequently owned between ninety and one hundred head of horses, but it so happened that he never could get his stock to count a hundred.

The Hites, Frys, Vanmeters, and many others, raised vast stocks of horses, cattle, hogs, &c. Tradition relates that Lord Fairfax, happening one day in Winchester to see a large drove of unusually fine hogs passing through the town, inquired from whence they came. Being informed that they were from the mountains west of Winchester, he remarked that when a new county should be laid off in that direction it ought to be called Hampshire, after a county in England celebrated for its production of fine hogs; and this, it is said, gave name to the present county of Hampshire.

The author will only add to this chapter, that, from the first settlement of the valley, to the breaking out of the war, on the part of the French and Indians, against our ancestors, in the year 1754, our country rapidly increased in numbers and in the acquisition of property, without interruption from the natives, a period of twenty-two years.

In my next chapter I shall give a brief account of the religion, habits and customs, of the primitive settlers.

—:o:—

CHAPTER V.

RELIGION, HABITS AND CUSTOMS, OF THE PRIMITIVE

SETTLERS.

A large majority of our first immigrants were from Pennsylvania, composed of native Germans or German extraction. There were, however, a number directly from Germany, several from Maryland and New Jersey, and a few from New York. These immigrants brought with them the religion, habits and customs, of their ancestors. They were composed generally of three religious sects, viz: Lutherans, Menonists* and Calvinists, with a few Tunkers. They generally settled in neighborhoods pretty much together.

---

*Simon Meno was one of the earliest German reformers, and the founder of this sect.

The territory now composing the county of Page, Powell's fort, and the Woodstock valley, between the West Fort mountain and North mountain, extending from the neighborhood of Stephensburg for a considerable distance into the county of Rockingham, was almost exclusively settled by Germans. They were very tenacious in the preservation of their language, religion, customs and habits. In what is now Page county they were almost exclusively of the Menonist persuasion: but few Lutherans or Calvinists settled among them. In other sections of the territory above described, there was a mixture of Lutherans and Calvinists. The Menonists were remarkable for their strict adherence to all the moral and religious observances required by their sect. Their children were early instructed in the principles and ceremonies of their religion, habits and customs. They were generally farmers, and took great care of their stock of different kinds. With few exceptions, they strictly inhibited their children from joining in the dance or other juvenile amusements common to other religious sects of the Germans.

In their marriages much ceremony was observed and great preparation made. Fatted calves, lambs, poultry, the finest of bread, butter, milk, honey, domestic sugar, wine, if it could be had; with every article necessary for a sumptuous feast in their plain way, were prepared in abundance. Previous to the performance of the ceremony, (the clergyman attending at the place appointed for the marriage,) four of the most respectable young females and four of the most respectable young men were selected as waiters upon the bride and groom. The several waiters were decorated with badges, to indicate their offices. The groomsmen, as they were termed, were invariably furnished with fine white aprons beautifully embroidered. It was deemed a high honor to wear the apron. The duty of the waiters consisted in not only waiting on the bride and groom, but they were required, after the marriage ceremony was performed, to serve up the wedding dinner, and to guard and protect the bride while at dinner from having her shoe stolen from her foot. This custom of stealing the bride's shoe, it is said, afforded the most heartfelt amusement to the wedding guest. To succeed in it, the greatest dexterity was used by the younger part of the company, while equal vigilance was manifested by the waiters to defend her against the theft; and if they failed, they were in honor bound to pay a penalty for the redemption of the shoe. This penalty was a bottle of wine or one dollar, which was commonly the price of a bottle of wine: and as a punishment to the bride, she was not permitted to dance until the shoe was restored. The successful thief, on getting hold of the shoe, held it up in great triumph to the view of the whole assemblage, which was generally pretty numerous. This custom was continued among the Germans from generation to generation, until since the war of the revolution. The author has conversed with many individuals, still living, who were eye-witnesses of it.

Throwing the stocking was another custom among the Germans.*—

---

*Throwing the stocking was not exclusively a German custom. It is celebrated by an Irish poet, in his "Irish Wedding." It is not improbable but it was common to the Celtic nations also.

When the bridge and groom were bedded, the young people were admitted into the room. A stocking, rolled into a ball, was given to the young females, who, one after the other, would go to the foot of the bed, stand with their backs towards it, and throw the stocking over their shoulders at the bride's head; and the first that succeeded in touching her cap or head was the next to be married. The young men then threw the stocking at the groom's head, in like manner, with the like motive. Hence the utmost eagerness and dexterity were used in throwing the stocking.— This practice, as well as that of stealing the bride's shoe, was common to all the Germans.

Among the Lutherans and Calvinists, dancing with other amusements was common, at their wedding parties particularly. Dancing and rejoicings were sometimes kept up for weeks together.*

The peaceable and orderly deportment of this hardy and industrious race of people, together with their perfect submission to the restraints of the civil authority, has always been proverbial. They form at this day a most valuable part of our community.

Among our early settlers, a number of Irish Presbyterians removed from Pennsylvania, and settled along Back creek, the North mountain and Opequon. A few Scotch and English families were among them.

The ancestors of the Glasses, Allens, Vances, Kerfotts, &c. were among the earliest settlers on the upper waters of the Opequon. The ancestors of the Whites, Russells, &c. settled near the North mountain. There were a mixture of Irish and Germans on Cedar creek and its vicinity; the Frys, Newells, Blackburns,† Wilsons, &c. were among the number. The Irish, like the Germans, brought with them the religion, customs and habits, of their ancestors. The Irish wedding was always an occasion of great hilarity, jollity and mirth. Among other scenes attending it, running for the bottle was much practiced. It was usual for the wedding parties to ride to the residence of the clergyman to have the ceremony performed. In their absence, the father or the next friend prepared, at the bride's residence, a bottle of the best spirits that could be obtained, around the neck of which a white ribbon was tied. Returning from the clergyman's, when within one or two miles of the home of the bride, some three or four young men prepared to run for the bottle. Taking an even start, their horses were put at full speed, dashing over mud, rocks, stumps, and disregarding all impediments. The race, in fact, was run with as much eagerness and desire to win, as is ever manifested on the turf by our sporting characters. The father or next friend of the bride, expecting the racers, stood with the bottle in his hand, ready to deliver to the successful competitor. On receiving it, he forthwith returned to meet the bride and groom. When met, the bottle was first presented to the bride, who must taste it at least, next to the groom, and then handed round to the company, every one of whom was required to swig it.

The Quakers differed from all other sects in their marriage ceremony.—

---

*Christian Miller, an aged and respectable man near Woodstock, related this custom to the author.

†Gen. Samuel Blackburn, it is said, descended from this family.

The parties having agreed upon the match, notice was given to the elders or overseers of the meeting, and a strict enquiry followed whether there had been any previous engagements by either of the parties to other individuals. If nothing of the kind appeared, the intended marriage was made known publicly; and if approved by all parties, the couple passed meeting. This ceremony was repeated three several times; when, if no lawful impediment appeared, a day was appointed for the marriage, which took place at the meeting-house in presence of the congregation. A writing, drawn up between the parties, purporting to be the marriage agreement, witnessed by as many of the bystanders as thought proper to subscribe their names, concluded the ceremony. They had no priest or clergyman to perform the rite of matrimony, and the whole proceeding was conducted with the utmost solemnity and decorum. This mode of marriage is still kept up, with but little variation.

Previous to the war of the revolution, it was the practice to publish the bans of matrimony, between the parties intending to marry, three successive Sabbath days in the church or meeting-house; after which, if no lawful impediment appeared, it was lawful for a licensed minister of the parish or county to join the parties in wedlock. It is probable that this practice, which was anciently used in the English churches, gave rise to the custom, in the Quaker society, of passing meeting. The peaceable and general moral deportment of the Quakers is too generally known to require particular notice in this work.

The Baptists were not among our earliest immigrants. About fourteen or fifteen families of that persuasion migrated from the state of New Jersey, and settled probably in 1742 or 1743 in the vicinity of what is now called Gerardstown, in the county of Berkeley.*

Mr. Semple, in his history of the Virginia Baptists, states, that in the year 1754, Mr. Stearns, a preacher of this sect, with several others, removed from New England. "They halted first at Opequon, in Berkeley county, Virginia, where he formed a Baptist church under the care of the Rev. John Gerard." This was probably the first Baptist church founded west of the Blue Ridge in our State.

It is said that the spot where Tuscarora meeting house now stands, in the county of Berkeley, is the first place where the gospel was publicly preached and divine service performed west of the Blue ridge.† This was and still remains a Presbyterian edifice.

---

*Mr. M'Cowan, an aged and respectable citizen of the neighborhood, communicated this fact to the author.

†This information was communicated to the author by a highly respectable old lady, of the Presbyterian church, in the county of Berkeley. She also stated that in addition to the general tradition, she had lately heard the venerable and reverend Dr. Matthews assert the fact. Mr. Mayers, now in his 87th year, born and raised on the Potomac, in Berkeley, stated his opinion to the author, that there was a house erected for public worship at the Falling Water about the same time that the Tuscarora meeting-house was built. Both these churches are now under the pastoral care of the Rev. James M. Brown.

It is not within the plan of this work to give a general history of the rise and progress of the various religious societies of our country. It may not, however, be uninteresting to the general reader to have a brief sketch of the difficulties and persecutions which the Quakers and Baptists had to encounter in their first attempts to propagate their doctrines and principles in Virginia.

In Hening's Statutes at Large, vol. i. pp. 532–33, the following most extraordinary law, if indeed it deserves the name, was enacted by the then legislature of Virginia, March, 1660:

"An act for the suppressing the Quakers.

"Whereas there is an vnreasonable and turbulent sort of people, commonly called Quakers, who contrary to the law do dayly gather together vnto them vnlaw'll assemblies and congregrations of people, teaching and publishing lies, miracles, false visions, prophecies and doctrines, which have influence vpon the comunities of men, both ecclesiasticall and civil, endeavouring and attempting thereby to destroy religion, lawes, comunities, and all bonds of civil societie, leaving it arbitrairie to everie vaine and vitious person whether men shall be safe, lawes established, offenders punished, and governours rule, hereby disturbing the publique peace and just interest : to prevent and restraine which mischiefe, *It is enacted*, That no master or commander of any shipp or other vessell do bring into this collonie any person or persons called Quakers, vnder the penalty of one hundred pounds sterling, to be leavied vpon him and his estate by order from the governour and council, or the comissioners in the severall counties where such ships shall arrive: That all such Quakers as have been questioned, or shall hereafter arrive, shall be apprehended wheresoever they shall be found, and they be imprisoned without baile or mainprize, till they do adjure this country, or putt in security with all speed to depart the collonie and not to return again: And if any should dare to presume to returne hither after such departure, to be proceeded against as contemners of the lawes and magistracy, and punished accordingly, and caused again to depart the country, and if they should the third time be so audacious and impudent as to returne hither, to be proceeded against as ffelons: That noe person shall entertain any of the Quakers that have heretofore been questioned by the governour and council, or which shall hereafter be questioned, nor permit in or near his house any assemblies of Quakers, in the like penalty of one hundred pounds sterling: That comissioners and officers are hereby required and authorized, as they will answer the contrary at their perill, to take notice of this act, to see it fully - effected and executed: And that no person do presume on their perill to dispose or publish their bookes, pamphlets or libells, bearing the title of their tenets and opinions."

This highhanded and cruel proceeding took place in the time of Oliver Cromwell's usurpation in England, and at a time when some glimmering of rational, civil, and religious liberty, manifested itself in the mother country. The preamble to this act is contradicted by the whole history of Quakerism, from its foundation to the present period. In all the written and traditional accounts handed down to us, the Quakers are represented as a most inoffensive, orderly, and strictly moral people, in all their deportment and habits.

This unreasonable and unwise legislation, it is presumed, was suffered to die a natural death, as, in the progress of the peopling of our country, we find that many Quakers, at a pretty early period, migrated and formed considerable settlements in different parts of the State.

It has already been noticed that the Baptists were not among the number of our earliest immigrants. Mr. Semple says: "The Baptists in Virginia originated from three sources. The first were immigrants from England, who about the year 1714 settled in the south east part of the State. About 1743 another party came from Maryland and founded a settlement in the north west.* A third party from New England, 1754."

This last was Mr. Stearns and his party. They settled for a short time on Capon river, in the county of Hampshire, but soon removed to North-Carolina. Mr. Stearns and his followers manifested great zeal and industry in the propagation of their doctrines and principles. Their religion soon took a wide range in the Carolinas and Virginia. They met with violent opposition from the established Episcopal clergy, and much persecution followed. To the credit of the people of our valley, but few if any acts of violence were committed on the persons of the preachers west of the Blue ridge. This is to be accounted for from the fact that a great majority of the inhabitants were dissenters from the Episcopal church. East of the Blue ridge, however, the case was widely different. It was quite common to imprison the preachers, insult the congregations, and treat them with every possible indignity and outrage. Every foul means was resorted to, which malice and hatred could devise, to suppress their doctrines and religion. But instead of success this persecution produced directly the contrary effect. "The first instance," says Mr. Semple, "of actual imprisonment, we believe, that ever took place in Virginia, was in the county of Spottsylvania. On the 4th June, 1768, John Waller, Lewis Craig, James Childs, &c., were seized by the sheriff, and hauled before three magistrates, who stood in the meeting-house yard, and who bound them in the penalty of $1000 to appear at court two days after. At court they were arraigned as disturbers of the peace, and committed to close jail." And in December, 1770, Messrs. William Webber and Joseph Anthony were imprisoned in Chesterfield jail.

The author deems it unnecessary to detail all the cases of persecution and imprisonment of the Baptist preachers. He will therefore conclude this narrative with the account of the violent persecution and cruel treatment of the late Rev. James Ireland, a distinguished Baptist preacher of our valley.

Mr. Ireland was on one occasion committed to the jail of Culpeper

*It is probable this is the party who settled in the neighborhood of Gerardstown. If so, Mr. S. is doubtless misinformed as to the place of their origin. The first Baptist immigrants who settled in Berkeley county were certainly from New Jersey.

county,* when several attempts were made to destroy him. Of these attempts he gives the following narrative:

"A number of my persecutors resorted to the tavern of Mr. Steward, at the court-house, where they plotted to blow me up with powder that night, as I was informed; but all they could collect was half a pound.— They fixed it for explosion, expecting I was sitting directly over it, but in this they were mistaken. Fire was put to it, and it went off with considerable noise, forcing up a small plank, from which I received no damage. The next scheme they devised was to smoke me with brimstone and Indian pepper. They had to wait certain opportunities to accomplish the same. The lower part of the jail door was a few inches above its sill. When the wind was favorable, they would get pods of Indian pepper, empty them of their contents, and fill them with brimstone, and set them burning, so that the whole jail would be filled with the killing smoke, and oblige me to go to cracks, and put my mouth to them in order to prevent suffocation. At length a certain doctor and the jailor formed a scheme to poison me, which they actually effected."

From this more than savage cruelty Mr. Ireland became extremely ill, was attended by several physicians, and in some degree restored to health and activity; but he never entirely recovered from the great injury which his constitution received.

The author had the satisfaction of an intimate personal acquaintance with Mr. Ireland, and lived a near neighbor to him for several years before his death. He was a native Scotsman; of course his pronunciation was a little broad. He had a fine commanding voice, easy delivery, with a beautiful natural elocution in his sermonizing. His language, perhaps, was not as purely classical as some of his cotemporaries; but such was his powerful elocution, particularly on the subject of the crucifixion and sufferings of our Savior, that he never failed to cause a flood of tears to flow from the eyes of his audience, whenever he touched that theme. In his younger years he was industrious, zealous, sparing no pains to propagate his religious opinions and principles, and was very successful in gaining proselytes: hence he became an object of great resentment to the established clergy, and they resorted to every means within their reach, to silence and put him down. But in this they failed. He at length triumphed over his persecutors, was instrumental in founding several church-

ORIGIN OF THE METHODIST RELIGION IN OUR VALLEY.

About the year 1775† two travelling strangers called at the residence of the late Maj. Lewis Stephens, the proprietor and founder of the town,

*In the life of Ireland, no dates are given. The time of his commitment was probably about the year 1771 or 1772.

†The author is not positive that he is correct as to the time this occurrence took place, but has been informed it was just before the commencement of the war of the Revolution. The late Dr. Tilden communicated this information to the writer—which he stated he learned from Mrs. Stephens.

now distinguished in the mail establishment as "Newtown Stephensburg," and enquired if they could obtain quarters for the night. Maj. Stephens happened to be absent; but Mrs. Stephens, who was remarkable for hospitality and religious impressions, informs them they could be accomodated. One of them observed to her, "We are preachers; and the next day being Sabbath, we will have to remain with you until Monday morning, as we do not travel on the Sabbath." To which the old lady replied, "if you are preachers, you are the more welcome."

John Hagerty and Richard Owens were the names of the preachers.— The next morning notice was sent through the town, and the strangers delivered sermons. This was doubtless the first Methodist preaching ever heard in our valley. It is said they travelled East of the Blue Ridge, (before they reached Stephensburg,) on a preaching tour, and probably crossed the Ridge at some place south of Stephensburg.

A number of the people were much pleased with them, and they soon got up a small church at this place. The late John Hite, Jr., his sister, Mrs. Elizabeth Hughes, (then a widow,) John Taylor and wife, Lewis Stephens, Sr. and wife, Lewis Stephens, Jr. and wife, and several others joined the church, and in a few years it began to flourish. The rapid spread of this sect throughout our country, needs no remarks from the author.

The first Camp Meeting held in our Valley, within the author's recollection, took place at what is called Chrisman's Spring, about two miles south of Stephensburg, on the great highway from Winchester to Staunton. This was probably in the month of August, 1806. It has been stated to the author, that the practice of Camp Meetings originated with a Baptist preacher somewhere about James River. It is said he was a man of great abilities and transcendant elocution; he however became too much of an Armenian in his doctrine to please the generality of his brethren, and they excommunicated him from their church, and attempted to silence him, but he would not consent to be silenced by them, and they refused him permission to preach in their meeting houses, and he adopted the plan of appointing meetings in the forest, where vast crowds of people attended his preaching, and they soon got up the practice of forming encampments. The author cannot vouch for the truth of this statement, but recollects it was communicated to him by a highly respectable member of the Baptist church.

In the year 1836, the author traveled through the South west counties on a tour of observation—he frequently passed places where Camp Meetings had been held; they are sometimes seen in dense forests, and some of them had the appearance of having been abandoned or disused for a considerable time. The author, however, passed one in Giles county which was the best fixed for the purpose he has ever seen. There is a large framed building erected probably spacious enough to shelter 2000 people or upwards, with a strong shingled roof, and some twelve or fifteen log houses, covered also with shingles, for the accommodation of visitors. A meeting had just been held at this place some two or three days before he passed it, at which, he was informed, several thousand people had at-

I

tended. It is situated very convenient to a most charming spring of delightful water, and stands on high ground. Its location is certainly very judicially selected for the purpose.

——:0:——

CHAPTER VI.

BREAKING OUT OF THE INDIAN WAR.

It has been noticed in a preceding chapter, that in the year 1753, emissaries from the Western Indians came among the Valley Indians, inviting them to cross the Allegany mountains, and that in the spring of the year 1754, the Indians suddenly and unexpectedly moved off, and entirely left the valley.

That this movement of the Indians was made under the influence of the French, there is but little doubt. In the year 1753, Maj. Geo. Washington (since the illustrious Gen. Washington,) was sent by governor Dinwiddie, the then colonial governor of Virginia, with a letter to the French commander on the western waters, remonstrating against his encroachments upon the territory of Virginia. This letter of remonstrance was disregarded by the Frenchman, and very soon afterwards the war, commonly called "Braddock's war," between the British government and France, commenced. In the year 1754, the government of Virginia raised an armed force with the intention of dislodging the French from their fortified places within the limits of the colony. The command of this army was given to Col. Fry, and George Washington was appointed lieutenant-colonel under him. Their little army amounted to three hundred men. "Washington advanced at the head of two companies of this regiment, early in April, to the Great Meadows, where he was informed by some friendly Indians, that the French were erecting fortifications in the forks between the Allegany and Monongahela rivers, and also that a detachment was on its march from that place towards the Great Meadows. War had not been formally declared between France and England, but as neither were disposed to recede from their claim to the lands on the Ohio, it was deemed inevitable, and on the point of commencing. Several circumstances were supposed to indicate a hostile intention on the part of the French detachment. Washington, under the guidance of some friendly Indians, on a dark rainy night surprised their encampment, and firing once, rushed in and surrounded them. The commander, Dumonville, was killed, with eight or nine others; one escaped, and all the rest immediately surrendered. Soon after this affair, Col. Fry died, and the command of the regiment devolved on Washington, who speedi-

ly collected the whole at the Great Meadows.   Two independent companies of regulars, one from South Carolina, soon after arrived at the same
place.   Col. Washington was now at the head of nearly four hundred
men.   A stockade, afterwards called Fort Necessity, was erected at the
Great Meadows, in which a small force was left, and the main body advanced with a view to dislodging the French from Fort Duquesne,* which
they had recently erected at the confluence of Allegany and Monongahela rivers.   They had not proceeded more than thirteen miles, when they
were informed by friendly Indians that the French, as numerous as pigeons
in the woods, were advancing in an hostile manner towards the English
settlements, and also that Fort Duquesne had been strongly reinforced.—
In this critical situation a council of war unanimously recommended a retreat to the Great Meadows, which was effected without delay, and every
exertion made to render Fort Necessity tenable, before the works intended for that purpose were completed.   Mons. de Villier, with a considerable force, attacked the fort.   The assailants were covered by trees and
high grass.†   The Americans received them with great resolution, and
fought some within the stockade, and others in the surrounding ditch.—
Washington continued the whole day on the outside of the fort, and conducted the defence with the greatest coolness and intrepidity.   The engagement lasted from 10 o'clock in the morning till night, when the French
commander demanded a parley, and offered terms of capitulation.   His
first and second proposals were rejected, and Washington would accept of
none but the following honorable ones, which were mutually agreed upon
in the course of the night: The fort to be surrendered on condition that
the garrison should march out with the honors of war, and be permitted to
retain their arms and baggage, and to march unmolested into the inhabited parts of Virginia."‡

In 1755 the British government sent Gen. Braddock, at the head of
two regiments, to this country.   Col. Washington had previously resigned the command of the Virginia troops.   Braddock invited him to join
the service as one of his volunteer aids, which invitation he readily accepted, and joined Braddock near Alexandria.§   The army moved on for
the west, and in their march out erected Fort Cumberland.‖   The cir-

---

*Fort Duquesne, so called in honor of the French commander, was, af-
ter it fell into the hands of the English, called Fort Pitt, and is now Pittsburgh.

†It is presumable that the grass here spoken of by Dr. Ramsey was of
the growth of the preceding year.   It is not probable that the grass, the
growth of the year 1754, so early in the season, had grown of sufficient
height to conceal a man.

‡Ramsey's Life of Washington.

§Then called Bellhaven.

‖Fort Cumberland was built in the year 1755, in the fork between Wills
creek and North branch of the Potomac, the remains of which are yet to
be seen.   It is about 55 miles north west of Winchester, on the Maryland side of the Potomac.   There is now a considerable town at this
place.   The garrison left at it was commanded by Maj. Livingston.   Mr.

cumstances attending the unfortunate defeat of Braddock, and the dreadful slaughter of his army near Pittsburgh, are too generally known to require a detailed account in this work: suffice it to say that the defeat was
attended with the most disastrous consequences to our country. The
whole western frontier was left exposed to the ravages of the forces of the
French and Indians combined.

After the defeat and fall of Braddock, Col. Dunbar, the next in command of the British army, retreated to Philadelphia, and the defence of
the country fell upon Washington, with the few troops the colonies were
able to raise. The people forthwith erected stockade forts in every part
of the valley, and took shelter in them. Many families were driven off,
some east of the Blue Ridge, and others into Maryland and Pennsylvania.

Immediately after the defeat of Braddock, Washington retreated to
Winchester, in the county of Frederick, and in the autumn of 1755 built
Fort Loudoun. The venerable and highly respectable Lewis Neill, who
was born on Opequon, about five miles east of Winchester, in 1747, stated to the author, that when he was about eight years of age, his father
had business at the fort, and that he went with him into it. Mr. Thomas
Barrett, another aged and respectable citizen, states that he has often
heard his father say, that Fort Loudoun was built the same year and immediately after Braddock's defeat. Our highly respectable and venerable
general, John Smith, who settled in Winchester in 1773, informed the author that he had seen and conversed with some of Washington's officers
soon after he settled in Winchester, and they stated to him that Washington marked out the site of the fort, and superintended the work; that he
bought a lot in Winchester, erected a smith's shop on it, and brought from
Mount Vernon his own blacksmith to make the necessary iron work for
the fort. These officers pointed out to Gen. Smith the spot where Gen.
Washington's huts or cabins were erected for his residence while in the
fort. The great highway leading from Winchester to the north passes
through the fort precisely where Washington's quarters were erected. It
stands at the north end of Loudoun street, and a considerable part of
the walls are now remaining. It covered an area of about half an acre;
within which area, a well, one hundred and three feet deep, chiefly thro'
a solid limestone rock, was sunk for the convenience of the garrison.*—
The labor of throwing up this fort was performed by Washington's regiment; so says Gen. Smith. It mounted six eighteen pounders, six twelve
pounders, six six-pounders, four swivels, and two howitzers, and contained

John Tomlinson gave the author this information. On the ancient site
of the fort, there are several dwelling houses, and a new brick Episcopal
church.

*The water in this well rises near the surface, and in great floods of
rain has been known to overflow and discharge a considerable stream of
water. The site of the fort is upon more elevated ground than the head
of any springs in its neighborhood. Upon what principle the water
should here rise above the surface the author cannot pretend to explain.

a strong garrison.* No formidable attempts were ever made by the enemy against it. A French officer once came to reconnoiter, and found it too strong to be attacked with any probability of success.†

For three years after the defeat of Braddock, the French and Indians combined carried on a most destructive and cruel war upon the western people. The French, however, in about three years after Braddock's defeat, abandoned Fort Duquesne, and it was immediately taken possession of by the British and colonial troops under the command of Gen. Forbes. Washington soon after resigned the command of the Virginia forces, and retired to private life. A predatory warfare was nevertheless continued on the people of the valley by hostile Indian tribes for several years after the French had been driven from their strong holds in the west; the particulars of which will form the subject of my next chapter.

——:o:——

CHAPTER VII.

INDIAN INCURSIONS AND MASSACRES.

AFTER the defeat of Braddock, the whole western frontier was left exposed to the incursions of the Indians and French. In the spring of the year 1756, a party of about fifty Indians, with a French captain at their head, crossed the Allegany mountains, committing on the white settlers every act of barbarous war. Capt. Jeremiah Smith, raised a party of twenty brave men, marched to meet this savage foe, and fell in with them at the head of Capon river, when a fierce and bloody battle was fought. Smith killed the captain with his own hand; five other Indians having fallen, and a number wounded, they gave way and fled. Smith lost two of his men. On searching the body of the Frenchman, he was found in possession of his commission and written instructions to meet another party of about fifty Indians at Fort Frederick,‡ to attack the fort, destroy it, and blow up the magazine.

---

*Gen. John Smith stated this fact to the author. The cannon were removed from Winchester early in the war of the revolution. Some further account of this artillery will be given in a future chapter. Mr. Henry W. Baker, of Winchester, gave the author an account of the number of cannon mounted on the fort.

†William L. Clark, Esq., is now the owner of the land including this ancient fortification, and has converted a part of it into a beautiful pleasure garden.

‡Fort Frederick was commenced in the year 1755, under the direction

The other party of Indians were encountered pretty low down the North branch of the Capon river, by Capt. Joshua Lewis, at the head of eighteen men; one Indian was killed when the others broke and ran off. Previous to the defeat of this party they had committed considerable destruction of the property of the white settlers, and took a Mrs. Horner and a girl about thirteen years of age prisoners. Mrs. Horner was the mother of seven or eight children; she never got back to her family. The girl, whose name was Sarah Gibbons, the sister of my informant,* was a prisoner about eight or nine years before she returned home. The intention of attacking Fort Frederick was of course abandoned.

Those Indians dispersed into small parties, and carried the work of death and desolation into several neighborhoods, in the counties now Berkeley, Frederick and Shenandoah. About eighteen or twenty of them crossed the North mountain at Mills's gap, which is in the county of Berkeley, killed a man by the name of Kelly, and several of his family, within a few steps of the present dwelling house of the late Mr. William Wilson, not more than half a mile from Gerardstown, and from thence passed on to the neighborhood of the present site of Martinsburg, the neighboring people generally taking shelter in John Evans' fort.† A small party of the Indians attacked the dwelling house of a Mr. Evans, brother to the owner of the fort; but being beaten off, they went in pursuit of a reinforcement. In their absence Mr. Evans and his family got safe to the fort. The Indians returned, and set fire to the house, the ruins of which are now to be seen from the great road leading to Winchester, three miles south of Martinsburg, at the head of what is called the Big Spring.

The same Indians took a female prisoner on the same day at John Strode's house. A boy by the name of Hackney, who was on his way to the fort, saw her previously, and advised her not to go to the house, saying that Strode's family were all gone to the fort, and that he suspected the Indians were then in the house. She however seeing a smoke at the house, disregarded the advice of the little boy, went to it, was seized by the Indians, taken off, and was about three years a prisoner, but finally

---

of Gov. Sharp, of Maryland, and was probably finished in 1776. It is still standing on the Maryland side of the Cohongoruton. Its walls are entirely of stone, four and a half feet thick at the base, and three at the top; they are at least twenty feet high, and have undergone but little dilapidation. Dr. John Hedges, and his son Capt. John C. Hedges, aided the author in the examination of this place, and measuring its area, height and thickness of the walls. Its location is not more than about twelve miles from Martinsburg, in Virginia, and about the same distance from Williamsport, in Maryland. It encloses an area of about one and a half acres, exclusive of the bastions or redoubts. It is said the erection of this fort cost about sixty-five thousand pounds sterling.

*Mr. Jacob Gibbons was born 10th Sept. 1745. Since the author saw him, he has departed this life—an honest, good old man.

†Evans' fort was erected within about two miles of Martinsburg, a stockade. The land is now owned by —— Fryatt, Esq.

got home. The boy went to the fort, and told what had happened; but the men had all turned out to bury Kelly and go in pursuit of the Indians, leaving nobody to defend the fort but the women and children. Mrs. Evans armed herself, and called on all the women, who had firmness enough to arm, to join her, and such as were too timed she ordered to run bullets. She then made a boy beat to arms on a drum; on hearing which, the Indians became alarmed, set fire to Strode's house,* and moved off. They discovered the party of white men just mentioned, and fired upon them, but did no injury. The latter finding the Indians too strong for them, retreated into the fort.†

From thence the Indians passed on to Opequon, and the next morning attacked Neally's fort, massacred most of the people, and took off several prisoners; among them George Stockton and Isabella his sister.— Charles Porterfield, a youth about 20 years of age, heard the firing from his father's residence, about one mile from the fort, armed himself and set off with all speed to the fort, but on his way was killed.‡

Among the prisoners were a man by the name of Cohoon, his wife, and some of his children. Mrs. Cohoon was in a state of pregnancy, and not being able to travel fast enough to please her savage captors, they forced her husband forward, while crossing the North mountain, and cruelly murdered her: her husband distantly heard her screams. Cohoon, however, that night made his escape, and got safely back to his friends.— George Stockton and his sister Isabella, who were also among the prisoners, were taken to the Indian towns. Isabella was eight or nine years of age, and her story is as remarkable as it is interesting. She was detained and grew up among the savages. Being a beautiful and interesting girl, they sold her to a Canadian in Canada, where a young Frenchman, named Plata, soon became acquainted with her, and made her a tender of his hand in matrimony.§ This she declined unless her parents' consent could be obtained,—a strong proof of her filial affection and good sense. The Frenchman immediately proposed to conduct her home, readily believing that his generous devotion and great attention to the daughter would lay the parents under such high obligations to him, that they would willingly consent to the union. But such were the strong prejudices existing at the time against everything French, that her parents and friends peremptorily objected. The Frenchman then prevailed on Isabella to elope with him; to effect which they secured two of her father's horses

---

*The present residence of the widow Showalter, three miles from Martinsburg.

†Mr. Joseph Hackney, Frederick county, stated these facts to the author. The little boy, mentioned above, grew up, married, was a Quaker by profession, and the father of my informant.

‡George Porterfield, Esq. now residing in the county of Berkeley, is a brother to the youth who was killed, and stated to the author the particulars of this unhappy occurrence. Capt. Glenn also stated several of the circumstances to the author.

§Mr. Mayers, of Berkeley county, gave the author the name of this young Frenchman.

and pushed off. They were, however, pursued by two of her brothers, overtaken, at Hunterstown, Pennsylvania, and Isabella forcibly torn from her protector and devoted lover, and brought back to her parents, while the poor Frenchman was warned that if he ever made any farther attempt to take her off, his life should pay the forfeit. This story is familiar to several aged and respectable individuals in the neighborhood of Martinsburg. Isabella afterwards married a man by the name of McClary, removed and settled in the neighborhood of Morgantown, and grew wealthy. George, after an absence of three years, got home also.

A party of fourteen Indians, believed to be part of those defeated by Capt. Smith, on their return to the west killed a young woman, and took a Mrs. Neff prisoner. This was on the South fork of the river Wappatomaka. They cut off Mrs. Neff's petticoat up to her knees, and gave her a pair of moccasins to wear on her feet. This was done to facilitate her travelling; but they proceeded no further than the vicinity of Fort Pleasant,* where, on the second night, they left Mrs. Neff in the custody of an old Indian, and divided themselves into two parties, in order to watch the fort. At a late hour in the night, Mrs. Neff discovering that her guard was pretty soundly asleep, ran off. The old fellow very soon awoke, fired off his gun, and raised a yell. Mrs. N. ran between the two parties of Indians, got safe into Fort Pleasant, and gave notice where the Indians were encamped. A small party of men, the same evening came from another small fort a few miles above, and joined their friends in Fort Pleasant. The Indians, after the escape of Mrs. Neff, had collected into one body in a deep glen, near the fort. Early the next morning, sixteen men, well mounted and armed, left the fort with a view to attack the Indians. They soon discovered their encampment. The whites divided themselves into two parties, intending to inclose the Indians between two fires; but unfortunately a small dog which had followed them, starting a rabbit, his yelling alarmed the Indians; upon which they cautiously moved off, passed between the two parties of white men unobserved, took a position between them and their horses, and opened a most destructive fire. The whites returned the fire with great firmness and bravery, and a desperate and bloody conflict ensued. Seven of the whites fell dead, and four were wounded. The little remnant retreated to the fort, whither the wounded also arrived. Three Indians fell in this battle, and several were wounded. The victors secured the white men's horses, and took them off.†

Just before the above action commenced, Mr. Vanmeter, an old man, mounted his horse, rode upon a high ridge, and witnessed the battle. He

---

*Fort Pleasant was a strong stockade with block houses, erected on the lands now owned by Isaac Vanmeter, Esq. on the South Branch of Potomac, a short distance above what is called the Trough.

†This battle, is called the "Battle of The Trough." Messrs. Vanmeter, McNeill and Heath, detailed the particulars to the author. A block house, with port holes, is now standing in Mr. D. McNeill's yard,—part of an old fort erected at the time of Braddock's war, the logs of which are principally sound.

returned with all speed to the fort, and gave notice of the defeat. The old man was killed by the Indians in 1757.

After committing to writing the foregoing account, the author received from his friend Dr. Charles A. Turley, of Fort Pleasant, a more particular narrative of the battle, which the author will subjoin, in the doctor's own words:

"The memorable battle of The Trough (says Dr. Turley) was preceded by the following circumstances. On the day previous, two Indian strollers, from a large party of sixty or seventy warriors, under the well known and ferocious chief Kill-buck, made an attack upon the dwelling of a Mrs. Brake, on the South fork of the South branch of the Potomac, about fifteen miles above Moorefield, and took Mrs. Brake and a Mrs. Neff prisoners. The former not being able to travel from her situation, was tomahawked and scalped, and the latter brought down to the vicinity of Town fort, about one and a half miles below Moorefield. There one of the Indians, under the pretence of hunting, retired, and the other laid himself down and pretended to fall asleep, with a view, as was believed, to let Mrs. Neff escape to the fort, and give the alarm. Every thing turned out agreeably to their expectations; for as soon as she reached the fort, and related the circumstances of her escape, 18 men from that and Buttermilk fort, five miles above, went in pursuit. They were men notorious for their valor, and who had been well tried on many such occasions.

"As soon as they came to the place indicated by Mrs. Neff, they found a plain trace left by the Indian, by occasionally breaking a bush. Mr. John Harness, who was well acquainted with the manners and mode of warfare of the Indians, pronounced that the hunter Indian had not returned to his comrade, or that they were in great force somewhere near and in ambush. They however pursued the trace, without discovering any signs of a larger party, until they arrived between two mountains, forming what from its resemblance is called The Trough. · Here, directly above a fine spring about 200 paces from the river, which at that time was filled to an impassable stage by a heavy fall of rain, these grim monsters of blood were encamped, to the number above stated. The western face of the ridge was very precipitous and rough, and on the north of the spring was a deep ravine, cutting directly up into the ridge above. Our little band of heroes, nothing daunted by the superior number of the enemy, dismounted unobserved, and prepared for battle, leaving their horses on the ridge. But by one of those unforeseen and almost unaccountable accidents which often thwart the seemingly best planned enterprises, a small dog which had followed them just at this juncture started a rabbit, and went yelping down the ridge, giving the Indians timely notice of their approach. They immediately flew to arms, and filing off up the ravine before described, passed directly into the rear of our little band, placing them in the very situation they had hoped to find their enemies, between the mountain and the swollen river. Now came the "tug of war," and both parties rushed to the onset, dealing death and slaughter at every fire. After an hour or two hard fighting, during which each of our little band had numbered his man, and more than half their number had fallen to rise no more, those

J

that remained were compelled to retreat, which could only be effected by swimming the river. Some who had been wounded, not being able to do this, determined to sell their lives as dearly as possible; and deliberately loading their rifles, and placing themselves behind some cover on the river bank, dealt certain death to the first adversary who made his appearance, and then calmly yielded to the tomahawk.

"We cannot here pass over without mentioning one of the many despotic acts exercised by the then colonial government and its officers towards the unoffending colonists. At the time of which we are speaking, there were quartered in Fort Pleasant, about one and a half miles above the battle ground, and within hearing of every gun, a company of regulars, commanded by a British officer named Wagner, who not only refused to march a man out of the fort, but, when the inhabitants seized their rifles and determined to rush to the aid of their brothers, ordered the gates to be closed, and suffered none to pass in or out. By marching to the western bank of the river, he might have effectually protected those who were wounded, without any danger of an attack from the enemy. And when the few who had escaped the slaughter, hailed and demanded admission into the fort, it was denied them. For this act of Capt. Wagner's the survivors of our Spartan band called him a coward; for which insult he thought it his duty to hunt them down like wolves, and when caught, to inflict corporal punishment by stripes.

"The Indian chief, Kill-buck, afterwards admitted, that although he had witnessed many sanguinary contests, this was the most so that he had ever experienced for the number of his enemies. Kill-buck was a Shawnee, a savage of strong mental powers, and well acquainted with all the families in the settlement before the war broke out. Col. Vincent Williams, whose father was inhumanly murdered by Kill-buck and his party on Patterson's creek, became personally acquainted with him many years afterwards, and took the trouble, when once in the state of Ohio, to visit him. He was far advanced in years, and had become blind. The colonel informed me that as soon as he told Kill-buck his name, the only answer he made was, "Your father was a brave warrior." The half brother of Col. Williams, Mr. Benjamin Casey, was with him. Mr. Peter Casey had once hired Kill-buck to catch and bring home a runaway negro, and was to have given him fourteen shillings. He paid him six shillings, and the war breaking out, he never paid him the other eight. At the vivist spoken of, Kill-buck inquired the name of his other visitor, and when the colonel told him it was Benjamin Casey,—'What, Peter Casey's son?' "Yes." "Your father owes me eight shillings; will you pay it?" said the old chief. The colonel at that time got all the particulars of the tragical death of his father, as well as the great heroism manifested by our little band at the battle of The Trough."

Dr. Turley refers in the foregoing narrative to the murder of Mr. Williams, on Patterson's creek. This melancholy tragedy the author is enabled to give, as it was related to him by Mr. James S. Miles, of Hardy.

Mr. Williams lived on Patterson's creek, on the farm now occupied by his grandson, Mr. James Williams. Hearing of the approach of the Indians, he repaired with his neighbors to Fort Pleasant (nine miles) for security. After remaining here a few days, supposing their houses might be revisited with safety, Mr. W. with seven others crossed the mountain for that purpose. They separated on reaching the creek; and Mr. W. went alone to his farm. Having tied his horse to a bush, he commenced salting his cattle, when seven Indians (as was afterwards said by Killbuck) got between him and his horse, and demanded his surrender. Mr. W. answered by a ball from his rifle, which killed one of the Indians, then retreated to his house, barricaded the door, and put his enemy at defiance. They fired at him at random through the door and windows, until the latter were filled with shot-holes. For greater security, Mr. W. got behind a hommony block in a corner, from which he would fire at his assailants through the cracks of the building, as opportunity offered. In this way he killed five out of the seven. The remaining two, resolved not to give up their prey, found it necessary to proceed more cautiously; and going to the least exposed side of the house, one was raised upon the shoulders of the other to an opening in the logs some distance above the level of Mr. W., who did not, consequently, observe the manœuvre, from which he fired, and shot Mr. W. dead. The body was instantly quartered, and hung to the four corners of the building, and the head stuck upon a fence stake in front of the door. This brave man was the father of the venerable Edward Williams, the clerk of Hardy county court until the election in 1830 under the new constitution, when his advanced age compelled him to decline being a candidate.

Sometime after the battle of The Trough, at a fort seven miles above Romney, two Indian boys made their appearance, when some of the men went out with the intention of taking them. A grown Indian made his appearance; but he was instantly shot down by Shadrach Wright. A numerous party then showed themselves, which the garrison sallied out and attacked; but they were defeated with the loss of several of their men, and compelled to retreat to the fort.*

Kill-buck, the chief before mentioned,. used frequently to command these marauding parties. Previous to the breaking out of the war, he was well acquainted with many of the white settlers on Wappatomaka, and lived a good part of his time among them. His intimate acquaintance with the country enabled him to lead his band of murderers from place to place, and to commit many outrages on the persons and property of the white inhabitants. In the progress of this work, some further notice will be taken of this distinguished warrior. There was another great Indian warrior called "Crane;" but the author has not been able to collect any particular traditionary accounts of the feats performed by him.

In the year 1757, a numerous body of Indians crossed the Allegany, and, as usual, divided themselves into small parties, and hovering about the different forts, committed many acts of murder and destruction of property. About thirty or forty approached Edward's fort,† on Capon river,

---

*Mr. James Parsons, near Romney, Hampshire county, gave the author this information.

†Edward's fort was located on the west side of Capon river, not more than three quarters of a mile above where the stage road from Winchester

killed two men at a small mill, took off a parcel of corn meal, and retreating along a path that led between a stream of water and a steep high
mountain, they strewed the meal in several places on their route. Immediately between this path and the stream is an abrupt bank, seven or
eight feet high, and of considerable length, under which the Indians concealed themselves, and awaited the approach of the garrison. Forty men
under the command of Capt. Mercer, sallied out, with the intention of
pursuing and attacking the enemy. But oh! fatal day! Mercer's party,
discovering the trail of meal, supposed the Indians were making a speedy
retreat, and, unapprised of their strength, moved on at a brisk step, until
the whole line was drawn immediately over the line of Indians under the
bank, when the latter discharged a most destructive fire upon them, sixteen falling dead at the first fire. The others attempting to save themselves by flight, were pursued and slaughtered in every direction, until,
out of the forty, but six got back to the fort. One poor fellow, who ran
up the side of the mountain, was fired at by an Indian: the ball penetrated just above his heel, ranged up his leg, shivering the bones, and lodged a little below his knee: he slipped under the lap of a fallen tree, there
hid himself, and lay in that deplorable situation for two days and nights before
he was found by his friends, it being that length of time before the people
at the fort would venture out to collect and bury the dead. This wounded
man recovered, and lived many years after, though he was always a crip-
ple from his wound. Capt. George Smith, who now resides on Back
creek, informed the author that he was well acquainted with him.

Sometime afterwards, the Indians, in much greater force, and aided, it
was believed, by several Frenchmen in person, determined to carry this
fort by storm. The garrison had been considerably reinforced; among others, by the late Gen. Daniel Morgan, then a young man. The Indians
made the assault with great boldness; but on this occasion they met with
a sad reverse of fortune. The garrison sallied out, and a desperate battle
ensued. The assailants were defeated with great slaughter, while the
whites lost comparatively but few men.

The remains of a gun of high finish, ornamented with silver mounting
and gold touch-hole, were plowed up near the battle ground about forty
years ago. It was supposed to have belonged to a French officer. Part
of a bomb shell was also found. Morgan in this action performed his
part with his usual intrepidity, caution and firmness, and doubtless did
much execution.*

Other parties of Indians penetrated into the neighborhood of Winchester, and killed several people about the Round hill; among others a man by
the name of Flaugherty, with his wife. Several inmates of a family by

---

to Romney crosses the river.

*Mr. William Carlile, now ninety-five years of age, and who resides
near the battle ground, informed the author that he removed and settled on
Capon soon after the battle was fought. He also stated that he had frequently heard it asserted that Morgan was in the battle, and acted with
great bravery, &c. Mr. Charles Carlile, son of this venerable man, stated the fact of the gun and part of a bomb shell being found.

the name of M'Cracken, on Back creek, about twelve miles from Winchester, were killed, and two of the daughters taken off as prisoners.—They, however, got back, after an absence of three or four years. Mr Lewis Neill informed the author that he saw and conversed with these women on the subject of their captivity after their return home. Jacob Havely and several of his family were killed near the present residence of Moses Russell, Esq. at the eastern base of the North mountain, fifteen or sixteen miles south west of Winchester. Dispennet, and several of his family, and Vance and his wife,* were also severally killed 'by the same party of Indians, in the same neighborhood.

The late respectable and intelligent Mrs. Rebecca Brinker, who was born 25th March, 1745, and who of course was upwards of ten years old when Braddock was defeated, related many interesting occurrences to the author ; among others, that a family of eighteen persons, by the name of Nicholls, who resided at the present residence of Mr. Stone, a little west of Maj. Isaac Hite's, were attacked, the greater number killed, and several taken off as prisoners: one old woman and her grandchild made their escape to a fort, a short distance from Middletown. This took place about 1756 or 1757, and it is probable by the same party who killed Havely and others.

In the year 1758, a party of about fifty Indians and four Frenchmen penetrated into the neighborhood of Mill creek, now in the county of Shenandoah, about 9 miles south of Woodstock. This was a pretty thickly settled neighborhood; and among other houses, George Painter had erected a large log one, with a good sized cellar. On the alarm being given, the neighboring people took refuge in this house. Late in the afternoon they were attacked. Mr. Painter, attempting to fly, had three balls shot through his body, and fell dead, when the others surrendered. The Indians dragged the dead body back to the house, threw it in, plundered the house of what they chose, and then set fire to it. While the house was in flames, consuming the body of Mr. Painter, they forced from the arms of their mothers four infant children, hung them up in trees, shot them in savage sport, and left them hanging. They then set fire to a stable in which were enclosed a parcel of sheep and calves, thus cruelly and wantonly torturing to death the inoffensive dumb animals. After these atrocities they moved off with forty-eight prisoners; among whom were Mrs. Painter, five of her daughters, and one of her sons; a Mrs. Smith and several of her children; a Mr. Fisher and several of his children, among them a lad of twelve or thirteen years old, a fine well grown boy, and remarkably fleshy. This little fellow, it will presently be seen, was destined to be the victim of savage cruelty.

Two of Painter's sons, and a young man by the name of Jacob Myers

---

*Moses Russell, Esq. is under the impression that these people were killed in the summer or fall of the year 1756. The author finds it impossible to fix the dates of the various acts of war committed by the savages. After the most diligent inquiry, he has not been able to find any person who committed to writing anything upon the subject at the time the several occurrences took place.

escaped being captured by concealment. One of the Painters, with Myers, ran over that night to Powell's fort, a distance of at least fifteen miles,
and to Keller's fort, in quest of aid. They had neither hat nor shoes,
nor any other clothing than a shirt and trowsers each. A small party of
men set out early the next morning, well mounted and armed, to avenge
the outrage. They reached Mr. Painter's early in the day; but on learning their strength, (from the other young Painter, who had remained concealed all that evening and night, and by that means was enabled to count
the number of the enemy,) they declined pursuit, being too weak in numbers to venture further. Thus this savage band got off with their prisoners and booty, without pursuit or interruption.

After six days' travel they reached their villages west of the Allegany
mountains, where they held a council, and determined to sacrifice their
helpless prisoner Jacob Fisher. They first ordered him to collect a quantity of dry wood. The poor little fellow shuddered, burst into tears, and
told his father they intended to burn him. His father replied, "I hope
not;" and advised him to obey. When he had collected a sufficient quantity of wood to answer their purpose, they cleared and smoothed a ring a-
round a sapling, to which they tied him by one hand, then formed a trail
of wood around the tree and set it on fire. The poor boy was then compelled to run round in this ring of fire until his rope wound him up to the
sapling, and then back until he came in contact with the flame, whilst his
infernal tormentors were drinking, singing and dancing around him, with
"horrid joy." This was continued for several hours; during which time
the savage men became beastly drunk, and as they fell prostrate to the
ground, the squaws would keep up the fire. With long sharp poles, prepared for the purpose, they would pierce the body of their victim whenever he flagged, until the poor and helpless boy fell and expired with the
most excruciating torments, whilst his father and brothers were compelled
to be witnesses of the heart-rending tragedy.

After an absence of about three years, Mrs. Painter, with her son and
two of her daughters; Mrs. Smith, who had the honor, if it could be so
deemed, of presenting her husband with an Indian son,* by a distinguished war chief; Fisher and his remaining sons; and several other prisoners,
returned home. Three of Mrs. Painter's daughters remained with the Indians. Mary, the youngest, was about nine years old when taken, and
was eighteen years a prisoner: two of the daughters never returned. A
man by the name of Michael Copple, who had himself been a prisoner a-
bout two years with the Indians, had learned their language, become an
Indian trader, and traveled much among them, at length found Mary
Painter with a wandering party of Cherokees. In conversing with her,
he discovered who she was—that he was acquainted with her family connections, and proposed to her to accompany him home, to which she re-

---

*Smith received his wife, and never maltreated her on this account; but
he had a most bitter aversion to the young chief. The boy grew up to
manhood, and exhibited the appearance and disposition of his sire. Attempts were made to educate him, but without success. He enlisted into the army of the revolution as a common soldier, and never returned.

fused her assent. He then said that her brothers had removed to Point Pleasant, and were desirous of seeing her; upon which she consented to accompany him that far to see her brothers; but finding, on arriving at the Point, that he had deceived her, she manifested much dissatisfaction, and attempted to go back to the Indians. Copple, however, after much entreaty, and promising to make her his wife, prevailed upon her to return home. He performed his promise of marriage, lived several years on Painter's land, and raised a family of children. Mary had lost her mother tung, learned a little English afterwards, but always conversed with her husband in the Indian language.* They finally removed to the west.

The garrison at Fort Cumberland was frequently annoyed by the Indians. There are two high knobs of the mountain, one on the Virginia side of the Cohongoruton on the South, the other on the Maryland side on the north east within a short distance of the fort. The Indians frequently took possession of these hights, and fired into the fort. Although they seldom did any injury in this way, yet it was disagreeable and attended with some danger. On a particular occasion a large party of Indians had taken possession of the knob on the Maryland side, and fired into the fort. A captain (the author regrets that he was not able to learn his name) and seventy-five brave fellows on a very dark night, volunteered to dislodge the enemy. They sallied out from the fort, surrounded the knob, and cautiously ascending until they were within reach of the foe, waited for daybreak to make the attack. Light appearing, they opened a tremendous fire, which threw the Indians into utter confusion, rendering them powerless for defence, while the whites continued from all sides to pour in volley after volley, spreading death and carnage. But few of the Indians escaped. The knob is called "Bloody Hill" to this day. This tradition the author received from several individuals in Cumberland: indeed, the story appears to be familiar with every aged individual in the neighborhood.

Shortly after this occurrence, Kill-buck attempted to take Fort Cumberland by stratagem. He approached it at the head of a large force of warriors; and under the guise of friendship, pretending to wish an amicable intercourse with the garrison, proposed to Maj. Livingston to admit himself and warriors. Some hints having been given to the commander to be upon his guard, Livingston seemingly consented to the proposal; but no sooner had Kill-buck and his chief officers entered than the gates were closed upon them. The wiley chief being thus entrapped, was roundly charged with his intended treachery, of which the circumstances were too self evident to be denied. Livingston, however, inflicted no other punisnment upon his captives than a mark of humiliating disgrace,

---

*The author deems a particular history of this woman necessary, because it is one among many instances of young white children, when taken prisoners, becoming attached to a savage life, and leaving it with great reluctance. Mr. George Painter, an aged and respectable citizen of Shenandoah county, who resides on the spot where this bloody tragedy was acted, and is a grandson of the man who was murdered and burnt, detailed these particulars to the author.

which to an Indian warrior was more mortifying than death. This stigma was, it is supposed, dressing them in petticoats, and driving them out of the fort.*

It has already been stated, that, previous to the breaking out of the war, Kill-buck lived a good part of his time among the white settlers in the neighborhood of Fort Pleasant. An Irish servant, belonging to Peter Casey, absconded, and Casey offered a pistole† reward for his recovery. Kill-buck apprehended the servant, and delivered him to his master; but from some cause or other, Casey refused to pay the reward. A quarrel ensued, and Casey knocked Kill-buck down with his cane. When the war broke out, Kill-buck sought every opportunity to kill Casey, but never could succeed. Many years afterwards, Casey's son obtained a lieutenancy, and was ordered to Wheeling, where Kill-buck then being, young Casey requested some of his friends to introduce him to him. When Kill-buck heard his name, he paused for a moment, and repeating, "Casey! Casey!" inquired of the young man whether he knew Peter Casey. The lieutenant replied, "Yes, he is my father." Kill-buck immediately exclaimed, "Bad man, bad man, he once knocked me down with his cane." On the young man's proposing to make up the breach, the old chief replied, "Will you pay me the pistole?" Young Casey refused to do this, but proposed to treat with a quart of rum, to which the old warrior assented, saying, "Peter Casey old man—Kill-buck old man:" and then stated that he had frequently watched for an opportunity to kill him, "but he was too lazy—would not come out of the fort: Kill-buck now friends with him, and bury the tomahawk."‡ This Indian chief, it is said was living about fourteen years ago, but had become blind from his great age, being little under, and probably over, one hundred years.

---

*The venerable John Tomlinson related this affair to the author. Mr. T. does not recollect the particular mark of disgrace inflicted on these Indians. The Rev. Mr. Jacobs, of Hampshire, suggested this as the most probable.

†The pistole is a piece of gold, equal to three dollars and seventy-five cents in value.

‡This anecdote is related, somewhat differently, by Dr. Turley, page 66 of this work.

CHAPTER VIII.

INDIAN INCURSIONS AND MASSACRES—Continued.

In a preceding chapter the erection of several stone dwelling-houses is noticed. These houses generally had small stockade forts about them; and whenever an alarm took place, the neighboring people took shelter in them, as places of security against their savage foe.*

The men never went out of the forts without their guns. The enemy were frequently lurking about them, and at every opportunity would kill some of the people. At the residence of Maj. Robert D. Glass, on Opequon, five miles south west of Winchester, part of his dwelling-house was erected in the time of the Indian war: the port-holes were plainly to be seen before the body was covered with weather-boarding. The people were closely "forted" for about three years. After the termination of hostilities between England and France, the incursions of the Indians were less frequent, and never in large parties; but they were continued at intervals until the year 1766 or 1767.

About the year 1758, a man by the name of John Stone, near what is called the White House, in the Hawksbill settlement, was killed by Indians. Stone's wife, with her infant child and a son about seven or eight years old, and George Grandstaff, a youth of sixteen years old, were taken off as prisoners. On the South Branch mountain, the Indians murdered Mrs. Stone and her infant, and took the boy and Grandstaff to their towns. Grandstaff was about three years a prisoner, and then got home. The little boy, Stone, grew up with the Indians, came home, and after obtaining possession of his father's property, sold it, got the money, returned to the Indians, and was never heard of by his friends afterwards.

The same Indians killed Jacob Holtiman's wife and her children, Holtiman escaping. They plundered old Brewbecker's house, piled up the chairs and spinning wheels, and set them on fire. A young woman who lived with Brewbecker had concealed herself in the garret; and after the Indians left the house, extinguished the fire, and saved the house from burning. Brewbecker's wife got information that the Indians were coming, and ran off with her children to where several men were at work, who conveyed her across the river to a neighboring house. Mr. John Brewbecker now resides on the farm where this occurrence took place.†

---

*The late Mrs. Rebecca Brinker, one of the daughters of George Bowman, on Cedar Creek, informed the author that she recollected when sixteen families took shelter in her father's house.

†Mr. Brewbecker resides on the west side of the South fork of the Shenandoah river, on Masinutton creek, in the new county of Page, and has erected a large and elegant brick house on the spot where the Indians plundered his father's dwelling.

K

The following singular tradition, as connected with this occurrence, has been related to the author:

About dusk on the evening previous, Mrs. Brewbecker told her husband and family that the Indians would attack them next morning, saying that she could see a party of them on the side of Masinutton mountain, in the act of cooking their supper. She also declared that she saw their fire, and could count the number of Indians. She pointed to the spot; but no other part of the family saw it; and it was therefore thought that she must be mistaken. Persisting in her declarations, she begged her husband to remove her and her children to a place of safety: but she was laughed at, told that it was mere superstition, and that she was in no danger. It was however afterwards ascertained that the savages had encamped that night at the place on the mountain pointed out by Mrs. B. It was about two miles off.*

These outrages of the Indians drove many of the white settlers below the Blue ridge.

Probably the same year, several Indians attacked the house of a man named Bingaman, near the present site of New Market. Bingaman, who was remarkably stout and active, defended his family with great resolution and firmness, and laid two of the assailants dead at his feet: they succeeded, however, in killing his wife and children, Bingaman escaping with several wounds, from which he finally recovered. The same party took Lewis Bingaman, (a nephew of the one spoken of,) a prisoner. He was a boy about thirteen or fourteen years old, grew up with the Indians, and became a man of distinction among them.

About the same time the Indians forcibly entered the house of Mr. Young, who resided on the farm now owned by William Smith, Esq. not more than a mile from Zane's old iron works, and killed several of his family. They took an infant, dashed its head against a rock, beat out its brains, and left it lying on the ground. Two of Young's daughters, pretty well grown, were carried off prisoners. Lieutenant Samuel Fry raised a force of between thirty and forty men, pursued, and came in sight of them, unobserved, at the Short mountain, near the Allegany. Fry's party prepared to fire; but unfortunately one of the white girls stepping accidentally before their guns, the intention was frustrated, and Fry being discovered the next moment, he ordered his men to charge. This was no sooner done than the Indians broke and ran off, leaving their guns, prisoners and plunder: the two young females were thus rescued and brought safely home.

Another family in the same neighborhood, by the name of Day, were attacked, several killed, and two of the daughters taken off. A party of eighteen or twenty whites pursued them. The girls, as they travelled through the mountains, expecting pursuit, took the precaution (unobserved by their captors) to tear off and frequently drop small scraps of white linen, as well as pluck off branches of bushes, and drop them as a trail, by which means their friends could readily discover their route. A bro-

*This tradition was given the author by Mr. Andrew Keyser, jr. who married a grand daughter of the woman who saw the Indians.

ther to the girls, a young man, was one of the pursuing party. The Indians were overtaken on the South Branch mountain; and as soon as seen, preparations were made to give them a deadly fire. But the young Day, in his eagerness to avenge the death of his father and family, prematurely fired, killing the object of his aim, when the others precipitately fled, leaving every thing behind them. They had cut off the girls' petticoats at the knees, in order that they should be able to make more speed in traveling. The girls were brought safe home.

There were several instances of the Indians committing murders on the whites about the Potomac and South Branch several years before Braddock's defeat. About the year 1752, a man by the name of James Davis was killed, pretty high up the Potomac; and in the succeeding year, William Zane and several of his family were taken prisoners on the South Branch, in the now county of Hardy. Isaac Zane, one of his sons, remained during his life with the Indians. The author saw this man at Chillicothe in the autumn of 1797, and had some conversation with him upon the subject of his captivity. He stated that he was captured when about nine years old; was four years without seeing a white person; had learned the Indian tung quite well, but never lost a knowledge of English, having learned to spell in two syllables, which he could still do, although pretty well advanced in years. He also said that a trader came to the Indian village four years after his captivity, and spoke to him in English, of which he understood every word; that when he grew up to manhood, he married a sister of the Wyandott king, and raised a family of seven or eight children. His sons were all Indians in their habits and dispositions; his daughters, four of them, all married white men, became civilized, and were remarkably fine women, considering the opportunities they had had for improvement.

This man possessed great influence with the tribes he was acquainted with; and as he retained a regard for his native countrymen, was several times instrumental in bringing about treaties of peace. The government of the United States granted him a patent for ten thousand acres of land, which he claimed as his private property; and when the author saw him he was on his way to Philadelphia to apply for a confirmation of his title. He was a near relation to the late Gen. Isaac Zane, of Frederick county, Virginia.

About the same time that Mr. Zane's family were taken prisoners, as just related, an Indian killed a white man near Oldtown, in Maryland, but was, in return, killed by the late Capt. Michael Cresap, then a boy, with a pistol, while he was in the act of scalping the white man.[*]

About the year 1758 there were two white men who disguised themselves in the habit of Indians, and appeared in the neighborhood of the present site of Martinsburg. They were pursued and killed, supposing them to be Indians.[†] It was no uncommon thing for unprincipled scoundrels to act in this manner. Their object was to frighten people to leave their homes, in order that they might rob and plunder them of their most

---

[*] Jacob's Life of Cresap.
[†] Related by Captain James Glenn.

valuable articles.* The Indians were frequently charged without outrages they never committed.

A man by the name of Edes, with his family, resided in a cave for several years, about three miles above the mouth of Capon. This cave is in a large rock, and when other people would take shelter at a fort in the neighborhood, Edes would remain in his cave. At length the Indians found them, by trailing the children when driving up their cows, and took Edes and his family prisoners.†

A Mr. Smith, a bachelor, resided on the west side of Capon river, in a small cabin. Three Indians one morning entered his house, split up his wooden bowls and trenchers (plates made of wood,) destroyed his household goods generally, and took him off as a prisoner. They crossed the Cohongoruton, and halted at a place called Grass lick, on the Maryland side, with the intention of stealing horses. Two of them went into a meadow for this purpose, while the third remained to guard Smith. The two men soon haltered a young unbroken horse, delivered him to the guard, and went in pursuit of more. The fellow who held the horse discovering the animal was easily frightened, several times scared him for his amusement, till at length he became so much alarmed that he made a sudden wheel, and ran off with the Indian hanging to the halter, dragging him a considerable distance. Smith took this opportunity to escape, and succeeded in getting off. The next morning a party of white men collected with the intention of giving pursuit. They went to Smith's cabin and found him mending his bowls and trenchers by sewing them up with wax-ends.‡

At Hedges' fort, on the present road from Martinsburg to Bath, west of Back creek, a man was killed while watching the spring.§

On Lost river there were two forts, one on the land now the residence of Jeremiah Inskeep, Esq. called Riddle's fort, where a man named Chesmer was killed; the other called Warden's fort,‖ where William Warden and a Mr. Taff were killed, and the fort burnt down.

Just before the massacre on Looney's creek, (related on the succeeding page,) seven Indians surrounded the cabin of Samuel Bingaman, not far distant from the present village of Petersburg, in the county of Hardy.— It was just before daybreak, that being the time when the Indians generally made their surprises. Mr. B's family consisted of himself and wife, his father and mother, and a hired man. The first four were asleep in the room below, and the hired man in the loft above. A shot was fired into the cabin, the ball passing through the fleshy part of the younger Mrs. Bingaman's left breast. The family sprung to their feet, Bingaman seizing his rifle, and the Indians at the same moment rushing in at the door. Bingaman told his wife and father and mother to get out of the way, under the bed, and called to the man in the loft to come down, who, how-

---

*Related by Lewis Neill.   †Capt. Glenn.
‡Related by Capt. Glenn.   §The same.
‖Warden's fort was at the present residence of Mr. Benjamin Warden, a grandson of the man that was killed, about thirty-five miles south west of Winchester.

ever, never moved. It was still dark, and the Indians were prevented from firing, by a fear of injuring one of their number. Bingaman, unrestrained by any fears of this kind, laid about him with desperation. At the first blow, his rifle broke at the breech, shivering the stock to pieces; but with the barrel he continued his blows until he cleared the room.— Daylight now appearing, he discovered that he had killed five, and that the remaining two were retreating across the field. He stepped out, and seizing a rifle which had been left by the party, fired at one of the fugitives, wounded, and tomahawked him. Tradition relates that the other fled to the Indian camp, and told his comrades that they had had a fight with a man who was a devil—that he had killed six of them, and if they went again, would kill them all. When Bingaman, after the battle, discovered that his wife was wounded, he became frantic with rage at the cowardice of the hired.man, and would have dispatched him but for the entreaties of Mrs. B. to spare his life. She recovered from her wound in a short time.*

It was the practice of the settlers on the Wappatomaka, in times of danger, to leave the forts in numbers, and assist each other in harvest.— About the year 1756, a party of nine whites left the fort opposite the present village of Petersburg, to assist Mr. Job Welton to cut his father's meadow and hunt his cattle. They took their rifles with them, as was invariably the practice whenever they left the fort. After collecting the cattle, they turned in and cut a portion of the meadow. As night approached, a proposition was made by Mr. Welton to return to the fort, which was rather opposed by the rest of the party, who, not having been molested during the day, were disposed to believe in their perfect security.— They repaired to the house of the elder Mr. Welton, fronting the meadow, and within two hundred yards of the present residence of Aaron Welton, Esq. Here they wished to remain, but the determination was resisted by Job Welton, who again advised a return to the fort. After some consultation it was agreed on to repair to the shelter of a large elm tree in the meadow where they had been mowing, and where they concealed themselves in a winnow of the grass, and soon fell into a sound sleep; from which they were sometime afterwards roused by the crack of a rifle. Mr. Welton was lying with his brother Jonathan under the same blanket, and the latter was shot through the heart. The party sprung to their feet and attempted to escape. In his alarm, Mr. W. forgot his rifle, and fled in company with a Mr. Delay. They had proceedeb about 200 yards, pursued by an Indian, when Delay wheeled and discharged his rifle, which brought his pursuer down. At the same instant that Delay wheeled, the Indian threw his tomahawk, which sunk into the back of Mr. Welton, severing two of his ribs. He fell to the ground, supposing himself

---

*The author received the particulars of this surprising adventure from Job Welton and Aaron Welton, Esqrs. of Petersburg. Mrs. Blue, wife of Mr. Garret Blue, also told the author, that when she was a small girl Bingaman frequently stopped at her father's residence on Cheat river, and she more than once heard him relate the circumstances of this affair, and say there were seven Indians.

mortally wounded by a rifle ball, while Delay continued onward pursued by another Indian. Mr. Welton soon recovered from his surprise, and proceeded cautiously in a direction towards the fort, very weak from the loss of blood. He soon heard Delay and the Indian in a parley; the former being exhausted by running and disposed to yield, and the latter demanding his surrender. Delay agreed to give up on condition that his enemy would spare his life, which being solemnly agreed to, he was re-conducted to the elm tree. Here a council was held, and Delay, with three others who had been taken, were inhumanly scalped, from which they died in two or three days afterwards. Mr. Welton was able to reach the fort, where he laid three months before his wound healed. Of the whole party, but three escaped; four were scalped and died, and two were killed at the first surprise. The escape of Mr. Kuykendall was remarkable. It was a bright moonlight night, while the shade of the elm rendered it quite dark under the tree. Mr. K. being an old man, was unable to fly with speed, and therefore remained still, while his companions fled across the meadow. The Indians passed over him, leaving the rear clear, when Mr. K. retreated at his leisure, and reached the fort in safety, one and a half miles.*

On the day following, the whites left the fort in pursuit, and overtook their enemy late at night on Dunkard bottom, Cheat river, where they had encamped. The pursuers dismounted, and the captain ordered Bingaman (the same whose prowess is related in a preceding page) to guard the horses. He however disobeyed, and loitered in the rear of the party.— To make the destruction of the enemy more certain, it was deemed advisable to wait for daylight before they began an attack: but a young man, whose zeal overcame his discretion, fired into the group, upon which the Indians sprung to their feet and fled. Bingaman singled out a fellow of giant-like size, whom he pursued, throwing aside his rifle that his speed might not be retarded—passed several smaller Indians in the chase— came up with him—and with a single blow of his hatchet, cleft his skull. When Bingaman returned to the battle ground, the captain sternly observed, "I ordered you to stay and guard the horses." Bingaman as sternly replied, "you are a rascal, sir: you intended to disgrace me; and one more insolent word, and you shall share the fate of that Indian," pointing towards the body he had just slain. The captain quailed under the stern menace, and held his peace. He and Bingaman had, a few days before, had a falling out. Several Indians fell in this affair, while the whites lost none of their party.

Dr. Turley stated to the author that he had often heard Mr. John Harness, who was one of the party that followed the Indians, relate that Delay was taken to Dunkard bottom, and when the Indians were then surprised, he was shot, but whether by his captors or accidentally, was not known, Delay himself not being able to tell. He was conveyed home on

---

*Messrs. Aaron and Job Welton related this tradition to the author. It was thought that Delay would have recovered but for the unskillfulness of the surgeon (if he deserved the name) who attended him. The late Gen. William Darke married his widow.

a litter, and died directly afterwards.   There were, however, two Delays, and the first relation may be true.

Mrs. Shobe, an aged and respectable lady, living on Mill creek, in Hardy county, informed the author that Delay was buried on the banks of the South Branch, and some years afterwards his skeleton was washed, out by a rising of the river.   She then heard Job Welton say that Delay had saved his life, and he would take care of his bones.

To show the spirit of the times, the following anecdote is related. Valentine Powers and his brother, with two or three others, left the fort near Petersburg,* on a visit to their farms, when they were fired upon by Indians from a thicket, and the brother of Powers killed.   Valentine ran, but soon calling to mind the saying, current among them, that "it was a bad man who took bad news home," he turned about and gave himself up and remained a prisoner five or six years.†

Martin Peterson was taken a prisoner on the South Branch, and carried to the Sandusky towns.   He used to accompany the Indians in their hunting excursions, and was permitted to have one load of powder and ball each day, which he always discharged at the game they met with.— As he gained on the confidence of his captors, they increased his allowance to two loads, and subsequently to three.   The same allowance was made to two other white prisoners.   These three, one day, after receiving their allowance, determined to attempt an escape; and left the towns accordingly.   As they ventured to travel only at night, guided by the north star, their progress was exceedingly slow and difficult.   On the second day one of their number died from fatigue, and Peterson took his ammunition.   A day or two afterwards, his remaining companion also gave out, and Peterson taking his ammunition, left him to perish.   He then pursued his way alone, and after a succession of hardships, came at length in sight of the fort.   But here, when within reach of his deliverance, his hopes were well-nigh blasted; for the sentry, mistaking him for an Indian, fired!   Happily the ball missed its aim, and he was able to make himself known before the fire was repeated.   This fort was on the farm now the residence of Mr. John Welton, near Petersburg, Hardy county.‡

Seybert's fort,§ was erected on the South fork of the South branch of

---

*Called Fort George.   The land is now owned by Job Welton, Esq.

†Related by Aaron Welton, Esq.

‡Related by Aaron Welton, Esq.

§The author, on a visit to Franklin, obtained some additional particulars in relation to the attack on Seybert's fort:—The party of Indians was commanded by the blood-thirsty and treacherous chief, Kill-buck.   Seybert's son, a lad about fifteen years of age, exhibited great firmness and bravery in the defence of the post.   He had with his rifle brought down two of his assailants, when Kill-buck called out to old Seybert, in English, to surrender, and their lives should be spared.   At that instant young Seybert, having charged his rifle, was in the act of presenting it at Kill-buck, when his father seized the gun, and took it from him, observing :— "We cannot defend the fort: we must surrender in order to save our lives," confiding in the assurances of the faithless Kill-buck.   The first the Potomac, on the land now owned by Mr. Ferdinand Lair, twelve miles north east of Franklin, the present county seat of Pendleton. In the year 1758, a party of Indians surprised the fort, in which were thirty persons. They bound ten, whom they conveyed without the fort, and then proceeded to massacre the others in the following manner: They seated them in a row upon a log, with an Indian standing behind each; and at a given signal, each Indian sunk his tomahawk into the head of his victim: an additional blow or two dispatched them. The scene was witnessed by James Dyer, a lad fourteen years old, who, not having been removed without the fort, supposed that he was to be massacred. He was however spared, and taken to Log town, sixteen miles below Fort Pitt, thence to the mouth of the Muskingum river, and thence to the spot where Chilicothe now stands, where he remained a prisoner one year and ten months. He had by this time gained the entire confidence of his captors, and was permitted to accompany them to Fort Pitt on a trading expedition.—When there he planned his escape, and happily succeeded. Being sent out for some bread with an Indian lad, he slipped into a hovel, unobserved by his companion, and implored the protection of the poor woman who occupied it. She told him to get behind a chest, the only furniture in the room, and threw upon him a bed. The Indians, on missing him, spent the afternoon in search, during which they looked into the very hovel where he was, and left the place the next morning on their return. Fort Pitt being then in possession of the English, a trooper very kindly conveyed him six or seven miles behind him, whence he made his way to his friends in Pennsylvania, where he remained two years longer, and then returned to South Fork.*

Another tradition says that Seybert's fort was not surprised. It had been invested for two or three days, and after two Indians had been killed, the garrison agreed to surrender on condition that their lives should be spared, which was solemnly pledged. The gate was then opened, and the Indians rushed in with demoniac yells. The whites fled with precipitation, but were retaken, with the exception of one man. The mas-

---

salutation he received, after surrendering the fort, was a stroke on his mouth from the monster, Kill-buck, with the pipe-end of his tomahawk, dislocating several of the old man's teeth; and immediately after he was massacred with the other victims. Young Seybert was taken off among the prisoners. He told Killbuck *he had raised his gun to kill him; but that his father had wrested it from him.* The savage laughed, and replied, "You little rascal, if you had killed me you would have saved the fort: for had I fallen my warriors would have immediately fled, and given up the siege in despair."

It is said there were three men in the fort, not one of whom manifested a disposition to aid its defence. Had they joined young Seybert, and acted with the same intrepidity and coolness, the place might have been saved, and the awful sacrifice of the inmates avoided.

*Related by Zebulon Dyer, Esq. clerk of Pendleton county, and son of the James Dyer mentioned.

sacre then took place, as before related, and ten were taken off as prisoners.

Another tradition says, that, on the fort's being given up, the Indians
seated twenty of the garrison in two rows, all of whom they killed except the wife of Jacob Peterson. When they reached her, an Indian interposed to save her life, and some altercation ensued. The friendly Indian at length prevailed ; and throwing her a pair of moccasons, told her
to march off with the prisoners. How long she remained in captivity is
not remembered.*

The Indians killed John Brake's wife on the South fork of the Wapp:-
tomaka. John Brake became conspicuous in the war of the revolution,
which will be noticed hereafter. Fredrick Jice had his whole family killed, with the exception of himself and one son. A man named Williams
and his wife were also killed. Richard Williams and his wife were taken prisoners : the latter was only eighteen months old when taken, remained with the Indians until she was thirteen, and was then brought
home. She had learned the Indian language perfectly; afterwards learned
to speak English, but there were some words she never could pronounce
plainly. She married Uriah Blue, on the South Branch.

About eight miles below Romney stood a fort. In time of harvest a
Mrs. Hogeland went out about three hundred yards to gather beans, two
men accompanying her as a guard. While gathering the beans, 8 or ten
Indians made their appearace. One of the guarde instantly fled ; the other, whose name was Hogeland, called to the woman to run to the fort ;
and placing himself between her and the enemy, with his rifle cocked and
presented, retreated from tree to tree until both entered it. Some old
men in the fort fired off their guns to alarm the harvest hands, who ran
into it, the Indians from the side of the mountain firing upon them, but
doing no injury. The same day the harvest hands were waylaid as they
returned to their work, fired upon, and Henry Newkirk wounded in the
hip. The whites returned the fire, and wounded an Indian, who dropped
his gun and fled. The others also made off, and the harvest hands proceeded to their work.

In 1756, while the Indians were lurking about Fort Pleasant, and constantly on the watch to cut off all communication therewith, a lad named
Higgins, aged about twelve years, was directed by his mother to go to
the spring, about a quarter of a mile without the fort, and bring a bucket
of water. He complied with much trepidation, and persuaded a companion of his, of about the same age, to accompany him. They repaired
to the spring as cautiously as possible, and after filling their buckets, ran
with speed towards the fort, Higgins taking the lead. When about half
way to the fort, and Higgins had got about thirty yards before his companion, he heard a scream from the latter, which caused him to increase
his speed to the utmost. He reached the fort in safety, while his companion was captured by the Indians, and taken to their settlements, where

---

*Mrs. Shobe informed the author that she had heard the wife of Jacob
Peterson frequently relate this.

L

he remained until the peace, and was then restored. The young Higgins subsequently became the active Capt. Robert Higgins in our revolutionary army, and after raising a numerous family in Virginia, removed with them to the west.[*]

In the neighborhood of Moorefield a party of men were mowing for Peter Casey. · They had placed their guns under a large tree in the edge of the meadow, and old Peter stood sentinel to watch and give the alarm should the enemy make their appearance. In a short time a party of Indians' discovered the hands at work; and cautiously crept through the brambles and shrubbery in order to get a position to make a deadly fire. One of them was in front of the others, and had approached very near old Peter before the latter saw him, when the old man flew at him with his cane raised, crying out, "By the Lord, boys, here they come!" The Indian, desperately frightened, took to his heels; the men flew to their guns; and the skulking savages retreated precipitately, without firing a single shot. It is not improbable that Casey still used the same stick with which he "knocked Kill-buck down."[†]

The author finding this chapter running to a tedious and perhaps tiresome length to the reader, will give his pen a short respite, and resume, his narrative of Indian outrages in the next chapter.

——:0:——

CHAPTER IX.

INDIAN INCURSIONS AND MASSACRES—Continued.

On Stony creek, five or six miles south-west of Woodstock, there was a a fort called "Wolfe's fort," where the people took shelter from the Indians for several years. Mr. Wolfe would sometimes venture out for the purpose of killing game, and was always accompanied by a favorite dog. On one particular occasion, this faithful animal saved his master's life.— Mr. W. walked out with his gun and dog, but had not proceeded far before the latter manifested great alarm, and used all his ingenuity to induce his master to return. He repeatedly crossed his path, endeavoring to obstruct his walk; would raise himself up, and place his feet against his master's breast, and strive to push him back; would run a few steps towards the fort, and then return whining. From the extraordinary manifestation of uneasiness on the part of the dog, Mr. Wolfe began to suspect there was some lurking danger, of course kept a sharp look out, and soon discovered an Indian at some distance behind a tree, watching and

---

*Related by Col. Isaac Vanmeter.   †The same.

waiting until he should come near enough to be a sure mark. Mr. W. made a safe retreat into the fort, and ever after felt the highest gratitude to his honest and faithful dog. The dog lived to be twenty-one years of age, and probably more.* Ulysses's dog "Argus" is much celebrated in history; but it is very questionable whether Argus ever rendered more important services to his lord and master. Ulysses was one of the commanding generals of the Greeks in the Trojan war, and was absent twenty years, it is said, from his home. The story of his dog is related by Homer in the following beautiful poetical effusion:†

Thus near the gates conferring as they drew,
Argus, the dog, his ancient master knew;
He, not unconscious of the voice and tread,
Lifts to the sound his ear, and rears his head;
Bred by Ulysses, nourish'd at his board,
But ah! not fated long to please his lord!
To him, his swiftness and his strength were vain;
The voice of glory call'd him o'er the main:
Till then in every sylvan chase renown'd,
With Argus, Argus, rung the woods around:
With him the youth pursu'd the goat or fawn,
Or trac'd the mazy leveret o'er the lawn.
Now left to man's ingratitude he lay,
Unhous'd, neglected in the public way;
And where on heaps the rich manure was spread,
Obscene with reptiles, took his sordid bed.
He knew his lord; he knew, and strove to meet;
In vain he strove to crawl, and kiss his feet,
Yet (all he could) his tail, his ears, his eyes,
Salute his master, and confess his joys.
Soft pity touch'd the mighty master's soul;
Adown his cheek a tear unbidden stole,
Stole unperceiv'd: he turn'd his head, and dried
The drop humane; then thus impassion'd cried:
"What noble beast in this abandon'd state,
Lies here all helpless at Ulysses' gate?
His bulk and beauty speak no vulgar praise;

---

*Moses Russell, Esq. of the county of Frederick, gave the author a detail of the particulars of this extraordinary story, and stated, that when he was a young man he once called at Mr. Wolfe's house and saw the dog. He appeared to be decrepit and suffering pain, and he asked Mr. Wolfe if he had not better kill the dog, and put him out of misery. Mr. Wolfe with much emphasis replied, "No, I would as readily consent to be killed myself as to kill that dog, or suffer him to be killed; he once saved my life;" and Mr. W. then related the above story. The dog was then twenty-one years old.

†It is said that Argus was the only creature that immediately recognized his master on his return to his palace from his twenty years' absence.

If, as he seems, he *was* in better days,
Some care his age deserves: or was he priz'd
For worthless beauty, therefore now despised?
Such dogs, and men there are, mere things of state,
And always cherish'd by their friends, the great."
   "Not Argus so, (Emmæus thus rejoin'd)
But serv'd a master of a nobler kind,
Who never, never, shall behold him more!
Long, long since perish'd on a distant shore!
O had you seen him, vigorous, bold and young,
Swift as a stag, and as a lion strong;
Him no fell savage on the plain withstood,
None scap'd him, bosom'd in the gloomy wood:
His eye how piercing, and his scent how true,
To wind the vapor in the tainted dew?
Such, when Ulysses left his natal coast,
Now years unnerve him, and his lord is lost,
The women keep the generous creature bare,
A sleek and idle race is all their care:
The master gone, the servants what restrains?
Or dwells humanity where riot reigns?
Jove fix'd it certain, that whatever day
Makes man a slave, takes half his worth away."
   This said, the honest herdsman strode before:
The musing monarch pauses at the door.
The dog whom fate had granted to behold
His lord when twenty tedious years had roll'd,
Takes a last look, and having seen him, dies;
So clos'd forever faithful Argus' eyes!

There was no poet at the time to transmit the name and fame of Mr. Wolfe's dog to posterity. European authors, in their prejudices, have on various occasions endeavored to disparage every thing of American production. The Count de Buffon is among the number. Englishmen delight in the disparagement of American quadrupeds. In the Family Encyclopedia, an English work, under the article "dogs," it is asserted that "when English dogs are transported to other countries, they degenerate, and become comparatively worthless!" It is believed the annals of the world may be safely challenged to produce an instance of greater manifestation of sagacity and faithful affection towards a master, than was exhibited by Mr. Wolfe's dog on the occasion spoken of. But to return.

At the Forks of Capon stockade. The men who occupied it had to go about four miles to cultivate a fine fertile field of low ground, to produce bread for their support. In the year 1757 or 1758, two men, one named Bowers, the other York, walked to the field to see how things were going on. On their return in the evening they were waylaid by seven Indians. Bowers was shot and fell dead; York ran, was pursued by three Indians, and took across a high ridge. One of his pursuers tired before he reached the top; the others continued the chase. After running a considerable distance, a second gave out. The third got so near that he several times extended his arm to seize York, but failed, and York got safe into the fort.*

On Patterson's creek, at the present site of Frankfort, Ashby's fort was erected. It was at this place that the celebrated race took place between the late Capt. John Ashby and three Indians. Capt. Ashby had walked out from the fort with his gun, and after proceeding some distance discovered three Indians, who knew him, but a little way off. He turned and ran: two of the Indians fired, but missed him: they all three then gave chase, but Ashby was too swift for them; and when they saw they could not overhaul him, one of them called out, "Run, Jack Ashby, run!" He replied, looking over his shoulder, "You fools, do you think I run booty?" —[with boots.]

Near the fort, Charles Keller was killed, the grandfather of Mr. Charles Keller, the present proprietor of the Frankfort Hotel.†

About the year 1756, Daniel Sullivan, at nine years of age, was taken prisoner by the Indians, with whom he remained nine years, when he was brought home. For some time he manifested a desire to return to the Indians, but at length became reconciled, and was afterwards their determined enemy. In his last battle with them, becoming desperately wounded, and his entrails falling out and in his way, he tore them off, and continued to fight until he fell and expired. The Indians after this considered him something more than man.‡

At the Rev. Mr. Jacob's present residence, on North Branch, a man by the name of Wade was killed.

Logan, the celebrated Indian, killed Benjamin Bowman, and took Humphrey Worstead prisoner. He compelled the latter to halter several of his own and Bowman's horses, and took them off.§

At a battle at Oldtown, John Walker killed an Indian and wounded another. Walker cut out a part of the dead Indian's flesh from the thick part of his thigh, and threw it to his dog, who ate it. He otherwise mutilated his body; and thrust parts of it into his mouth.

Thomas Higgins was one of the earliest settlers on the Cohongoruton. He lived about four miles from Bath, but was driven thence, and removed to the neighborhood of Gerardstown, in the county of Berkeley. After his removal, three of his sons were taken off as prisoners, and never returned. At the close of Dunmore's war, one of them was seen at Wheeling by a man who was acquainted with his family, and asked why he did not come home, since his father had left him a good tract of land. He replied that he did not wish to live with white people; they would always call him Indian; and he had land enough.‖

The wife of the late Walter Denny, of Frederick county, was taken by

---

*Related by Mr. John Largent.

†Mr. Keller stated this fact to the author.

‡Isaac Kuykendall, Esq. of the South Branch, near Romney, stated this fact to the author, and added that Sullivan was his near relation.

§Related by Mr. Gerrit Blue, of the North Branch.

‖Related by Mr. James Higgins, of the North Branch.

the Indians when a small child, and grew up among them. Her maiden name was Flaugherty. After returning from her captivity, she married Walter Denny, who resided some time after his marriage in the neighborhood of Pittsburgh. In 1774 the Indians advised him to move off, as they intended to go to war with the whites. Mr. Denny removed and settled in the county of Frederick. The author recollects frequently seeing this man. A Miss Williams was also taken about the same time: she, too, grew up with the Indians. These two female children were taken on Patterson's creek.

There is a tradition of a battle fought on Patterson's creek, between the whites and Indians, the spring before Braddock's defeat; but the author was not able to obtain the particulars, except that the Indians were defeated.

The Indians killed Oliver Kremer, in Short Gap, and took his wife prisoner.

· In the year 1764, a party of eighteen Delawares crossed the mountains. Furman's fort was about one mile above the Hanging Rock, on the South Branch. William Furman and Nimrod Ashby had gone out from the fort to watch a deer lick in the Jersey mountain.* The Indians discovered and killed them both, and passed on into the county of Frederick, where they divided into two parties. One party of eight moved on to the Cedar creek settlement; the other of ten attacked the people in the neighborhood of the present residence of Maj. John White. On this place Dr. White, the ancestor of the White family, had settled, and on his land a stockade was erected. The people in the neighborhood had taken the alarm, and were on their way to the fort, when they were assaulted by these ten Indians. They killed David Jones and his wife, two old people. Some of Mrs. Thomas' family were killed, and she and one daughter taken off. An old man by the name of Llyod, and his wife, and several of his children, were killed. Esther Lloyd, their daughter, about thirteen years old, received three tomahawk wounds in the head, was scalped, and left lying, supposed to be dead. Henry Clouser and two of his sons were killed, and his wife and four of his daughters taken. The youngest daughter was about two years old; and as she impeded the mother's travelling, when they reached the North mountain, the poor little innocent babe was taken by its heels, its head dashed against a tree, and the brains beaten out, and left lying on the ground. Mrs. Thomas was taken to the Wappatomaka; but the river being pretty full, and deep fording, they encamped near Furman's fort for the night. The next morning a party of white men fired off their guns at the fort, which alarmed the Indians, and they hurried across the river, assisting all their female prisoners except Mrs. Thomas, who being quite stout and strong, was left to shift for herself. The current, however, proved too strong for her, and she floated down the river—but lodged against a rock, upon which she crawled, and saved herself from drowning. Before her capture she had concealed half a loaf of bread in her bosom, which, during her struggles in the water washed out, and, on her reaching the rock, floated to her

---

*So called from its being first settled by immigrants from New Jersey.

again. In this instance, the text of scripture, "Cast thy bread upon the waters, for thou shalt find it after many days,"* might have some application. It was not "many days," but there appears to have been something providential in it, for it saved her from extreme suffering. The next morning Mrs. Thomas made her way to William's fort, about two miles below the Hanging Rock, on the South Branch.†

The author has received from Maj. John White, of Frederick, another account of the foregoing outrages, which he will give in Maj. W.'s own words:

"In July, 1763, information was received by the late Maj. Robert White, (who had a small fort around his house as an asylum for the people in the neighborhood,) that Indians had been seen on that or the preceding day on Capon. He immediately went to the several families living near the base of the North mountain, as far as to Owen Thomas', five or six miles from the fort, told them of the report, and advised them to go into the fort until the danger should be over. It being harvest time, Owen Thomas was unwilling to leave home, and mounted a horse to go to his neighbor Jacob Kackley's, who had several sons grown, to propose to arm themselves and work together in their respective grain fields; but on his way to Mr. Kackley's he was shot dead and scalped, the Indians having concealed themselves behind two logs that lay one across the other near the road.

"In June, 1764, similar information of Indians being seen was received at the fort. Maj. White, as on the former occasion, went in the afternoon to warn the people of their danger; when the widow Thomas, Mr. Jones and Mr. Clouser, set off with their families for the fort; but night coming on when they reached Mr. Lloyd's, (about two miles from the fort,) they concluded to stay there all night. In the morning, as soon as day appeared, they resumed their journey; but before they were out of sight of the house, the Indians attacked them, and killed, wounded, or took prisoners twenty-two or twenty-three persons. Evan Thomas, a son of the man killed the preceding summer, a boy of seven years old, ran back into the house, and hid himself behind some puncheons that he placed across a corner of the room, and remained concealed, notwithstanding the Indians brought the prisoners into the house, among whom were his mother and sister, both tied, and kept them there till they fried bacon and ate their breakfast; they then set fire to the house in two places, and went away. Evan said he continued in the house as long as he could on account of the fire; that he saw through a chink in the wall the direction the Indians went; and not knowing which way to go, he concluded to take the contrary course from the one taken by them. He rambled about all that day and the most of the next before he found any person, the houses which he passed having been abandoned by their owners going to the fort. The Indians encamped the first night at a spring on the Romney road, between the North river and Little Capon; and on the next day

---

*Ecclesiastics, 11th chap. 1st verse.

†Mr. Gerrit Blue stated to the author that he was then a small boy, but well recollects seeing Mrs. Thomas when she got into the fort.

they stopped on the bank of the South Branch, near where Romney now stands, to eat their dinner. While thus engaged, a party who were stationed in a fort a mile or two lower down the river, and who had just returned from a scout, discharged their guns in order to clean them, which alarmed the Indians, and they hurried across the river, assisting all their female prisoners excepting Mrs. Thomas, who being a large fat woman, it was supposed would perish, as the water was rapid and deep. She floated down the stream, however, until almost exhausted, when she had the good fortune to get on a rock, and save herself from drowning. She had put a piece of bread in her bosom the morning she was taken, and lost it in the water; but it happened to float so near her while on the rock that she caught it and ate it; which, as she said, so revived and strengthened her that she plunged into the water again, and providentially got out on the east side of the river. She reached Williams' fort, two miles below the Hanging Rock, on the same day. It was often remarked by Mrs. Thomas' acquaintances, that after her return she would minutely relate the circumstances attending the murder of her husband and children, and her own sufferings, without shedding a tear. Either five or seven of the persons wounded by the Indians, were taken to the fort at Maj. Robert White's, and attended by Dr. M'Donald, though but one recovered, Hester Lloyd, who had two scalps taken from her."

Mrs. Thomas' daughter, and Mrs. Clouser and her three small daughters, were taken to the Indian towns, and after an absence of about six months, were released from captivity, and all returned home safely.

There is something remarkable in the history of the three Miss Clousers, who were all prisoners at the same time. The eldest was about ten years old, the next eldest about seven, and the youngest between five and six. They all returned home from their captivity, grew up, were married, raised families of children, and are now widows, living in the same neighborhood, not more than five or six miles apart. Two of them, Mrs. Shultz and Mrs. Snapp, reside about one and a half miles from the residence of the author, and the third, Mrs. Fry, not exceeding six miles.

Miss Lloyd, who was "tomahawked and scalped," was soon discovered not to be dead. The late Dr. M'Donald was sent for, who trepanned her in the several fractures in her head. She recovered and lived many years after. There are several respectable individuals now living who knew this woman.*

The other party of eight Indians committed several murders on Cedar creek. It is probable this party killed a Mr. Lyle, a Mr. Butler, and some others. Mr. Ellis Thomas, the husband of the woman whose story has just been given, was killed the harvest preceding. This party of eight Indians took off two female prisoners, were pursued by a party of white men, overtaken in the South Branch mountain, and fired upon, when one of the Indians was killed. The others fled, leaving their guns,

---

*General Smith, Maj. R. D. Glass, Miss Susan Glass, Mrs. Shultz, and Mrs. Snapp, severally stated to the author that they frequently saw this woman after she recovered from her wounds. Mrs. Shultz states that it was on the first day of June the outrage was committed.

prisoners, and plunder.* The prisoners and property were brought home. Two of the fugitives overtook the party in the Alleghany mountain who had Mrs. Clouser, her daughters, and other prisoners, in custody. The fugitives appeared in desperate ill humor, and proposed to murder the prisoners; but the others peremptorily objected, and would not suffer their prisoners to be injured.†

The same year, 1764, a party of eight Indians, with a white man by the name of Abraham Mitchell, killed George Miller, his wife and two children, within about two miles of Strasburg. They also the same day killed John Dellinger on the land now the residence of Capt. Anthony Spengler, adjoining the town, and took Rachel Dellinger, with her infant child, prisoners. It was a male child, very stout, and heavy of its age. In crossing Sandy ridge, west of Capon river, this child had its brains beaten out against a tree. A party of white men pursued them, overtook them in the South Branch mountain, fired upon them, and killed one, when the others fled, leaving every thing behind. Rachel Dellinger was brought home, and stated that the unprincipled scoundrel Mitchell was with the Indians. About twelve months before, Mitchell had been punished for a petty act of theft, while the people were at Bowman's fort.— Miller and Dellinger inflicted the punishment.‡

At the massacre of the people near White's fort, one of Mrs. Thomas' daughters, when the people were preparing to go to the fort, was requested by Mrs. Clouser to take a bottle of milk in her hand, and carry it to the fort. When the Indians assailed them, this young woman concealed herself behind a tree, and finally escaped. As soon as she could run off without being discovered, she started and ran eight or nine miles with the bottle of milk in her hand. She was met by two of the Fawcetts, near their residence, informed them of what had happened, and they forthwith removed their families to Stephens' fort.§

A little son of Mrs. Thomas concealed himself under a pile of flax, which the Indians set on fire. As the fire progressed, the little fellow kept in a direction to avoid it, while the smoke concealed him from the sight of the enemy, and he got safe to the fort.

Thomas Pugh resided at the time on the farm, late the residence of Mr. John M'Cool, eight or nine miles north west of Winchester. The same party of Indians who committed the outrage near White's fort, on the night after were lurking about Mr. Pugh's house. His dog gave the alarm; and from his singular behavior, and manifestations of rage, (as if he were

---

*Moses Russell, Esq.

†Mrs. Shultz and Mrs. Snapp.

‡The late Mrs. Brinker related the particulars of these occurrences to the author. Major Isaac Hite recollects when Miller and Dellinger were killed.

§Stephen's fort was at the spot where Zane's iron works were afterwards erected on Cedar creek. Mr. Elisha Fawcett, a near neighbor of the author, a highly respectable and intelligent man, stated to the author that he had frequently heard his father and uncle speak of this occurrence.

M

engaged in a furious battle,) Mr. Pugh cautiously looked out at a window and although it was rather a dark night, he discovered several Indians looking over a cluster of briars but a short distance from his house. He and his wife and children immediately retreated through a back door and pushed off. They had not gone far, before Pugh recollected his money; he turned back, got into the house, secured his money, took it with him, and saved himself and family from injury. During the whole time Pugh and his family were making their escape, the dog continued his uproar, and as soon as they were out of danger, followed them.* The Indians broke into the house, robbed it of what they chose, and destroyed the furniture; but they did not burn the building. It is said they burnt comparatively but a few houses, because they expected to reconquer the country, and return to inhabit it; in which event they would have comfortable houses ready built to their hands; hence they generally spared the buildings.

About the year 1765, the Indians made their appearance in the neighborhood of Woodstock, in the county of Shenandoah. On Narrow Passage creek, eighteen or twenty women and children had collected together, in order to go to the fort at Woodstock. An old man by the name of George Sigler was with them. Five Indians attacked them. Sigler, after firing, and wounding one in the leg, clubbed his gun and fought to desperation. While he was thus engaged, the women and children made their escape, and got safe from the fort. Sigler broke his gun over the heads of the enemy, wounded several of them pretty severely, and received himself several wounds, but continued the fight until he fell from the loss of blood, when his merciless enemies mangled his body in a manner shocking to behold.†

In 1766 the Indians made another visit to the neighborhood of Woodstock. Two men, by the name of Sheetz and Taylor, had taken their wives and children into a wagon, and were on their way to the fort. At the Narrow Passage, three miles south of Woodstock, five Indians attacked them. The two men were killed at the first onset, and the Indians rushed to seize the women and children. The women, instead of swooning at the sight of their bleeding, expiring husbands, seized their axes, and with Amazonian firmness, and strength almost superhuman, defended themselves and children. One of the Indians had succeeded in getting hold of one of Mrs. Sheetz's children, and attempted to drag it out of the wagon; but with the quickness of lightning she caught her child in one hand, and with the other made a blow at the head of the fellow, which caused him to quit his hold to save his life. Several of the Indians received pretty sore wounds in this desperate conflict, und all at last ran off, leaving the two women with their children to pursue their way to the fort.

---

*Mr. Joseph Hackney informed the author that he had frequently heard Mr. Pugh relate this occurrence. This is another instance of the extraordinary evidence of the sagacity and affection of the dog, and is little inferior to the story of Mr. Wolfe's dog.

†Mr. Christian Miller, a very aged and intelligent man, gave the author this narrative.

In the latter part of August, the same year, a party of eight Indians and a worthless villian of a white man crossed Powell's Fort mountain, to the South fork of the Shenandoah, at the late residence of John Gatewood, Esq. where the Rev. John Roads, a Menonist preacher of the Gospel, then lived. Mr. R., his wife, and three of his sons, were murdered. Mr. Roads was standing in his door, when he was shot and fell dead.— Mrs. Roads and one of her sons were killed in the yard. One of the young men was at the distance of about one hundred and fifty yards from the house, in a corn field. Hearing the report of the guns at the house, he ascended a pear tree to see what it meant, where he was discovered by an Indian and instantly killed. The third poor young lad attempted to save himself by flight, and to cross the river, but was pursued and killed in the river. The place is called the Bloody ford to this day. The enemy demanded of the youth who was killed in the yard, where his father kept his money; and was told that if he did not immediately point out the place, they would kill him; but if he would show them the money, his life should be spared. On his declaring he could not tell them, he was instantly shot and fell dead. Mr. Roads' eldest daughter Elizabeth caught up her little sister, a child about sixteen or eighteen months old, ran into the barn, and secured the door. An Indian discovered and pursued her, and attempted to force open the door; but not succeeding, he with many oaths and threats ordered her to open it. On her refusing, the fellow ran back to the house to get fire; and while he was gone, Elizabeth crept out a hole on the opposite side of the barn, with her little sister in her arms, ran through a field of tall hemp, crossed the river, and got safe to a neighboring house, and thus saved herself and sister.

After plundering the house of such articles as they chose to take, the Indians set fire to all the buildings, and left the dead body of Mr. Roads to be consumed in the flames.* They then moved off, taking with them two of the sons and two of the daughters prisoners. The youngest prisoner was a weak, sickly little boy, eight or nine years of age: he of course was not able to stand the fatigue of traveling; and crossing the head of Powell's fort, they killed him. His two sisters then refusing to go any farther with them, were barbarously murdered, and their bodies left a prey to wolves and other wild beasts. The other boy was taken off and remained about three years in captivity before he returned home. It was generally believed at the time, that the white scoundrel who was with the Indians, induced them to commit this horrid murder, in order to rob Mr. Roads of his money; but he missed his object. Mr. Roads kept his money and title papers in a niche in the cellar wall, the dampness and coolness of which preserved them from injury. They were all found safe.

It was quite a common thing with the Germans to have garners fixed

---

*Mrs. Stover, the mother of Daniel Stover, Esq., now of Page county, stated to the author that she was then about fifteen years old, and distinctly saw the houses in flames from her father's residence, about two miles off, on the opposite side of the river: and the next day the neighboring people collecting to bury the dead, found Mr. Roads' body about half consumed.

in their garrets to preserve their grain. There was a quantity of rye aloft in the dwelling house, which was burnt to coal; and as the floors gave way to the flames, the rye fell in a considerable body into the cellar. At any time upon digging into the ruins of the cellar, the grains of rye, or rather coal, can be found—the shape of the grain being as perfect as when in its natural state.

With this bloody tragedy ended the irruptions of the savages upon the people of the valley. This was the last great outrage of savage warfare committed east of the North mountain.

There are several other interesting occurrences which the author overlooked and omitted to record in due order of time. They are of a character too interesting to be lost in the history of our country. He will therefore proceed to relate them.

About the year 1760, two Indians were discovered lurking in the neighborhood of Mill creek. Matthias Painter, John Painter and William Moore, armed themselves and went in pursuit. They had not proceeded far, before they approached a large fallen pine, with a very bushy top.—As they neared the tree, Matthias' Painter observed, "We had better look sharp; it is quite likely the Indians are concealed under the tops of this tree." He had scarcely uttered the words before one of the Indians rose up and fired. The ball grazed the temple of John Painter. Moore and Painter fired at the same instant; one of their balls passed through the Indian's body, and he fell, they supposed dead enough. The other fellow fled, leaving his gun and every thing else behind. The white men pursued him some distance, but the fugitive was too fleet for them. Finding they could not overhaul him, they gave up the chase and returned to the pine tree: but to their astonishment, the supposed dead Indian had moved off with both guns and a large pack of skins, &c. They pursued his trail, and when he found they were gaining upon him, he got into a sink hole, and as soon as they approached pretty near, commenced firing at them. He had poured out a quantity of powder on dry leaves, filled his mouth with bullets, and using a musket which was a self-primer, he was enabled to load with astonishing quickness. He thus fired at least thirty times before they could get a chance to dispatch him. At last Mr. Moore got an opportunity, and shot him through the head. Moore and Painter had many disputes which give the fellow the first wound. Painter, at length, yielded, and Moore got the premium allowed by law for Indian scalps.*

The fugitive who made his escape, unfortunately met with a young woman on horseback, named Seehon, whom he tore from her horse, and forced off with him. This occurred near the present site of Newmarket, in the county of Shenandoah. After traveling about twenty miles, chiefly in the night, and getting nearly opposite Keisletown, in the county of Rockingham, it is supposed the poor girl broke down from fatigue, and the savage monster beat her to death with a heavy pine knot. Her screams were heard by some people that lived upwards of a mile from the

---

*Mr. George Painter communicated this adventure to the author.

scene of horror, and who next day on going to the place to ascertain the cause, found her stripped naked, and weltering in her blood.*

At the attack on George Miller's family, the persons killed were a short distance from the house, spreading flax in a meadow. One of Miller's little daughters was sick in bed. Hearing the firing, she jumped up, and looking through a window and seeing what was done, immediately passed out at a back window, and ran about two or three miles, down to the present residence of David Stickley, Esq. and from thence to Geo. Bowman's on Cedar creek, giving notice at each place. Col. Abraham Bowman, of Kentucky, then a lad of sixteen or seventeen, had but a few minutes before passed close by Miller's door, and at first doubted the little girl's statement. He however armed himself, mounted his horse, and in. riding to the scene of action, was joined by several others who had turned out for the same purpose, and soon found the information of the little girl too fatally true.

The late Mr. Thomas Newell, of Shenandoah county, informed the author that he was then a young man. His father's residence was about one mile from Miller's house ; and hearing the firing, he instantly took his rifle, and ran to see what it meant. When he arrived at the spot, he found Miller, his wife, and two children, weltering in their blood, and still bleeding. He was the first person who arrived ; and in a very few minutes Bowman and several others joined him. From the scene of murder they went to the house, and on the sill of the door lay a large folio German Bible, on which a fresh killed cat was thrown. On taking up the Bible it was discovered that fire had been placed in it ; but after burning through a few leaves, the weight of that part of the book which lay uppermost, together with the weight of the cat, had so compressed the leaves as to smother and extinguish the fire.†

In the year 1768, Capt. William White, a brave and active Indian fighter, made a visit to Col. Wm. Crawford, who had removed and settled at the Meadows in the Allegany mountains. White lived on Cedar creek, and Crawford had lived on Bull-skin. They had been out together on Indian expeditions ; of course were well acquainted. Crawford had an Irish servant, a pretty stout and active man, who was permitted to accompany White on a hunting excursion. They had not been out long before they discovered two Indians in the glades. The latter, the moment they discovered the two white men, flew behind trees, and prepared for battle. White and his Irishman, however, soon out-generaled them, and killed them both. They were soon after apprehended, and committed to Winchester jail on a charge of murder. But White had rendered

---

*Mrs. Branaman, an aged and respectable old lady near Pennybacker's iron works, gave the author this information.

†This Bible is now in the possession of Mr. George Miller, of Shenandoah county, about one a half miles south of Zane's old iron works. The author saw and examined it. The fire had been placed about the centre of the 2d book of Samuel, burnt through fourteen leaves, and entirely out at one end. It is preserved in the Miller family, as a sacred relic or memento of the sacrifice of their ancestors.

his neighbors too many important services, and was too popular, to be permitted to languish loaded with irons in a dungeon for killing Indians. Although the Indian hostilities had entirely ceased, too many individuals were smarting under a recollection of the outrages they had but recently experienced at the hands of their merciless, savage, and implacable foe. Soon after White and his partner in the charge were committed to jail, Capt. Abraham Fry raised a party of fifty-five or sixty volunteers, well armed and mounted, to effect their rescue. They dismounted near the present site of Mr. Isaac Hollingsworth's dwelling house, where they left their horses under a guard of a few men, and marched into Winchester about daybreak next morning. They repaired directly to the jail door, knocked up the jailer, and demanded the keys. The jailer hesitated, and attempted to remonstrate. Fry presented his rifle, cocked it, and peremptorily demanded the keys, telling the jailer he would be a dead man in one minute if he did not deliver them. The jailer quailed under the fiery countenance and stern menaces of Fry, and complied. Fry placed a guard at the door, went in, knocked off their irons, and took the prisoners out. The late Robert Rutherford attempted to harangue the mob upon the impropriety and danger of their proceedings; but he might as well have addressed himself to so many lions or tigers. As Fry's party marched into the town, it created considerable alarm and excitement.—The women, half dressed, were seen running from house to house and calling out, "Well done, brave fellows, good luck to you brave boys."—This cheering of Fry's party at once convinced them that the public sympathy and good feeling were on their side. The prisoners were taken off and set at liberty. Capt. White afterwards distinguished himself at the bloody battle of the Point, under Col. Sevier.

The author had heard something of this story more than forty years ago. The late Capt. James Wilson, of the neighborhood of Stephensburg, had stated some of the particulars, but not sufficiently connected to give to the world. The author was therefore apprehensive that he would not be able at this late period to collect the facts. Whilst engaged in obtaining materials for this work, he called on the late Thomas Newell, of Shenandoah, and among other things inquired of him whether he had any knowledge or recollection of the affair. This venerable man, then ninety-three years of age, in his second childhood, and his recollection of recent events entirely gone, the moment the inquiry was made, with much animation and a cheerful countenance, replied, "Yes, my friend, I reckon I can tell you, when I was one of the very boys." The author then asked the old gentleman whether he would have any objection to his name being given as authority, and as one of Fry's party. He replied with equal animation and emphasis, "No, my friend, I always gloried in what I did." Moses Russe'l, Esq. informed the author that his two elder brothers were of Fry's party, and that if he had been old enough, he would doubtless have been among them. But he had more than once heard one of his brother's speak of this occurrence with great regret, and lament the part he had taken in it. Gen. Smith recollects hearing much said on this subject soon after he came to Winchester to live. To say the least of it, it was a dangerous precedent in a civilized society. There is another individual, now living in the neighborhood of the author's residence, who was of Fry's party, and is now about eighty years of age, who was an active and useful character in the war of the revolution, and from him the author obtained many particulars of this occurrence; but as he never formally authorized the use of his name publicly, it is withheld. It was from the information of this individual that the author was enabled to find the year when this important occurrence took place.

After the most diligent inquiry, the author could not ascertain whether the murder of these two Indians was followed by any acts of retaliation on the part of the savages.

The same year (1768) a worthless character by the name of John Price committed a most wanton and unprovoked murder on the body of a popular young Indian chief. Price had resided several years in the Hawks-bill settlement. He went out to the Indian country under the character of an Indian trader, and soon formed an acquaintance with this young war chief. Price was an expert marksman and experienced hunter, and soon acquired the confidence and attachment of the young warrior. They frequently took hunting excursions; in the last of which, having wandered a considerable distance from the Indian habitations, Price shot the young man dead, robbed him of his rifle, a few silver ornaments and hunting dress, and left him lying in the wilderness; then pushed home, boasting of what he had done, and showed his ill-gotten booty.

A few days after Price's return home, Lewis Bingaman, who was taken prisoner when a boy, and who grew up and became a distinguished man, (which has been heretofore noticed,) came in at the head of thirty warriors in pursuit of Price. He made himself known to Frederick Offenberger, and told what Price had done; said that he would go to Price, and propose to take a hunt; that his warriors were concealed in the Masinutton mountain; and if he succeeded in decoying Price into their hands, they would be perfectly satisfied, and do no injury to any other person; but if they did not succeed in getting Price, they would revenge the death of their young chief upon the first white persons they could find, and the lives of many innocent women and children would be sacrificed to appease their vengeance. Offenberger kept Bingaman's communication to himself, believing that Price deserved punishment. He was accordingly decoyed into the hands of the thirty warriors, and never heard from afterwards; of course he expiated his base and treacherous murder of the young Indian, by the most lingering and painful death which savage ingenuity could devise.

Tradition relates a story of a Mr. Hogeland, who on a certain occasion killed an Indian in the following manner. Hogeland went out in the evening from Furman's fort, in pursuit of the milch cows. He heard the bell in a deep glen, and from its peculiar sound, suspected some stratagem. Instead of pursuing the hollow therefore, he took up a high ridge, and passed the spot where the bell was ringing: then cautiously descending the hollow, he discovered an Indian with the bell (which he had taken from the cow,) suspended to a small sapling, which he shook gently to keep the bell in motion. Whilst the savage was thus engaged with a view to decoy the owner within the reach of his rifle, Hogeland took deliberate aim at him, and shot him through the body.; upon which another Indian started up, ran, and got off. Thus this wiley savage fell into the snare he believed he had adroitly prepared for killing the owner of the cattle.*

The author has heard another version of this story. It is said there was a young man with Hogeland; and when the Indian was seen with the bell, Hogeland at the same instant discovered the other standing at a tree, with his gun raised ready to fire at whoever should come for the cows. Hogeland pointed him out to the young man, and observed, "Now take deliberate aim, whilst I take the fellow with the bell." They both fired and both Indians fell dead.†

Thus ends the author's narrative of the many important occurrences and great events from the commencement of Indian hostilities, in the year 1754, until their final termination in 1766, a period of twelve years.

From the termination of hostilities in 1766, until the commencement of Dunmore's war in 1774, the people of the valley enjoyed uninterrupted peace and tranquility, and the country settled and increased with great rapidity. Several families of distinction removed from the lower country and settled in the valley. The ancestors of the Washingtons, Willeses, Throckmortons, and Whitings, severally settled in the neighborhood of Long marsh and Bull-skin.

The author did not find it convenient to obtain the several treaties made with the Indian tribes during the period from the commencement of Braddock's war until the final termination of hostilities. Nor does he consider it very material, as those treaties were no sooner made than broken. Should this be deemed a material defect, he will endeavor to supply it in another edition.

The commencement and termination of Dunmore's war will form the subject of the next chapter.

---

*Samuel Kercheval, jr. of Romney, related this tradition to the author.
†William Naylor, Esq. gave the author this version of the story.

CHAPTER X.

DUNMORE'S WAR WITH THE INDIANS.

In the year 1773, the Indians killed two white men on the Hockhock-ing river, to-wit, John Martin and Guy Meeks, (Indian traders,) and rob-bed them of about £200 worth of goods. About the 1st of May, 1774, they killed two other men in a canoe on the Ohio, and robbed the canoe of its contents.* There were other similar occurrences, which left no doubt upon the minds of the western people, that the savages had deter-mined to make war upon them; and of course acts of retaliation were resorted to on the part of the whites.

The late Col. Angus M'Donald, near Winchester, and several other in-dividuals, went out in the spring of 1774, to survey the military bounty lands, lying on the Ohio and Kanawha rivers, allowed by the king's pro-clamation to the officers and soldiers of the army, for their services in a preceding war with the Indians, but were driven off.

Col. M'Donald forthwith waited on Gov. Dunmore in person, and gave him an account of the hostile disposition of the Indians. The governor authorized him to raise a regiment of four hundred men, and immediately proceed to punish the enemy. He soon succeeded in raising his little ar-my, and in the month of June marched into the Indian country, destroyed several of their villages, cut off their corn, and returned. He had two or three running fights with the Indians, but there was little blood shed on either side.

This act of war produced a general combination of the various nations north-west of the Ohio; and hence arose the necessity of speedily raising a powerful army to save the western people from being entirely cut off, or driven from their habitations.

Lord Dunmore issued his orders to Col. A. Lewis, of Augusta county, to raise a body of one thousand men, and immediately proceed to the Ohio river, where he (Dunmore) would join him with an equal number, to be raised in the northern counties of Virginia. Dunmore very soon raised the requisite number of men, principally volunteers from the counties of Ber-keley, Hampshire, Frederick and Shenandoah.† Capt. Daniel Cresap went to South Carolina, and brought in one hundred and twenty Catawba Indian warriors at his own expense and responsibility, which he intended employing against the western enemy. He soon after marched at the head of this band of warriors, with the addition of sixteen white volun-teers, with the design of breaking up and destroying the Moravian In-dian towns on Cheat river. These people professed christianity and neu-

---

*Mr. Jacob's Life of Cresap.
†General John Smith.

N

trality in the war then going on between the red and white people. But they were charged by the white people with secretly aiding and abetting the hostile Indians ; hence Cresap's determination to break up their settlements and drive them off. In crossing the Allegany, 7 Indians under the guise of friendship, fell in with Cresap's party and in the most treacherous manner contrived to kill seven of the white volunteers, and then fled. They were instantly pursued by the Catawbas, and two of them taken prisoners and delivered up to Cresap, who, after reproaching them with their base treachery, discharged them, and retreated into the settlement with his Indians and remaining white volunteers. The Catawba Indians soon after left Cresap and returned to their nation. The late generals, Daniel Morgan and James Wood, were captains in Dunmore's campaign, each of whom had served under M'Donald as captains the preceding spring.*

For further particulars of this war, the author will give copious extracts from Mr. Doddridge's "Notes on the wars west of the Allegany," and from Mr. Jacob's "Life of Cresap." These two authors have detailed the causes which led to this disastrous and destructive war, and are directly at issue on some of the most important particulars. In this controversy the author of this work will not partake so far as to express an opinion which of these two divines have truth on their side ; but he considers it is his duty, as an impartial and faithful historian, to give both these reverend gentlemen's accounts, at full length, of the original causes and consequences of this war.

It appears however evident, that the late Capt. Michael Cresap has had injustice done to his character, both by Mr. Jefferson and Mr. Doddridge. Mr. Jefferson, in his "Notes on Virginia," charges Cresap with being "infamous for his many Indian murders, and murdering Logan's family in cold blood." Mr. Doddridge repeats the charge of the murder of Logan's family, and adds the further charge "that Cresap was the cause of Dunmore's war." How far these charges are refuted by Mr. Jacob, an impartial world will determine.

It is to be regretted that Mr. Jacob's vindication of the character of his friend Cresap cannot have a circulation co-extensive with Mr. Jefferson's charges against him. The celebrity of Mr. Jefferson's character, together with the beautiful specimen of Indian oratory in the Logan speech, has probably caused his work to be circulated and read all over the civilized world.

The author will only add that he has obtained permission, from the proprietors of those works, to use them as he deems proper. The Hon. Philip Doddridge, shortly before his death, in a letter to the author, stated that he considered there would be no impropriety in appending any part of his brother's book to this publication ; and Mr. Jacob, in the most liberal and unqualified terms, permits him to append the whole or any part of his "Life of Cresap."

---

*Mr. John Tomlinson related the particulars of these occurrences to the author, and added that he himself was one of Cresap's party, and that he was then a youth of seventeen or eighteen years of age.

REV. MR. DODDRIDGE'S ACCOUNT OF DUNMORE'S WAR.

After the conclusion of the Indian wars, by the treaty made with the chiefs by Sir William Johnson at the German flats, in the latter part of 1764, the western settlements enjoyed peace until the spring of 1774.

During this period of time, the settlements increased with great rapidity along the whole extent of the western frontier. Even the shores of the Ohio, on the Virginia side, had a considerable population as early as the year 1774.

Devoutly might humanity wish that the record of the causes which led to the destructive war of 1774, might be blotted from the annals of our country. But it is now too late to efface it; the "black-lettered list" must remain, a dishonorable blot in our national history. Good however may spring out of evil. The injuries inflicted upon the Indians, in early times by our forefathers, may induce their descendants to shew *justice* and *mercy* to the diminished posterity of those children of the wilderness, whose ancestors perished, in cold blood, under the tomahawk and scalping knife of the white savages.

In the month of April, 1774, a rumor was circulated that the Indians had stolen several horses from some land jobbers on the Ohio and Kanawha rivers. No evidences of the fact having been adduced, led to the conclusion that the report was false. This report, however, induced a pretty general belief that the Indians were about to make war upon the frontier settlements, but for this apprehension there does not appear to have been the slightest foundation.

In consequence of this apprehension of being attacked by the Indians, the land jobbers ascended the river, and collected at Wheeling. On the 27th of April, it was reported in Wheeling that a canoe, containing two Indians and some traders, was coming down the river, and then not far from the place. On hearing this, the commandant of the station, Capt. Cresap, proposed to go up the river and kill the Indians. This project was vehemently opposed by Col. Zane, the proprietor of the place. He stated to the captain that the killing of those Indians would inevitably bring on a war, in which much innocent blood would be shed, and that the act in itself would be an atrocious murder, and a disgrace to his name forever. His good counsel was lost. The party went up the river. On being asked, at their return, what had become of the Indians? they coolly answered that "they had fallen overboard into the river!" Their canoe, on being examined, was found bloody, and pierced with bullets. This was the first blood which was shed in this war, and terrible was the vengeance which followed.

In the evening of the same day, the party, hearing that there was an encampment of Indians at the mouth of Captina, went down the river to the place, attacked the Indians, and killed several of them. In this affair one of Cresap's party was severely wounded.

The massacre at Captina, and that which took place at Baker's, about forty miles above Wheeling, after that at Captina, were unquestionably the sole causes of the war of 1774. The last was perpetrated by thirty-two men, under the command of Daniel Greathouse. The whole num-her killed at this place, and on the river opposite to it, was twelve, besides several wounded. This horrid massacre was effected by an hypocritical stratagem, which reflects the deepest dishonor on the memory of those who were agents in it.

The report of the murders committed on the Indians near Wheeling, induced a belief that they would immediately commence hostilities; and this apprehension furnished the pretext for the murder above related. The ostensible object for raising the party under Greathouse, was that of defending the family of Baker, whose house was opposite to a large encampment of Indians, at the mouth of Big Yellow creek. The party were concealed in ambuscade, while their commander went over the river, under the mask of friendship, to the Indian camp, to ascertain their number.—— While there, an Indian woman advised him to return home speedily, saying that the Indians were drinking and angry on account of the murder of their people down the river, and might do him some mischief. On his return to his party, he reported that the Indians were too strong for an open attack. He returned to Baker's, and requested him to give any Indians who might come over, in the course of the day, as much rum as they might call for, and get as many of them drunk as he possibly could. The plan succeeded. Several Indian men and women came over the river to Baker's, who had previously been in the habit of selling rum to the Indians. The men drank freely, and became intoxicated. In this state they were all killed by Greathouse and a few of his party. I say a few of his party; for it is but justice to state, that not more than five or six of the whole number had any participation in the slaughter at the house.—— The rest protested against it as an atrocious murder. From their number, being by far the majority, they might have prevented the deed; but alas! they did not. A little Indian girl alone was saved from the slaughter, by the humanity of some of the party, whose name is not now known.

The Indians in the camp, hearing the firing at the house, sent a canoe with two men in it to inquire what had happened. These two Indians were both shot down as soon as they landed on the beach. A second and larger canoe was then manned with a number of Indians in arms; but in attempting to reach the shore, some distance below the house, they were received by a well directed fire from the party, which killed the greater number of them, and compelled the survivors to return. A great number of shots were exchanged across the river, but without damage to the white party, not one of whom was even wounded. The Indian men who were murdered were all scalped.

The woman who gave the friendly advice to the commander of the party when in the Indian camp, was amongst the slain at Baker's house.

The massacres of the Indians at Captina and Yellow creek, comprehended the whole of the family of the famous but unfortunate Logan, who before these events had been a lover of the whites, a strenuous advocate for peace; but in the conflict which followed them, by way of revenge for the death of his people, he became a brave and sanguinary chief among the warriors.

The settlers along the frontiers, knowing that the Indians would make war upon them for the murder of their people, either moved off to the interior, or took up their residence in forts. The apprehension of war was soon realized. In a short time the Indians commenced hostilities along the whole extent of our frontier.

Express was speedily sent to Williamsburg, the then seat of government of the colony of Virginia, communicating intelligence of the certainty of the commencement of an Indian war. The assembly was then in session.

A plan for a campaign, for the purpose of putting a speedy conclusion to the Indian hostilities, was adopted between the earl of Dunmore, governor of the colony, and Gen. Lewis, of Botetourt county. General Lewis was appointed to the command of the southern division of the forces to be employed on this occasion, with orders to raise a large body of volunteers and drafts from the south-eastern counties of the colony with all dispatch. These forces were to rendezvous at Camp Union, in the Greenbrier country. The earl of Dunmore was to raise another army in the northern counties of the colony, and in the settlements west of the mountains, and assemble them at Fort Pitt, and from thence descend the river to Point Pleasant, at the mouth of the great Kanawha, the place appointed for the junction of the two armies, for the purpose of invading the Indian country and destroying as many of their villages as they could reach in the course of the season.

On the 11th of September, the forces under Gen. Lewis, amounting to eleven hundred men, commenced their march from Camp Union to Point Pleasant, a distance of one hundred and sixty miles. The space of country between these two points was at that time a trackless desert. Capt. Matthew Arbuckle, the pilot, conducted the army by the nearest and best route to their place of destination. The flour and ammunition were wholly transported on pack horses, as the route was impassable for wheel carriages. After a painful march of nineteen days, the army arrived, on the 1st of October, at Point Pleasant,* where an encampment was made.

---

*Of the battle of the Point, the author has obtained some further particulars, which may not be uninteresting to the reader. He saw and conversed with three individuals who participated in that desperate struggle, viz :—Joseph Mays, Andrew Reed, and James Ellison.

The two first named informed the author that Col. Lewis ordered out a body of three hundred men to meet and disperse the Indians as they were approaching his encampment. The detachment was overpowered by the numerical force of the Indians, not less than a thousand strong ; the whites, contending, however, for every inch of ground in their retreat. They were driven back several hundred yards, when Col. Lewis ordered forward a second detachment of three hundred men, who rushed forward with impetuosity to the relief of the first, which movement at once checked the savages, and partially changed the aspect of the fight. Col. Chas. Lewis, who had arrayed himself in a gorgeous scarlet waistcoat, against the advice of his friends, thus rendering himself a conspicuous mark for the Indians, was mortally wounded early in the action : yet was able to walk back after receiving the wound, into his own tent, where he expired. He was met on his way by the commander-in-chief, his

Gen. Lewis was exceedingly disappointed at hearing no tidings of the earl of Dunmore, who, according to previous arrangements, was to form a junction with him at this place. He immediately dispatched some scouts, to go by land in the direction of Fort Pitt, to obtain intelligence of the route which the earl had taken, and then return with the utmost dispatch. On the 9th, three men, who had formerly been Indian traders, arrived in the camp, on express from the earl, to inform Lewis that he had changed his plan of operations, and intended to march to the Indian towns by the way of Hoekhocking, and directing Gen. Lewis to commence his march immediately for the old Chilicothe towns.

Very early in the morning of the 10th, two young men set out from the camp to hunt up the river. Having gone about three miles, they fell upon a camp of the Indians, who were then in the act of preparing to march to attack the camp of Gen. Lewis. The Indians fired on them and killed one of them; the other ran back to the camp with the intelligence that the Indians, in great force, would immediately give battle.

Gen. Lewis immediately ordered out a detachment of the Botetourt troops under Col. Fleming, and another of the Augusta troops under Col. Charles Lewis, remaining himself with the reserve for the defence of the camp. The detachment marched out in two lines, and met the Indians in the same order about 400 yards from the camp. The battle commenced a little after sunrise, by a heavy firing from the Indians. At the onset our troops gave back some distance; until met by a reinforcement, on the arrival of which the Indians retreated a little way and formed a line behind logs and trees, reaching from the bank of the Ohio to that of the Kanawha. By this maneuver, our army and camp were completely invested, being inclosed between two rivers, with the Indian line of battle in front, so that no chance of retreat was left. An incessant fire was kept up on both sides, with but little change of position until sundown, when the Indians retreated, and in the night recrossed the Ohio, and the next day commenced their march to their towns on the Scioto.

---

brother, Col. Andrew Lewis, who remarked to him, "I expected something fatal would befall you," to which the wounded officer calmly replied, "It is the fate of war." About two o'clock, Col. Christie arrived in the field at the head of five hundred men—the battle still raging—a reinforcement which decided the issue almost immediately. The Indians fell back about two miles, obstinately fighting the whole distance; and such was the persevering spirit of the savages, though they were fairly beaten, that the contest was not entirely closed till the setting of the sun, when they relinquished the field. Shortly after the battle, several traders with the Indians, regarded as neutral in war, called at the Point, and informed Captain Arbuckle, commandant of the station, that there were not less than twelve hundred Indians in this memorable action. Cornstalk, confident of success, had placed a body of some two hundred Indians on the opposite bank of the Kanawha, to cut off the retreat of the whites; and that the loss of the Indians in killed and wounded was not short of three hundred men.

Our loss in this destructive battle was seventy-five killed, and one hundred and forty wounded. Among the killed were Col. Chas. Lewis, Col. Fields, Captains Buford, Murray, Ward, Wilson and M'Clenachan; lieutenants Allen, Goldsby and Dillon, and several subaltern officers.

Col. Lewis, a distinguished and meritorious officer, was mortally wounded by the first fire of the Indians, but walked into the camp and expired in his own tent.

The number of Indians engaged in the battle of the Point was never ascertained, nor yet the amount of their loss. On the morning after the engagement, twenty-one were found on the battle ground, and twelve more were afterwards found in the different places where they had been concealed. A great number of their dead were said to have been thrown into the river during the engagement. Considering that the whole number of our men engaged in the conflict were riflemen, and from habit sharp shooters of the first order, it is presumable that the loss on the side of the Indians was at least equal to ours.

The Indians during the battle were commanded by the Cornstalk warrior, the king of the Shawnees. This son of the forest, in his plans of attack and retreat, and in all his maneuvers throughout the engagement, displayed the skill and bravery of the consummate general. During the whole of the day, he was heard from our lines, vociferating, with the voice of a Stentor, "Be strong! be strong!" It is even said that he killed one of his men with his own hand for cowardice.

The day following the battle, after burying the dead, entrenchments were thrown up round the camp, and a competent guard were appointed for the care and protection of the sick and wounded. On the succeeding day Gen. Lewis commenced his march for the Shawnee towns on the Scioto. This march was made through a trackless desert, and attended with almost insuperable difficulties and privations.

In the meantime the earl of Dunmore, having collected a force and provided boats at Fort Pitt, descended the river to Wheeling, where the army halted for a few days, and then proceeded down the river in about one hundred canoes, a few keel boats and perouges, to the mouth of Hockhocking, and from thence over land until the army had got within eight miles of the Shawnee town Chilicothe, on the Scioto. Here the army halted, and made a breastwork of fallen trees and intrenchments of such extent as to include about twelve acres of ground, with an inclosure in the center containing about one acre, surrounded by intrenchments. This was the citidal which contained the markees of the earl and his superior officers.

Before the army had reached that place, the Indian chiefs had sent several messengers to the earl asking peace. With this request he soon determined to comply, and therefore sent an express to Gen Lewis with an order for his immediate retreat. This order Gen. Lewis disregarded, and continued his march until his lordship in person visited his camp, was formally introduced to his officers, and gave the order in person. The army of Gen. Lewis then commenced their retreat.

It was with the greatest reluctance and chagrin that the troops of Gen. Lewis returned from the enterprise in which they were engaged. The massacres of their relatives and friends at the Big Levels and Muddy creek, and above all their recent loss at the battle of the Point, had inspired these "Big-knives," as the Indians called the Virginians, with an inveterate thirst for revenge, the gratification of which they supposed was shortly to take place, in the total destruction of the Indians and their towns along the Scioto and Sandusky rivers. The order of Dunmore was obeyed, but with every expression of regret and disappointment.

The earl with his officers having returned to his camp, a treaty with the Indians was opened the following day.

In this treaty, every precaution was used on the part of our people to prevent the Indians from ending a treaty in the tragedy of a massacre.— Only eighteen Indians, with their chiefs, were permitted to pass the outer gate of their fortified encampment, after having deposited their arms with the guard at the gate.

The treaty was opened by Cornstalk, the war chief of the Shawnees, in a lengthy speech, in which he boldly charged the white people with having been the authors of the commencement of the war, in the massacres of the Indians at Captina and Yellow creek. This speech he delivered in so loud a tone of voice, that he was heard all over the camp.— The terms of the treaty were soon settled and the prisoners delivered up.

Logan, the Cayuga chief, assented to the treaty; but still indignant at the murder of his family, he refused to attend with the other chiefs at the camp of Dunmore. According to the Indian mode in such cases, he sent his speech in a belt of wampum by an interpreter, to be read at the treaty.

Supposing that this work may fall into the hands of some readers who have not seen the speech of Logan, the author thinks it not amiss to insert the celebrated morsel of Indian eloquence in this place, with the observation that the authenticity of the speech is no longer a subject of doubt. The speech is as follows :

"I appeal to any white man to say, if he ever entered Logan's cabin hungry, and he gave him not meat: if ever he came cold and naked, and he clothed him not. During the course of the last long and bloody war, Logan remained idle in his cabin, an advocate for peace. Such was my love for the whites, that my countrymen pointed as they passed, and said, 'Logan is the friend of the white men.' I had even thought to have lived with you, but for the injuries of one man. Col. Cresap, the last spring in cold blood, and unprovoked, murdered all the relations of Logan, not even sparing my women and children. There runs not a drop of my blood in the veins of any living creature. This called on me for revenge. I have sought it: I have killed many: I have fully glutted my vengeance: for my country I rejoice at the beams of peace. But do not harbor a thought that mine is the joy of fear. Logan never felt fear. He will not turn on his heel to save his life. Who is there to mourn for Logan?— Not one."

Thus ended, at the treaty of Camp Charlotte, in the month of November, 1774, the disastrous war of Dunmore. It began in the wanton and unprovoked murders of the Indians at Captina and Yellow creek, and ended with an awful sacrifice of life and property to the demon of revenge.

On our part we obtained at the treaty a cessation of hostilities and a surrender of prisoners, and nothing more.

The plan of operations adopted by the Indians in the war of Dunmore, shews very clearly that their chiefs were by no means deficient in the foresight and skill necessary for making the most prudent military arrangements for obtaining success and victory in their mode of warfare. At an early period they obtained intelligence of the plan of the campaign against them, concerted between the earl of Dunmore and Gen. Lewis. With a view therefore, to attack the forces of these commanders seperately, they speedily collected their warriors, and by forced marches reached the Point before the expected arrival of the troops under Dunmore. Such was the privacy with which they conducted their march to Point Pleasant, that Gen. Lewis knew nothing of the approach of the Indian army until a few minutes before the commencement of the battle, and it is very probable, that if Cornstalk, the Indian commander, had had a little larger force at the battle of the Point, the whole army of Gen. Lewis would have been cut off, as the wary savage had left them no chance of retreat. Had the army of Lewis been defeated, the army of Dunmore, consisting of little more than one thousand men, would have shared the fate of those armies which at different periods have suffered defeats in consequence of venturing too far into the Indian country, in numbers too small, and with munitions of war inadequate to sustain a contest with the united forces of a number of Indian nations.

It was the general belief among the officers of our army, at the time, that the earl of Dunmore, while at Wheeling, received advice from his government of the probability of the approaching war between England and the colonies, and that afterwards, all his measures, with regard to the Indians, had for their ultimate object an alliance with those ferocious warriors for the aid of the mother country in their contest with us. This supposition accounts for his not forming a junction with the army of Lewis at Point Pleasant. This deviation from the original plan of the campaign jeopardized the army of Lewis, and well nigh occasioned its total destruction. The conduct of the earl at the treaty, shews a good understanding between him and the Indian chiefs. He did not suffer the army of Lewis to form a junction with his own, but sent them back before the treaty was concluded, thus risking the safety of his own forces; for at the time of the treaty, the Indian warriors were about his camp in force sufficient to have intercepted his retreat and destroyed his whole army.

REV. MR. JACOB'S ACCOUNT OF DUNMORE'S WAR.

At this period, to wit, in the commencement of the year 1774, there existed between our people and the Indians, a kind of doubtful, precarious and suspicious peace. In the year 1773, they killed a certain John Martin and Guy Meeks, (Indian traders,) on the Hockhocking, and robbed them of about £200 worth of goods.

They were much irritated with our people, who were about this time beginning to settle Kentucky, and with them they waged an unceasing and destructive predatory war; and whoever saw an Indian in Kentucky, saw an enemy; no questions were asked on either side but from the muzzles of their rifles. Many other circumstances at this period combined to show that our peace with the Indians rested upon such dubious and uncertain ground, that it must soon be dispersed by a whirlwind of carnage and war. And as I consider this an all-important point in the thread of our history, and an interesting link in the chain of causes combining to produce Dunmore's war, I will present the reader with another fact directly in point. It is extracted from the journal of a 'squire M'Connel, in my possession. The writer says that about the 3d day of March, 1774, while himself and six other men, who were in company with him, were asleep in their camp in the night, they were awakened by the fierce barking of their dogs, and thought they saw something like men creeping towards them. Alarmed at this, they sprang up, seized their rifles, and flew to trees. By this time one Indian had reached their fire; but hearing them cock their guns, he drew back, stumbled and fell. The whole party now came up, and appearing friendly, he ordered his men not to fire, and shook hands with his new guests. They tarried all night, and appearing so friendly, prevailed with him and one of his men to go with them to their town, at no great distance from their camp; but when they arrived he was taken with his companion to their council, or war house, a war dance performed around them, the war club shook at or over them, and they detained close prisoners and narrowly guarded for two or three days. A council was then held over them, and it was decreed that they should be threatened severely and discharged, provided they would give their women some flour and salt. Being dismissed, they set out on their journey to the camp, but met on their way about twenty-five warriors and some boys. A second council was held over them, and it was decreed that they should not be killed, but robbed, which was accordingly done; and all their flour, salt, powder and lead, and all their rifles that were good, were taken from them; and being further threatened, the Indians left them, as already noticed. This party consisted of seven men, viz. 'squire M'Connel, Andrew M'Connel, Lawrence Darnel, William Ganet, Matthew Riddle, John Laferty, and Thos. Canady.

We have also in reserve some more material facts, that go to show the aspect of affairs at this period, and that may be considered as evident precursors to an impending war. And it is certainly not a trifling item in the catalogue of these events, that early in the spring of 1774, whether precedent or subsequent to Connolly's famous circular letter I am not prepared to say, having no positive data; but it was, however, about this time that the Indians killed two men in a canoe belonging to a Mr. Butler, of Pittsburgh, and robbed the canoe of the property therein. This was about the first of May, 1774, and took place near the mouth of Little Beaver, a small creek that empties into the Ohio between Pittsburgh and Wheeling; and this fact is so certain and well established, that Benj. Tomlinson, Esq. who is now living (1826,) and who assisted in burying the dead, can and will bear testimony to its truth. And it is presumed it was this circumstance which produced that prompt and terrible vengeance taken on the Indians at Yellow creek immediately afterwards, to wit, on the 3d day of May, which gave rise to, and furnished matter for, the pretended lying speech of Logan, which I shall hereafter prove a counterfeit, and if it was genuine, yet a genuine fabrication of lies.

Thus we find from an examination into the state of affairs in the west, that there was a predisposition to war, at least on the part of the Indians. But may we not suspect that other latent causes, working behind the scenes and in the dark, were silently marching to the same result?

Be it remembered, then, that this Indian war was but as a portico to our revolutionary war, the fuel for which was then preparing, and which burst into a flame the ensuing year.

Neither let us forget that the earl of Dunmore was at this time governor of Virginia; and that he was acquainted with the views and designs of the British cabinet, can scarcely be doubted. What then, suppose ye, would be the conduct of a man possessing his means, filling a high official station, attached to the British government, and master of consummate diplomatic skill?

Dunmore's penetrating eye could not but see, and he no doubt did see, two all-important objects, that, if accomplished, would go to subserve and promote the grand object of the British cabinet, namely, the establishment of an unbounded and unrestrained authority over our North American continent.

These two objects were, first, setting the new settlers on the west side of the Allegany by the ears; and secondly, embroiling the western people in a war with the Indians. These two objects accomplished, would put it in his power to direct the storm to any and every point conducive to the grand object he had in view. But as in the nature of the thing he could not, and policy forbidding that he should, always appear personally in promoting and effectuating these objects, it was necessary he should obtain a confidential agent attached to his person and to the British government, and one that would promote his views either publicly or covertly, as circumstances required.

The materials for his first object were abundant, and already prepared. The emigrants to the western country were almost all from the three states of Virginia, Maryland and Pennsylvania. The line between the two states of Virginia and Pennsylvania was unsettled, and both these States claimed the whole of the western country. This motley mixture of men from different States did not harmonize. The Virginians and Marylanders disliked the Pennsylvania laws, nor did the Pennsylvanians relish those of Virginia. Thus many disputes, much warm blood, broils, and sometimes battles, called *fisticuffs*, followed.

The earl of Dunmore, with becoming zeal for the honor of the "ancient dominion," seized upon this state of things so propitious to his views; and having found Dr. John Connoly, a Pennsylvanian, with whom I think he could not have had much previous acquaintance, by the art of hocuspocus or some other art, converted him into a stanch Virginian, and appointed him vice governor and commandant of Pittsburgh and its dependencies, that is to say, of all the western country. Affairs on that side of the mountain began to wear a serious aspect; attempts were made by both States to enforce their laws; and the strong arm of power and coercion was let loose by Virginia. Some magistrates acting under the authority of Pennsylvania were arrested, sent to Virginia, and imprisoned.

But that the reader may be well assured that the hand of Dunmore was in all this, I present him with a copy of his proclamation. It is however deficient as to date:

"WHEREAS, I have reason to apprehend that the government of Pennsylvania, in prosecution of their claims to Pittsburgh and its dependencies, will endeavor to obstruct his majesty's government thereof, under my administration, by illegal and unwarrantable commitment of the officers I have appointed for that purpose, and that settlement is in some danger of annoyance from the Indians also; and it being necessary to support the dignity of his majesty's government and protect his subjects in the quiet and peaceable enjoyment of their rights; I have therefore thought proper, by and with the consent and advice of his majesty's council, by this proclamation in his majesty's name, to order and require the officers of the militia in that district to embody a sufficient number of men to repel any insult whatsoever; and all his majesty's liege subjects within this colony are hereby strictly required to be aiding and assisting therein, or they shall answer the contrary at their peril; and I further enjoin and require the several inhabitants of the territories aforesaid to pay his majesty's quitrents and public dues to such officers as are or shall be appointed to collect the same within this dominion, until his majesty's pleasure therein shall be known."

It is much to be regretted that my copy of this proclamation is without date. There can, however, be no doubt it was issued either in 1774 or early in 1775, and I am inclined to think it was issued in 1774; but it would be satisfactory to know precisely the day, because chronology is the soul of history

But this state of things in the west, it seems from subsequent events, was not the mere effervescence of a transient or momentary excitement, but continued a long season. The seeds of discord had fallen unhappily on ground too naturally productive, and were also too well cultivated by the earl of Dunmore, Connoly, and the Pennsylvania officers, to evaporate in an instant.

We find by recurring to the history of our revolutionary war, that that awful tornado, if it had not the effect to sweep away disputes about state rights and local interests, yet it had the effect to silence and suspend every thing of that nature pending our dubious and arduous struggle for national existence: but yet we find, in fact, that whatever conciliatory effect this state of things had upon other sections of the country, and upon the nation at large, it was not sufficient to extinguish this fire in the west.—For in the latter end of the year 1776, or in the year 1777, we find these people petitioning Congress to interpose their authority, and redress their grievances. I have this petition before me, but it is too long to copy: I therefore only give a short abstract.

It begins with stating that whereas Virginia and Pennsylvania both set up claims to the western country, it was productive of the most serious and distressing consequences: that as each State pertinaciously supported their respective pretensions, the result was, as described by themselves, "frauds, impositions, violences, depredations, animosities," &c. &c.

These evils they ascribe (as indeed the fact was,) to the conflicting claims of the two States; and so warm were the partisans on each side, as in some cases to produce battles and shedding of blood. But they superadd another reason for this ill-humor, namely, the proceedings of Dunmore's warrant officers, in laying land warrants on land claimed by others, and many other claims for land granted by the crown of England to individuals, companies, &c., covering a vast extent of country, and including most of the lands already settled and occupied by the greatest part of the inhabitants of the western country; and they finally pray Congress to erect them into a seperate State and admit them into the Union as a fourteenth State.

As the petition recites the treaty of Pittsburgh, in October 1775, it is probable we may fix its date (for it has none,) to the latter part of 1776 or 1777. I rather think the latter, not only from my own recollection of the circumstances of that period, but especially from the request in the petition to be erected into a new State, which certainly would not have been thought of before the Declaration of Independence.

But the unhappy state of the western country will appear still more evident, when we advert to another important document which I have also before me. It is a proclamation issued by the delegates in Congress from the States of Pennsylvania and Virginia, and bears date Philadelphia, July 25, 1775.

But the heat of fire, and inflexible obstinacy of the parties engaged in this controversy, will appear in colors still stronger, when we see the unavailing efforts made by the delegates in Congress from the two States of Virginia and Pennsylvania in the year 1775. These gentlemen, it was obvious, under the influence of the best of motives, and certainly with a view to the best interests, peace, and happiness of the western people, sent them a proclamation, couched in terms directly calculated to restore tranquillity and harmony among them : but the little effect produced by this proclamation, their subsequent petition just recited, and sent the next year or year after to Congress, fully demonstrates.

But as I consider this proclamation an important document, and as it is nowhere recorded, I give it to the reader entire :

"To the Inhabitants of Pennsylvania and Virginia,
on the west side of the Laurel Hill.

"FRIENDS AND COUNTRYMEN :—It gives us much concern to find that disturbances have arisen, and still continue among you, concerning the boundaries of our colonies. In the character in which we now address you, it is unnecessary to inquire into the *origin* of those unhappy disputes, and it would be improper for us to express our approbation or censure on either side ; but as representatives of two of the colonies, united among many others for the defence of the liberties of America, we think it our duty to remove, as far as lies in our power, every obstacle that may *prevent her sons* from co-operating as vigorously as they would wish to do towards the attainment of this great and important end. Influenced sole-

ly by this motive, our joint and earnest request to you is, that all animosities, which have heretofore subsisted among you, as inhabitants of distinct colonies, may now give place to generous and concurring efforts for
the preservation of every thing that can make our common country dear
to us.

"We are fully persuaded that you, as well as we, wish to see your differences terminate in this happy issue. For this desirable purpose we re-
commend it to you that all bodies of *armed men, kept under either pro-*
vince, be dismissed; that all those on either side, who *are in confinement,*
or under bail for taking a part in the contest, be discharged; and that until the dispute be decided, every person be permitted to retain his possessions unmolested.

"By observing these directions, the public tranquillity will· be secured
without injury to the titles on either side. The period, we flatter ourselves, will soon arrive, when this unfortunate dispute, which has produced much mischief, and as far as we can learn no good, will be peaceably
and constitutionally determined.

"We are your friends and countrymen,
        ·P. Henry, Richard Henry Lee, Benjamin Harrison, Th.
        Jefferson, John Dickinson, Geo. Ross, B. Franklin, Jas.
        Wilson, Charles Humphreys.
"Philadelphia, July 25, 1775."

But to conclude this part of our subject, I think the reader cannot but
see from Dunmore's proclamation; the violent measures of his lieutenant
Connoly and the Virginia officers, and from the complexion of the times,
and the subsequent conduct of both Dunmore and Connoly, as we shall
see hereafter; that this unhappy state of things, if not actually produced,
was certainly improved by Dunmore to subserve the views of the British
court.

We now proceed to examine the question, how far facts and circumstances justify us in supposing the earl of Dunmore himself instrumental
in producing the Indian war of 1774.

It has been already remarked that this Indian war was but the precur-
sor to our revolutionary war of 1775—that Dunmore, the then governor of
Virginia, was one of the most inveterate and determined enemies to the
revolution—that he was a man of high talents, especially for intrigue and
diplomatic skill—that occupying the station of commander-in-chief of the
large and respectable State of Virginia, he possessed means and power to
do much to serve the views of Great Britain. And we have seen, from
the preceding pages, how effectually he played his part among the inhabitants of the western country. I was present myself when a Pennsylvania
magistrate, of the name of Scott, was taken into custody, and brought
before Dunmore, at Prestone old fort; he was severely threatened and dismissed, perhaps on bail, but I do not recollect how; another Pennsylvania magistrate was sent to Staunton jail. And I have already shewn in
the preceding pages, that there was a sufficient preparation of materials
for this war in the predisposition and hostile attitude of our affairs with
the Indians; that it was consequently no difficult matter with a Virginia

governor.to direct the incipient state of things to any point most conducive to the grand end he had in view, namely, weakening our national strength in some of its best and most efficient parts. If, then, a war with the Indians might have a tendency to produce this result, it appears perfectly natural and reasonable to suppose that Dunmore would make use of all his power and influence to promote it; and although the war of 1774 was brought to a conclusion before the year was out, yet we know that this fire was scarcely extinguished before it burst out into a flame with tenfold fury, and two or three armies of the whites were sacrificed before we could get the Indians subdued; and this unhappy state of our affairs with the Indians happening during the severe conflict of our revolutionary war, had the very effect, I suppose, Dunmore had in view, namely, dividing our forces and enfeebling our aggregate strength; and that the seeds of these subsequent wars with the Indians were sown in 1774 and 1775, appears almost certain.

Yet still, however, we admit that we are not in possession of materials to substantiate this charge against the earl; and all we can do is to produce some facts and circumstances that deserve notice, and have a strong bearing on the case.

And the first we shall mention* is a circular letter sent by Maj. Connoly, his proxy, early in the spring of the year 1774; warning the inhabitants to be on their guard—that the Indians were very angry, and manifested so much hostility, that he was apprehensive they would strike somewhere as *soon as the season would permit*, and enjoining the inhabitants to prepare and retire into forts, &c. It might be useful to collate and compare this letter with one he wrote to Capt. Cresap on the 14th July following; see hereafter. In this letter he declares there is war or danger of war, before the war is properly begun; in that to Capt. Cresap he says the Indians deport themselves peaceably, when Dunmore and Lewis and Cornstalk are all on their march for battle.

This letter was sent by express in every direction of the country. Unhappily we have lost or mislaid it, and consequently are deficient in a most material point in its date. But from one expression in the letter, namely, that the Indians will strike when the season permits, and this season is generally understood to mean when the leaves are out, we may fix it in the month of May. We find from a subsequent letter from Pentecost and Connoly to Capt. Reece, that this assumed fact is proved: see hereafter.

Therefore this letter cannot be of a later date than sometime in the month of April; and if so, before Butler's men were killed on Little Beaver; and before Logan's family were killed on Yellow creek, and was in fact the fiery red-cross and harbinger of war, as in days of yore among the Scottish clans. That this was the fact is I think absolutely certain, because no mention is made in Connoly's letter of this affair, which certainly would not have been omitted, if precedent to his letter.

---

*The remark, as it should seem incidentally made, in Dunmore's proclamation, as to the Indian war, (see page 108,) deserves notice, as it has no connection with the subject of that proclamation.

This letter produced its natural result. The people fled into forts, and put themselves into a posture of defence, and the tocsin of war resounded from Laurel hill to the banks of the Ohio. Capt. Cresap, who was peaceably at this time employed in building houses and improving lands on the Ohio, received this letter, accompanied, it is believed, with a confirmatory message from Col. Croghan and Maj. M'Gee, Indian agents and interpreters;* and he thereupon immediately broke up his camp, and ascended the river to Wheeling fort, the nearest place of safety, from whence it is believed he intended speedily to return home; but during his stay at this place, a report was brought into the fort that two Indians were coming down the river. Capt. Cresap, supposing from every circumstance, and the general aspect of affairs, that war was inevitable, and in fact already begun, went up the river with his party; and two of his men, of the name of Chenoweth and Brothers, killed these two Indians. Beyond controversy this is the only circumstance in the history of this Indian war, in which his name can in the remotest degree be identified with any measure tending to produce this war; and it is certain that the guilt or innocence of this affair will appear from its date. It is notorious, then, that those Indians were killed not only after Capt. Cresap had received Connoly's letter, and after Butler's men were killed in the canoe, but also after the affair at Yellow creek, and after the people had fled into forts. But more of this hereafter, when we take up Mr. Doddrige and his book; simply, however, remarking here, that this affair of killing these two Indians has the same aspect and relation to Dunmore's war that the battle of Lexington has to the war of the revolution.

But to proceed. Permit us to remark, that it is very difficult at this late period to form a correct idea of these times, unless we can bring distinctly into view the real state of our frontier. The inhabitants of the western country were at this time thinly scattered from the Allegany mountain to the eastern banks of the Ohio, and most thinly near that river.— In this state of things, it was natural to suppose that the few settlers in the vicinity of Wheeling, who had collected into that fort, would feel extremely solicitous to detain captain Cresap and his men as long as possible, especially until they could see on what point the storm would fall.— Capt. Cresap, the son of a hero, and a hero himself, felt for their situation; and getting together a few more men in addition to his own, and not relishing the limits of a little fort, nor a life of inactivity, set out on what was called a scouting party, that is, to reconnoiter and scour the frontier border; and while out and engaged in this business, fell in with and had a running fight with a party of Indians, nearly about his equal in numbers, when one Indian was killed, and Cresap had one man wounded. This affair took place somewhere on the banks of the Ohio. Doddridge says it was at the mouth of Captina; be it so—it matters not; but he adds, it was on the same day the Indians were killed in the canoe. In this the doctor is most egregiously mistaken, as I shall prove hereafter.

But may we not ask, what were these Indians doing here at this time, on the banks of the Ohio? They had no town near this place, nor was

*I had this from Capt. Cresap himself, a short time after it occurred.

it their hunting season, as it was about the 8th or 10th of May. Is it not then probable, nay almost certain, that this straggling banditti were prepared and ready to fall on some parts of our exposed frontier, and that their dispersion saved the lives of many helpless women and children?

But the old proverb, *cry mad-dog and kill him!* is, I suppose, equally as applicable to heroes as to dogs.

Capt. Cresap soon after this returned to his family in Maryland; but feeling most sensibly for the inhabitants on the frontier in their perilous situation, immediately raised a company of volunteers, and marched back to their assistance; and having advanced as far as Catfish camp, the place where Washington, Pa., now stands, he was arrested in his progress by a peremptory and insulting order from Connoly, commanding him to dismiss his men and to return home.

This order, couched in offensive and insulting language, it may be well supposed, was not very grateful to a man of Captain Cresap's high sense of honor and peculiar sensibility, especially conscious as he was of the purity of his motives, and the laudable end he had in view. He nevertheless obeyed, returned home and dismissed his men, and with the determination, I well know from what he said after his return, never again to take any part in the present Indian war, but to leave Mr. Commandant at Pittsburgh to fight it out as he could. This hasty resolution was however of short duration. For however strange, contradictory, and irreconcilable the conduct of the earl of Dunmore and his vice-governor of Pittsburgh, &c. may appear, yet it is a fact, that on the 10th of June, the earl of Dunmore, unsolicited, and to Capt. Cresap certainly unexpected, sent him a captain's commission of the militia of Hampshire county, Virginia, notwithstanding his residence was in Maryland. This commission reached Capt. C. a few days after his return from the expedition to Catfish camp, just above mentioned; and inasmuch as this commission, coming to him in the way it did, carried with it a tacit expression of the governer's approbation of his conduct—add to which, that about the same time his feelings were daily assailed by petition after petition, from almost every section of the western country, praying, begging, and beseeching him to come over to their assistance—it is not surprising that his resolution should be changed. Several of these petitions and Dunmore's commission have escaped the wreck of time and are in my possession.

This commission coming at the time it did, and in the way and under the circumstances above recited, aided and strengthened as it was by the numberless petitioners aforesaid, broke down and so far extinguished all Capt. Cresap's personal resentment against Connoly that he once more determined to exert all his power and influence in assisting the distressed inhabitants of the western frontier, and accordingly immediately raised a company, placed himself under the command of Maj. Angus M'Donald, and marched with him to attack the Indians, at their town of Wappatomachie, on the Muskingum. His popularity, at this time, was such, and so many men flocked to his standard, that he could not consistently with the rules of an army, retain them in his company, but was obliged to transfer them, much against their wills, to other captains, and the result

P

was, that after retaining in his own company as many men as he could consistently, he filled completely the company of his nephew Capt. Michael Cresap, and also partly the company of Capt. Hancock Lee.   This little army of about four hundred men, under Maj. M'Donald, penetrated the Indian country as far as the Muskingum ; near which they had a skirmish with a party of Indians under Capt. Snake, in which M'Donald lost six men, and killed the Indian chief Snake.

A little anecdote here will go to show what expert and close shooters we had in those days among our riflemen.   When M'Donald's little army arrived on the near bank of the Muskingum, and while lying there, an Indian on the opposite shore got behind a log or old tree, and was lifting up his head occasionally to view the white men's army.   One of Capt. Cresap's men, of the name of John Harness, seeing this, loaded his rifle with two balls, and placing himself on the bank of the river, watched the opportunity when the Indian raised his head, and firing at the same instant, put both balls through the Indian's neck, and laid him dead ;* which circumstance no doubt had great influence in intimidating the Indians.

M'Donald after this had another running fight with the Indians, drove them from their towns, burnt them, destroyed their provisions, and, returning to the settlement, discharged his men.

But this affair at Wappatomachie and expedition of M'Donald were only the prelude to more important and efficient measures.   It was well understood that the Indians were far from being subdued, and that they would now certainly collect all their force, and to the utmost of power return the compliment of our visit to their territories.

The governor of Virginia, whatever might have been his views as to the ulterior measures, lost no time in preparing to meet this storm.   He sent orders immediately to Col. Andrew Lewis, of Augusta county, to raise an army of about one thousand men, and to march with all expedition to the mouth of the Great Kanawha, on the Ohio river, where, or at some other point, he would join him, after he had got together another army, which he intended to raise in the northwestern counties, and command in person.   Lewis lost no time, but collected the number of men required, and marched without delay to the appointed place of rendezvous.

But the earl was not quite so rapid in his movements, which circumstance the eagle eye of old Cornstalk, the general of the Indian army, saw, and was determined to avail himself of, foreseeing that it would be much easier to destroy two separate columns of an invading army before than after their junction and consolidation.   With this view he marched with all expedition to attack Lewis, before he was joined by the earl's army from the north calculating, confidently no doubt, that if he could destroy Lewis, he would be able to give a good account of the army of the earl.

The plans of Cornstalk appear to have been those of a consummate and skillful general, and the prompt and rapid execution of them displayed the energy of a warrior.   He therefore, without loss of time, attack-

---

*The Muskingum at this place is said to be about 200 yards wide.

ed Lewis at his post. The attack was sudden, violent, and I believe unexpected. It was neverthelesss well fought, very obstinate, and of long
continuance: and as both parties fought with rifles, the conflict was dreadful; many were killed on both sides, and the contest was only finished
with the approach of night. The Virginians, however, kept the field, but
lost many valuable officers and men, and among the rest, Col. Charles
Lewis, brother to the commander-in-chief.

Cornstalk and Blue Jacket, the two Indian captains, it is said, performed prodigies of valor; but finding at length all their efforts unavailing,
drew off their men in good order, and with the determination to fight no
more, if peace could be obtained upon reasonable terms.

This battle of Lewis' opened an easy and unmolested passage for Dunmore through the Indian country;* but it is proper to remark here, however, that when Dunmore arrived with his wing of the army at the mouth
of Hockhocking, he sent Capt. White-eyes, a Delaware chief, to invite
the Indians to a treaty, and he remained stationary at that place until
White-eyes returned, who reported that the Indians would not treat about
peace. I presume, in order of time, this must have been just before Lewis' battle; because it will appear in the sequel of this story, that a great
revolution took place in the minds of the Indians after the battle.

Dunmore, immediately upon the report of White-eyes that the Indians
were not disposed for peace, sent an express to Col. Lewis to move on
and meet him near Chilicothe, on the Scioto, and both wings of the army were put in motion. But as Dunmore approached the Indian towns,
he was met by flags from the Indians, demanding peace, to which he acceded, halted his army, and runners were sent to invite the Indian chiefs,
who cheerfully obeyed the summons, and came to the treaty—save only
Logan, the great orator, who refused to come. It seems, however, that
neither Dunmore nor the Indian chiefs considered his presence of much
importance, for they went to work and finished the treaty without him—
referring, I believe, some unsettled points for future discussion, at a treaty
to be held the ensuing summer or fall at Pittsburgh. This treaty, the articles of which I never saw, nor do I know that they were ever recorded,
concluded Dunmore's war, in September or October, 1774. After the
treaty was over, old Cornstalk, the Shawnee chief, accompanied Dunmore's army until they reached the mouth of Hockhocking, on the Ohio;
and what was most singular, rather made his home in Capt. Cresap's tent,
with whom he continued on terms of the most friendly familiarity. I consider this circumstance as positive proof that the Indians themselves nei-

---

*A little anecdote will prove that Dunmore was a general, and also the
high estimation in which he held Capt. Cresap. While the army was
marching through the Indian country, Dunmore ordered Capt. Cresap
with his company and some more of his best troops in the rear. This
displeased Cresap, and he expostulated with the earl, who replied, that
the reason of this arrangement was, because he knew that if he was attacked in front, all those men would soon rush forward into the engagement. This reason, which was by the by a handsome compliment, satisfied Cresap, and all the rear guard.

ther considered Capt. Cresap the murderer of Logan's family, nor the cause of the war. It appears, also, that at this place the earl of Dunmore received dispatches from England. Doddridge says he received these on his march out.

But we ought to have mentioned in its proper place, that after the treaty between Dunmore and the Indians commenced near Chilicothe, Lewis arrived with his army, and encamped two or three miles from Dunmore, which greatly alarmed the Indians, as they thought he was so much irritated at losing so many men in the late battle that he would not easily be pacified; nor would they be satisfied until Dunmore and old Cornstalk went into Lewis' camp to converse with him.

Doct. Doddridge represents this affair in different shades of light from this statement. I can only say I had my information from an officer who was present at the time.

But it is time to remind the reader, that, although I have wandered into such a minute detail of the various occurrences, facts and circumstances of Dunmore's war; and all of which as a history may be interesting to the present and especially to the rising generation; yet it is proper to remark that I have two leading objects chiefly in view—first, to convince the world, that whoever and whatever might be the cause of the Indian war of 1774, it was not Capt. Cresap; secondly, that from the aspect of our political affairs at that period, and from the known hostility of Dunmore to the American revolution, and withal from the subsequent conduct of Dunmore, and the dreadful Indian war that commenced soon after the beginning of our war with Great Britain—I say, from all these circumstances, we have infinitely stronger reasons to suspect Dunmore than Cresap; and I may say that the dispatches above mentioned that were received by Dunmore at Hockhocking, although after the treaty, were yet calculated to create suspicion.

But if, as we suppose, Dunmore was secretly at the bottom of this Indian war, it is evident that he could not with propriety appear personally in a business of this kind; and we have seen and shall see, how effectually his sub-governor played his part between the Virginians and Pennsylvanians; and it now remains for us to examine how far the conduct of this man (Connoly) will bear us out in the supposition that there was also some foul play, some dark intriguing work to embroil the western country in an Indian war.

And I think it best now, as we have introduced this man Connoly again, to give the reader a short condensed history of his whole proceedings, that we may have him in full view at once. We have already presented the reader with his circular letter, and its natural result and consequences and also with his insulting letter and mandatory order to Capt. Cresap, at Catfish camp, to dismiss his men and go home; and that the reader may now see a little of the character of this man, and understand him, if it is possible to understand him, I present him with the copy of a letter to Capt. Reece.

"As I have received intelligence that Logan, a Mingo Indian, with about twenty Shawnees and others, were to set off for war last Monday, and I have reason to believe that they may come upon the inhabitants about Wheeling, I hereby order, require and command you, with all the men you can raise, immediately to march and join *any of the companies already out and under the pay of government*, and upon joining your parties together, scour the frontier and become a barrier to our settlements, and endeavor to fall in with their tracks, and pursue them, using your utmost endeavors to chastise them as open and avowed enemies.

"I am, sir, your most humble servant,

"DORSEY PENTECOST, for

"JOHN CONNOLY.

"To Capt. Joel Reece, use all expedition, May 27, 1774."

Now here is a fellow for you. A very short time before this, perhaps two or three days before the date of this letter, Capt. Cresap, who had a fine company of volunteers, is insulted, ordered to dismiss his men and go home; and indeed it appears from one expression in this letter, namely, "the companies who are already out," that these companies must have been actually out at the very time Cresap is ordered home.

Now if any man is skilled in the art of legerdemain, let him unriddle this enigma if he can.

But as so many important facts crowd together at this eventful period, it may be satisfactory to the reader, and have a tendency more clearly to illustrate the various scenes interwoven in the thread of this history, to present to his view a chronological list of these facts; and I think the first that deserves notice is Connoly's circular letter, which we date the 25th day of April; secondly, the two men killed in Butler's canoe we know was the first or second day of May; thirdly, the affair at Yellow creek was on the third or fourth day of May; fourthly, the Indians killed in the canoe above Wheeling the fifth or sixth day of May; fifthly, the skirmish with the Indians on the river Ohio, about the eighth or tenth day of May; after which, Capt. Cresap returned to Catfish camp about the twenty-fifth of May. Indeed this fact speaks for itself; it could not be earlier, when it is considered that he rode home from the Ohio, a distance of about one hundred and forty miles, raised a company and marched back as far as Catfish, through bad roads, near one hundred and twenty miles; and all, agreeably to my statement, in seventeen days: then it is evident that he was not at Catfish camp sooner than the 25th of May; and if so, he was ordered home at the very time when scouts were out, and the settlement threatened with an attack from the Indians, as is manifest from Connoly's own letter to Capt. Reece, dated May 27, 1774.

But the hostility of Connoly to Capt. Cresap was unremitting and without measure or decency; for on the 14th of July, of the same year, we find one of the most extraordinary, crooked, malignant, Grubstreet epistles, that ever appeared upon paper: but let us see it.

"*Fort Dunmore.** July 14, 1774.

"Your whole proceedings, so far as relate to our disturbances with the Indians, have been of a nature so extraordinary, that I am much at a loss

---

*During the government of Connoly in this place, he changed the name from Pitt to Dunmore; but subsequent events have blotted out Dunmore's name.

to account for the cause; but when I consider your late steps, tending directly to ruin the service here, by inveigling away the militia of this garrison by your preposterous proposals, and causing them thereby to embezzle the arms of government, purchased at an enormous expense, and at the same time to reflect infinite disgrace upon the honor of this colony, by attacking a set of people, which, notwithstanding the injury they have sustained by you in the loss of their people, yet continue to rely upon the professions of friendship which I have made, and deport themselves accordingly; I say when I consider these matters, I must conclude you are actuated by a spirit of discord, so prejudicial to the peace and good order of society, that the conduct calls for justice, and due execution thereof can only check. I must once again order you to desist from your pernicious designs, and require of you, if you are an officer of militia, to send the deserters from this place back with all expedition, that they may be dealt with as their crimes merit.

"I am, sir, your servant,
"JOHN CONNOLY."

This letter, although short, contains so many things for remark and animadversion, that we scarcely know where to begin. It exhibits, however, a real picture of the man, and a mere superficial glance at its phraseology will prove that he is angry, and his nerves in a tremor. It is, in fact, an incoherent jumble of words and sentences, all in the disjunctive.

But it is a perfect original and anomaly in the epistolary line; and contains in itself internal marks of genuine authenticity.

The first thing in this letter that calls for our attention is the language he uses towards the people he calls "*militia deserters.*" That they may be dealt with, he says, as their crimes merit. Now I pray you who were those people? Doubtless the respectable farmers and others in the vicinity of Pittsburgh. And what does this Mogul of the west intend to do with them? Why hang them, to be sure; for this is military law. But the true state of this case doubtless is, that these militia considered themselves free men; that they were not well pleased either with Connoly or garrison duty; that viewing their country in danger, and their wives and children exposed to savage barbarity, they preferred more active service, and joined the standard of Capt. Cresap. And is this a new thing, or reprehensible? How often do our militia enter into the regular army, and whoever dreamed of hanging them for so doing?

But, secondly, we say it is possible Capt. Cresap did not know from whence these men came; and if he did, he deserves no censure for receiving them; and as to the charge of inveigling away the militia from the garrison, we know this must be positively false, because he was not in Pittsburgh in the year 1774, either personally or by proxy.

As to the general charge against Capt. Cresap, of attacking the Indians, and the great injury he had done them, I need only say that this charge is refuted again and again in the course of this history, and its unparalleled impudence especially, or the date of this letter, merits the deepest contempt. But the most extraordinary feature in this most extraordinary letter is couched in these words, namely: "That the Indians relied upon the expressions of friendship he made them and deported themselves accordingly."

Be astonished, O ye nations of the earth, and all ye kindreds of people at this! For be it remembered this is the 14th day of July 1774, when Connoly has the unblushing impudence to assert that the Indians relied upon his expressions of friendship, and deported themselves accordingly, when at this very time we were engaged in the hottest part of Dunmore's war; when Dunmore himself was raising an army and personally on his way to take the command; when Lewis was on his march from Augusta county, Virginia, to the Ohio; when Cornstalk, with his Indian army, was in motion to meet Lewis; and when Capt. Cresap was actually raising a company to join Dunmore when he arrived. And it was while engaged in this business, that he received this letter from Connoly.

Now if any man can account for this strange and extraordinary letter upon rational principles, let him do so if he can: he has more ingenuity and a more acute discernment than I have.

Soon after receiving this letter, Capt. Cresap left his company on the west side of the mountain and rode home, where he met the earl of Dunmore at his house, and where he (the earl) remained a few days in habits of friendship and cordiality with the family. One day while the earl was at his house, Capt. Cresap, finding him alone, introduced the subject of Connoly's ill treatment, with a view, I suppose, of obtaining redress, or of exposing the character of a man he knew to be high in the estimation and confidence of the earl. But what effect, suppose ye, had this remonstrance on the earl? I'll tell you; it lulled him into a profound sleep. Aye, aye, thinks I to myself (young as I then was,) this will not do, captain; there are wheels within wheels, dark things behind the curtain between this noble earl and his sub-satellite.

Capt. Cresap was himself open, candid and unsuspicious, and I do not know what he thought, but I well remember my own thoughts upon this occasion.

But let us, as nearly as possible, finish our business with Connoly, although we must thereby get a little ahead of our history: yet, as already remarked, we think it less perplexing to the reader, than to give him here a little and there a little of this extraordinary character.

We find, then, that in the year 1775, Connoly, discovering that his sheep-skin could not cover him much longer, threw off the mask and fled to his friend Dunmore, who also, about the same time, was obliged to take sanctuary on board a British ship of war in the Chesapeake bay.—From this place, i. e. Portsmouth in Virginia, Connoly wrote the following letter to Col. John Gibson, who, no doubt, he supposed possessed sentiments congenial to his own. It happened, however, that he was mistaken in his man, for Gibson exposed him, and put his letter into the hands of the commissioners who were holding a treaty with the Indians.

But let us see this letter: it is dated Portsmouth, August 9, 1775.

"Dear Sir: I have safely arrived here, and am happy in the greatest degree at having so fortunately escaped the narrow inspection of my enemies, the enemies to their country's good order and government. I should esteem myself defective in point of friendship towards you, should I neglect to caution you to avoid an over zealous exertion of what is now ridiculously called patriotic spirit, but on the contrary to deport yourself with that moderation for which you have always been so remarkable, and which must in this instance tend to your honor and advantage. You may rest assured from me, sir, that the greatest unanimity now prevails at home, and the innovating spirit among us here is looked upon as ungenerous and undutiful, and that the utmost exertions of the powers in government (if necessary) will be used to convince the infatuated people of their folly.

"I would, I assure you, sir, give you such convincing proofs of what I assert, and from which every reasonable person may conclude the effects, that nothing but madness could operate upon a man so far as to overlook his duty to the present constitution, and to form unwarrantable associations with *enthusiasts*, whose ill-timed folly must draw down upon them inevitable destruction. His lordship desires you to present his hand to Captain White-eyes, [a Delaware Indian chief,] and to assure him he is sorry he had not the pleasure of seeing him at the treaty, [a treaty held by Connoly in his name,] or that the situation of affairs prevented him from coming down.

"Believe me, dear sir, that I have no motive in writing my sentiments thus to you, further than to endeavor to steer you clear of the misfortunes which I am confident must involve but unhappily too many. I have sent you an address from the people of Great Britain to the people of America, and desire you to consider it attentively, which will I flatter myself convince you of the idleness of many determinations and the absurdity of an intended slavery.

"Give my love to George, [his brother, afterwards a colonel in the revolutionary war,] and tell him he shall hear from me, and I hope to his advantage. Interpret the inclosed speech to Capt. White-eyes from his lordship. Be prevailed upon to shun the popular error, and judge for yourself, as a good subject, and expect the rewards due to your services.
"I am, &c.   JOHN CONNOLY."

The inclosed speech to White-eyes we shall see in its proper place, after we have finished our business with Connoly. It seems, then, that either a mistaken notion of his influence, or greatly deceived by his calculations on the support of Col. Gibson, his brother and friends, or in obedience to the solicitations of his friend Dunmore, he undertakes (*incog.*) a hazardous journey from the Chesapeake bay to Pittsburgh, in company, if I recollect right, with a certain Doct. Smith; but our Dutch republicans of Fredericktown, Maryland, smelt a rat, seized, and imprisoned him, from whence he was removed to the Philadelphia jail, where we will leave him awhile to cool.

But let us now look at these two characters; Connoly uses every effort to destroy us and subvert our liberties, and Cresap marches to Boston with a company of riflemen to defend his country. If then men's actions afford us the true and best criterion to judge of their merit or demerit, we can be at no loss to decide on this occasion. Nor can there be any doubt that this man, so full of tender sensibility and sympathy for the sufferings of the Indians, when arrested with his colleague (Smith) in Frederick, had a Pandora's box full of fire-brands, arrows and death, to scatter among the inhabitants of the west.

But it is probable the reader, as well as the writer, is weary of such company: we therefore bid him adieu, and once more attend his excellency the governor of Virginia, whom we left, I think, on board a British sloop of war, in the Chesapeake bay.

The reader has not forgotten, that we long since stated it as our opinion, that it was probable, and that we had strong reasons to believe, that Dunmore himself, from political motives, though acting behind the scenes, was in reality at the bottom of the Indian war of 1774.

We have already alluded to several circumstances previous to and during that war; but we have in reserve several more evincive of the same fact subsequent to the war.

It may be remembered, that at the treaty of Chilicothe, it was remarked that some points were referred for future discussion at Pittsburgh, in the ensuing fall; and it appears that a treaty was actually held by Connoly, in Dunmore's name, with the chiefs of the Delaware, and some Mingo tribes in the summer ensuing. This is historically a fact, and matter of record, which I extract from the minutes of a treaty, held in the autumn of the same year, with several tribes of Indians, by commissioners from the Congress of the United States and from Virginia.*

But to understand this perfectly, the reader must be informed, that, previous to this treaty, Capt. Jas. Wood, afterwards governor of Virginia, was sent by that State as the herald of peace, with the olive branch in his hand, to invite all the Indian tribes bordering on the Ohio and its waters, to a treaty at Pittsburgh, on the 10th day of September following. Capt. Wood kept a journal, which is incorporated in the proceedings of the treaty, from which journal I copy as follows: "July the 9th, I arrived (says he) at Fort Pitt, where I received information that the chiefs of the Delawares and a few of the Mingos had lately been treating with Maj. Connoly agreeably to instructions from lord Dunmore, and that the Shawnees had not come to the treaty," &c.

Capt. Wood however acknowledges, in a letter he wrote to the convention of Virginia from this place, that this treaty held by Connoly was *in the most open and candid manner, that it was held in the presence of the committee, and that he laid the governor's instructions before them.* Very good. But why these remarks respecting Connoly and Dunmore? Does not this language imply jealousy and suspicion, which Capt. Wood, who certainly was deceived, was anxious to remove? But to proceed. He says:

"July 10. White-eyes came with an interpreter to my lodging. He

---

*The original minutes of this treaty are in my own possession. They were presented to me by my friend John Madison, secretary to the commissioners, with I think this remark, that they were of no use to them, but might be of some to me.

Q

informed me, he was desirous of going to Williamsburg with Mr. Connoly to see lord Dunmore, who had promised him his interest in procuring a grant from the king for the lands claimed by the Delawares; that they were all desirous of living as the white people do, and under their laws and protection; that lord Dunmore had engaged to make him some satisfaction for his trouble in going several times to the Shawnee towns, and serving with him on the campaign, &c. &c. He told me he hoped I would advise him whether it was proper for him to go or not. I was then under the necessity of acquainting him with the disputes subsisting between lord Dunmore and the people of Virginia, and engaged, whenever the assembly met, that I would go with him to Williamsburg, &c. &c. He was very thankful, and appeared satisfied."

The reader must observe this is July the 10th, 1775, and he will please to refer to pages 119 and 120, where he wil see from Connoly's letter of Aug. 9th, how much reliance was to be placed on his candor and sincerity, as stated by Capt. Wood to the convention on the 9th day of July. Thus we find that about thirty days after Capt. Wood's testimony in his favor, Connoly threw away the mask, and presented himself in his true character; and from his own confession and the tenor of his letter to Gibson, it is plain that the current of suspicion ran so strongly against him that he declared himself "most happy in escaping the vigilance of his enemies."

We owe the reader an apology for introducing this man again; but the fact is, that Dunmore and Connoly are so identified in all the political movements of this period, that we can seldom see one without the other; and Connoly is the more prominent character; especially in the affairs of the west.

But we now proceed with Capt. Wood's journal. He tells us that on the 20th July, he met Gerrit Pendergrass about 9 o'clock; that he had just left the Delaware towns; that two days before, the Delawares had just returned from the Wyandott towns, where they had been at a grand council with a French and English officer, and the Wyandotts; that Monsieur Baubee and the English officer told them to be on their guard, that the white people intended to strike them very soon, &c. &c.

July 21. At 1 o'clock, arriving at the Moravian Indian town, examined the minister (a Dutchman), concerning the council lately held with the Indians, &c. who confirmed the account before stated.

July 22. About 10 o'clock, arrived at Coshocton, (a chief town of the Delawares,) and delivered to their council a speech, which they answered on the 23d. After expressing their thankfulness for the speech and willingness to attend the proposed treaty at Pittsburgh, they delivered to Capt. Wood a belt and string they said was sent to them by an Englishman and Frenchman from Detroit, accompanied with a message that the people of Virginia were determined to strike them; that they would come upon them two different ways, the one by the way of the lakes, and the other by the way of the Ohio, and to take their lands, that they must be constantly on their guard, and not to give any credit to whatever you said, as you were a people not to be depended upon; that the Virginians would invite them to a treaty, but that they must not go at any rate, and to take particular notice of the advice they gave, which proceeded from motives of real friendship.

Now by comparing and collating this with the speech sent by Dunmore, enclosed in Connoly's letter, it will furnish us with a squinting at the game that was playing with the Indians by the earl of Dunmore and other British officers; to be convinced of which, read the following speech from Dunmore, which was enclosed in a letter to Gibson:

"Brother Capt. White-eyes, I am glad to hear your good speeches as sent to me by Maj. Connoly, and you may be assured I shall put one end of the belt you have sent me into the hands of our great king, who will be glad to hear from his brothers the Delawares, and will take strong hold of it. You may rest satisfied that our foolish young men shall never be permitted to have your lands; but on the contrary the great king will protect you, and preserve you in the possession of them.

"Our young people in this country have been very foolish, and done many imprudent things, for which they must soon be sorry, and of which I make no doubt they have acquainted you; but must desire you not to listen to them, as they would be willing you should act foolishly with themselves; but rather let what you hear pass in at one ear and out of the other, so that it may make no impression on your heart, *until you hear from me fully*, which shall be as soon as I can give further information.

"Capt. Waite-eyes will please acquaint the Cornstalk with these my sentiments, as well as the chiefs of the Mingos, and other six nations.

          (Signed)   "DUNMORE."

It is scarcely necessary to remark here, that the flight of Dunmore from Williamsburg, of Connoly from Pittsburgh, this speech of Dunmore's, and the speech of the Delawares to Capt. Wood, are all nearly cotemporaneous, and point the reader pretty clearly to the aspect of our affairs with the Indians at this period. Dunmore's speech, as you have it above, although pretty explicit, is yet guarded, as it had to pass through an equivocal medium; but he tells Capt. White-eyes he shall hear from him *hereafter*, and this *hereafter* speech was no doubt in Connoly's portmanteau when he was arrested in Frederick.

But to conclude this tedious chapter, nothing more now seems necessary than to call the attention of the reader to those inferences that the facts and circumstances detailed in the foregoing pages seem to warrant.

The first circumstance in the order of events seems to be the extraordinary and contradictory conduct of Dunmore and Connoly respecting Captain Cresap. They certainly understood each other, and had one ultimate end in view; yet we find on all occasions Dunmore treats Cresap with the utmost confidence and cordiality, and that Connoly's conduct was continually the reverse, even outrageously insulting him, while under the immediate orders of Dunmore himself.

Secondly, we find Dunmore acting with duplicity and deception with Col. Lewis and his brigade, from Augusta county. So says Doddridge.

Thirdly, we find Capt. Cresap's name foisted into Logan's pretended speech, when it is evident, as we shall hereafter prove, that no names at all were mentioned in the original speech made for Logan.

Fourthly, it appears pretty plainly that much pains were taken by Dunmore, at the treaty of Chilicothe, to attach the Indian chiefs to his person, as appears from facts that afterwards appeared.

Fifthly, the last speech from Dunmore to Capt. White-eyes and other Indian chiefs, sent in Connoly's letter to Gibson; to all which we may add, his lordship's nap of sleep while Cresap was stating his complaints against Connoly, and all Connoly's strange and unaccountable letters to Cresap.

I say, from all which it will appear that Dunmore had his views, and those views hostile to the liberties of America, in his proceedings with the Indians in the war of 1774, the circumstances of the times, in connection with his equivocal conduct, lead us almost naturally to infer that he knew pretty well what he was about, and among other things, that he knew a war with the Indians at this time would materially subserve the views and interest of Great Britain, and consequently he perhaps might feel it a duty to promote said war, and if not, why betray such extreme solicitude to single out some conspicuous character, and make him the scape-goat, to bear all the blame of this war, that he and his friend Connoly might escape?

——:0:——

CHAPTER XI.

WAR OF THE REVOLUTION.

It is not within the plan of this work, to go into a general detail of the war of the revolution. The author will only give an account of it so far as it is connected with the immediate history of the valley.

At the beginning of the war the late Daniel Morgan was appointed a captain, and very soon raised a company of brave and active young men, with whom he marched to join Gen. Washington at Boston. John Humphreys was Morgan's first lieutenant. Morgan was soon promoted to the rank of major, and Humphreys was made his captain. It is believed this was one of the first regular companies raised in Virginia, which marched to the north. Morgan with his company was ordered to join Gen. Montgomery, and march to the attack on Quebec; in which attack Montgomery was killed, and Morgan, after performing prodigies of valor, compelled to surrender himself and his brave troops prisoners of war. Capt. Humphreys was killed in the assault. The reverend Mr. Peter Muhlenburg, a clergyman of the Lutheran* profession, in the county of Shenandoah, laid off his gown and took up the sword. He was appointed a colonel, and soon raised a regiment, called the 8th, consisting chiefly of young men of German extraction. Abraham Bowman was appointed to a majoralty in it, as was also Peter Helphinstine, of Winchester. It was frequently called the "German regiment." Muhlenburg was ordered to the south in 1776, and the unhealthiness of the climate proved fatal to many of his men.

James Wood, of Winchester, was also appointed a colonel. He soon raised another regiment, marched to the north, and joined Gen. Washington's main army.

Maj. Morgan, after several months' captivity, was exchanged together with his troops, promoted to the rank of colonel, and again joined his country's standard in the northern army. Muhlenburg returned from his southern campaign, and in 1777 also joined the northern army. He was promoted to the rank of brigadier-general, and Abraham Bowman to the rank of colonel. Helphinstine contracted a lingering disease in the south, returned home on furlow, and died in Winchester in the autumn of 1776. Col. Morgan, with a picked regiment of riflemen, was ordered to join Gen. Gates, to meet and oppose Gen. Burgoyne. It is universally admitted that Morgan, with his brave and expert rifle regiment, contributed much towards achieving the victory which followed.

After the capture of Burgoyne and his army, (17th Oct. 1777,) Morgan, for his great personal bravery, and superior military talents displayed on all occasions, was promoted to the rank of brigadier-general. He joined the standard of Washington, and soon distinguished himself in harassing the British army in the neighborhood of Philadelphia.

Numerous calls for the aid of the militia were made from time to time to assist our country in the defence of its rights and liberties; which calls were generally promptly obeyed. The spirit of patriotism and love of country was the prevailing passion of a vast majority of the people of the valley; and with one exception, which will be noticed hereafter, our character was not tarnished by any thing like a tory insurrection. The author most devoutly wishes, for the honor of his native country, that this exception could be blotted out of our history, and consigned to eternal oblivion.

Our valley, at the commencement of the war, was comparatively thinly populated. The first official return, for the county of Frederick, of the effective militia, to the executive of Virginia, amounted only to 923; the whole number of people in Winchester was 800, probably a small fraction over. This return and enumeration was made in the year 1777.

In 1777 Gen. Sullivan "gained possession of some records and papers belonging to the Quakers, which, with a letter, were forwarded to Congress, and referred to a committee." On the 28th of August, the committee reported, "That the several testimonies which have been published since the commencement of the present contest betwixt Great Britain and America, and the uniform tenor of the conduct and conversation of a num-

---

*The author is mistaken; he was an Episcopalian.

ber of persons of considerable wealth, who profess themselves to belong to the society of people commonly called Quakers, render it certain and notorious that those persons are with much rancor and bitterness disaffected to the American cause; that as those persons will have it in their power, so there is no doubt it will be their inclination, to communicate intelligence to the enemy, and in various other ways to injure the councils and arms of America; that when the enemy, in the month of December, 1776, were bending their progress towards the city of Philadelphia, a certain seditious publication, addressed 'To our friends and brethren in religious profession, in these and the adjacent provinces,' signed John Pemberton, 'in and on behalf of the meeting of sufferers, held at Philadelphia, for Pennsylvania and New Jersey, the 26th of the 12th month, 1776,' was published, and as your committee is credibly informed, circulated amongst many members of the society called Quakers, throughout the different States; that the seditious paper aforesaid originated in Philadelphia, and as the persons' names who are under-mentioned, have uniformly manifested a disposition highly inimical to the cause of America; therefore, *Resolved*, That it be earnestly recommended to the supreme executive council of the State of Pennslvania, forthwith to apprehend and secure the persons of Joshua Fisher, Abel James, James Pemberton, Henry Drinker, Israel Pemberton, John Pemberton, John James, Samel Pleasants, Thomas Wharton, sen., Thomas Fisher son of Joshua, and Samuel Fisher son of Joshua, together with all such papers in their possession as may be of a political nature.

"And whereas there is strong reason to apprehend that these persons maintain a correspondence and connection highly prejudicial to the public safety, not only in this State, but in the several States of America; *Resolved*, That it be recommended to the executive powers of the respective States, forthwith to apprehend and secure all persons, as well among the Quakers as others, who have in their general conduct and conversation evinced a disposition inimical to the cause of America; and that the persons so seized be confined in such places, and treated in such manner, as shall be consistent with their respective characters and security of their persons: that the records and papers of the meetings of sufferings in the respective States, be forthwith secured and carefully examined, and that such parts of them as may be of a political nature, be forthwith transmitted to Congress."

The said report being read, and several the paragraphs considered and debated, and the question put severally thereon, the same was agreed to. *Ordered*, That the board of war remove under guard to a place of security out of the State of Pennsylvania, the Hon. John Penn, Esq. and Benjamin Chew, Esq.; and that they give orders for having them safely secured and entertained agreeable to their rank and station in life." A number of Quakers besides those mentioned, and several persons of a different denomination, were taken up by the supreme executive council of Pennsylvania, concerning whom Congress resolved, on the 8th of September, "That it be recommended to the said council to order the immediate departure of such of said prisoners as refuse to swear or affirm allegiance to the State of Pennsylvania, to Staunton, in Augusta county, Virginia."*

In conformity with the recommendation of Congress, a number of Quakers, together with one druggist and a dancing master, were sent to Winchester under guard, with a request from the executive of Pennsylvania, directed to the county lieutenant of Frederick, to secure them. General John Smith was then the county lieutenant. When the prisoners were delivered into his custody, he proposed to them, that if they would pledge their honors not to abscond, they should not be placed in confinement.— Among the prisoners were three of the Pembertons, two of the Fishers, an old Quaker preacher named Hunt, and several others, amounting in all to twelve, and, with the druggist and dancing master, fourteen. One of the Fishers was a lawyer by profession. He protested in his own name, and on behalf of his fellow prisoners, against being taken into custody by Col. Smith; stated that they had protested against being sent from Philadelphia; that they had again protested at the Pennsylvania line, against being taken out of the State; had repeated their protest at the Maryland line, against being taken into Virginia; that there was no existing law which justified their being deprived of their liberty, and exiled from their native homes and families, and treated as criminals. To which Colonel Smith replied, "It is true that I know of no existing law which will justify your detention; but as you are sent to my care by the supreme executive authority of your native State, and represented as dangerous characters and as having been engaged in treasonable practices with the enemy, I consider it my duty to detain you, at least until I can send an express to the governor of Virginia for his advice and direction what to do in the premises." He accordingly dispatched an express to Williamsburg, with a letter to the governor, who soon returned with the orders of the executive to secure the prisoners. Col. Smith again repeated that "if they would pledge themselves not to abscond, he would not cause them to be confined." Upon which one of the Pembertons spoke and observed to Fisher, "that *his protest* was unavailing, and that they must patiently submit to their fate." Then addressing himself to Col. Smith, he observed, "they would not enter into any pledges, and he must dispose of them as he thought proper." The colonel then ordered them to be placed under guard.

Shortly before this, three hundred Hessian prisoners had been sent to Winchester; there was consequently a guard ready prepared to receive these exiles, and they remained in custody about eight or nine months; during which time two of them died, and the whole of them became much dejected; and it is probable more of them would have died of broken hearts, had they not been permitted to return.

Some time after the British left Philadelphia, these exiles employed the

---

*See Gordon's History of the American Revolution, vol. ii. pp. 222, 223.

It was at the instance of the late General Isaac Zane, of Frederick county, Virginia, that the place of exile was changed from Staunton to Winchester.

late Alexander White, Esq. a lawyer near Winchester, for which they paid him one hundred pounds Virginia currency in gold coin, to go to Philadelphia, and negotiate with the executive authority of the State to permit them to return to their families and friends; in which negotiation White succeeded; and to the great joy and heartfelt satisfaction of these captives, they returned to their native homes.

In the absence of the exiles, Sir William Howe, the British general, had taken up his head quarters in John Pemberton's dwelling house. It was a splendid building, and had been much abused by the British, who also occupied several other houses belonging to Pemberton, which were much injured. Pemberton owned an elegant carriage, which Sir William had taken the liberty of using in his parties of pleasure. When Pemberton saw the situation of his property, he obtained permission from the proper authority, and waited on Sir William Howe, and demanded indemnification for the injury done to his buildings and carriage. The plain and independent language he used to the British general on this subject, was as remarkable for its bluntness, as it was for its fearless character. "Thee has (said he) done great damage to my buildings, and thee suffered thy w****s to ride in my carriage; and my wife will not use it since: thee must pay me for the injury, or I will go to thy master (meaning the king of England,) and lay my complaint before him." Sir William could but smile at the honest bluntness of the man, and thought it best to compromise, and pay him a sum of money, with which the old Quaker was satisfied.*

In 1779 there was a considerable increase of British prisoners at Winchester, and in 1780 barracks were erected about four miles west of the town, to which the prisoners were removed, and a regular guard kept over them. In 1781 the number of prisoners increased to about 1600.

It was this year, in the month of January, that Gen. Morgan, at the battle of the Cowpens, in South Carolina, gave the British Col. Tarlton a most signal defeat. In this action Morgan displayed the most consummate military skill and bravery. Whilst the two armies were closely engaged, Morgan, discovering the enemy were thrown into some confusion, called out in his usual stentorian voice, "Hurra, my brave boys! another close fire, and the day is ours. *Remember, Morgan has never been beaten!*" The author cannot now recollect his authority for this statement, but has repeatedly heard it asserted by different individuals who were acquainted with the fact.

In the year 1813 the author travelled through South Carolina, and called to see Mr. William Calmes, with whom he had an intimate acquaintance when quite a youth, having been school-fellows in this county (Frederick.) Mr. Calmes was well acquainted with Gen. Morgan, and related the following anecdote, in relation to Morgan and Tarlton.

There were two brothers, by the name of ———, citizens of South Carolina, men of considerable wealth and respectability, who joined the British standard, and both obtained colonel's commissions. One of them was at Cornwallis' head-quarters the day Tarlton set out determined to

---

*Gen. John Smith detailed the foregoing particulars to the author.

take Morgan at all hazards. Meeting with Col. ———, he accosted him to the following effect: "Well, colonel, if you will be at his lordship's head-quarters (naming the day,) you shall have the pleasure of dining with the old wagoner." To which Col. ——— replied, "I wish you success, Col. Tarlton, but permit me to caution you: you will find Morgan hard to take." On which Tarlton flew into a passion, and threatened to arrest the colonel for using such language in hearing of his officers. The latter calmly replied, "Col. Tarlton, I have staked every thing dear to me in this life upon the issue of the present contest. I own a fine estate. My family and my personal liberty are in danger. If America succeeds in establishing her independence, my estate will be forfeited, my family reduced to beggary and the least I can expect, (if I escape with my life,) will be perpetual exile. Hence, sir, I most ardently wish your success. But permit me again to caution you. Morgan is a cunning, artful officer, and you will find him hard to take." Tarlton, however, pushed off in high glee, determined at every risk to capture Morgan and his little band of warriors. The result was soon known at his lordship's head-quarters; and it so happened, when Tarlton returned, Col. ——— was present. The moment Tarlton saw him he apologized to him for the harsh language he had used towards him, and exclaimed, "By ———! Morgan is truly a great man!" This extorted praise from this haughty British officer speaks volumes for the high military talents of General Morgan.

At the close of the war this refugee colonel took shelter for himself and family in the British dominions of Canada, and his fine estate was confiscated. He however petitioned the government of South Carolina; and from his general good character in private life, an act of pardon, together with the restoration of his estate, was passed, and he returned to its enjoyment with all the privileges of a free citizen. After his return Mr. Calmes became acquainted with him, and received the above statement of facts from him.

The brother of this officer, from some acts of ferocious cruelty practiced upon the friends of the American cause, had his estate also confiscated. The goverment refused to restore it, and passed an act of perpetual banishment against him.

In 1781 Cornwallis entered Virginia at the head of a large army, and in the month of June a party of tories raised the British standard on Lost river, then in the county of Hampshire (now Hardy.) John Claypole, a Scotsman by birth, and his two sons, were at the head of the insurrection.* Claypole had the address to draw over to his party a considerable majority of the people on Lost river, and a number on the South fork of the Wappatomaka. They first manifested symptoms of rebellion by refusing

---

*Moses Russell, Esq., informed the author, that it was reported and believed at the time that Claypole's two sons went to North Carolina, and had an interview with Lord Cornwallis, who appointed and commissioned them both captains in the British service, and sent the commission of colonel to their father.

R

to pay their taxes and refusing to furnish their quota of men to serve in the militia.   The sheriffs, or collectors of the revenue, complained to Col. Vanmeter, of the county of Hampshire, that they were resisted in their attempts to discharge their official duties, when the colonel ordered a captain and thirty men to their aid.   The insurgents armed themselves, and determined to resist.   Among them was John Brake, a German of considerable wealth, who resided about fifteen miles above Moorefield, on the South fork of the river, and whose house became the place of rendezvous for the insurgents.   When the sheriff went up with the militia posse, fifty men appeared in arms.   The posse and tories unexpectedly met in the public road.   Thirty-five of the latter broke and ran about one hundred yards, and then formed, while fifteen stood firm.   The captain of the guard called out for a parley, when a free conversation took place, in which this dangerous proceeding on the part of the tories was pointed out, with the terrible consequences which must inevitably follow. It is said that had a pistol been fired, a dreadful scene of carnage would have ensued.*   The two parties, however, parted without bloodshed.— But instead of the tory party retiring to their respective homes and attending to their domestic duties, the spirit of insurrection increased.— They began to organize, appointed officers, and made John Claypole their commander-in-chief, with the intention of marching off in a body to Cornwallis, in the event of his advancing into the valley or near it.

Several expresses were sent to Col. Smith, requesting the aid of the militia, in the counties immediately adjoining, to quell this rebellion. He addressed letters to the commanding officers of Berkeley and Shenandoah, beat up for volunteers in Frederick, and in a few days an army of four hundred rank and file were well mounted and equipped. Gen. Morgan, who, after the defeat of Tarlton and some other military services, had obtained leave of absence from the army, and was now reposing on his farm (Saratoga) in Frederick, and whose name was a host in itself, was solicited to take the command, with which he readily complied. About the 18th or 20th of June the army marched from Winchester, and in two days arrived in the neighborhood of this tory section of Hardy county.— They halted at Claypole's house,† and took him prisoner.   Several young men fled; among them William Baker.   As he ran across Claypole's meadow he was hailed and ordered to surrender; but disregarding the command, Capt. Abraham Byrd, of Shenandoah county, an excellent marksman, raised his rifle, fired, and wounded him in the leg.‡ He fell, and several of Morgan's party went to him to see the result.   The ball had penetrated just above the heel; ranged up the leg, and shivered the

---

*Isaac Vanmeter, Esq., then about eighteen years of age, was one of the posse, and related these facts to the author.

†Claypole's former residence is now owned by Mr. Miller, and is about forty-five or fifty miles south-west of Winchester, on Lost river in Hardy county.

‡The spot was pointed out to the author; by Mr. Miller, where Byrd stood when he fired at Baker, and where Baker fell.   The distance is about four hundred yards.

bones. As the poor fellow begged for mercy, he was taken to the house, and his wound dressed by the surgeon of the regiment. He recovered, and is still living. They took from Claypole provisions for themselves and horses, Col. Smith (who was second in command,) giving him a certificate for their value.

From Claypole's the army moved up Lost river, and some young men in the advance took a man named Matthias Wilkins prisoner, placed a rope round his neck, and threatened to hang him. Col. Smith rode up, saw what was going on, and ordered them instantly to desist. They also caught a man named John Payne, and branded him on the posteriors with a red hot spade, telling him they would make him a freemason.—Claypole solemnly promised to be of good behavior, gave bail and was set at liberty.

The army thence crossed the South Branch mountain. On or near the summit they saw a small cabin, which had probably been erected by some hunters. Gen. Morgan ordered it to be surrounded, observing, "It is probable some of the tories are now in it." As the men approached the cabin, ten or a dozen fellows ran out and fled. An elderly man, named Mace, and two of his sons, were among them. Old Mace, finding himself pretty closely pursued, surrendered. One of the pursuers was Capt. William Snickers, who an aid-de-camp of Morgan, who being mounted on a fine horse, was soon alongside of him. One of Mace's sons looking round at this instant, and seeing Snickers aiming a blow with a drawn sword at his father, drew up his rifle and fired at him. The ball passed through the crest of his horse's neck; he fell, and threw the rider over his head. Snickers was at first thought by his friends to be killed; and in the excitement of the moment, an Irishman, half drunk, who had been with Morgan for some time as a waiter, and had seen much tory blood shed in the Carolinas, ran up to the prisoner (Mace) with a cocked pistol in his hand, and shot the poor man, who fell, and instantly expired. Capt. Snickers soon recovered from the bruises received in his fall, as did his horse also from the wound in his neck.

The army proceeded on to pay their respects to Mr. John Brake, an old German, who had a fine farm with extensive meadows, a mill, large distillery, and many fat hogs and cattle. He was an exception, in his political course, to his countrymen, as they were almost to a man, true whigs, and friends to their country. Brake, as before observed, had joined the tory band, and his house was their place of rendezvous, where they feasted on the best he had. All this appearing unquestionable, Morgan marched his army to his residence, there halted, and spent two days and nights with his reluctant host. His troops lived on the best his fine farm, mill and distillery afforded, feasting on his pigs, fatted calves, young beeves, lambs, poultry, &c., while their horses, fared no less luxuriously upon his fine unmown meadows, oat fields, &c. As Brake had entertained and feasted the tories, Morgan concluded that he should feast them in turn.

The third day, in the morning, the army moved on down the river, passed by Moorefield, and returned to Winchester, where it was disbanded, after a service of only about eight or ten days. Thus was this tory insurrection crushed in the bud. The party themselves became ashamed of their conduct, and in some degree to atone for it, and wipe off the stain, several of the young men volunteered their services and marched to aid in the capture of Cornwallis.

Within three or four days after these men were disbanded, two expresses in one day arrived at Winchester, and informed Col. Smith that Tarlton was on his way to rescue the British prisoners at the Winchester barracks. Col. Smith had again to call out the militia; and ordering four hundred men as a guard, removed the prisoners to Fort Frederick, in Maryland, at which place they remained to the end of the war.*

The summer of 1781 was emphatically the summer of militia campaigns. There were frequent alarms that Tarlton and his legion (of devils, some people termed them,) were on their way to visit our valley; and sometimes it was reported that Cornwallis and his whole army would be upon us. The militia was almost constantly marching and countermarching.

It however pleased Heaven so to order things, that Cornwallis and his large army should be entrapped and captured at Yorktown, in Virginia.—This put an end to the scourge of the war; and our people being permitted to enjoy the blessings of peace and agriculture, commerce and the mechanical arts improved in a most astonishing degree. The French and British armies circulated immense sums of money in gold and silver coin, which had the effect of driving out of circulation the wretched paper currency which had till then prevailed. Immense quantities of British and French goods were soon imported: our people imbibed a taste for foreign fashions and luxury; and in the course of two or three years, from the close of the war, such an entire change had taken place in the habits and manners of our inhabitants, that it almost appeared as if we had suddenly become a different nation. The staid and sober habits of our ancestors, with their plain home-manufactured clothing, were suddenly laid aside, and European goods of fine quality adopted in their stead. Fine ruffles, powdered heads, silks and scarlets, decorated the men; while the most costly silks, satins, chintzes, calicoes, muslins, &c., &c., decorated our females. Nor was their diet less expensive; for superb plate, foreign spirits, wines, &c., &c., sparkled on the sideboards of many farmers. The natural result of this change of the habits and customs of the people —this aping of European manners and morals,—was to suddenly drain our country of its circulating specie; and as a necessary consequence, the people ran in debt, times became difficult, and money hard to raise.

The sufferings and hard dealings with the Quakers deserve some notice in this place. The unfortunate proceedings of the Philadelphia Quakers drew down upon the whole order the strong prejudices and even hatred of the friends to the American cause. The treasonable proceedings of a few individuals ought not to have been visited upon the whole order of Quakers. It must be admitted, however, that this proceeding was a great

---

*Gen. John Smith communicated all the particulars of the foregoing narrative to the author, with the exception of branding Payne with the spade; this fact was stated by Mr. Chrisman on Lost River.

blot upon Quaker character, and stamped the individuals concerned in it, with base hypocrisy, and gave the lie to their religious professions.— Whilst they professed to hold it unlawful to shed human blood; whilst they disclaimed all concern with the war; they were secretly giving intelligence to the enemy, and aiding and abetting them in every way they could, except resorting to arms. But it is again repeated that it was unjust with one fell sweep to condemn the whole order, for the malconduct of a few individuals. The Quakers in the valley, notwithstanding their entire neutrality, were unquestionably the greatest sufferers by the war.— They refused to bear arms, they refused to pay war taxes, and hence the sheriffs or collectors were compelled to destrain and sell their property to raise their respective proportion of the public burthens.

At the beginning of the war, attempts were made to compel them to bear arms, and serve in the militia; but it was soon found unavailing.— They would not perform any military duty required of them: not even the scourge would compel them to submit to discipline. The practice of coercion was therefore abandoned, and the Legislature enacted a law to levy a tax upon their property to hire substitutes to perform militia duty in their stead. This, with other taxes, bore peculiarly heavy upon them. Their personal property was sold under the hammer to raise these public demands; and before the war was over, many of them were reduced to great distress in their pecuniary circumstances.

There is an amusing story told of James Gotharp, who resided on Apple-pie ridge. He was forced to march with a militia company, and on one particular occasion was placed as sentry at a baggage wagon, with orders to suffer no man to go into the wagon without a written order from the commanding officer. One of the officers walking to the wagon to go in, Gotharp demanded his written authority: the officer cursed him and stepped upon the houns of the wagon. Gotharp seized him by his legs and pulled his feet off the houns. The officer fell with his face upon the houns and had his nose and mouth sorely bruised.

This selling of Quakers' property afforded great opportunity for designing individuals to make profitable speculations. They continued to refuse to pay taxes for several years after the war, holding it unlawful to contribute their money towards discharging the war debt. This being at length adjusted, no part of our citizens pay their public demands with more punctuality, (except their muster fines which they still refuse to pay.) Owing to their industrious and sober habits, they soon recovered from their pecuniary distress produced by the war, and are generally speaking the most independent part of our community. Vast numbers of them have migrated to the western country, and several of their meetings are entirely broken up. There is however, still a considerable number of them in the counties of Frederick and Berkeley. They continued their ancient practice of depending upon their household manufactures for their clothing; and it was a long time before they gave into the practice of purchasing European goods. A few of them entered into the mercantile business; several others erected fine merchant mills; others engaged in mechanical pursuits; but the great body of them are farmers, and are generally most excellent cultivators of the soil.

The greater part of the Germans, also, were a long time dependent up-on their domestic manufactures for their clothing; but they, too, have imbibed a taste for foreign finery. They however manage to effect their purchases by bartering, in a considerable degree, their own household manufactures in exchange.

Some three or four years ago the author called at the house of a farmer in the southwest part of Shenandoah county, where he saw five spinning wheels at work. The old lady, three of her daughters, and a hired girl, were busily engaged in spinning finely prepared hemp. The author en-quired of the old lady, whether she sold any part of her domestic goods. To which she replied, "Yes; when de gals wants to puy some fine dings in de sthore, dey bay for it in linen und linsey; und I puy sugar and gof-fee, und salt, und any dings we wants, und I bay for it all in our own coods."

The author stopped at a neighboring house, and inquired of the in-mates how their neighbor I—— got along. "O," replied the man, "Mr. I. buys a plantation every four or five years, and always pays the money down."

————:o:————

CHAPTER XII.

MODE OF LIVING OF THE PRIMITIVE SETTLERS.

THE first houses erected by the primitive settlers were log cabins, with covers of split clapboards, and weight poles to keep them in place. They were frequently seen with earthen floors; or if wood floors were used, they were made of split puncheons, a little smoothed with the broad-axe. These houses were pretty generally in use since the author's recollection. There were, however, a few framed and stone buildings erected previous to the war of the revolution. As the country improved in population and wealth, there was a corresponding improvement in the erection of build-ings.

When this improvement commenced, the most general mode of build-ing was with hewn logs, a shingle roof and plank floor, the plank cut out with a whip saw. As it is probable some of my young readers have ne-ver seen a whip saw, a short description of it may not be uninteresting. It was about the length of the common mill saw, with a handle at each end transversely fixed to it. The timber intended to be sawed was first squared with the broad-axe, and then raised on a scaffold six or seven feet high. Two able-bodied men then took hold of the saw, one standing on the top of the log and the other under it, and commenced sawing. The labor was excessively fatiguing, and about one hundred feet of plank or scantling was considered a good day's work for the two hands. The introduction of saw mills, however, soon superseded the use of the whipsaw, but they were not entirely laid aside until several years after the war of the revolution.

The dress of the early settlers was of the plainest materials—generally of their own manufacture; and if a modern "belle" or "beau" were now to witness the extreme plainness and simplicity of their fashions, the one would be almost thrown into a fit of hysterics, and the other frightened at the odd and grotesque appearance of their progenitors.

Previous to the war of the revolution, the married men generally shaved their heads, and either wore wigs or white linen caps. When the war commenced, this fashion was laid aside, partly from patriotic considerations, and partly from necessity. Owing to the entire interruption of the intercourse with England, wigs could not easily be obtained, nor white linen for caps.

The men's coats were generally made with broad backs, and straight short skirts, with pockets on the outside having large flaps. The waistcoats had skirts nearly half way down to the knees, and very broad pocket flaps. The breeches were so short as barely to reach the knee, with a band surrounding the knee, fastened with either brass or silver buckles.— The stocking was drawn up under the knee-band, and tied with a garter (generally red or blue) below the knee, so as to be seen. The shoes were of coarse leather, with straps to the quarters, and fastened with either brass or silver buckles. The hat was either wool or fur, with a round crown not exceeding three or four inches high, with a broad brim.* The dress for the neck was usually a narrow collar to the shirt, with a white linen stock drawn together at the ends, on the back of the neck, with a broad metal buckle. The more wealthy and fashionable were sometimes seen with their stock, knee and shoe buckles, set either in gold or silver with brilliant stones. The author can recollect, when a child, if he happened to see any of those finely dressed "great folk," as they were then termed, he felt awed in their presence, and viewed them as something more than man.

The female dress was generally the short gown and petticoat made of the plainest materials. The German women mostly wore tight calico caps on their heads, and in the summer season they were generally seen with no other clothing than a linen shift and petticoat—the feet, hands, and arms bare. In hay and harvest time, they joined the men in the labor of the meadow and grain fields. This custom, of the females laboring in the time of harvest, was not exclusively a German practice, but was common to all the northern people. Many females were most expert mowers and reapers. Within the author's recollection, he has seen several female reapers who were equal to the stoutest males in the harvest field. It was no uncommon thing to see the female part of the family at

---

*The Quakers were remarkable for their broad brim hats. They were sometimes called "Broadbrims," by way of distinguishing them from other people.

the hoe or plow; and some of our now wealthiest citizens frequently boast of their grandmothers, aye mothers too, performing this kind of heavy labor.

The natural result of this kind of rural life was, to produce a hardy and vigorous race of people. It was this race of people who had to meet and breast the various Indian wars and the storms of the revolution.

The Dutchman's barn was usually the best building on his farm. He was sure to erect a fine large barn, before he built any other dwelling-house than his rude log cabin. There were none of our primitive immigrants more uniform in the form of their buildings than the Germans.— Their dwelling-houses were seldom raised more than a single story in height, with a large cellar beneath; the chimney in the middle, with a very wide fire-place in one end for the kitchen, in the other end a stove room. Their furniture was of the simplest and plainest kind; and there was always a long pine table fixed in one corner of the stove room, with permanent benches on one side. On the upper floor, garners for holding grain were very common. Their beds were generally filled with straw or chaff, with a fine feather bed for covering in the winter. The author has several times slept in this kind of a bed; and to a person unaccustomed to it, it is attended not unfrequently with danger to the health. The thick covering of the feathers is pretty certain to produce a profuse perspiration, which an exposure to cold, on rising in the morning, is apt to check suddenly, causing chillness and obstinate cough. The author, a few years ago, caught in this way the most severe cold, which was followed by a long and distressing cough, he was ever afflicted with.

Many of the Germans have what they call a drum, through which the stove pipe passes in their upper rooms. It is made of sheet iron, something in the shape of the military drum. It soon fills with heat from the pipe, by which the rooms become agreeably warm in the coldest weather. A piazza is a very common appendage to a Dutchman's dwelling-house, in which his saddles, bridles, and very frequently his wagon or plow harness are hung up.

The Germans erect stables for their domestic animals of every species: even their swine are housed in the winter season. Their barns and stables are well stored with provender, particularly fine hay: hence their quadrupeds of all kinds are kept throughout the year in the finest possible order. This practice of housing stock in the winter season is unquestionably great economy in husbandry. Much less food is required to sustain them, and the animals come out in the spring in fine health and condition. It is a rare occurrence to hear of a Dutchman's losing any part of his stock with poverty. The practice of housing stock in the winter is not exclusively a German custom, but it is common to most of the northern people, and those descended from immigrants from the north. The author recollects once seeing the cow stalls adjoining a farmer's dwelling.

The German women, many of them, are remarkably neat housekeepers. There are some of them, however, extremely slovenly, and their dwellings are kept in the worst possible condition. The effluvia arising

from this want of cleanlines is in the highest degree disgusting and offensive to persons unaccustomed to such fare. The same remarks are applicable to the Irish; nay to some native Virginians. The Germans are
remarkable for their fine bread, milk and butter. They consume in their
diet less animal flesh, and of course more vegetables, than most other people. Their "sour krout"* in the winter constitutes a considerable part of
their living. They generally consume less, and sell more of the product
of their labor, than any other class of our citizens. A Dutchman is proverbial for his patient perseverance in his domestic labors. Their farms
are generally small and nicely cultivated. In his agricultural pursuits,
his meadows demand his greatest care and attention. His little farm is
laid off in fields not exceeding ten or twelve acres each. It is rarely seen
that a Dutchman will cultivate more than about ten or twelve acres in Indian corn any one year. They are of opinion that the corn crop is a great
exhauster of the soil, and they make but little use of corn for any other
purpose than feeding and fattening their swine.

Previous to the war of the revolution, and for several years after, considerable quantities of tobacco were raised in the lower counties of the
valley. The cultivation of this crop was first introduced and pursued by
immigrants from the eastern counties of Virginia. From the newly
cleared lands, two crops of tobacco in succession were generally taken,
and it was then appropriated to the culture of other crops. The crop of
tobacco left the soil in the finest possible state for the production of other
crops. Corn, wheat, rye, flax, oats, potatoes, and every thing else, were
almost certain to produce abundant crops, after the crop of tobacco.

In the year 1794 the French revolution broke out, when bread stuffs of
every kind suddenly became enormously high; in consequence of which
the farmers in the valley abandoned the cultivation of tobacco, and turned
their attention to wheat, which they raised in vast quantities for several
years. It was no uncommon thing for the farmer, for several years after
the commencement of the French revolution, to sell his crops of wheat
from one to two, and sometimes at two and a half dollars per bushel, and
his flour from ten to fourteen dollars per barrel in our seaport towns.

In the year 1796, the Hessian fly first made its appearance in Virginia.

---

*"Sour krout" is made of the best of cabbage. A box about three
feet in length, and six or seven inches wide, with a sharp blade fixed
across the bottom, something on the principle of the jack plane, is used
for cutting the cabbage. The head being separated from the stalk, and
stripped of its outer leaves, is placed in this box, and run back and forth.
The cabbage thus cut up is placed in a barrel, a little salt sprinkled on
from time to time, then pressed down very closely, and covered over at
the open head. In the course of three or four weeks it acquires a sour-
ish taste, and to persons accustomed to the use of it, is a very agreeable
and wholesome food. It is said that the use of it, within the last few
years, on board of ships, has proved it to be the best preventive known
for the scurvy. The use of it is becoming pretty general among all clas-
ses of people in the valley.

S

Its ravages that year were limited, and but little damage was sustained in the crops of wheat. The crop of 1797, in the counties contiguous to the Potomac, was generally destroyed, and the same year partial injury was discovered in Frederick county. The crop of 1798, throughout the county of Frederick, was nearly destroyed. Ever since which time the farmers have annually suffered more or less from the ravages of this destructive destroyer. This insect had prevailed in some of the northern States for several years before it reached Virginia. It is said it first appeared on Long Island, and was believed to have been imported by the Hessian troops in their straw bedding in the time of the war of the revolution.— If this be true, it was a woful curse upon our country—of which it probably will never be relieved. The present generation have abundant cause to execrate the inhuman policy of our parent State in bringing upon us this heavy calamity, and all future generations will probably join in condemning the British ministry who forced upon our ancestors that unrighteous and disastrous war.

——:0:——

CHAPTER XIII.

NORTHERN NECK OF VIRGINIA.

CHARLES II., king of England, granted to the ancestors of the late lord Fairfax all the lands lying between the head waters of the Rappahannock and Potomac to the Chesapeake bay. This immense grant included the territory now comprising the counties of Lancaster, Northumberland, Richmond, Westmoreland, Stafford, King George, Prince William, Fairfax, Loudon, Fauquier, Culpeper, Madison, Page, Shenandoah, Hardy, Hampshire, Morgan, Berkeley, Jefferson and Frederick. It is said that the first grant to the ancestors of Fairfax was only intended to include the territory in the Northern Neck east of the Blue ridge; but after Fairfax discovered that the Potomac river headed in the Allegany mountains, he returned to England, and instituted his petition in the court of king's bench for extending his grant into the Allegany mountains, so as to include the territory composing the present counties of Page, Shenandoah, Hardy, Hampshire, Morgan, Berkeley, Jefferson and Frederick.— A compromise took place between Fairfax and the crown: but previous to the institution of Fairfax's suit, several individuals had obtained grants for large bodies of land west of the Blue ridge, from the colonial government of Virginia. In the compromise it was expressly stipulated that the holders of lands, under what were then called the king's grants, were to be quieted in their right of possession.

Joist Hite and his partners had obtained grants for a large body. Fair-fax, under the pretext that Hite, &c., had not complied with the terms of their grants, took it upon himself to grant away large quantities of these lands to other individuals. This arbitrary and high-handed proceeding on the part of his lordship, produced a lawsuit, which Hite and his partners instituted in the year 1736, and in the year 1786 it was decided.—Hite and partners recovered a large amount of money for the rents and profits, and a considerable quantity of land.*

The immense Fairfax estate has passed out of the hands of Fairfax's heirs. The lands (as observed in a preceding chapter) were granted by Fairfax in fee simple to his tenants, subject to an annual rent of two shillings sterling per hundred acres. This small rent amounted in the aggregate to a very large sum; added to which, Fairfax required the payment of ten shillings sterling on each fifty acres, (what he termed composition money,) which was paid on issuing the grant.

About the year 1742, his lordship opened his office in the county of Fairfax for granting out the land. A few years after, he removed to the county of Frederick, and settled at what he called "Greenway-Court," about 12 or 14 miles south-east of Winchester, where he kept his land office during his life. He died in the autumn of 1781, very soon after the surrender of Cornwallis. It is said that as soon as he heard of the capture of Cornwallis and his army, he called to his servant to assist him to bed, observing, "It is time for me to die;" and truly the old man never again left his bed until he was consigned to the tomb. His body was deposited under the communion-table in the then Episcopal church in Winchester.†

---

*In the year 1736, Fairfax entered a caveat against Hite, &c., alledging that the lands claimed by them were within the bounds of the Northern Neck, and consequently his property. This was the beginning of the controversy, and led to the suit instituted by Hite and partners against him. All the parties died before the suit was decided. Hite in 1731 purchased from John and Isaac Vanmeter their right or warrant for locating 40,000 acres: Hite and McKay obtained a warrant for locating 100,-000 acres more in their own names: and in order to obtain settlers, took in Robert Green and William Duff as partners. Hence the firm of Joist Hite, Robert McKay, Robert Green, and William Duff. Green and Duff settled in Culpeper county, and are the ancestors of the families of those names in that county, and of Gen. Duff Green, of Washington City.

†Lord Fairfax made a donation to the Episcopal society, of a lot of land, upon which a large stone building was erected as a place of worship. The lot is in the center of the town; and, attached to the church, was a large burial ground, in which a great number of bodies were deposited. The Episcopal society lately sold at auction this ancient building and lot for twelve thousand dollars. The purchasers caused the skeletons to be removed, and there are now three elegant brick houses erected on the lot. With the money arising from the sale the Episcopal society purchased a lot on Boscowen and Washington streets, and have built a splendid new church. It is to be regretted that no account was taken of the number

In the year 1785 the Legislature of Virginia passed an act which among other provisions (in relation to the Northern Neck,) is the following :

"And be it further enacted, that the landholders within the said district of the Northern Neck shall be forever hereafter exonerated and discharged from composition and quitrents, any law, custom or usage, to the contrary notwithstanding."* This act of the State freed the people from a vexatious and troublesome kind of taxation. Fairfax's representatives soon sold out their interest in his private estate in this country, and it is believed there is no part of this vast landed estate remaining in the hands of any branch of the Fairfax family. Chief Justice Marshall, the late Raleigh Colston, Esq., and the late Gen. Henry Lee, purchased the right of Fairfax's legatees (in England) to what is called the Manor of Leeds,† South Branch Manor, Patterson's Creek Manor, and various other tracts of land of immense value—the most of which had been leased out for long terms or lives. This estate has been the cause of more litigation probably than any other estate in Virginia. Suits growing out of the case of Hite, &c., against Fairfax, are yet depending in our courts—and some of the tenants in the Manor of Leeds have lately taken it in their heads that the Fairfax title is defective, and refuse to pay rents to the present claimants. This refusal has produced a lawsuit, which will doubtless be a long time pending.

This profligate manner of granting away lands in immense bodies was unquestionably founded in the most unwise and unjust policy. Instead of promoting the speedy settlement and improvement of the country—instead of holding out to the bulk of society every possible encouragement to make the most speedy settlement and improvement of the new country —monopolies in several instances were given, or pretended to be sold to a few favorites of the governing powers, whereby these favorites were enabled to amass vast estates, and to lord it over the great majority of their fellow men. Such are the blessings of kingly governments. But the people of this free and happy republic have abundant cause to rejoice and bless their God that this wretched kind of policy and high-handed injustice is done away, in the freedom and wisdom of our institutions, and that we have no longer our ears assailed, nor our understandings outraged, with the disgusting, high sounding title of "My lord!" applied to poor frail human beings.

Lord Fairfax was the county lieutenant for Frederick for several years.

of skeletons removed. The author inquired of several persons, who were concerned in the removal, no one of whom could give any account of the number. It is probable there were not less than 1,000—the skeleton of Lord Fairfax among them.

*See Revised Code of the Laws of Virginia, vol. i. p. 351.

†The Manor of Leeds is located in the counties of Culpeper, Fauquier and Frederick, and contains about 150,000 acres; the South Branch Manor in Hardy, 55,000; Patterson's creek in Hampshire, 9,000 acres.— Goony-Run Manor, which adjoins the Manor of Leeds, contains about 13,000 acres, and lies chiefly in Shenandoah county.

On looking into the record of the proceedings of the court-martial, the author found the following entry:

"At a council of war, held for regulating the militia of Frederick county, in order to take such steps as shall be thought most expedient in the present critical conjuncture, the 14th day of April, 1756; present, the Rt. Hon. the lord Fairfax, county lieutenant; John Hite, major; John Lindsey, Isaac Parkins, Richard Morgan, Saml. Odell, Edward Rodgers, Jeremiah Smith,* Thomas Caton, Paul Long, captains.

"Proposals having been sent to the several captains of the militia, signed by the commanding officer of the said militia, and dated the 7th day of April, 1756, to get what volunteers they could encourage to go in search of the Indian enemy who are daily ravaging our frontiers and committing their accustomed cruelties on the inhabitants; and the aforesaid officers being met together, and finding the number of men insufficient to go against the enemy, it is considered that the men be discharged, being only fifteen.   FAIRFAX."

From this it appears that lord Fairfax, among others, was an attentive officer in the time of the Indian wars. In truth it behooved his lordship to be active. He had more at stake, and the command of greater funds, than any other individual member of society. The Indian hostilities retarded the settlement of his large domain, and of course lessened his revenue. It is said that his lordship was remarkable for his eccentricities and singularity of disposition and character, and that he had an insatiable passion for hoarding up English gold.† He never married; of course left no child to inherit his vast estate; but devised his property, or a large portion of it, to the Rev. Denny Martin, his nephew in England, on condition that he would apply to the parliament of Great Britain for an act to authorize him to take the name of lord Fairfax. This was done; and Denny Lord Fairfax, like his uncle, never marrying, he devised the estate to Gen. Philip Martin, who, never marrying, and dying without issue, devised the estate to two old maiden sisters, who sold it to Messrs. Marshall, Colston and Lee.

He devised that part of his estate on which he resided, and which he called "Greenway-Court Manor," (containing ten thousand acres, with a large part of his slaves, &c.,) to another nephew, the late Col. Thomas Bryan Martin, who had resided with him for many years previous to his death. Col. Martin, like the others, never married. But he contrived to make a daughter by a Mrs. Crawford, who Lord Fairfax had employed as a housekeeper. After Fairfax's death, Martin kept this woman as a mistress for several years: she died, and the daughter grew up and married

---

*Capt. Jeremiah Smith, the same who defeated the party of fifty Indians, and killed the French captain, noticed in a preceding chapter.

†Some four or five years ago the slaves of the Rev. Mr. Kennerly, the present proprietor of "Greenway-Court," in quarrying stone, not far from Fairfax's ancient dwelling-house, found about $250 worth of gold coin, supposed to have been hidden there by his lordship.

the late Francis Geldart, who was a captain in the British service in the
war of the revolution. She died soon after her marriage without issue.
Martin gave Geldart about one thousand acres of land, part of "Greenway-Court Manor," with a number of slaves, &c. Col. Martin, after the
death of his daughter, employed a white housekeeper, a Miss Powers, to
whom he devised Greenway-Court, with one thousand acres of land, a
number of slaves, and all the residue of his personal estate of every description, (with the exception of part of his stock, slaves, and money.)
Miss Powers, after the death of Martin, married the late Mr. W. Carna-
gy, by whom she had an only daughter, who is now the wife of the Rev.
Mr. Thomas Kennerly. Col. Martin directed by his will the sale of all
the residue of his estate, and the money arising from the sale to be remit-
ted and paid to his two maiden sisters in England.* Shortly after his
death an attempt was made to escheat the landed estate, and the suit was
depending some sixteen or eighteen years before its final decision. The
Court of Appeals at length decided the question in favor of Martin's legatees.

It is proper, before the subject of lord Fairfax's immense grant is dismissed, to inform the reader, that a few years after the war of the revolution an attempt was made to confiscate all that part of his landed estate
devised to his nephew Denny Martin (afterwards Denny Lord Fairfax.)
But Messrs. Marshall, Colston and Lee, having purchased the estate, a
compromise took place between them and the state government, for the
particulars of which the reader is referred to the first volume of the Revised Code of the Laws of Virginia, pp. 352, 353.

The sale of the estate of lord Fairfax by his legatees in England, and
the devise and sale of the estate of the late Col. T. B. Martin, is the last
chapter in the history of the Fairfax interest in the Northern Neck, a
territory comprising about one fourth of the whole of the present limits of
Virginia.

The State of Maryland has lately set up a claim to a considerable tract
of territory on the north-west border of Virginia, including a part of the
Northern Neck. As the claim was pushed with much earnestness, the
executive of our State appointed Charles James Faulkner, Esq., of Martinsburg, a commissioner to collect and embody the necessary testimony,
on behalf of Virginia, on this interesting question. Mr. Faulkner's able
report the author deems of sufficient interest to his readers generally to
insert in this work. It follows :

REPORT OF CHARLES JAMES FAULKNER, RELATIVE TO THE BOUNDARY LINE BETWEEN VIRGINIA AND MARYLAND.

MARTINSBURG, Nov. 6, 1832.

SIR: In execution of a commission addressed to me by your excellency, and made out in pursuance of a joint resolution of the General Assembly of this State, of the 20th of March last, I have directed my at-

---

*The estate sold for about one hundred thousand dollars.

tention to the collection of such testimoney as the lapse of time and the nature of the inquiry have enabled me to procure touching "the settlement and adjustment of the western boundary of Maryland." The division line which now separates the two States on the west, and which has heretofore been considered as fixed by positive adjudication and long acquiescence, commences at a point where the *Fairfax stone* is planted, at the head spring of the Potomac river, and runs thence due north to the Pennsylvania line. This is the boundary by which Virginia has held for near a century; it is the line by which she held in 1786, when the compact made by the Virginia and Maryland commissioners was solemnly ratified by the legislative authorities of the two States.

An effort is now made by the General Assembly of Maryland, to enlarge her territory by the establishment of a different division line. We have not been informed which fork of the South Branch she will elect as the new boundary, but the proposed line is to run from *one* of the forks of the South Branch, thence due north to the Pennsylvania *terminus*. It is needless to say that the substitution of the latter, no matter at which fork it may commence, would cause an important diminution in the already diminished territorial area of this State. It would deprive us of large portions of the counties of Hampshire, Hardy, Pendleton, Randolph and Preston, amounting in all to almost half a million of acres—a section of the commonwealth which, from the quality of its soil, and the character of its population, might well excite the cupidity of a government resting her claims upon a less substantial basis than a stale and groundless pretension of more than a century's antiquity. Although my instructions have directed my attention more particularly to the collection and preservation of the evidence of such living witnesses "as might be able to testify to any facts or circumstances in relation to the settlement and adjustment of the western boundary," I have consumed but a very inconsiderable portion of my time in any labor or inquiry of that sort, for who indeed, now living, could testify to any "facts or circumstances" which occurred nearly a century since? And if such individuals were now living, why waste time in taking depositions as to those "facts," in proof of which the most ample and authentic testimony was taken in 1736, as the basis of a royal adjudication? I have consequently deemed it of more importance to procure the original documents where possible, if not, authentic copies of such papers as would serve to exhibit a connected view of the origin, progress and termination of that controversy with the crown, which resulted, after the most accurate and laborious surveys, in the ascertainment of those very "facts and circumstances" which are now sought to be made again the subjects of discussion and inquiry. In this pursuit I have succeeded far beyond what I had any ground for anticipation; and from the almost forgotten rubbish of past years, have been enabled to draw forth documents and papers whose interest may survive the occasion which redeemed them from destruction.

To enable your excellency to form a just conception of the weight and importance of the evidence herewith accompanying this report, I beg leave to submit with it a succinct statement of the question in issue between the governments of Virginia and Maryland, with some observations shewing the relevancy of the evidence to the question thus presented.

The territory of Maryland granted by Charles I. to lord Baltimore in June 1632, was described in the grant as "that region bounded by a line drawn from Watkins' point on Chesapeake bay to the ocean on the east; thence to that part of the estuary of Delaware on the north which lieth under the 40th degree, where New England is terminated; thence in a right line by the degree aforesaid, *to the meridian of the fountain of the Potomac;* thence following its course by its farther bank to its confluence." (*Marshall's Life of Washington, vol.* 1, *chap.* II, *pp.* 78—81, 1*st edition*)

It is plain that the western boundary of this grant was the meridian of the fountain of the Potomac, from the point where it cut the 40th degree of north latitude to the fountain of the river; and that the extent of the grant depended upon the question, what stream was the Potomac? So that the question now in controversy grows immediately out of the grant. The territory granted to lord Baltimore was undoubtedly within the chartered limits of Virginia: (*See* 1*st charter of April* 1606, *sec.* 4, *and the* 2*d charter of May* 1609, *sec.* 6, 1*st Hen. Stat. at Large, pp.* 58—88.)— And Marshall says that the grant "was the first example of the dismemberment of a colony, and the creation of a new one within its limits, by the mere act of the crown;" and that the planters of Virginia presented a petition against it, "which was heard before the privy council (of England) in July 1633, when it was declared that lord Baltimore should retain his patent, and the petitioners their remedy at law. To this remedy they never thought proper to resort."

Whether there be any record of this proceeding extant, I have never been able to learn. The civil war in England broke out about ten years after, and perhaps the journals of the proceedings of the privy council were destroyed. Subsequently to this, we are informed by Graham, the planters, "fortified by the opinion of eminent lawyers whom they consulted, and who scrupled not to assure them that the ancient patents of Virginia still remained in force, and that *the grant of Maryland, as derogatory to them, was utterly void,*they presented an application to the parliament complaining of the unjust invasion which their privileges had undergone." (*Graham's History, vol.* 2, *p.* 12.) But as the parliaments of those days were but the obsequious ministers of the crown, that application, it is presumed, likewise shared the fate of their former petition to the privy council.

The present claim of Maryland, then, must be founded on the supposition that the stream which *we* call the Potomac was *not;* and that the stream now called the South Branch of the Potomac, *was* in fact *the* Potomac intended in the grant to lord Baltimore. I have never been informed which fork of the South Branch she claims as the Potomac (for there is a North and a South fork of the South Branch); neither have I been able to learn what is the evidence, or kind of evidence, on which she relies to ascertain that the stream which is *now* called the *South Branch* of the Potomac, but which *at the date of the grant to lord Baltimore* was not known at all, and when known, known for many years only as the *Wappacomo,* was *the* Potomac intended by lord Baltimore's grant. For this important geographical fact, I refer to the numerous early maps of the chartered limits of Virginia and Maryland, some of which are to be seen in the public libraries of Washington and Richmond.

The question, which stream was the Potomac? is simply a question which of them, if either, bore the name. The name is matter of general reputation. If there be any thing which depends wholly upon general acceptation, which ought and must be settled by prescription, it is this question, which of these rivers was and is *the* Potomac? The accompanying papers, it is believed, will ascertain this fact to the satisfaction of every impartial inquirer.

In the twenty-first year of Charles II. a grant was made to lord Hopton and others, of what is called the *Northern Neck* of Virginia, which was sold by the other patentees to lord Culpeper, and confirmed to him by letters patent in the fourth year of James II. This grant carried with it nothing but the right of soil and the incidents of ownership; for it was expressly subjected to the jurisdiction of the government of Virginia. Of this earlier patent I believe there is no copy in Virginia. The *original* charter from James II. to lord Culpeper accompanies this report, marked No. 1. They are both recited in the colonial statute of 1736. (1 *Rev. Code, ch.* 89.) The tract of country thereby granted, was "all that entire tract, territory and parcel of land, lying and being in America, and bounded by and within the heads of the rivers Tappahannock *alias* Rappahannock, and Quiriough *alias* Potomac rivers, the course of said rivers as they are commonly called and known by the inhabitants, and description of their parts and Chesapeake bay."

As early as 1729, in consequence of the eagerness with which lands were sought on the Potomac and its tributary streams, and from the difficulties growing out of conflicting grants from lord Fairfax and the crown, the boundaries of the Northern Neck proprietary became a subject which attracted deep and earnest attention. At this time the Potomac had been but little explored; and although the stream itself above its confluence with the Shenandoah was known as the Cohongoroota, or Upper Potomac, it had never been made the subject of any very accurate surveys and examinations, nor had it yet been settled, by any competent authority, which of its several tributaries was entitled to be regarded as the main or principal branch of the river. It became important, therefore, to remove all further doubt upon that question.

In June, 1729, the lieutenant-governor of Virginia addressed a communication to the lords commissioners of trade and plantation affairs, in which he solicits their attention to the ambiguity of the lord proprietor's charter, growing out of the fact that there were several streams which might be claimed as the head springs of Potomac river, among which he enumerates the Shenandoah, and expresses his determination "to refuse the suspension of granting of patents, until the case should be fairly stated and determined according to the genuine construction of the proprietor's charter." This was followed by a petition to the king in council, agreed to by the house of burgesses of Virginia, in June, 1730, in which it is set forth, among other matters of complaint, "that the head

springs of the Rappahannock and Potomac are not yet known to any of
your majesty's subjects ; that much inconvenience had resulted to grantees therefrom, and praying the adoption of such measures as might lead
to its ascertainment to the satisfaction of all interested.   Lord Fairfax,.
who, by his marriage with the only daughter of lord Culpeper, had now
succeeded to the proprietorship of the Northern Neck, feeling it likewise
due to *his* grantees to have the question relieved from all further difficulty, preferred his petition to the king in 1733, praying that his majesty
would be pleased to order a commission to issue, for running out, marking, and ascertaining the bounds of his patent, according to the true in-
tent and meaning of his charter.   An order to this effect was accordingly
directed by the king ; and three commissioners were appointed on behalf
of the crown, and the same number on behalf of lord Fairfax-   The duty which devolved upon them was to ascertain, by actual examination
and survey, the true fountains of the Rappahannock and Potomac rivers.
To enable them more perfectly to discharge the important trust confided
to them, they were authorised to summon persons before them, to take
depositions and affidavits, to search papers, and employ surveyors, chain-
carriers, markers, and other necessary attendants.   The commissioners
convened in Fredericksburg, on the 26th of September, 1736, and proceeded to discharge their duties, by taking depositions, appointing surveyors, and making every needful and requisite preparation for the survey.   They commenced their journey of observation and survey on the
12th day of October, 1736, and finished it on the 14th of December, of
the same year ;   on which day they discovered what they marked
and reported to be the first fountain of the Potomac river.   Separate reports were made by the commissioners, which reports, with all the accompanying documents, papers, surveys, plans, &c., were, on the 21st
of December, 1738, referred to the council for plantation affairs.   That
board, after hearing counsel, made a report on the 6th day of April, 1745,
in which they state, "that having examined into the several reports, returns, plans, and other papers transmitted to them by the commissioners
appointed on behalf of the crown, as likewise of lord Fairfax, and having
been attended by council on behalf of your majesty, as likewise of lord
Fairfax, and having heard all that they had to offer thereupon, and the question being concerning that boundary which ought to be drawn from the first
head or spring of the river Rappahannock to the first head or spring of the
river Potomac, the committee do agree humbly to report to your majesty as
their opinion, that within the words and meaning of the letters patent, granted by king James II. bearing date the 27th day of September, in the fourth
year of his reign, the said boundary ought to begin at the first spring of
the South branch of the river Rappahannock, and that the said boundary
be from thence drawn in a straight line north-west *to the place in the Al-*
leghany mountains where that part of the Potomac river, which is now
called Cohongoroota, first rises."   The Cohongoroota is known to be
the stream which the Maryland writers term the *North branch* of the
Potomac, but which is recognised in Virginia, and described on all the
maps and surveys which I have ever yet seen, as *the Potomac river,*
from its first fountain, where the Fairfax stone is located, to its confluence

with the Shenandoah; there being, properly speaking, no such stream as the North branch of the Potomac. This report of the council for plantation affairs was submitted to the king in council on the 11th of April, 1745, and fully confirmed by him, and a further order made, directing the appointment of commissioners to run and mark the dividing line agreeably to his decision thus made. Commissioners were accordingly appointed, who, having provided themselves with surveyors, chain-carriers, markers, &c., commenced their journey on the 18th of September, 1746. On the 17th of October they planted the *Fairfax stone* at the spot which had been described and marked by the preceding commissioners as the true head spring of the Potomac river, and which has continued to be regarded, from that period to the present time, as the southern point of the western boundary between Maryland and Virginia. A joint report of these proceedings was made by the commissioners to the king, accompanied with their field notes; which report was received and ordered to be filed away among the records of his majesty's privy council. Thus terminated, after a lapse of sixteen years, a proceeding, which had for its object, among other matters, the ascertainment of the *first fountain of the Potomac river*, and which resulted in the establishment of that "fact" by a tribunal of competent jurisdiction. This decision has now been acquiesced in for near a century; and all topographical description and sketches of the country have been made to conform to it. I say *acquiesced in*, for it is impossible to regard the varying, fluctuating legislation of Maryland upon the subject, at one session of her general assembly *recognizing* the line as now established, (see compact of 1785, Session Acts of 1803, 1818, and others,) at another authorizing the appointment of commissioners to *adjust* the boundary, as a grave resistance of its conclusiveness, or such a *continual claim*, as under the usages of international law, would bar an application of the principles of *usucaption* and *prescription*. (See Vattel, p. 251. Grotius, lib. 2, cap. 4. Wolfius Jus. Nat. par. 3.)

Jurisdiction in all cases relating to boundaries between provinces, the dominion and proprietary government, is by the common law of England exclusively vested in the *king and council*. (1 Ves. sen. p. 447.) And notwithstanding it may be a question of boundary between the crown and the lord proprietor of a province, (such as that between lord Fairfax and the crown,) the king is the only judge, and is presumed to act with entire impartiality and justice in reference to all persons concerned, as well those who are parties to the proceeding before him, as others not parties who may yet be interested in the adjustment. (Vesey, ib.) Such is the theory and practice of the English constitution; and although it may not accord precisely with our improved conceptions of juridical practice, it is nevertheless the law which must now govern and control the legal aspect of the territorial dispute between Virginia and Maryland.

It does not appear by the accompanying papers, that Charles lord Baltimore, the then proprietor of Maryland, deputed an agent to attend *upon his part in the examination and survey of the Potomac river*. It is possible he conceived his interests sufficiently protected in the aspect which the controversy had then assumed between lord Fairfax and the crown. Certain it is, that it nowhere appears that he ever considered himself aggrieved by the result of that adjustment. That his government was fully apprised of what was in progress, can scarcely admit of a rational doubt. For it is impossible to conceive that a controversy so deeply affecting not only the interests of lord Baltimore, but all who were concerned in the purchase of land in that section of the country, and conducted with so much solemnity and notoriety, could have extended through a period of sixteen years without attracting the attention of the government of Maryland—a government ever jealous, because ever doubtful of the original tenure by which her charter was held. But had lord Baltimore even considered himself aggrieved by the result of that settlement, it is difficult now to conceive upon what ground he would have excepted to its justice, or question its validity. Could he have said that the *information* upon which the decision was founded was imperfect? Or that the proceedings of the commissioners were characterized by haste, favoritism or fraud? This, the proceedings of that board, still preserved, would contradict. For never was there an examination conducted with more deliberation, prosecuted with more labor, or scrutinised with a more jealous or anxious vigilance. Could he have shewn that some other stream *ought* to have beeen fixed upon as the true head spring of the Potomac? This, it is believed, is impossible; for although it may be true that the South branch is a longer stream, it nevertheless wants those more important characteristics which were then considered by the commissioners, and have been subsequently regarded by esteemed geographers as essential in distinguishing a tributary from the main branch of a river. (See Flint's Geography, vol. 2, p. 88.) Lastly, would he have questioned the *authority* of the crown to settle the boundaries of lord Fairfax's charter, without having previously made him a *party* to the proceeding? I have before shewn the futility of such an idea. Besides, this would have been at once to question the authority under which he held his own grant; for Baltimore held by virtue of an arbitrary act of the second Charles. His grant was manifestly made in violation of the chartered rights of Virginia, and carried into effect not only without the acquiescence, but against the solemn and repeated remonstrances of her government. Was Virginia consulted in the "dismemberment" of her territory? Was she made a party to that proceeding, by which, "for the first time in colonial history, one new province was created within the chartered limits of another by the mere act of the crown?" But the fact is, that Charles lord Baltimore, *who lived for six years* after the adjustment of this question, never did contest the propriety of the boundary as settled by the commissioners, but from all that remains of his views and proceedings, fully acquieseed in its accurary and justice. (See the treaty with the Six Nations of Indians, at Lancaster, in June, 1744.)

The first evidence of dissatisfaction with the boundary as established, which the researches of the Maryland writers have enabled them to exhibit, are certain instructions from Frederick lord Baltimore (successor of Charles) to Governor Sharp, which were presented by the latter to his council in August, 1753. I have not been able to procure a copy of those instructions, but a recent historian of Maryland, and an ingenious advocate of her present claim, referring to them, says, "His instructions were predicated upon the supposition that the survey might possibly have been made *with the knowledge and concurrence of his predecessor*, and hence he denies the *power* of the latter to enter into *any arrangement* as to the *boundaries*, which could extend *beyond his life estate*, or conclude those in remainder." (See M'Mahon's History of Maryland, p. 53.)

What were the precise limitations of those *conveyances* made by the proprietors of Maryland, and under which Frederick lord Baltimore denies the power of his predecessor to enter into any arrangement as to the boundaries, which could extend beyond his life estate, I am unable to say—my utmost researches have failed to furnish me with a copy of them —but they were so far satisfactory to his lordship's legal conceptions, as to induce him to resist even the execution of a decree pronounced by lord Hardwicke, in 1750, (1 Ves. sen. pp. 444–46) upon a written compact as to boundaries, which had been executed by his predecessor and the Penns, in 1732. To enforce submission to that decree, the Penns filed a bill of reviver in 1754, and after an ineffectual struggle of six years, lord Baltimore was compelled with a bad grace to submit, and abide by the *arrangement* as to the boundaries which had been made by his predecessor. To this circumstance, in all probability, was lord Fairfax indebted for his exemption from the further demands of the proprietor of Maryland. For lord Frederick, no ways averse to litigation, had by this time doubtless become satisfied that the *power* of his predecessor did extend beyond his life estate, and might even *conclude those in remainder*. Be that as it may, however, certain it is that the records of Maryland are silent upon the subject of this pretension, from September, 1753, until ten years subsequent to the compact between Virginia and Maryland in 1785.

An opinion prevails among our most distinguished jurists, resting solely upon traditional information, that about 1761, Frederick lord Baltimore presented a petition to the king and council, praying a revision of the adjustment made in 1745, which petition was rejected, or after a short time abandoned as hopeless. If there ever was such a proceeding, I can find nothing of it in the archives of Virginia.

Be that as it may, it is certain that ever since 1745 lord Fairfax claimed and held, and the commonwealth of Virginia constantly to this day has claimed and held by the Cohongoroota, that is by the northern branch, as *the* Potomac, and whatever lord Baltimore or his heirs, and the State of Maryland may have *claimed*, she has *held* by the same boundary. There was no reason why lord Fairfax, being in actual possession, should have controverted the claim of lord Baltimore, or Maryland. If lord Baltimore, or Maryland, ever controverted the boundary, the question must, and either has been decided against them, or it must have been abandoned as hopeless. If they never controverted it, the omission to do so, can only be accounted for, upon the supposition that they knew it to be hopeless. If Maryland ever asserted the claim—seriously asserted it I mean— it must have been before the revolution, or at least during it, when we all know, she was jealous enough of the extended territory of Virginia. *The claim must have had its origin before the compact between the two states, of*

March. 1795, (1 Rev. Code, ch. 18.)   We then held by the same boundary by which we now hold ; we held to what *we* called and now call the Potomac : she then held to what *we* call the Potomac.   Is it possiole to doubt that this is *the* Potomac recognised by the *compact ?*   That compact is now forty-seven years old.

I have diligently inquired whether, as the Potomac above the confluence of the Shenandoah was called the Cohongoroota, the stream now called the South branch of the Potomac ever had any peculiar name, known to and established among the English settlers—for it is well known it bore the Indian name of Wappacomo.   I never could learn that it was known by any other name, but that which it yet bears, the South branch of the Potomac.   Now that very name of itself sufficiently evinces, that it was regarded as a *tributary* stream of another river, and that river the Potomac ; and that the river of which the South branch was the tributary, was regarded as the main stream.

But let us for a moment concede that the decision of the king in council was not absolutely conclusive of the present question ; let us concede that the long acquiescence of Maryland in that adjustment has not precluded a further discussion of its merits ; let us even suppose the compact of 1785 thrown out of view, with all the subsequent recognitions of the present boundary by the legislative acts of that state, and the question between the two streams now for the first time presented as an original question of preference ;—what are the facts upon which Maryland would rely to show that any other stream, than the one bearing the name, is entitled to be regarded as the main branch of the Potomac ?   It were idle to say that the South branch is the Potomac, because the South branch is a longer or even larger stream than the North branch which Virginia claims to hold by.   According to that sort of reasoning, the Missouri, above its confluence with the Mississippi, is the Mississippi, being beyond comparison the longer and larger stream.   The claim of the South branch, then, would rest solely upon *its great length*   In opposition to this it might be said that the Cohongoroota is more frequently navigable—that it has a larger volume of water—*that the valley of the South branch is, in the grand scale of conformation, secondary to that of the Potomac—that the South branch has not the general direction of that river, which it joins nearly at right angles—that the valley of the Potomac is wider than that of the South branch, as is also the river broader than the other.*   And lastly that the course of the river and the direction of the valley are the same above and below the junction of the South branch.   (See letters accompanyidg this report, No. 26.)   These considerations have been deemed sufficient to establish the title to the "father of waters," to the name which he has so long borne.   (See History and Geography of Western States, vol. 2, Missouri.)   And as they exist in an equal extent, so should they equally confirm the pre-eminence which the Cohongoroota has now for near a century so proudly and peacefully enjoyed.

The claim of Maryland to the territory in question, is by no means so reasonable as the claim of the great Frederick of Prussia to Silesia, which that prince asserted and maintained, but which he tells us himself he ne-

ver would have thought of asserting, if his father had not left him an o-
verflowing treasury and a powerful army.

With this brief historical retrospect, presented as explanatory of the accompanying testimony, I will now lay before your excellency, in chronological order, a list of the documents and papers referred to in my preceding observations.

No. 1. Is the original grant from king James II. to Thomas lord Culpeper, made on the 27th September, in the fourth year of his reign.

No. 2. Copy of a letter from Major Gooch, lieutenant governor of Virginia, to the lords commissioners for trade and plantations, dated at Williamsburg, June 29, 1729.

No. 3. Petition to the king in Council, in relation to the Northern
Neck grants and their boundaries, agreed to by the house of burgesses,
June 30th, 1730.

No. 4. The petition of Thomas lord Fairfax, to his majesty in council,
preferred in 1733, setting forth his grants from the crown, and that there
had been divers disputes between the governor and council in Virginia
and the petitioner, and his agent Robert Carter, Esq., touching the boundaries of the petitioner's said tract of land, and praying that his majesty
would be pleased to order a commission to issue for running out, marking
and ascertaining the bounds of the petitioner's said tract of land.

No. 5. A copy of an order of his majesty in his privy council, bearing
date 29th of November, 1733, directing William Gooch, Esq. lieutenant-
governor of Virginia, to appoint three or more commissioners, (not exceeding five) who in conjunction with a like number to be named and
deputed by the said lord Fairfax, are to survey and settle the marks and
boundaries of the said district of land, agreeably to the terms of the patent under which the lord Fairfax claims.

No. 6. Copy of the commission from lieutenant-governor Gooch to
William Byrd of Westover, *John Robinson* of Piscataway, and *John
Grymes* of Brandon, appointing them commissioners on behalf of his ma-
jesty, with full power, authority, &c.

[I have not been able to meet with a copy of the commission of lord
Fairfax to his commissioners—they were *William Beverly, William Fairfax* and *Charles Carter.* It appears by the accompanying report of their
proceedings, that "his lordship's commissioners delivered to the king's
commissioners an attested copy of their commission," which having been
found upon examination more restricted in its authority than that of the
commissioners of the crown, gave rise to some little difficulty which was
subsequently adjusted.]

No. 7. Copy of the instructions on behalf of the right honorable lord
Fairfax, to his commissioners.

No. 8. Minutes of the proceedings of the commissioners apppointed on
the part of his majesty and the right honorable Thomas lord Fairfax, from
their first meeting at Fredericksburg, September 25th, 1736.

No. 9. Original correspondence between the commissoners during the
years 1736 and 1737, in reference to the examination and survey of the
Potomac river.

No. 10. The original field notes of the survey of the Potomac river, the mouth of the Shenandoah to the head spring of said Potomac river, by Mr. Benjamin Winslow.

No. 11. The original plat of the survey of the Potomac river.

No. 12. Original letter from John Savage, one of the surveyors, dated January 17, 1737, stating the grounds upon which the commissioners had decided in favor of the Cohongorouta over the Wappacomo, as the main branch of the Potomac. The former, he says, is both wider and deeper than the latter.

No. 13. Letter from Charles Carter, Esq. dated January 20, 1737, exhibiting the result of a comparative examination of the North and South branches of the Potomac. The North Branch at its mouth, he says, is twenty-three poles wide, the South branch sixteen, &c.

No. 14. A printed map of the Northern Neck of Virginia, situate betwixt the rivers Potomac and Rappahannock, drawn in the year 1737, by William Mayo, one of the king's surveyors, according to his actual survey in the preceding year.

No. 15. A printed map of the course of the rivers Rappahannock and Potomac, in Virginia, as surveyed according to order in 1736 and 1737, (supposed to be by lord Fairfax's surveyors.)

No. 16. A copy of the separate report of the commissioners appointed on the part of the crown. [I have met with no copy of the separate report of lord Fairfax's commissioners.]

No. 17. Copy of lord Fairfax's observations upon and exceptions to the report of the commissioners of the crown.

No. 18. A copy of the report and opinion of the right honorable the lords of the committee of council for platation affairs, dated 6th April, 1745.

No. 19. The decision of his majesty in council, made on the 11th of April, 1745, confirming the report of the council for plantation affairs, and further ordering the lieutenant-governor of Virginia to nominate three or more persons, (not exceeding five,) who, in conjunction with a like number to be named and deputed by lord Fairfax, are to run and mark out the boundary and dividing line, according to his decision thus made.

No. 20. The original commissioners from Thomas lord Fairfax to the honorable Wm. Fairfax, Charles Carter and William Beverly, Esqrs., dated 11th June, 1745.

[Col. Joshua Fry, Col. Lunsford Lomax, and Maj. Peter Hedgeman, were appointed commissioners on the part of the crown.]

No. 21. Original agreement entered into by the commissioners, preparatory to their examination of the Potomac river.

No. 22. The original journal of the journey of the commissioners, surveyors, &c., from the head spring of the Rappahannock to the head spring of the Potomac, in 1746. [This is a curious and valuable document, and gives the only authentic narrative now extant of the planting of the Fairfax stone.]

No. 23. The joint report of the commissioners appointed as well on the part of the crown as of lord Fairfax, in obedience to his majesty's order of 11th April, 1735.

No. 24. A manuscript map of the head spring of the Potomac river, executed by Col. George Mercer of the regiment commanded in 1756 by General Washington.

No. 25. Copy of an act of the general assembly of Maryland, passed February 19, 1819, authorizing the appointment of commissioners on the part of that state, to meet such commissioners as may be appointed for the same purpose by the commonwealth of Virginia, to settle and adjust, by mutual compact between the two governments, the western limits of that state and the commonwealth of Virginia, *to commence at the most western source of the North branch of the Potomac river, and to run a due north course thence to the Pennsylvania line.*

No. 26. Letters from intelligent and well informed individuals, residing in the country watered by the Potomac and its branches, addressed to the undersigned, stating important geographical facts bearing upon the present controversy.

There are other papers in my possession, not listed nor referable to any particular head, yet growing out of and illustrating the controversy between lord Fairfax and the crown; these are also herewith transmitted.

There are other documents again not at all connected with my present duties, which chance has thrown in my way, worthy of preservation in the archives of the state. Such, for example, as the original *"plan of the line between Virginia and North Carolina, which was run in the year 1728, in the spring and fall, from the sea to Peter's creek, by the Hon. William Byrd, Wm. Dandridge and Richard Fitzwilliams, Esqrs. commissioners, and Mr. Alex'r Irvine and Mr. Wm. Mayo, surveyors--and from Peter's creek to Steep rock creek, was continued in the fall of the year 1749, by Joshua Fry, and Peter Jefferson."* Such documents, should it accord with the views of your excellency, might be deposited with "the Virginia Historical and Philosophical Society," an institution of recent origin, yet founded upon the most expanded views of public utility, and which is seeking by its patriotic appeals to individual liberality, to wrest from the ravages of time the fast perishing records and memorials of our early history and institutions.

With sentiments of regard, I am, very respectfully, your obedient servant,

CHARLES JAS. FAULKNER.

To John Floyd, Esq. Governor of Virginia.

After perusing this masterly exposition, the reader will be at a loss to conceive on what grounds Maryland can rest her claims to the territory in question, and what authorities she can adduce to support them. The controversy is still pending, and, in addition to Mr. Faulkner, Col. John B. D. Smith, of Frederick, and John S. Gallaher, Esq. of Jefferson, have been appointed commissioners on the part of Virginia.

U

CHAPTER XIV.

——:0:——

THE two counties of Frederick and Augusta were laid off at the same session of the colonial legislature, in the year 1738, and included all the vast region of country west of the Blue Ridge. Previous to that time the county of Orange included all the territory west of the mountains.—Orange was taken from Spottsylvania in the year 1734, Spottsylvania having previously crossed the Blue Ridge, and took in a considerable part of what is now the county of Page. Previous to laying off the county of Orange, the territory west of the Blue Ridge, except the small part which lay in Spottsylvania, does not appear to have been included in any county. Spottsylvania was laid off in the year 1720; the act for which is worded as follows :

"Preamble. That the frontiers towards the high mountains are exposed to danger from the Indians, and the late settlements of the French to the westward of the said mountains : Enacted, Spotsylvania county bounds upon Snow creek up to the mill ; thence by a southwest line to the River North Anna ; thence up the said river as far as convenient, and thence by a line to be run over the high mountains to the river on the north west side thereof,[*] so as to include the northern passage through the said mountains ; thence down the said river until it comes against the head of the Rappahannock ; thence by a line to the head of Rappahannock river ; and down that river to the mouth of Snow creek; which tract of land, from the first of May, 1721, shall become a county, by the name of Spotsylvania county."

Thus it appears that a little more than one hundred years ago Spotsylvania was a frontier county, and that the vast region west of the Blue ridge, with its millions of people, has been settled and improved from an entire wilderness. The country for more than a thousand miles to the west has been within this short period rescued from a state of natural barbarism, and is now the seat of the fine arts and sciences, of countless millions of wealth, and the abode of freedom, both religious and political. Judging from the past, what an immense prospect opens itself to our view for the future. Within the last half century, our valley has poured out thousands of emigrants, who have contributed towards peopling the Carolinas, Georgia, Tennessee, Kentucky, Ohio, and other regions south and west, and migrations still continue.

It has already been stated that Frederick county was laid off in the year 1738. The first court of justice held in the county was in the year 1743. This delay, it is presumable, arose from the want of a sufficient

——
[*]South fork of the Shenandoah.

number of Magistrates to form a quorum for the legal transaction of business.   The first court was composed of the following justices, to wit : Morgan Morgan, David Vance, Marquis Calmes, Thomas Rutherford, William M'Mahon, Meredith Helm, George Hoge and John White.— James Wood, clerk.   This court sat the first time, on Friday 11th day of November, 1743.   At this term of the court is to be found on record the following entry : 'Ordered, that the sheriff of this county build a twelve foot square log house, logged above and below, to secure his prisoners, he agreeing to be satisfied with what shall be allowed him for such building by two of the court, and he not to be answerable for escapes.'   This was the first jail erected in the county of Frederick.

The county of Hampshire was the next laid off, and was taken from Frederick and Augusta.   This was done in the year 1753.   The first court held in this county was in December, 1757.   Thomas B. Martin, James Simpson, William Miller, Solomon Hedges and Nathaniel Kuykendall, justices, composed the court, and Gabriel Jones the clerk.

Berkeley and Dunmore were taken from Frederick in the year 1772.— In October, 1777, the legislature altered the name of Dunmore county to Shenandoah.   It does not appear, from the language of the law, for what particular reasons this alteration was made.   It had been named after and in honor of lord Dunmore, the then governor under the royal government. But his lordship took a most decidedly active part in opposition to the American revolution ; and in order to have the liberty of wearing his head, took shelter on board of a British armed vessel.   His conduct is pretty fully related in Mr. Jacob's account of Dunmore's war, given in the preceding pages ; and it was doubtless owing to this cause that the name of Dunmore county was altered to that of Shenandoah.

In the year 1769, Botetourt county was taken from Augusta.   In the act is to be found the following clause : "And whereas the people situated on the Mississippi, in the said county of Botetourt, will be very remote from the court house, and must necessarily become a separate county, as soon as their numbers are sufficient, which probably will happen in a short time ; Be it therefore enacted, by the authority aforesaid, that the inhabitants of that part of the said county of Botetourt, which lies on the said waters, shall be exempted from the payment of any levies to be laid by the said county court for the purpose of building a court house and prison for the said county."   Thus it appears that Virginia, at that period, claimed the jurisdiction and territory of that vast region of country westward to the Mississippi.

In 1772 the county of Fincastle was taken from Botetourt ; and in 1776 Fincastle was divided into the counties of Kentucky, Washington and Montgomery, and the name of Fincastle became extinct.

In the year 1777 Rockbridge county was taken from Augusta and Botetourt.   Rockingham county, the same year, was taken from Augusta, and Greenbrier from Augusta and Botetourt.   The years 1776 and 1777 were remarkable for the many divisions of the western counties.   West Augusta, in the year 1775, by the convention assembled for the purpose of devising a plan for resisting the oppressions of the mother country, among other proceedings determined, that "the landholders of the district of West Augusta shall be considered as a distinct county, and have the liberty of sending two delegates to represent them in general convention as aforesaid."

This is the first account which the author has been able to find in our ancient statutes in relation to West Augusta as a separate district or county. In fact, it does not appear that we ever had a county legally established by this name. It is presumable that it acquired the name by general usage, from its remote and western locality from the seat of justice. Be this as it may, it appears that the district of West Augusta never had its bounds laid off and defined until the month of October 1776, when it was divided into three distinct counties, viz: Ohio, Yohogania, and Monongalia. By the extension of the western boundary between Pennsylvania and Virginia, the greater part of the county Yohogania falling within the limits of Pennsylvania, the residue was, by an act of assembly of 1785, added to Ohio, and Yohogania became extinct.

Harrison county was established in 1784, taken from Monongalia. In 1785 Hardy county was laid off, taken from Hampshire. In 1786 Randolph county was laid off, taken from Harrison. In 1785 Russell county was taken from Washington. In 1787 Pendleton county was taken from Augusta, Hardy and Rockingham. In 1788 Kanawha was taken from Greenbrier and Montgomery. In 1789 Wythe county was taken from Montgomery, and a part of Botetourt added to Montgomery. In 1790 Bath county was taken from Augusta, Botetourt and Greenbrier. In 1792 Lee county was taken from Russell; and in the same year, Grayson county was taken from Wythe.

The author has deemed it an interesting part of his work to give a particular history of the establishment of our counties, because it goes to shew the rapid increase of our population, and improvement of our country, since the termination of the war of the revolution. To an individual born and raised in the valley, and who is old enough to recollect the passing events for the last half century—who was acquainted with the state of our country fifty years ago, its sparse population, rude log buildings, and uncultivated manners and customs of our ancestors—the great improvement of every thing calculated to better the condition of human life—the astonishing change in the appearance of our country—its elegant buildings, finely cultivated farms, improved state of society, &c.—are calculated almost to raise doubts in his mind whether these vast changes could possibly have taken place within his little span of existence. The author's destiny, when a youth, thew him into a business which gave him an opportunity of exploring a considerable part of the lower counties of the valley, and he has lately made it his business again to explore the same counties; and if he had been for the last forty years shut up in a dungeon, and recently set at liberty, he would almost doubt his own senses and believe himself in another country. A great part of our valley may be said to be elegantly improved*

---

*Capt. James Russell, of Berkeley, some years ago built a brick barn 150 feet long and 55 wide.

The late Mr. John Hite, in the year 1785, built the first brick house e-

CHAPTER XV.

——:0:——

ABOUT the year 1738, there were two cabins erected near the run in Winchester.† The author regrets that he has not been able to ascertain the names of the first settlers in this town. Tradition however relates that they were German families.

In the year 1752 the legislature passed "an act for the establishing of the town of Winchester." In the preamble are the following words :

"Whereas it has been represented to this general assembly, that James Wood, gentleman, did survey and lay out a parcel of land at the court house‡ in Frederick county, in twenty-six lots, of half an acre each, with streets for a town, by the name of Winchester, and made sale of the said lots to divers persons who have since settled and built and continue building and settling thereon ; but because the same was not laid off and erected into a town by act of assembly, the freeholders and inhabitants thereof will not be entitled to the like privileges enjoyed by the freeholders and inhabitants of other towns in this colony, Be it enacted, &c. that the said parcel of land lately claimed by the said James Wood, lying and being in the county of Frederick aforesaid, together with fifty-four other lots of half an acre each, twenty-four thereof in one or two streets on the east side of the former lots, the street or streets to run parallel with the street already laid off, and the remaining thirty lots to be laid off at the north end of the aforesaid twenty-six, with a commodious street or streets in such manner as the proprietor thereof, the right honorable Thomas lord Fairfax, shall see fit, be and is hereby constituted, enacted, and established a town, in the manner already laid out, to be called by and retain the

———

ver erected west of the Blue ride. This is but a small one story building, and is now owned by the heirs of the late Mr. A. Neill, at the north end of Stephensburg, in the county of Frederick. In 1787 Mr. Hite built a merchant mill, which was at that time considered the finest mill in the valley. It is now hardly considered a second rate mill.

†A very aged woman, by the name of Sperry, informed the author that when she first saw the place where Winchester now stands, she was 22 years of age, and from her age at the time the author conversed with her, (which was in 1809,) he found the year in which she first saw Winchester to be in 1738, at which time she stated there were but two small log cabins, and those near the run.

‡Mr. Jacob Gibbon informed the author that he was in Winchester in 1755, and that the court house was a small cabin, and that he saw the court sitting in this cabin.

name of Winchester, and that the freeholders of the said town shall forever hereafter enjoy the same privileges which the freeholders of other towns erected by act of assembly enjoy." This act further provides that fairs may be held in the town twice in each year.

Thus it appears that the late Col. James Wood was the founder of Winchester, and not lord Fairfax as has generally been believed. The latter made an addition to the town. Tradition relates that Fairfax was much more partial to Stephensburg than he was to Winchester, and used all his influence to make Stephensburg the seat of justice, but that Wood out-generaled his lordship, and by treating one of the justices with a bowl of toddy secured his vote in favor of Winchester, which settled the question, and that Fairfax was so offended at the magistrate who thus sold his vote, that he never after spoke to him.*

The late Robert Rutherford, Esq. opened the first store ever established in Winchester. There was soon a mixed population of Germans, Irish, and a few English and Scotch. The national prejudices which existed between the Dutch and Irish produced much disorder and many riots. It was customary for the Dutch, on St. Patrick's day, to exhibit the effigy of the saint, with a string of Irish potatoes around his neck, and his wife Sheeley, with her apron loaded also with potatoes. This was always followed by a riot. The Irish resented the indignity offered to their saint and his holy spouse, and a battle followed. On St. Michael's day the Irish would retort, and exhibit the saint with a rope of *"sour krout"* about his neck. Then the Dutch, like the Yankee, *"felt chock full of fight,'* and at it they went, pell mell, and many a black eye, bloody nose, and broken head, was the result.† The author recollects one of these riots since the war of the revolution. The practice was at last put down by the rigor with which our courts of justice punished the rioters.

In the month of September, 1758, the town of Stephensburg, in the county of Frederick, was established. This town was first founded by Peter Stephens, who came to Virginia with Joist Hite, in the year 1732. The ruins of Stephens's first cabin are yet to be seen. Lewis Stephens, the late proprietor of the town, was the son of Peter Stephens. He laid out the town in form, and applied to the general assembly to have it established by law, which was done in the year 1758.

This town was first settled almost exclusively by Germans; and the religion, habits and customs, of their ancestors, were preserved with great tenacity for many years. The German language was generally used in this village since the author's acquaintance with it, which acquaintance commenced in the year 1784.

In the month of November, 1761, Strasburg, (commonly called Stover's town,) was established by law. This town was settled entirely by

---

*The late John S. Woodcock, Esq. communicated this fact to the author, and stated that he had the information from the late Col. Martin.

†Gen. Smith informed the author that this practice was kept up for several years after he settled in Winchester, and that several very dangerous riots took place, in which he with other magistrates had to interpose, to preserve the peace.

Germans, and to this day the German language is in general use, though the English language is now generally understood, and also spoken by the inhabitants. It was laid off by Peter Stover.

Staunton, in the county of Augusta, was laid off by William Beverly, Esq. and established by act of the general assembly in November, 1761. The first settlers were principally Irish.

In March, 1761, Woodstock, then in the county of Frederick, was established by law. Jacob Miller laid off twelve hundred acres of land, ninety-six of which were divided into half acre lots, making one hundred and ninety-two building lots—the remainder into streets and five acre lots, commonly called out lots. This town appears to have been originally laid out upon a larger scale than any of our ancient villages. Like the most of our towns it was settled exclusively by Germans, and their religion, customs, habits, manners and language, were for a long time preserved, and to this day the German language is generally in use by the inhabitants.

Mecklenburg (Shepherdstown,) then in the county of Frederick, now in Jefferson, was established by law in the month of November, 1762.— This village is situated immediately on the bank of the Cohongoroota (Potomac) about twelve miles above Harpers-Ferry. It was laid off by the late Capt. Thomas Shepherd, and was first settled chiefly by German mechanics. It is remarkable for its being the place where *the first steam boat was ever constructed in the world.* Mr. James Rumsey, in the year 1788, built a boat, which was propelled by steam against a brisk current. There are some of the remnants of the machinery now to be seen, in the possession of Capt. Haines, in that place.

Romney, in the county of Hampshire, was laid off by the late lord Fairfax, and established by law in the month of November, 1762. His lordship laid off fifty acres into streets and half acre lots ; but the town improved but slowly. It does not contain more than fifty families at this time. It is nevertheless a place of considerable business ; has a bank, printing office, several stores and taverns. The new Parkersburg turnpike road passes through it, which will doubtless, when completed, give it many great advantages.

In February, 1772, Fincastle, in the county of Botetourt, was established. Israel Christian made a present of forty acres of land to the justices of Botetourt court, for the use of the county. The court laid off the said forty acres of land into lots, and applied to the legislature to have the town established by law, which was done accordingly.

In October, 1776, first year of the commonwealth, the town of Bath, at the warm springs, in the county of Berkeley, (now the seat of justice for Morgan county,) was established, and laid off by act of assembly.

Preamble. "Whereas it hath been represented to this general assembly, that the laying off fifty acres of land in lots and streets for a town at the warm springs, in the county of Berkeley, will be of great utility, by encouraging the purchasers thereof to build convenient houses for accommodating numbers of infirm persons, who frequent those springs yearly for the recovery of their health ; Be it enacted, &c. that fifty acres of land adjoining the said springs, being part of a larger tract of land, the property of the right honorable Thomas lord Fairfax, or other person or persons holding the same by a grant or conveyance from him, be and the same is hereby vested in Bryan Fairfax, Thomas Bryan Martin, Warner Washington, the Reverend Charles Mynn Thruston, Robert Rutherford, Thomas Rutherford, Alexander White, Philip Pendleton, Samuel Washington, William Ellzey, Van Swearingen, Thomas Hite, James Edmundson, and James Nourse, gentlemen, trustees, to be by them, or any seven of them, laid out into lots of one quarter of an acre each, with convenient streets, which shall be and the same is hereby established a town, by the name of Bath."

The author has been the more particular in making the foregoing extract from the act of the legislature, because this appears to be the first instance under our republican government in which the legislature took the authority of establishing and laying out a town upon the land of private individuals, without the consent of the owner of the land. It is possible lord Fairfax assented to the laying off of this town ; but if he did, there is nothing in the language of the act which goes to show it.

In the month of October, 1777, Lexington, in the county of Rockbridge, was established. Extract from the law: "And be it further enacted, that at the place which shall be appointed for holding courts in the said county of Rockbridge, there shall be laid off a town, to be called Lexington, thirteen hundred feet in length and nine hundred in width.*— And in order to make satisfaction to the proprietors of the said land, the clerk of the said county shall, by order of the justices, issue a writ directed to the sheriff, commanding him to summon twelve able and disinterested freeholders, to meet on the said land on a certain day, not under five nor over ten days from the date, who shall upon oath value the said land, in so many parcels as there shall be separate owners, which valuation the sheriff shall return, under the hands and seals of the said jurors, to the clerk's office ; and the justices, at laying their first county levy, shall make provision for paying the said proprietors their respective proportions thereof; and the property of the said land, on the return of the said valuation, shall be vested in the justices and their successors, one acre thereof to be reserved for the use of the said county, and the residue to be sold and conveyed by the said justices to any persons, and the money arising from such sale to be applied towards lessening the county levy: and the public buildings for the said county shall be erected on the land reserved as aforesaid." From this it appears that the name of the town was fixed by law before the site is marked out.

Moorefield was also established in the month of October, 1777, in the county of Hampshire, now the seat of justice for the county of Hardy.— Extract from the act of assembly : "Whereas it hath been represented to this present general assembly, that the establishing a town on the lands of Conrad Moore in the county of Hampshire, would be of great advantage to the inhabitants, by encouraging tradesmen to settle amongst them ; Be it therefore enacted, &c. that sixty-two acres of land belonging to the said Conrad Moore, in the most convenient place for a town,

---

*This was truly upon a small scale.

Be, and the same is hereby vested in Garret Vanmeter, Abel Randall, Moses Hutton, Jacob Read, Jonathan Meath, Daniel M'Neil, and George Rennoek, gentlemen, trustees, to be by them, or any four of them, laid out into lots of half an acre each, with convenient streets, which shall be and the same is hereby established a town, by the name of Moorefield."

Martinsburg was established in the month of October, 1778. Extract from the law : " Whereas it hath been represented to this present general assembly, that Adam Stephen, Esq. hath lately laid off one hundred and thirty acres of land in the county of Berkeley, where the court house now stands, in lots and streets for a town, &c.; Be it enacted, &c. that the said one hundred and thirty acres of land laid out into lots and streets, agreeable to a plan and survey thereof made, containing the number of two hundred and sixty-nine lots, as, by the said plan and survey, relation thereunto being had, may more fully appear, be and the same is hereby vested in James M'Alister, Joseph Mitchell, Anthony Noble, Jas. Strode, Robert Carter Willis, William Patterson and Philip Pendleton, gentlemen, trustees, and shall be established a town by the name of Martinsburg." This town was named after the late Col. T. B. Martin.

Tradition relates that an animated contest took place between the late Gen. Adam Stephen and Jacob Hite, Esq.; in relation to fixing the seat of justice for this county ; Hite contending for the location thereof on his own land, at what is now called Leetown, in the county of Jefferson, Stephen advocating Martinsburg. Stephen prevailed, and Hite became so disgusted and dissatisfied, that he sold out his fine estate, and removed to the frontier of South Carolina. Fatal remove ! He had not been long settled in that state, before the Indians murdered him and several of his family in the most shocking and barbarous manner.* It is said that the evening before this bloody massacre took place, an Indian squaw, who was much attached to Mrs. Hite,† called on her and warned her of the intended massacre, and advised her to remove with her little children to a place of safety. Mrs. Hite immediately communicated this intelligence to her husband, who disbelieved the information, observing, "the Indians were too much attached to him to do him any injury." The next morning, however, when it was fatally too late to escape, a party of Indians, armed and painted in their usual war dress, called on Hite, and told him they had determined to kill him. It was in vain that he pleaded his friendship for them, and the many services he had rendered their nation : their fell purpose was fixed, and nothing could appease them but his blood, and that of his innocent, unoffending and helpless wife and children. They commenced their operations by the most cruel tortures upon Mr. Hite, cutting him to pieces, a joint at a time ; and whilst he was thus in the most violent agonies, they barbarously murdered his wife and several

*Col. James Hite, of Jefferson county, related this tradition to the author.

†Mrs. Hite was the sister of the late Col. J. Madison, of Orange county, Virginia, and of course aunt to ex-president Madison.

V

of her little offspring. After Mr. Hite, his wife, and several of the children were dispatched, they took two of his daughters, not quite grown, and all his slaves as prisoners. They also carried off what plunder they chose, and their booty was considerable.

Mr. Hite kept a large retail store, and dealt largely with the Creek and Cherokee tribes. It is said a man by the name of Parish, who went to Carolina with Hite, and to whom Hite had been very friendly, growing jealous of Hite's popularity with the Indians, instigated the savages to commit the murder. About the year 1784 or 1785, the author saw the late Capt. George Hite, (who had been an officer in the revolutionary army,) and who had just returned from an unsuccessful search after his two young sisters, who were taken captives at the time of the murder of his father. He had traversed a great part of the southern country, among the various tribes of Indians, but never could hear any thing of them. Capt. Hite, some short time after the war of the revolution, recovered a part of his father's slaves, who had been taken off by the Indians, one of whom is now owned by Maj. Isaac Hite, of Frederick county. This woman brought home an Indian son, whom the author has frequently seen, and who had all the features of an Indian. A part of Hite's slaves are to this day remaining with the Indians, and are kept in rigorous slavery. In the winter of 1815–16, the author fell in with Col. William Triplett, of Wilkes county, Georgia, who informed him, that in the autumn of the year 1809 he was traveling through the Creek country, and saw an old negro man who told him he was one of Jacob Hite's slaves, taken when his master and family were murdered in South Carolina. He further informed Col. Triplett, that there were then sixty negroes in possession of the Indians, descended from slaves taken from Hite, the greater number of whom were claimed by the little Tallapoosa king.

In October, 1778, the town of Abingdon was established in Washington county.

In the month of May, 1780, the town of Harrisonburg, in the county of Rockingham, was established. It appears that Mr. Thomas Harrison had laid off fifty acres of his land into lots and streets, and the legislature simply confirmed what Mr. Harrison had done, without appointing trustees for the town, as was the usual practice. The privileges, however, granted by law to the citizens of other incorporated towns, were given to the inhabitants of Harrisonburg.

In the month of October, 1782, the town of Lewisburg, in the county of Greenbrier, was established. The act of assembly appropriates forty acres of land at the court house, to be laid off into half acre lots and streets. Samuel Lewis, James Reid, Samuel Brown, Andrew Donnelly, John Stuart, Archer Matthews, William Ward, and Thomas Edgar, gentlemen, were appointed trustees.

In October, 1785, Clarksburg, in the county of Harrison, was established. Wm. Haymond, Nicholas Carpinert, John Myers, John M'Ally, and John Davison, gentlemen, were appointed trustees.

In the same month and year, Morgantown, in the county of Monongalia, was established. The act appropriates fifty acres of land, the property of Zackquell Morgan, to be laid off into lots and streets for a town: Samuel Hanway, John Evans, David Scott, Michael Kearnes, and James Daugherty, trustees.

In October, 1786, Charlestown, in the county of Berkeley, (now the seat of justice for the county of Jefferson,) was established. This town was laid off by the late Col. Charles Washington, a brother to the illustrious Gen. George Washington, on his own land. Eighty acres were divided into lots and streets; and John Augustine Washington, William Drake, Robert Rutherford, James Crane, Cato Moore, Magnus Tate, Benjamin Rankin, Thornton Washington, Wm. Little, Alexander White, and Richard Ranson, were appointed trustees. This town bears the christian name of its proprietor.

In the year 1787, Frankfort, in Hampshire county, was established. One hundred and thirty-nine acres of land was laid off into lots and streets, with out-lots, by John Sellers. John Mitchell, Andrew Cooper, Ralph Humphreys, John Williams, sen., James Clark, Richard Stafford, Hezekiah Whiteman, and Jacob Brookhart, trustees.

In the month of October, 1787, the town of West-Liberty, in the county of Ohio, was established. Sixty acres of land was laid off into lots and streets by Reuben Foreman and Providence Mounts. Moses Chapline, George M'Cullough, Charles Willis, Van Swearingen, Zachariah Sprigg, James Mitchell, and Benjamin Briggs, were appointed trustees.

In the same month and year, Middletown, in the county of Berkeley, (commonly called Gerrardstown,) was established. This town was laid off by the late Rev. Mr. David Gerrard, and contained one hundred lots. William Henshaw, James Haw, John Gray, Gilbert M'Kewan, and Robt. Allen, were appointed trustees.

The same year and month, the town of Watson, (commonly called Capon Springs,) in the county of Hampshire, was established—twenty acres of land to be laid off in lots and streets. Elias Poston, Henry Fry, Isaac Hawk, Jacob Hoover, John Winterton, Valentine Swisher, Rudolph Bumgarner, Paul M'Ivor, John Sherman Woodcock, and Isaac Zane, gentlemen, trustees.

In 1788, Front Royal was established, in the county of Frederick. Fifty acres of land, the property of Solomon Vanmeter, James Moore, Robert Haines, William Cunningham, Peter Halley, John Smith, Allen Wiley, Original Wroe, George Chick, William Morris, and Henry Trout, was laid out into lots and streets; and Thomas Allen, Robert Russell, William Headly, William Jennings, John Hickman, Thomas Hand, and Thomas Buck, gentlemen, trustees.

The same year and month, Pattonsburg, in the county of Botetourt, on James river, was established. Crowsville, in Botetourt, was established at the same time.

In 1790, Beverly was laid off and established a town at Randolph court-house.

Frontville, at the Sweet Springs, and Springfield, in the county of Hampshire, were severally laid off and established in October, 1790.

In October, 1791, Darksville in Berkeley, Keisletown in Rockingham, and Charlestown in Ohio, were severally established. This concludes the author's account of the establishment of the various towns west of the Blue ridge, within the present western limits of Virginia, from the earliest settlement of the country to the year 1792 inclusive.

This history of the establishment of the towns in Western Virginia, from the earliest settlement of the country, to the year 1792 inclusive, is gathered from Hening's Statutes at Large, which brings the acts of the legislature no further than that period. To continue the list to the present time, would require an examination of the various session acts since 1792, which it would be difficult to obtain, perhaps, except in Richmond, to which place it would not suit the author's present convenience to make a journey. As he confidently anticipates a demand for a second edition of this work, he will in the mean time make perfect this portion of the history of our country for future insertion.

NOTES

ON THE SETTLEMENT AND INDIAN WARS

OF THE

WESTERN PARTS OF VIRGINIA AND PENNSYLVANIA,

From the year 1763 until the year 1783 inclusive.

TOGETHER WITH

A VIEW OF THE STATE OF SOCIETY AND MANNERS OF THE FIRST SETTLERS OF THAT COUNTRY.

BY THE REV. DR. JOSEPH DODDRIDGE.

NOTES, &c.

——:o:——

CHAPTER I.

PRELIMINARY OBSERVATIONS ON THE CHARACTER OF THE INDIAN MODE OF WARFARE, AND ITS ADOPTION BY THE WHITE PEOPLE.

THIS is a subject which presents human nature in its most revolting features, as subject to a vindictive spirit of revenge, and a thirst of human blood, leading to an indiscriminate slaughter of all ranks, ages and sexes, by the weapons of war, or by torture.

The history of man is, for the most part, one continued detail of bloodshed, battles and devastations. War has been, from the earliest periods of history, the almost constant employment of individuals, clans, tribes and nations. Fame, one of the most potent objects of human ambition, has at all times been the delusive, but costly reward of military achievement. The triumph of conquest, the epithet of greatness, the throne and the sceptre, have uniformly been purchased by the conflict of battle and garments rolled in blood.

If the modern European laws of warfare have softened in some degree the horrid features of national conflicts, by respecting the rights of private property, and extending humanity to the sick, wounded and prisoners; we ought to reflect that this amelioration is the effect of civilization only. The natural state of war knows no such mixture of mercy with cruelty. In his primitive state, man knows no object in his wars, but that of the extermination of his enemies, either by death or captivity.

The wars of the Jews were exterminatory in their object. The destruction of a whole nation was often the result of a single campaign. Even the beasts themselves were sometimes included in the general massacre.

The present war between the Greeks and Turks is a war upon the ancient model—a war of utter extermination.

It is, to be sure, much to be regretted, that our people so often followed the cruel examples of the Indians, in the slaughter of prisoners,

and sometimes women and children: yet let them receive a candid hearing at the bar of reason and justice, before they are condemned as barbarians, equally with the Indians themselves.

History scarcely presents an example of a civilized nation carrying on
a war with barbarians without adopting the mode of warfare of the barbarous nation.   The ferocious Suwarrow, when at war with the Turks,
was as much of a savage as the Turks themselves.   His slaughters were
as indiscriminate as theirs; but during his wars against the French, in
Italy, he faithfully observed the laws of civilized warfare.

Were the Greeks now at war with a civilized nation, we should hear
nothing of the barbarities which they have committed on the Turks; but
being at war with barbarians, the principle of self defence compels them
to retaliate on the Turks the barbarities which they commit on them.

In the last rebellion in Ireland, that of the United Irishmen, the government party were not much behind the rebels in acts of lawless cruelty.
It was not by the hands of the executioner alone they perished. Summary justice, as it was called, was sometimes inflicted. How many
perished under the torturing scourge of the drummer for the purpose of
extorting confessions!   These extra-judicial executions were attempted
to be justified on the ground of the necessity of the case.

Our revolutionary war has a double aspect: on the one hand we carried on a war with the English, in which we observed the maxims of
civilized warfare with the utmost strictness; but the brave, the potent,
the magnanimous nation of our forefathers had associated with themselves, as auxiliaries, the murderous tomahawk and scalping knife of the
Indian nations around our defenseless frontiers, leaving those barbarous
sons of the forest to their own savage mode of warfare, to the full indulgence of all their native thirst for human blood.

On them, then, be the blame of all the horrid features of this war between civilized and savage men, in which the former was compelled, by
every principle of self defense, to adopt the Indian mode of warfare, in
all its revolting and destructive features.

Were those who were engaged in the war against the Indians, less
humane than those who carried on the war against their English allies?
No, they were not.   Both parties carried on the war on the same principle of reciprocity of advantages and disadvantages.   For example, the
English and Americans take each one thousand prisoners: they are exchanged: neither army is weakened by this arrangement.   A sacrifice is
indeed made to humanity, in the expense of taking care of the sick,
wounded and prisoners; but this expense is mutual.   No disadvantages
result from all the clemency of modern warfare, excepting an augmenta-
tion of the expenses of war.   In this mode of warfare, those of the nation,
not in arms, are safe from death by the hands of soldiers.   No civilized
warrior dishonors his sword with the blood of helpless infancy, old age,
or that of the fair sex.   He aims his blows only at those whom he finds
in arms against him.   The Indian kills indiscriminately.   His object is
the total extermination of his enemies.   Children are victims of his vengeance, because, if males, they may hereafter become warriors, or if
females, they may become mothers.   Even the fetal state is criminal in

his view. It is not enough that the fetus should perish with the murdered mother; it is torn from her pregnant womb, and elevated on a stick or pole, as a trophy of victory and an object of horror to the survivors of the slain.

If the Indian takes prisoners, mercy has but little concern in the transaction. He spares the lives of those who fall into his hands, for the purpose of feasting the feelings of ferocious vengeance of himself and his comrades, by the torture of his captive; or to increase the strength of his nation by his adoption into an Indian family; or for the purpose of gain, by selling him for an higher price, than his scalp would fetch, to his christian allies of Canada; for be it known that those allies were in the constant practice of making presents for scalps and prisoners, as well as furnishing the means for carrying on the Indian war, which for so many years desolated our defenseless frontiers. No lustration can ever wash out this national stain. The foul blot must remain, as long as the page of history shall convey the record of the foul transaction to future generations.

The author would not open wounds which have, alas! already bled so long, but for the purpose of doing justice to the memory of his forefathers and relatives, many of whom perished in the defense of their country, by the hands of the merciless Indians.

How is a war of extermination, and accompanied with such acts of atrocious cruelty, to be met by those on whom it is inflicted? Must it be met by the lenient maxims of civilized warfare? Must the Indian captive be spared his life? What advantage would be gained by this course? The young white prisoners, adopted into Indian families, often become complete Indians; but in how few instances did ever an Indian become civilized. Send a cartel for an exchange of prisoners; the Indians know nothing of this measure of clemency in war; the bearer of the white flag for the purpose of effecting the exchange would have exerted his humanity at the forfeit of his life.

Should my countrymen be still charged with barbarism, in the prosecution of the Indian war, let him who harbors this unfavorable impression concerning them, portray in imagination the horrid scenes of slaughter, which frequently met their view in the course of the Indian war. Let him, if he can bear the reflection, look at helpless infancy, virgin beauty, and hoary age, dishonored by the ghastly wounds of the tomahawk and scalping knife of the savage. Let him hear the shrieks of the victims of the Indian torture by fire, and smell the surrounding air, rendered sickening by the effluvia of their burning flesh and blood. Let him hear the yells, and view the hellish features of the surrounding circle of savage warriors, rioting in all the luxuriance of vengeance, while applying the flaming torches to the parched limbs of the sufferers, and then suppose those murdered infants, matrons, virgins and victims of torture, were his friends and relations, the wife, sister, child or brother; what would be his feelings! After a short season of grief, he would say, "I will now think only of revenge."

Philosophy shudders at the destructive aspect of war in any shape:

christianity, by teaching the religion of the good Samaritan, altogether forbids it: but the original settlers of the western regions, like the greater part of the world, were neither philosophers nor saints. They were "men of like passions with others;" and therefore adopted the Indian mode of warfare from necessity and a motive of revenge; with the exception of burning their captives alive, which they never did. If the bodies of savage enemies were sometimes burned, it was not until after they were dead.

Let the voice of nature and the law of nations plead in favor of the veteran pioneers of the desert regions of the west. War has hitherto been a prominent trait in the moral system of human nature, and will continue such, until a radical change shall be effected in favor of science, morals and piety, on a general scale.

In the conflicts of nations, as well as those of individuals, no advantages are to be conceded. If mercy may be associated with the carnage and devastations of war, that mercy must be reciprocal; but a war of utter extermination must be met by a war of the same character, or by an overwhelming force which may put on end to it, without a sacrifice of the helpless and unoffending part of the hostile nation. Such a force was not at the command of the first inhabitants of this country. The sequel of the Indian war goes to show that in a war with savages the choice lies between extermination and subjugation. Our government has wisely and humanely pursued the latter course.

Tho author begs to be understood that the foregoing observations are not intended as a justification of the whole of the transactions of our people with regard to the Indians during the course of the war. Some instances of acts of wanton barbarity occurred on our side, which have received and must continue to receive the unequivocal reprobation of all the civilised world. In the course of this history, it will appear that more deeds of wanton barbarity took place on our side than the world is now acquainted with.

CHAPTER II.

——:0:——

THE treaty of peace between his British majesty and the kings of France, Spain and Portugal, concluded at Paris on the 10th of February, 1763, did not put an end to the Indian war against the frontier parts and back settlements of the colonies of Great Britain.

The spring and summer of 1763, as well as those of 1764, deserve to be memorable in history, for the great extent and destructive results of a war of extermination, carried on by the united force of all the Indian nations of the western country, along the shore of the northern lakes, and throughout the whole extent of the frontier settlements of Pennsylvania, Virginia and North Carolina.

The events of this war, as they relate to the frontier of Pennsylvania and the shores of the lakes, are matters of history already, and therefore shall be no farther related here than is necessary to give a connected view of the military events of those disastrous seasons. The massacres by the Indians in the southwestern part of Virginia, so far as they have come to the knowledge of the author, shall be related more in detail.

The English historians (Hist. of England, vol. x. p. 399,) attribute this terrible war to the influence of the French Jesuits over the Indians; but whether with much truth and candor, is, to say the least of it, extremely doubtful.

The peace of 1763, by which the provinces of Canada were ceded to Britain, was offensive to the Indians, especially as they very well knew that the English government, on the ground of this treaty, claimed the jurisdiction of the western country generally; and as an Indian sees no difference between the right of jurisdiction and that of possession, they considered themselves as about to be dispossessed of the whole of their country, as rapidly as the English might find it convenient to take possession of it. In this opinion they were confirmed by the building of forts on the Susquehanna, on lands to which the Indians laid claim. The forts and posts of Pittsburg, Bedford, Ligonier, Niagara, Detroit, Presque Isle, St. Joseph and Michilimackinac, were either built, or improved and strengthened, with additions to their garrisons. Thus the Indians saw themselves surrounded on the north and east by a strong line of forts, while those of Bedford, Ligonier and Pittsburg, threatened an extension of them into the heart of their country. Thus circumstanced, the aboriginals of the country had to choose between the prospect of being driven to the inhospitable regions of the north and west, of negotiating with the British government for continuance of the possession of their own land, or of taking up arms for its defense. They chose the lat

ter course, in which a view of the smallness of their numbers, and the
scantiness of their resources, ought to have taught them, that although
they might do much mischief, they could not ultimately succeed; but the
Indians, as well as their brethren of the white skin, are often driven by
their impetuous passions to rash and destructive enterprises, which reason, were it permitted to give it counsels, would disapprove.

The plan resolved on by the Indians for the prosecution of the war,
was that of a general massacre of all the inhabitants of the English settlements in the western country, as well as of those on the lands on the
Susquehanna, to which they laid claim.

Never did military commanders of any nation display more skill, or
their troops more steady and determined bravery, than did those red men
of the wilderness in the prosecution of their gigantic plan for the recovery
of their country from the possession of the English. It was indeed a war
of utter extermination on an extensive scale,—a conflict which exhibited
human nature in its native state, in which the cunning of the fox is associated with the cruelty of the tiger. We read the history of this war with
feelings of the deepest horror; but why? On the part of the savages,
theirs was the ancient mode of warfare, in which there was nothing of
mercy. If science, associated with the benign influence of the christian
system, has limited the carnage of war to those in arms, so as to give the
right of life and hospitality to women, infancy, old age, the sick, wounded
and prisoners, may not a farther extension of the influence of those powerful but salutary agents put an end to war altogether? May not future
generations read the history of our civilized warfare with equal horror and
wonder, that with our science and piety we had wars at all!

The English traders among the Indians were the first victims in this
contest. Out of one hundred and twenty of them, among the different
nations, only two or three escaped being murdered. The forts of Presque
Isle, St. Joseph and Michilimackinac were taken, with a general slaughter of their garrisons.

The fortresses of Bedford, Ligonier, Niagara, Detroit and Pitt, were
with difficulty preserved from being taken.

It was a principal object with the Indians to get possession of Detroit
and Fort Pitt, either by assault or famine. The former was attempted
with regard to Detroit. Fort Pitt, being at a considerable distance from
the settlements, where alone supplies could be obtained, determined the
savages to attempt its reduction by famine.

In their first attempt on Fort Detroit, the Indians calculated on taking
possession of it by stratagem. A large number of Indians appeared before the place under pretence of holding a congress with Maj. Gladwin,
the commandant. He was on his guard and refused them admittance.
On the next day, about five hundred more of the Indians arrived in arms,
and demanded leave to go into the fort, to hold a treaty. The commandant refused to admit a greater number than forty The Indians understood his design of detaining them as hostages, for the good conduct of
their comrades on the outside of the fort, and therefore did not send them
into the place. The whole number of men in the fort and on board two
vessels of war in the river, did not exceed one hundred and ten or twelve;

but by means of the cannon they possessed, they made shift to keep the Indians at a distance, and convince them that they could not take the place. When the Indians were about to retire, Capt. Dalyel arrived at the fort with a considerable reinforcement for the relief of the place. He made a sortie against the breastworks which the Indians had thrown up, with two hundred and forty-five men. This detachment was driven back with the loss of seventy men killed and forty-two wounded. Capt. Dalyel was among the slain. Of one hundred men who were escorting a large quantity of provisions to Detroit, sixty-seven were massacred.

Fort Pitt had been invested for some time, before Capt Ecayer had the least prospect of relief. In this situation he and his garrison had resolved to stand it out to the last extremity, and even perish of famine, rather than fall into the hands of the savages, notwithstanding the fort was a bad one, the garrison weak, and the country between the fort and Ligonier in possession of the savages, and his messengers killed or compelled to return back. In this situation, Col. Bouquet was sent by Gen Amhurst to the relief of the place, with a large quantity of provisions under a strong escort. This escort was attacked by a large body of Indians, in a narrow defile on Turtle creek, and would have been entirely defeated, had it not been for a successful stratagem employed by the commander for extricating themselves from the savage army. After sustaining a furious contest from one o'clock till night, and for several hours the next morning, a retreat was pretended, with a view to draw the Indians into a close engagement. Previous to this movement, four companies of infantry and grenadiers were placed in ambuscade. The plan succeeded. When the retreat commenced, the Indians thought themselves secure of victory, and pressing forward with great vigor, fell into the ambuscade, and were dispersed with great slaughter. The loss on the side of the English was above one hundred killed and wounded; that of the Indians could not have been less. The loss was severely felt by the Indians, as in addition to the number of warriors who fell in the engagement, several of the most distinguished chiefs were among the slain. Fort Pitt, the reduction of which they had much at heart, was now placed out of their reach, by being effectually relieved and supplied with the munitions of war.

The historian of the western region of our country cannot help regarding Pittsburg, the present flourishing emporium of the northern part of that region, and its immediate neighborhood, as classic ground, on account of the memorable battles which took place for its possession in the infancy of our settlements. Braddock's defeat, Maj. Grant's defeat, its conquest by Gen. Forbes, the victory over the Indians above related by Maj. Bouquet, serve to show the importance in which this post was held in early times, and that it was obtained and supported by the English government, at the price of no small amount of blood and treasure. In the neighborhood of this place, as well as in the war-worn regions of the old world, the plowshare of the farmer turns up from beneath the surface of the earth, the broken and rusty implements of war, and the bones of the slain in battle.

It was in the course of this war that the dreadful massacre at Wyoming

took place, and desolated the fine settlements of the New-England peo‑
ple along the Susquehanna.

The extensive and indiscriminate slaughter of both sexes and all ages
by the Indians, at Wyoming and other places, so exasperated a large
number of men, denominated the "Paxton boys," that they rivalled the
most ferocious of the Indians themselves in deeds of cruelty, which have
dishonored the history of our country, by the record of the shedding of
innocent blood without the slightest provocation—deeds of the most atro‑
cious barbarity.

The Conestoga Indians had lived in peace for more than a century in
the neighborhood of Lancaster, Pa. Their number did not exceed forty.
Against these unoffending descendants of the first friends of the famous
William Penn, the Paxton boys first directed their more than savage ven‑
geance. Fifty-seven of them, in military array, poured into their little
village, and instantly murdered all whom they found at home, to the
number of fourteen men, women and children. Those of them who did
not happen to be at home at the massacre, were lodged in the jail of
Lancaster for safety. But alas! this precaution was unavailing. The
Paxton boys broke open the jail door, and murdered the whole of them,
in number about fifteen to twenty. It was in vain that these poor de‑
fenseless people protested their innocence and begged for mercy on their
knees. Blood was the order of the day with those ferocious Paxton
boys. The death of the victims of their cruelties did not satisfy their
rage for slaughter; they mangled the dead bodies of the Indians with
their scalping knives and tomahawks in the most shocking and brutal
manner, scalping even the children and chopping off the hands and feet
of most of them.

The next object of those Paxton boys was the murder of the christian
Indians of the villages of Wequetank and Nain. From the execution
of this infernal design they were prevented by the humane interference of
the government of Pennsylvania, which removed the inhabitants of both
places under a strong guard to Philadelphia for protection. They re‑
mained under guard from November, 1763, until the close of the war in
December, 1764: the greater part of this time they occupied the barracks
of that city. The Paxton boys twice assembled in great force, at no
great distance from the city, with a view to assault the barracks and mur‑
der the Indians; but owing to the military preparations made for their re‑
ception, they at last reluctantly desisted from the enterprise.

While we read, with feelings of the deepest horror, the record of the
murders which have at different periods been inflicted on the unoffending
christian Indians of the Moravian profession, it is some consolation to
reflect, that our government has had no participation in those murders;
but on the contrary, has at all times afforded them all the protection which
circumstances allowed.

The principal settlements in Greenbrier were those of Muddy Creek
and the Big Levels, distant about fifteen or twenty miles from each other.
Before these settlers were aware of the existence of the war, and suppo‑
sing that the peace made with the French comprehended their Indian
allies also, about sixty Indians visited the settlement on Muddy Creek.

They made the visit under the mask of friendship. They were cordially received and treated with all the hospitality which it was in the power of these new settlers to bestow upon them; but on a sudden, and without any previous intimation of any thing like an hostile intention, the Indians murdered, in cold blood, all the men belonging to the settlement, and made prisoners of the women and children.

Leaving a guard with their prisoners, they then marched to the settlements in the Levels, before the fate of the Muddy Creek settlement was known. Here, as at Muddy Creek, they were treated with the most kind and attentive hospitality, at the house of Archibald Glendennin, who gave the Indians a sumptuous feast of three fat elks, which he had recently killed. Here a scene of slaughter, similar to that which had recently taken place at Muddy Creek, occurred at the conclusion of the feast. It commenced with an old woman, who having a very sore leg, showed it to an Indian, desiring his advice how she might cure it. This request he answered with a blow of the tomahawk, which instantly killed her. In a few minutes all the men belonging to the place shared the same fate. The women and children were made prisoners.

In the time of the slaughter, a negro woman at the spring near the house where it happened, killed her own child for fear it should fall into the hands of the Indians, or hinder her from making her escape.

Mrs. Glendennin, whose husband was among the slain, and herself with her children prisoners, boldly charged the Indians with perfidy and cowardice, in taking advantage of the mask of friendship to commit murder. One of the Indians exasperated at her boldness, and stung, no doubt, at the justice of her charge against them, brandished his tomahawk over her head, and dashed her husband's scalp in her face. In defiance of all his threats, the heroine still reiterated the charges of perfidy and cowardice against the Indians.

On the next day, after marching about ten miles, while passing through a thicket, the Indians forming a front and rear guard, Mrs. Glendennin gave her infant to a neighbor woman, stepped into the bushes without being perceived by the Indians, and made her escape. The cries of the child made the Indians inquire for the mother. She was not to be found. "Well," says one of them, "I will soon bring the cow to her calf;" and taking the child by the feet, beat its brains out against a tree. Mrs. Glendennin returned home in the course of the succeeding night, and covered the corpse of her husband with fence rails. Having performed this pious office for her murdered husband, she chose, as a place of safety, a cornfield, where, as she related, her heroic resolution was succeeded by a paroxysm of grief and despondency, during which she imagined she saw a man with the aspect of a murderer standing within a few steps of her. The reader of this narrative, instead of regarding this fit of despondency as a feminine weakness on the part of this daughter of affliction, will commiserate her situation of unparalleled destitution and distress. Alone, in the dead of night, the survivor of all the infant settlements of that district, while all her relatives and neighbors of both settlements were either prisoners or lying dead, dishonored by ghastly wounds of the tomahawk and scalping knife of the savages, her husband and her children amongst the slain.

It was some days before a force could be collected in the eastern part of Botetourt and the adjoining country for the purpose of burying the dead.

Of the events of this war, on the southwestern frontier of Virginia, and in the country of Holstein, the then western part of North Carolina, the author has not been informed, farther than that, on the part of the Indians, it was carried on with the greatest activity, and its course marked with many deeds of the most atrocious cruelty, until late in the year 1764, when a period was put to this sanguinary contest, by a treaty made with the Indian nations by Sir William Johnston, at the German Flats.

The perfidy and cruelties practiced by the Indians during the war of 1763 and 1764, occasioned the revolting and sanguinary character of the Indian wars which took place afterwards. The Indians had resolved on the total extermination of all the settlers of our north and southwestern frontiers, and being no longer under the control of their former allies, the French, they were at full liberty to exercise all their native ferocity, and riot in the indulgence of their innate thirst for blood.

[Next follows, in Dr. Doddrige's work, his account of Dunmore's war, which the author of this history has transferred to the chapter under that head in the preceding pages. The chapter which follows relates to an event which occurred during that war.]

------:o:------

CHAPTER III.

THE DEATH OF CORNSTALK.

This was one of the most atrocious murders committed by the whites during the whole course of the war. [Dunmore's war.]

In the summer of 1777, when the confederacy of the Indian nations, under the influence of the British government, was formed, and began to commit hostilities along our frontier settlements, Cornstalk, and a young chief of the name of Red-hawk, with another Indian, made a visit to the garrison at the Point, commanded at that time by Capt. Arbuckle. Cornstalk stated to the captain, that, with the exception of himself and the tribe to which he belonged, all the nations had joined the English, and that unless protected by the whites, "they would have to run with the stream."

Capt. Arbuckle thought proper to detain the Cornstalk chief and his two companions as hostages for the good conduct of the tribe to which they belonged. They had not been long in this situation before a son of Cornstalk, concerned for the safety of his father, came to the opposite side of the river and hallooed; his father knowing his voice, answered him. He was brought over the river. The father and son mutually embraced each other with the greatest tenderness.

On the day following, two Indians, who had concealed themselves in the weeds on the bank of the Kanawha opposite the fort, killed a man of the name of Gilmore, as he was returning from hunting. As soon as the dead body was brought over the river, there was a general cry amongst the men who were present, "Let us kill the Indians in the fort." They immediately ascended the bank of the river with Capt. Hall at their head, to execute their hasty resolution. On their way they were met by Capt. Stuart and Capt. Arbuckle, who endeavored to dissuade them from killing the Indian hostages, saying that they certainly had no concern in the murder of Gilmore; but remonstrance was in vain. Pale as death with rage, they cocked their guns and threatened the captains with instant death, if they should attempt to hinder them from executing their purpose.

When the murderers arrived at the house where the hostages were confined, Cornstalk rose up to meet them at the door, but instantly received seven bullets through his body; his son and his other two fellow-hostages were instantly despatched with bullets and tomahawks.

Thus fell the Shawnee war chief Cornstalk, who, like Logan, his companion in arms, was conspicuous for intellectual talent, bravery and misfortune.

The biography of Cornstalk, as far as it is now known, goes to show that he was no way deficient in those mental endowments which constitute true greatness. On the evening preceding the battle of Point Pleasant, he proposed going over the river to the camp of Gen. Lewis, for the purpose of making peace. The majority in the council of warriors voted against the measure. "Well," said Cornstalk, "since you have resolved on fighting, you shall fight, although it is likely we shall have hard work to-morrow; but if any man shall attempt to run away from the battle, I will kill him with my own hand," and accordingly fulfilled his threat with regard to one cowardly fellow.

After the Indians had returned from the battle, Cornstalk called a council at the Chillicothe town, to consult what was to be done next. In this council he reminded the war chiefs of their folly in preventing him from making peace, before the fatal battle of Point Pleasant, and asked, "What shall we do now? The Long-knives are coming upon us by two routes. Shall we turn out and fight them?" All were silent. He then asked, "Shall we kill our squaws and children, and then fight until we shall all be killed ourselves?" To this no reply was made. He then rose up and struck his tomahawk in the war post in the middle of the council house, saying, "Since you are not inclined to fight, I will go and make peace;" and accordingly did so.

On the morning of the day of his death, a council was held in the fort at the Point, in which he was present. During the sitting of the council, it is said that he seemed to have a presentiment of his approaching fate. In one of his speeches, he remarked to the council, "When I was young, every time I went to war I thought it likely that I might return no more; but I still lived. I am now in your hands, and you may kill me if you choose. I can die but once, and it is alike to me whether I die now or at another time." When the men presented themselves before the door, for the purpose of killing the Indians, Cornstalk's son manifested signs of fear, on observing which, his father said, "Don't be afraid, my son; the Great Spirit sent you here to die with me, and we must submit to his will. It is all for the best."

------:o:------

CHAPTER IV.

WAPPATOMICA CAMPAIGN.

UNDER the command of Col. Angus M'Donald, four hundred men were collected from the western part of Virginia by the order of the earl of Dunmore, the then governor of Virginia. The place of rendezvous was Wheeling, some time in the month of June, 1774. They went down the river in boats and canoes to the mouth of Captina, from thence by the shortest route to Wappatomica town, about sixteen miles below the present Coshocton. The pilots were Jonathan Zane, Thomas Nicholson and Tady Kelly. About six miles from the town, the army were met by a party of Indians, to the number of forty or fifty, who gave a skirmish by the way of ambuscade, in which two of our men were killed and eight or nine wounded. One Indian was killed and several wounded. It was supposed that several more of them were killed, but they were carried off. When the army came to the town, it was found evacuated. The Indians had retreated to the opposite shore of the river, where they had formed an ambuscade, supposing the party would cross the river from the town. This was immediately discovered. The commanding officer then sent sentinels up and down the river, to give notice, in case the Indians should attempt to cross above or below the town. A private in the company of Capt. Cresap, of the name of John Harness, one of the sentinels below the town, displayed the skill of a backwoods sharpshooter. Seeing an Indian behind a blind across the river, raising up his head, at times, to look over the river, Harness charged his rifle with a second ball, and taking deliberate aim, passed both balls through the neck of the Indian. The Indians dragged off the body and buried it with the honors of war. It was found the next morning and scalped by Harness.

Soon after the town was taken, the Indians from the opposite shore

:sued for peace. The commander offered them peace on condition of their sending over their chiefs as hostages. Five of them came over the river and were put under guard as hostages. In the morning they were marched in front of the army over the river. When the party had reached the western bank of the Muskingum, the Indians represented that they could not make peace without the presence of the chiefs of the other towns: on which one of the chiefs was released to bring in the others. He did not return in the appointed time. Another chief was permitted to go on the same errand, who in like manner did not return. The party then moved up the river to the next town, which was about a mile above the first, and on the opposite shore. Here we had a slight skirmish with the Indians, in which one of them was killed and one of our men wounded. It was then discovered, that during all the time spent in the negotiation, the Indians were employed in removing their women and children, old people and effects, from the upper towns. The towns were burned and the corn cut up. The party then returned to the place from which they sat out, bringing with them the three remaining chiefs, who were sent to Williamsburg. They were released at the peace the succeeding fall.

The army were out of provisions before they left the towns, and had to subsist on weeds, one ear of corn each day, with a very scanty supply of game. The corn was obtained at one of the Indian towns.

———.0.———

CHAPTER V.

GEN. M'INTOSH'S CAMPAIGN.

In the spring of the year 1773, government having sent a small force of regular troops, under the command of Gen. M'Intosh, for the defense of the western frontier, the general, with the regulars and militia from Fort Pitt, descended the Ohio about thirty miles, and built Fort M'Intosh, on the site of the present Beaver town. The fort was made with strong stockades, furnished with bastions, and mounted with one 6-pounder. This station was well selected as a point for a small military force, always in readiness to pursue or intercept the war parties of Indians, who frequently made incursions into the settlements on the opposite side of the river in its immediate neighborhood. The fort was well garrisoned and supplied with provisions during the summer.

Sometime in the fall of the same year, Gen. M'Intosh received an order from government to make a campaign against the Sandusky towns. This order he attempted to obey with one thousand men; but owing to the delay in making necessary outfits for the expedition, the officers, on reaching Tuscarawa, thought it best to halt at that place, build and garrison a fort, and delay the farther prosecution of the campaign until the next spring. Accordingly they erected Fort Laurens on the bank of the Tuscarawa. Some time after the completion of the fort, the general returned with the army to Fort Pitt, leaving Col. John Gibson with a command of one hundred and fifty men to protect the fort until spring. The Indians were soon acquainted with the existence of the fort, and soon convinced our people, by sad experience, of the bad policy of building and attempting to hold a fort so far in advance of our settlements and other forts.

The first annoyance the garrison received from the Indians was some time in the month of January. In the night time they caught most of the horses belonging to the fort, and taking them off some distance into the woods, they took off their bells, and formed an ambuscade by the side of a path leading through the high grass of a prairie at a little distance from the fort. In the morning the Indians rattled the horse bells at the further end of the line of the ambuscade. The plan succeeded; a fatigue of sixteen men went out for the horses and fell into the snare. Fourteen were killed on the spot, two were taken prisoners, one of whom was given up at the close of the war, the other was never afterwards heard of.

Gen. Benjamin Biggs, then a captain in the fort, being officer of the day, requested leave of the colonel to go out with the fatigue party, which fell into the ambuscade. "No," said the colonel, "this fatigue party does not belong to a captain's command. When I shall have occasion to employ one of that number, I shall be thankful for your service; at present you must attend to your duty in the fort." On what trivial circumstances do life and death sometimes depend!

In the evening of the day of the ambuscade, the whole Indian army, in full war dress and painted, marched in single file through a prairie in view of the fort. Their number, as counted from one of the bastions, was eight hundred and forty-seven. They then took up their encampment on an elevated piece of ground at a small distance from the fort, on the opposite side of the river. From this camp they frequently held conversations with the people of our garrison. In these conversations, they seemed to deplore the long continuance of the war and hoped for peace; but were much exasperated at the Americans for attempting to penetrate so far into their country. This great body of Indians continued the investment of the fort, as long as they could obtain subsistence, which was about six weeks.

An old Indian by the name of John Thompson, who was with the American army in the fort, frequently went out among the Indians during their stay at their encampment, with the mutual consent of both parties. A short time before the Indians left the place, they sent word to Col. Gibson, by the old Indian, that they were desirous of peace, and that if he would send them a barrel of flour they would send in their proposals the next day; but although the colonel complied with their request, they marched off without fulfilling their engagement.

The commander, supposing the whole number of the Indians had gone off, gave permission to Col. Clark, of the Pennsylvania line, to escort the invalids, to the number of eleven or twelve, to Fort M'Intosh. The whole number of this detachment was fifteen. The wary Indians had left a party behind, for the purpose of doing mischief. These attacked this party of invalids and the escort, about two miles from their fort, and killed the whole of them with the exception of four, amongst whom was the captain, who ran back to the fort. On the same day a detachment went out from the fort, brought in the dead, and buried them with the honors of war, in front of the fort gate.

In three or four days after this disaster, a relief of seven hundred men, under Gen. M'Intosh, arrived at the fort with a supply of provisions, a great part of which was lost by an untoward accident. When the relief had reached within about one hundred yards of the fort, the garrison gave them a salute of a general discharge of musketry, at the report of which the pack horses took fright, broke loose and scattered the provisions in every direction through the woods, so that the greater part of them could never be recovered again.

Among other transactions which took place about this time, was that of gathering up the remains of the fourteen men for interment, who had fallen in the ambuscade during the winter, and which could not be done during the investment of the place by the Indians. They were found mostly devoured by the wolves. The fatigue party dug a pit large enough to contain the remains of all of them, and after depositing them in the pit, merely covering them with a little earth, with a view to have revenge on the wolves for devouring their companions, they covered the pit with slender sticks, rotten wood and bits of bark, not of sufficient strength to bear the weight of a wolf. On the top of this covering they placed a piece of meat, as a bait for the wolves. The next morning seven of them were found in the pit. They were shot and the pit filled up.

For about two weeks before the relief arrived, the garrison had been put on short allowance of half a pound of sour flour and an equal weight of stinking meat for every two days. The greater part of the last week, they had nothing to subsist on but such roots as they could find in the woods and prairies, and raw hides. Two men lost their lives by eating wild parsnip roots by mistake. Four more nearly shared the same fate, but were saved by medical aid.

On the evening of the arrival of the relief, two days' rations were issued to each man in the fort. These rations were intended as their allowance during their march to Fort M'Intosh; but many of the men, supposing them to have been back rations, ate up the whole of their allowance before the next morning. In consequence of this imprudence, in eating immoderately after such extreme starvation from the want of provisions, about forty of the men became faint and sick during the first day's march. On the second day, however, the sufferers were met by a great number of their friends from the settlements to which they belonged, by whom they were amply supplied with provisions, and thus saved from perishing.

Maj. Vernon, who succeeded Col. Gibson in the command of Fort Laurens, continued its possession until the next fall, when the garrison, after being, like their predecessors, reduced almost to starvation, evacuated the place.

Thus ended the disastrous business of Fort Laurens, in which much fatigue and suffering were endured and many lives lost, but without any beneficial result to the country.

——:o:——

CHAPTER VI.

THE MORAVIAN CAMPAIGN.

THIS ever memorable campaign took place in the month of March, 1782. The weather, during the greater part of the month of February, had been uncommonly fine, so that the war parties from Sandusky visited the settlements, and committed depredations earlier than usual. The family of a William Wallace, consisting of his wife and five or six children, were killed, and John Carpenter taken prisoner. These events took place in the latter part of February. The early period at which those fatal visitations of the Indians took place, led to the conclusion that the murderers were either Moravians, or that the warriors had had their winter quarters at their towns on the Muskingum. In either case, the Moravians being in fault, the safety of the frontier settlements required the destruction of their establishments at that place.

Accordingly, between eighty and ninety men were hastily collected together for the fatal enterprise. They rendezvoused and encamped the first night on the Mingo bottom, on the west side of the Ohio river. Each man furnished himself with his own arms, ammunition and provision. Many of them had horses. The second days march brought them within one mile of the middle Moravian town, where they encamped for the night. In the morning the men were divided into two equal parties, one of which was to cross the river about a mile above the town, their videttes having reported that there were Indians on both sides of the river. The other party was divided into three divisions, one of which was to take a circuit in the woods, and reach the river a little distance below the town, on the east side. Another division was to fall into the middle of the town, and the third at its upper end.

When the party which designed to make the attack on the west side had reached the river, they found no craft to take them over, but something like a canoe was seen on the opposite bank. The river was high with some floating ice. A young man of the name of Slaughter swam the river and brought over, not a canoe, but a trough designed for holding sugar water. This trough could carry but two men at a time. In order to expedite their passage, a number of men stripped off their clothes, put them into the trough, together with their guns, and swam by its sides, holding its edges with their hands. When about sixteen had crossed the river, their two sentinels, who had been posted in advance, discovered an Indian whose name was Shabosh. One of them broke one of his arms by a shot. A shot from the other sentinel killed him. These heroes then scalped and tomahawked him.

By this time about sixteen men had got over the river, and supposing that the firing of the guns which killed Shabosh would lead to an instant discovery, they sent word to the party designed to attack the town on the east side of the river to move on instantly, which they did.

In the mean time, the small party which had crossed the river, marched with all speed to the main town on the west side of the river. Here they found a large company of Indians gathering the corn which they had left in their fields the preceding fall when they removed to Sandusky. On the arrival of the men at the town, they professed peace and good will to the Moravians, and informed them that they had come to take them to Fort Pitt for their safety. The Indians surrendered, delivered up their arms, and appeared highly delighted with the prospect of their removal, and began with all speed to prepare victuals for the white men and for themselves on their journey.

A party of white men and Indians was immediately dispatched to Salem, a short distance from Gnadenhutten, where the Indians were gathering in their corn, to bring them into Gnadenhutten. The party soon arrived with the whole number of the Indians from Salem.

In the mean time the Indians from Gnadenhutten were confined in two houses some distance apart, and placed under guard; and when those from Salem arrived, they were divided, and placed in the same houses with their brethren of Gnadenhutten.

The prisoners being thus secured, a council of war was held to decide on their fate. The officers, unwilling to take on themselves the whole responsibility of the decision, agreed to refer the question to the whole number of the men. The men were accordingly drawn up in a line. The commandant of the party, Col. David Williamson, then put the question to them in form, "Whether the Moravian Indians should be taken prisoners to Pittsburg, or put to death, and requested that all those who were in favor of saving their lives should step out of the line and form a second rank." On this sixteen, some say eighteen, stepped out of the rank, and formed themselves into a second line; but alas! this line of mercy was far too short for that of vengeance.

The fate of the Moravians was then decided on, and they were told to prepare for death.

The prisoners, from the time they were placed in the guard-house, foresaw their fate, and began their devotions by singing hymns, praying, and exhorting each other to place a firm reliance in the mercy of the Savior of men. When their fate was announced to them, these devoted people embraced, kissed, and bedewing each others' faces and bosoms with their mutual tears, asked pardon of the brothers and sisters for any offense they might have given them through life. Thus, at peace with their God and each other, on being asked by those who were impatient for the slaughter, "Whether they were ready to die?" they answered "that they had commended their souls to God, and were ready to die."

The particulars of this dreadful catastrophe are too horrid to relate. Suffice it to say, that in a few minutes these two slaughter-houses, as they were then called, exhibited in their ghastly interior, the mangled, bleeding remains, of these poor unfortunate people, of all ages and sexes, from the aged grayheaded parent, down to the helpless infant at the mother's breast, dishonored by the fatal wounds of the tomahawk, mallet, war club, spear and scalping-knife.

Thus, O Brainard and Zeisberger! faithful missionaries, who devoted your whole lives to incessant toil and sufferings in your endeavors to make the wilderness of paganism "rejoice and blossom as the rose," in faith and piety to God! thus perished your faithful followers, by the murderous hands of the more than savage white men. Faithful pastors! Your spirits are again associated with those of your flock, "where the wicked cease from troubling and the weary are at rest!"

The number of the slain, as reported by the men on their return from the campaign, was eighty-seven or eighty-nine; but the Moravian account, which no doubt is correct, makes the number ninety-six. Of these, sixty-two were grown persons, one-third of whom were women; the remaining thirty-four were children. All these, with a few exceptions, were killed in the houses. Shabosh was killed about a mile above the town, on the west side of the river. His wife was killed while endeavoring to conceal herself in a bunch of bushes at the water's edge, on the arrival of the men at the town, on the east side of the river. A man at the same time was shot in a canoe, while attempting to make his escape from the east to the west side of the river. Two others were shot while attempting to escape by swimming the river. A few men, who were supposed to be warriors, were tied and taken some distance from the slaughter houses, to be tomahawked. One of these had like to have made his escape at the expense of the life of one of the murderers. The rope by which he was led was of some length. The two men who were conducting him to death fell into a dispute who should have the scalp. The Indian, while marching with a kind of dancing motion, and singing his death song, drew a knife from a scabbard suspended round his neck, cut the rope, and aimed at stabbing one of the men; but the jerk of the rope occasioned the men to look round. The Indian then fled towards the woods, and while running, dexterously untied the rope from his wrists. He was instantly pursued by several men who fired at him, one of whom wounded him in the arm. After a few shots the firing was forbidden, for fear the men might kill each other as they were running in a straggling manner. A young man then mounted on a horse and pursued the Indian, who when overtaken struck the horse on the head with a club. The rider sprang from the horse, on which the Indian seized, threw him down and drew his tomahawk to kill him. At that instant, one of the party got near enough to shoot the Indian, which he did merely in time to save the life of his companion.

Of the whole number of the Indians at Gnadenhutten and Salem, only two made their escape. These were two lads of fourteen or fifteen years of age. One of them, after being knocked down and scalped, but not killed, had the presence of mind to lie still among the dead, until the dusk of the evening, when he silently crept out of the door and made his escape. The other lad slipped through a trap door into the cellar of one of the slaughter houses, from which he made his escape through a small cellar window.

These two lads were fortunate in getting together in the woods the same night. Another lad, somewhat larger, in attempting to pass through the same window, it is supposed stuck fast and was burnt alive.

The Indians of the upper town were apprised of their danger in due time to make their escape, two of them having found the mangled body of Shabosh. Providentially they all made their escape, although they might have been easily overtaken by the party, if they had undertaken their pursuit. A division of the men were ordered to go to Shonbrun; but finding the place deserted, they took what plunder they could find, and returned to their companions without looking farther after the Indians.

After the work of death was finished, and the plunder secured, all the buildings in the town were set on fire and the slaughter houses among the rest. The dead bodies were thus consumed to ashes. A rapid retreat to the settlements finished the campaign.

Such were the principal events of this horrid affair. A massacre of innocent, unoffending people, dishonorable not only to our country, but human nature itself.

Before making any remarks on the causes which led to the disgraceful events under consideration, it may be proper to notice the manner in which the enterprise was conducted, as furnishing evidence that the murder of the Moravians was intended, and that no resistance from them was anticipated.

In a military point of view, the Moravian campaign was conducted in the very worst manner imaginable. It was undertaken at so early a period, that a deep fall of snow, a thing very common in the early part of March in former times, would have defeated the enterprise. When the army came to the river, instead of constructing a sufficient number of rafts to transport the requisite number over the river at once, they commenced crossing in a sugar trough, which could carry only two men at a time, thus jeopardizing the safety of those who first went over. The two sentinels who shot Shabosh, according to military law ought to have been executed on the spot for having fired without orders, thereby giving premature notice of the approach of our men. The truth is, nearly the whole number of the army ought to have been transported over the river; for after all their forces employed, and precaution used in getting possession of the town on the east side of the river, there were but one man and one squaw found in it, all the others being on the other side. This circumstance they ought to have known beforehand, and acted accordingly. The Indians on the west side of the river amounted to about eighty, and among them above thirty men, besides a number of young lads, all possessed of guns and well accustomed to the use of them; yet this large

Y

number was attacked by about sixteen men. If they had really anticipated resistance, they deserved to lose their lives for their rashness.   It is
presumable, however, that having full confidence in the pacific principles
of the Moravians, they did not expect resistance; but calculated on blood
and plunder without having a shot fired at them.   If this was really the
case, the author leaves it to justice to find, if it can, a name for the transaction.

One can hardly help reflecting with regret, that these Moravians did
not for the moment lay aside their pacific principles and do themselves
justice.   With a mere show of defense, or at most a few shots, they might
have captured and disarmed those few men, and held them as hostages
for the safety of their people and property until they could have removed
them out of their way.   This they might have done on the easiest terms,
as the remainder of the army could not have crossed the river without their
permission, as there was but one canoe at the place, and the river too high
to be forded.   But alas! these truly christian people suffered themselves
to be betrayed by hypocritical professions of friendship, until "they were
led as sheep to the slaughter."   Over this horrid deed humanity must
shed tears of commisseration, as long as the record of it shall remain.

Let not the reader suppose that I have presented him with a mere imaginary possibility of defense on the part of the Moravians.   This defense
would have been an easy task.   Our people did not go on that campaign
with a view of fighting.   There may have been some brave men among
them; but they were far from being all such.   For my part, I cannot suppose for a moment that any white man, who can harbor a thought of
using his arms for the killing of women and children in any case, can be
a brave man.   No, he is a murderer.

The history of the Moravian settlements on the Muskingum, and the
peculiar circumstances of their inhabitants during the revolutionary contest between Great Britain and America, deserve a place here.

In the year 1772, the Moravian villages were commenced by emigra-
tions from Friedenshutten on the Big Beaver, and from Wyalusing and
Sheshequon on the Susquehanna.   In a short time they rose to considerable extent and prosperity, containing upwards of four hundred people.
During the summer of Dunmore's war, they were much annoyed by war
parties of the Indians, and disturbed by perpetual rumors of the ill intentions of the white people of the frontier settlements towards them; yet
their labors, schools and religious exercises, went on without interruption.

In the revolutionary war, which began in 1775, the situation of the
Moravian settlements was truly deplorable.   The English had associated
with their own means of warfare against the Americans, the scalping
knife and tomahawk of the merciless Indians.   These allies of England
committed the most horrid depredations along the whole extent of our
defenseless frontier.   From early in the spring until late in the fall, the
early settlers of the western parts of Virginia and Pennsylvania had to
submit to the severest hardships and privations.   Cooped up in little
stockade forts, they worked their little fields in parties under arms guarded by sentinels, and were doomed from day to day to witness or hear re-

ports of the murders or captivity of their people, the burning of their houses, and the plunder of their property.

The war with the English fleets and armies, on the other side of the mountains, was of such a character as to engage the whole attention and resources of our government, so that, poor as the first settlers of this country were, they had to bear almost the whole burden of the war during the revolutionary contest. They chose their own officers, furnished their own means, and conducted the war in their own way. Thus circumstanced, "they became a law unto themselves," and on certain occasions perpetrated acts which government was compelled to disapprove. This lawless temper of our people was never fully dissipated until the conclusion of the whiskey rebellion in 1794.

The Moravian villages were situated between the settlements of the whites and the towns of the warriors, about sixty miles from the former, and not much farther from the latter. On this account they were denominated "the half-way houses of the warriors." Thus placed between two rival powers engaged in furious warfare, the preservation of their neutrality was no easy task, perhaps impossible. If it requires the same physical force to preserve a neutral station among belligerent nations that it does to prosecute a war, as is unquestionably the case, this pacific people had no chance for the preservation of theirs. The very goodness of their hearts, their aversion to the shedding of human blood, brought them into difficulties with both parties. When they sent their runners to Fort Pitt, to inform us of the approach of the war parties, or received, fed, secreted and sent home prisoners, who had made their escape from the savages, they made breaches of their neutrality as to the belligerent Indians. Their furnishing the warriors with a resting place and provisions was contrary to their neutral engagements to us; but their local situation rendered those accommodations to the warriors unavoidable on their part, as the warriors possessed both the will and the means to compel them to give whatever they wanted from them.

The peaceable Indians first fell under suspicion with the Indian warriors and the English commandant at Detroit, to whom it was reported that their teachers were in close confederacy with the American congress, for preventing not only their own people, but also the Delawares and some other nations, from associating their arms with those of the British for carrying on the war against the American colonies.

The frequent failures of the war expeditions of the Indians was attributed to the Moravians, who often sent runners to Fort Pitt to give notice of their approach. This charge against them was certainly not without foundation. In the spring of the year 1781 the war chiefs of the Delawares fully apprised the missionaries and their followers of their danger both from the whites and Indians, and requested them to remove to a place of safety from both. This request was not complied with, and the almost prophetic predictions of the chiefs were literally fulfilled.

In the fall of the year 1781, the settlements of the Moravians were broken up by upwards of three hundred warriors, and the missionaries taken prisoners, after being robbed of almost every thing. The Indians were left to shift for themselves in the barren plains of Sandusky, where most of their horses and cattle perished from famine during the winter. The missionaries were taken prisoners to Detroit; but after an examination by the governor, were permitted to return to their beloved people again.

In the latter part of February, a party of about one hundred and fifty of the Moravian Indians returned to their deserted villages on the Muskingum, to procure corn to keep their families and cattle from starving. Of these, ninety-six fell into the hands of Williamson and his party, and were murdered.

The causes which led to the murder of the Moravians are now to be detailed.

The pressure of the Indian war along the whole of the western frontier, for several years preceding the event under consideration, had been dreadfully severe. From early in the spring, until the commencement of winter, from day to day murders were committed in every direction by the Indians. The people lived in forts which were in the highest degree uncomfortable. The men were harrassed continually with the duties of going on scouts and campaigns. There was scarcely a family of the first settlers who did not, at some time or other, lose more or less of their number by the merciless Indians. Their cattle were killed, their cabins burned, and their horses carried off. These losses were severely felt by a people so poor as we were at that time. Thus circumstanced, our people were exasperated to madness by the extent and severity of the war. The unavailing endeavors of the American congress to prevent the Indians from taking up the hatchet against either side in the revolutionary contest, contributed much to increase the general indignation against them, at the same time those pacific endeavors of our government divided the Indians amongst themselves on the question of war or peace with the whites. The Moravians, part of the Delawares, and some others, faithfully endeavored to preserve peace, but in vain. The Indian maxim was, "he that is not for us is against us." Hence the Moravian missionaries and their followers were several times on the point of being murdered by the warriors. This would have been done had it not been for the prudent conduct of some of the war chiefs.

On the other hand, the local situation of the Moravian villages excited the jealousy of the white people. If they took no direct agency in the war, yet they were, as they were then called, "half-way houses" between us and the warriors, at which the latter could stop, rest, refresh themselves, and traffick off their plunder. Whether these aids, thus given to our enemies, were contrary to the laws of neutrality between belligerents, is a question which I willingly leave to the decision of civilians. On the part of the Moravians they were unavoidable. If they did not give or sell provisions to the warriors, they would take them by force. The fault was in their situation, not in themselves.

The longer the war continued, the more our people complained of the situation of these Moravian villages. It was said that it was owing to their being so near us, that the warriors commenced their depredations so early in the spring, and continued them until so late in the fall.

In the latter end of the year 1781, the militia of the frontier came to a

.determination to break up the Moravian villages on the Muskingum. For this purpose a detachment of our men went out under the command of Col. David Williamson, for the purpose of inducing the Indians with their teachers to move farther off, or bring them prisoners to Fort Pitt. When they arrived at the villages they found but few Indians, the greater number of them having removed to Sandusky. These few were well treated, taken to Fort Pitt, and delivered to the commandant of that station, who after a short detention sent them home again.

This procedure gave great offense to the people of the country, who thought the Indians ought to have been killed. Col. Williamson, who, before this little campaign, had been a very popular man, on account of his activity and bravery in war, now became the subject of severe animadversion on account of his lenity to the Moravian Indians. In justice to his memory I have to say, that although at that time very young, I was personally acquainted with him, and from my recollection of his conversation, I say with confidence that he was a brave man, but not cruel. He would meet an enemy in battle, and fight like a soldier, but not murder a prisoner. Had he possessed the authority of a superior officer in a regular army, I do not believe that a single Moravian Indian would have lost his life; but he possessed no such authority. He was only a militia officer, who could advise, but not command. His only fault was that of too easy a compliance with popular opinion and popular prejudice. On this account his memory has been loaded with unmerited reproach.

Several reports unfavorable to the Moravians had been in circulation for some time before the campaign against them. One was, that the night after they were liberated at Fort Pitt, they crossed the river and killed or made prisoners a family of the name of Monteur. A family on Buffalo creek had been mostly killed in the summer or fall of 1781 ; and it was said by one of them, who, after being made a prisoner, made his escape, that the leader of the party of Indians who did the mischief was a Moravian. These, with other reports of similar import, served as a pretext for their destruction, although no doubt they were utterly false.

Should it be asked what sort of people composed the band of murderers of these unfortunate people? I answer, they were not miscreants or vagabonds; many of them were men of the first standing in the country : many of them were men who had recently lost relations by the hands of the savages. Several of the latter class found articles which had been plundered from their own houses, or those of their relations, in the houses of the Moravians. One man, it is said, found the clothes of his wife and children, who had been murdered by the Indians a few days before : they were still bloody ; yet there was no unequivocal evidence that these people had any direct agency in the war. Whatever of our property was found with them had been left by the warriors in exchange for the provisions which they took from them. When attacked by our people, although they might have defended themselves, they did not: they never fired a single shot. They were prisoners, and had been promised protection. Every dictate of justice and humanity required that their lives should be spared. The complaint of their villages being "half-way houses for the warriors," was at an end, as they had been removed to Sandusky the fall before. It was therefore an atrocious and unqualified murder. But by whom committed—by a majority of the campaign? For the honor of my country, I hope I may safely answer this question in the negative. It was one of those convulsions of the moral state of society, in which the voice of the justice and humanity of a majority is silenced by the clamor and violence of a lawless minority. Very few of our men imbrued their hands in the blood of the Moravians. Even those who had not voted for saving their lives, retired from the scene of slaughter with horror and disgust. Why then did they not give their votes in their favor? The fear of public indignation restrained them from doing so. They thought well, but had not heroism enough to express their opinion. Those who did so, deserve honorable mention for their intrepidity. So far as it may hereafter be in my power, this honor shall be done them, while the names of the murderers shall not stain the pages of history, from my pen at least.

——:o:——

CHAPTER VII.

THE INDIAN SUMMER.

As connected with the history of the Indian wars of the western country, it may not be amiss to give an explanation of the term "Indian summer."

This expression, like many others, has continued in general use, notwithstanding its original import has been forgotten. A backwoodsman seldom hears this expression without feeling a chill of horror, because it brings to his mind the painful recollection of its original application. Such is the force of the faculty of association in human nature.

The reader must here be reminded, that, during the long continued Indian wars sustained by the first settlers of the west, they enjoyed no peace excepting in the winter season, when, owing to the severity of the weather, the Indians were unable to make their excursions into the settlements. The onset of winter was therefore hailed as a jubilee by the early inhabitants of the country, who, throughout the spring and early part of the fall, had been cooped up in their little uncomfortable forts, and subjected to all the distresses of the Indian war.

At the approach of winter, therefore, all the farmers, excepting the owner of the fort, removed to their cabins on their farms, with the joyful feelings of a tenant of a prison, recovering his release from confinement. All was bustle and hilarity in preparing for winter, by gathering in the corn, digging potatoes, fattening hogs, and repairing the cabins. To our forefathers the gloomy months of winter were more pleasant than the zephyrs and the flowers of May.

It however sometimes happened, after the apparent onset of winter, the weather became warm; the smoky time commenced, and lasted for a considerable number of days. This was the Indian summer, because it afforded the Indians another opportunity of visiting the settlements with their destructive warfare. The melting of the snow saddened every countenance, and the genial warmth of the sun chilled every heart with horror. The apprehension of another visit from the Indians, and of being driven back to the detested fort, was painful in the highest degree, and the distressing apprehension was frequently realized.

Toward the latter part of February we commonly had a fine spell of open warm weather, during which the snow melted away. This was denominated the "pawwawing days," from the supposition that the Indians were then holding their war councils, for planning off their spring campaigns into the settlements. Sad experience taught us that in this conjecture we were not often mistaken.

Sometimes it happened that the Indians ventured to make their excursions too late in the fall or too early in the spring for their own convenience.

A man of the name of John Carpenter was taken early in the month of March, in the neighborhood of what is now Wellsburg. There had been several warm days, but on the night preceding his capture there was a heavy fall of snow. His two horses, which they took with him, nearly perished in swimming the Ohio. The Indians as well as himself suffered severely with the cold before they reached the Moravian towns on the Muskingum. In the morning after the first day's journey beyond the Moravian towns, the Indians sent out Carpenter to bring in the horses, which had been turned out in the evening, after being hobbled. The horses had made a circuit, and fallen into the trail by which they came, and were making their way homewards.

When Carpenter overtook them, and had taken off their fetters, he had, as he said, to make a most awful decision. He had a chance and barely a chance to make his escape, with a certainty of death should he attempt it without success; while on the other hand, the horrible prospect of being tortured to death by fire presented itself. As he was the first prisoner taken that spring, of course the general custom of the Indians, of burning the first prisoner every spring, doomed him to the flames.

After spending a few minutes in making his decision, he resolved on attempting an escape, and effected it by way of forts Laurens, M'Intosh and Pittsburg. If I recollect rightly, he brought both his horses home with him. This happened in the year 1782. The capture of Mr. Carpenter, and the murder of two families about the same time, that is to say, in the two or three first days of March, contributed materially to the Moravian campaign, and the murder of that unfortunate people.

————:0:————

CHAPTER VIII.

This, in one point of view at least, is to be considered as a second Moravian campaign, as one of its objects was that of finishing the work of murder and plunder with the christian Indians at their new establishment on the Sandusky. The next object was that of destroying the Wyandot towns on the same river. It was the resolution of all those concerned in this expedition, not to spare the life of any Indians that might fall into their hands, whether friends or foes. It will be seen in the sequel that the result of this campaign was widely different from that of the Moravian campaign the preceding March.

It should seem that the long continuance of the Indian war had debased a considerable portion of our population to the savage state of our nature. Having lost so many relatives by the Indians, and witnessed their horrid murders and other depredations on so extensive a scale, they became subjects of that indiscriminate thirst for revenge, which is such a prominent feature in the savage character; and having had a taste of blood and plunder, without risk or loss on their part, they resolved to go on and kill every Indian they could find, whether friend or foe.

Preparations for this campaign commenced soon after the close of the Moravian campaign, in the month of March; and as it was intended to make what was called at that time "a dash," that is, an enterprise conducted with secrecy and despatch, the men were all mounted on the best horses they could procure. They furnished themselves with all their outfits, except some ammunition, which was furnished by the lieutenant colonel of Washington county.

On the 25th of May 1782, four hundred and eighty men mustered at the old Mingo towns, on the western side of the Ohio river. They were all volunteers from the immediate neighborhood of the Ohio, with the exception of one company from Ten Mile, in Washington county. Here an election was held for the office of commander-in-chief for the expedition. The candidates were Col. Williamson and Col. Crawford. The latter was the successful candidate. When notified of his appointment, it is said that he accepted it with apparent reluctance.

The army marched along "Williamson's trail," as it was then called, until they arrived at the upper Moravian town, in the fields belonging to which there was still plenty of corn on the stalks, with which their horses were plentifully fed during the night of their encampment there.

Shortly after the army halted at this place, two Indians were discovered by three men, who had walked some distance out of the camp. Three shots were fired at one of them, but without hurting him. As soon as the news of the discovery of Indians had reached the camp, more than one half of the men rushed out, without command, and in the most tumultuous manner, to see what happened. From that time, Col. Crawford felt a presentiment of the defeat which followed.

The truth is, that notwithstanding the secrecy and dispatch of the enterprise, the Indians were beforehand with our people. They saw the rendezvous on the Mingo bottom, and knew their number and destination. They visited every encampment immediately on their leaving it, and saw from their writing on the trees and scraps of paper, that "no quarter was to be given to any Indian, whether man, woman, or child."

Nothing material happened during their march until the 6th of June, when their guides conducted them to the site of the Moravian villages, on one of the upper branches of the Sandusky river; but here, instead of meeting with Indians and plunder, they met with nothing but vestiges of desolation. The place was covered with high grass; and the remains of a few huts alone announced that the place had been the residence of the people whom they intended to destroy, but who had moved off to Scioto some time before.

In this dilemma, what was to be done? The officers held a council, in which it was determined to march one day longer in the direction of Upper Sandusky, and if they should not reach the town in the course of the day, to make a retreat with all speed.

The march was commenced on the next morning through the plains of Sandusky, and continued until about two o'clock, when the advance guard was attacked and driven in by the Indians, who were discovered in large numbers in the high grass with which the place was covered. The Indian army was at that moment about entering a piece of woods, almost entirely surrounded by plains; but in this they were disappointed by a rapid movement of our men. The battle then commenced by a heavy fire from both sides. From a partial possession of the woods which they had gained at the onset of the battle, the Indians were soon dislodged. They then attempted to gain a small skirt of wood on our right flank, but were prevented from doing so by the vigilance and bravery of Maj. Leet, who commanded the right wing of the army at that time. The firing was incessant and heavy until dark, when it ceased. Both armies lay on their arms during the night. Both adopted the policy of kindling large fires along the line of battle, and then retiring some distance in the rear of them, to prevent being surprised by a night attack. During the conflict of the afternoon three of our men were killed and several wounded.

In the morning our army occupied the battle ground of the preceding day. The Indians made no attack during the day, until late in the evening, but were seen in large bodies traversing the plains in various directions. Some of them appeared to be employed in carrying off their dead and wounded.

In the morning of this day a council of the officers was held, in which a retreat was resolved on, as the only means of saving their army, the Indians appearing to increase in numbers every hour. During the sitting of this council, Col. Williamson proposed taking one hundred and fifty volunteers, and marching directly to Upper Sandusky. This proposition

Z

the commander-in-chief prudently rejected, saying, "I have no doubt but that you would reach the town, but you would find nothing there but empty wigwams; and having taken off so many of our best men, you would leave the rest to be destroyed by the host of Indians with which we are now surrounded, and on your return they would attack and destroy you. They care nothing about defending their towns—they are worth nothing. Their squaws, children and property, have been removed from them long since. Our lives and baggage are what they want, and if they can get us divided they will soon have them. We must stay together and do the best we can."

During this day preparations were made for a retreat by burying the dead and burning fires over their graves to prevent discovery, and preparing means for carrying off the wounded. The retreat was to commence in the course of the night. The Indians, however, became apprised of the intended retreat, and about sundown attacked the army with great force and fury, in every direction excepting that of Sandusky.

When the line of march was formed by the commander-in-chief, and the retreat commenced, our guides prudently took the direction of Sandusky, which afforded the only opening in the Indian lines and the only chance of concealment. After marching about a mile in this direction, the army wheeled about to the left, and by a circuitous route gained the trail by which they came, before day. They continued their march the whole of the next day, with a trifling annoyance from the Indians, who fired a few distant shots at the rear guard, which slightly wounded two or three men. At night they built fires, took their suppers, secured the horses and resigned themselves to repose, without placing a single sentinel or vidette for safety. In this careless situation, they might have been surprised and cut off by the Indians, who, however, gave them no disturbance during the night, nor afterwards during the whole of their retreat. The number of those composing the main body in the retreat was supposed to be about three hundred.

Most unfortunately, when a retreat was resolved on, a difference of opinion prevailed concerning the best mode of effecting it. The greater number thought it best to keep in a body and retreat as fast as possible, while a considerable number thought it safest to break off in small parties, and make their way home in different directions, avoiding the route by which they came. Accordingly many attempted to do so, calculating that the whole body of the Indians would follow the main army. In this they were entirely mistaken. The Indians paid but little attention to the main body of the army, but pursued the small parties with such activity, that but very few of those who composed them made their escape.

The only successful party who were detached from the main army, was that of about forty men under the command of a Capt. Williamson, who, pretty late in the night of the retreat, broke through the Indian lines under a severe fire and with some loss, and overtook the main army on the morning of the second day of the retreat.

For several days after the retreat of our army, the Indians were spread over the whole country, from Sandusky to the Muskingum, in pursuit of the straggling parties, most of whom were killed on the spot. They even pursued them almost to the banks of the Ohio. A man of the name of Mills was killed, two miles to the eastward of the site of St. Clairsville, in the direction of Wheeling from that place. The number killed in this way must have been very great: the precise amount, however, was never fairly ascertained.

At the commencement of the retreat, Col. Crawford placed himself at the head of the army, and continued there until they had gone about a quarter of a mile, when missing his son John Crawford, his son-in-law Maj. Harrison, and his nephews Maj. Rose and William Crawford, he halted and called for them as the line passed, but without finding them. After the army had passed him, he was unable to overtake it, owing to the weariness of his horse. Falling in company with Dr. Knight and two others, they traveled all the night, first north, and then to the east, to avoid the pursuit of the Indians. They directed their coures during the night by the north star.

On the next day they fell in with Capt. John Biggs and Lieut. Ashley, the latter of whom was severely wounded. There were two others in company with Biggs and Ashley. They encamped together the succeeding night. On the next day, while on their march, they were attacked by a party of Indians, who made Col. Crawford and Dr. Knight prisoners. The other four made their escape; but Capt. Biggs and Lieutenant Ashley were killed the next day.

Col. Crawford and Dr. Knight were immediately taken to an Indian encampment, at a short distance from the place where they were captured. Here they found nine fellow prisoners and seventeen Indians. On the next day they were marched to the old Wyandot town, and on the next morning were paraded, to set off, as they were told, to go to the new town. But alas! a very different destination awaited these captives! Nine of the prisoners were marched off some distance before the colonel and the doctor, who were conducted by Pipe and Wingemond, two Delaware chiefs. Four of the prisoners were tomahawked and scalped on the way, at different places.

Preparations had been made for the execution of Col. Crawford, by setting a post about fifteen feet high in the ground, and making a large fire of hickory poles about six yards from it. About half a mile from the place of execution, the remaining five of the nine prisoners were tomahawked and scalped by a number of squaws and boys.

When arrived at the fire, the colonel was stripped and ordered to sit down. He was then severely beaten with sticks, and afterwards tied to the post, by a rope of such length as to allow him to walk two or three times round it, and then back again. This done, they began the torture by discharging a great number of loads of powder upon him, from head to foot; after which they began to apply the burning ends of the hickory poles, the squaws in the mean time throwing coals and hot ashes on his body, so that in a little time he had nothing but coals to walk on. In the midst of his sufferings, he begged of the noted Simon Girty to take pity on him and shoot him. Girty tauntingly answered, "You see I have no gun, I cannot shoot;" and laughed heartily at the scene. After suffering about three hours he became faint and fell down on his face. An Indian then scalped·him, and an old squaw threw a quantity of burning coals on the place, from which the scalp was taken. After this he rose and walked round the post a little, but did not live much longer. After he expired, his body was thrown into the fire and consumed to ashes. Col. Crawford's son and son-in-law were executed at the Shawnee towns.

Dr. Knight was doomed to be burned at a town about forty miles distant from Sandusky, and committed to the care of a young Indian to be taken there. The first day they traveled about twenty-five miles, and encamped for the night. In the morning, the gnats being very troublesome, the doctor requested the Indian to untie him, that he might help him to make a fire to keep them off. With this request the Indian complied. While the Indian was on his knees and elbows, blowing the fire, the doctor caught up a piece of a tent pole which had been burned in two, about eighteen inches long, with which he struck the Indian on the head with all his might, so as to knock him forward into the fire. The stick however broke, so that the Indian, although severely hurt, was not killed, but immediately sprang up. On this the doctor caught up the Indian's gun to shoot him, but drew back the cock with so much violence that he broke the main spring. The Indian ran off with a hideous yelling. Dr. Knight then made the best of his way home, which he reached in twenty-one days, almost famished to death. The gun being of no use, after carrying it a day or two he left it behind. On his journey he subsisted on roots, a few young birds and berries.

A Mr. Slover, who had been a prisoner among the Indians, and was one of the pilots of the army, was also taken prisoner to one of the Shawnee towns on the Scioto. After being there a few days, and as he thought, in favor with the Indians, a council of the chiefs was held, in which it was resolved that he should be burned. The fires were kindled, and he was blackened and tied to a stake, in an uncovered end of the council-house. Just as they were about commencing the torture, there came on suddenly a heavy thunder gust, with a great fall of rain, which put out the fires. After the rain was over the Indians concluded that it was then too late to commence and finish the torture that day, and therefore postponed it till the next day. Slover was then loosed from the stake, conducted to an empty house, to a log of which he was fastened with a buffalo tug round his neck, while his arms were pinioned behind him with a cord. Until late in the night the Indians sat up smoking and talking. They frequently asked Slover how he would like to eat fire the next day. At length one of them laid down and went to sleep; the other continued smoking and talking with Slover. Sometime after midnight, he also laid down and went to sleep. Slover then resolved to make an effort to get loose if possible, and soon extricated one of his hands from the cord, and then fell to work with the tug round his neck, but without effect. He had not been long engaged in these efforts, before one of the Indians got up and smoked his pipe awhile. During this time Slover kept very still for fear of an examination. The Indian laying down, the prisoner renewed his efforts, but for some time without effect, and he resigned himself to his fate. After resting for awhile, he resolved to make another and a last effort, and as he related, put his hand to the tug, and without dif-

ficulty slipped it over his head. The day was just then breaking. He
sprang over a fence into a cornfield, but had proceeded but a little distance
in the field, before he came across a squaw and several children, lying
asleep under a mulberry tree. He then changed his course for part of
the commons of the town, on which he saw some horses feeding. Passing over the fence from the field, he found a piece of an old quilt. This
he took with him, and was the only covering he had. He then untied
the cord from the other arm, which by this time was very much swelled.
Having selected, as he thought, the best horse on the commons, he tied
the cord to his lower jaw, mounted him and rode off at full speed. The
horse gave out about 10 o'clock, so that he had to leave him. He then
traveled on foot with a stick in one hand, with which he put the weeds
behind him, for fear of being tracked by the Indians. In the other he
carried a bunch of bushes to brush the gnats and musketoes from his
naked body. Being perfectly acquainted with the route, he reached the
river Ohio in a short time, almost famished with hunger and exhausted
with fatigue.

Thus ended this disastrous campaign. It was the last one which took
place in this section of the country during the revolutionary contest of the
Americans with the mother country. It was undertaken with the very
worst of views, those of murder and plunder. It was conducted without
sufficient means to encounter, with any prospect of success, the large
force of Indians opposed to ours in the plains of Sandusky. It was conducted without that subordination and discipline, so requisite to insure
success in any hazardous enterprise, and it ended in a total discomfiture.
Never did an enterprise more completely fail of attaining its object.
Never, on any occasion, had the ferocious savages more ample revenge
for the murder of their pacific friends, than that which they obtained on
this occasion.

Should I be asked what considerations led so great a number of people
into this desperate enterprise?—why with so small a force and such slender means they pushed on so far as the plains of Sandusky?—I reply,
that many believed that the Moravian Indians, taking no part in the war,
and having given offense to the warriors on several occasions, their belligerent friends would not take up arms in their behalf. In this conjecture they were sadly mistaken. They did defend them with all the force
at their command, and no wonder, for notwithstanding their christian and
pacific principles, the warriors still regarded the Moravians as their relations, whom it was their duty to defend.

The reflections which naturally arise out of the history of the Indian
war in the western country, during our revolutionary contest with Great
Britain, are not calculated to do honor to human nature, even in its civilized state. On our side, indeed, as to our infant government, the case
is not so bad. Our congress faithfully endeavored to prevent the Indians
from taking part in the war on either side. The English government, on
the other hand, made allies of as many of the Indian nations as they could,
and they imposed no restraint on their savage mode of warfare. On the
contrary, the commandants at their posts along our western frontier received and paid the Indians for scalps and prisoners. Thus the skin of a

white man's or even a woman's head served in the hands of the Indian as current coin, which he exchanged for arms and ammunition, for the farther prosecution of his barbarous warfare, and clothing to cover his half naked body. Were not these rewards the price of blood?—of blood, shed in a cruel manner, on an extensive scale; but without advantage to that government which employed the savages in their warfare against their relatives and fellow-christians, and paid for their murders by the piece!

The enlightened historian must view the whole of the Indian war, from the commencement of the revolutionary contest, in no other light than a succession of the most wanton murders of all ages, from helpless infancy to decrepit old age, and of both sexes, without object and without effect.

On our side, it is true, the pressure of the war along our Atlantic border was such that our government could not furnish the means for making a conquest of the Indian nations at war against us. The people of the western country, poor as they were at that time, and unaided by government, could not subdue them. Our campaigns, hastily undertaken, without sufficient force and means, and illy executed, resulted in nothing beneficial. On the other hand, the Indians, with the aids their allies could give them in the western country, were not able to make a conquest of the settlement on this side of the mountains. On the contrary, our settlements and the forts belonging to them became stronger and stronger from year to year during the whole continuance of the wars. It was therefore a war of mutual, but unavailing slaughter, devastation and revenge, over whose record humanity still drops a tear of regret, but that tear cannot efface its disgraceful history.

----:o:----

CHAPTER IX.

ATTACK ON RICE'S FORT.

This fort consisted of some cabins and a small block-house, and was, in dangerous times, the residence and place of refuge for twelve families of its immediate neighborhood. It was situated on Buffalo creek, about twelve or fifteen miles from its junction with the river Ohio.

Previously to the attack on this fort, which took place in the month of September, 1782, several of the few men belonging to the fort had gone to Hagerstown, to exchange their peltry and furs for salt, iron and ammunition, as was the usual custom of those times. They had gone on this journey somewhat earlier that season than usual, because there had been "a still time," that is, no recent alarms of the Indians.

A few days before the attack on this fort, about three hundred Indians had made their last attack on Wheeling fort. On the third night of the investment of Wheeling, the Indian chiefs held a council, in which it was determined that the siege of Wheeling should be raised, two hundred of the warriors return home, and the remaining hundred of picked men make a dash into the country and strike a heavy blow somewhere before their return. It was their determination to take a fort somewhere and massacre all its people, in revenge for their defeat at Wheeling.

News of the plan adopted by the Indians, was given by two white men, who had been made prisoners when lads, raised among the Indians and taken to war with them. These men deserted from them soon after their council at the close of the siege of Wheeling. The notice was indeed but short, but it reached Rice's fort about half an hour before the commencement of the attack. The intelligence was brought by Mr. Jacob Miller, who received it at Dr. Moore's in the neighborhood of Washington. Making all speed home, he fortunately arrived in time to assist in the defense of the place. On receiving this news, the people of the fort felt assured that the blow was intended for them, and in this conjecture they were not mistaken. But little time was allowed them for preparation.

The Indians had surrounded the place before they were discovered; but they were still at some distance. When discovered, the alarm was given, on which every man ran to his cabin for his gun, and took refuge in the block-house. The Indians, answering the alarm with a war whoop from their whole line, commenced firing and running towards the fort from every direction. It was evidently their intention to take the place by assault; but the fire of the Indians was answered by that of six brave and skillful sharpshooters. This unexpected reception prevented the intended assault, and made the Indians take refuge behind logs, stumps, and trees. The firing continued with little intermission for about four hours.

In the intervals of the firing, the Indians frequently called out to the people of the fort, "Give up, give up, too many Indian; Indian too big; no kill." They were answered with defiance, "Come on, you cowards; we are ready for you;—shew us your yellow hides, and we will make holes in them for you."

During the evening, many of the Indians, at some distance from the fort, amused themselves by shooting the horses, cattle, hogs and sheep until the bottom was strewed with their dead bodies.

About ten o'clock at night the Indians set fire to a barn about thirty yards from the fort. It was large and full of grain and hay. The flame was frightful, and at first it seemed to endanger the burning of the fort, but the barn stood on lower ground than the fort. The night was calm, with the exception of a slight breeze up the creek. This carried the flame and burning splinters in a different direction, so that the burning of the barn, which at first was regarded as a dangerous, if not fatal occurrence, proved in the issue the means of throwing a strong light to a great distance in every direction, so that the Indians durst not approach the fort to set fire to the cabins, which they might have done at little risk, under the cover of darkness.

After the barn was set on fire, the Indians collected on the side of the fort opposite the barn, so as to have the advantage of the light, and kept up a pretty constant fire, which was as steadily answered by that of the fort, until about two o'clock, when the Indians left the place and made a hasty retreat.

Thus was this little place defended by a Spartan band of six men, against one hundred chosen warriors, exasperated to madness by their failure at Wheeling fort. Their names shall be inscribed in the list of heroes of our early times. They were Jacob Miller, George Lefler, Peter Fullenweider, Daniel Rice, George Felebaum and Jacob Lefler, junr. George Felebaum was shot in the forehead, through a port-hole, at the second fire of the Indians, and instantly expired, so that in reality the defense of the place was made by only five men.

The loss of the Indians was four, three of whom were killed at the first fire, from the fort, the other was killed about sundown. There can be no doubt but that a number more were killed and wounded in the engagement, but were concealed or carried off.

A large division of these Indians, on their retreat, passed within a little distance of my father's fort. In following their trail, a few days afterwards, I found a large poultice of chewed sassafras leaves. This is the dressing which the Indians usually apply to recent gunshot wounds. The poultice which I found having become too old and dry, was removed and replaced with a new one.

Examples of personal bravery and hair breadth escapes are always acceptable to readers of history. An instance of both of these happened during the attack on this fort, which may be worth recording.

Abraham Rice, one of the principal men belonging to the fort of that name, on hearing the report of the deserters from the Indians, mounted a very strong active mare and rode in all haste to another fort, about three and a half miles distant from his own, for further news, if any could be had, concerning the presence of a body of Indians in the neighborhood. Just as he reached the place he heard the report of the guns at his own fort. He instantly returned as fast as possible, until he arrived within sight of the fort. Finding that it still held out, he determined to reach it and assist in its defense, or perish in the attempt. In doing this, he had to cross the creek, the fort being some distance from it on the opposite bank. He saw no Indians until his mare sprang down the bank of the creek, at which instant about fourteen of them jumped up from among the weeds and bushes and discharged their guns at him. One bullet wounded him in the fleshy part of the right arm above the elbow. By this time several more of the Indians came up and shot at him. A second ball wounded him in the thigh a little above the knee, but without breaking the bone, and the ball passed transversely through the neck of the mare. She however sprang up the bank of the creek, fell to her knees, and stumbled along about a rod before she recovered. During this time several Indians came running up to tomahawk him. Yet he made his escape, after having about thirty shots fired at him from a very short distance. After riding about four miles, he reached Lamb's fort, much exhausted with the loss of blood. After getting his wounds dressed and resting awhile, he sat off late in the evening with twelve men, determined if possible to reach the fort under cover of the night. When they got within about two hundred yards of it, they halted: the firing still continued. Ten of the men, thinking the enterprise too hazardous, refused to go any further, and retreated. Rice and two other men crept silently along towards the fort; but had not proceeded far before they came close upon an Indian in his concealment. He gave the alarm yell, which was instantly passed round the lines with the utmost regularity. This occasioned the Indians to make their last effort to take the place and make their retreat under cover of the night. Rice and his two companions returned in safety to Lamb's fort.

About ten o'clock next morning, sixty men collected at Rice's fort for the relief of the place. They pursued the Indians, who kept in a body for about two miles. The Indians had then divided into small parties and took over the hills in different directions, so that they could be tracked no farther. The pursuit was of course given up.

A small division of the Indians had not proceeded far after their separation, before they discovered four men coming from a neighboring fort in the direction of that which they had left. The Indians waylaid the path, and shot two of them dead on the spot: the others fled. One of them being swift on foot, soon made his escape: the other being a poor runner, was pursued by an Indian, who after a smart chase came close to him. The man then wheeled round and snapped his gun at the Indian. This he repeated several times. The Indian then threw his tomahawk at his head, but missed him. He then caught hold of the ends of his belt which was tied behind in a bow knot. In this again the Indian was disappointed, for the knot came loose, so that he got the belt, but not the man, who wheeled round and tried his gun again, which happened to go off and laid the Indian dead at his feet.

—:0:—

CHAPTER X.

EXPECTED ATTACK ON DODDRIDGE'S FORT.

When we received advice, at my father's fort, of the attack on Rice's block-house, which was but a few miles distant, we sent word to all those families who were out on their farms, to come immediately to the fort. It became nearly dark before the two runners had time to give the alarm to the family of a Mr. Charles Stuart, who lived about three quarters of a mile off from the fort.

They returned in great haste, saying that Stuart's house was burned down, and that they had seen two fires between that and the fort, at which the Indians were encamped. There was therefore no doubt that an attack would be made on our fort early in the morning.

In order to give the reader a correct idea of the military tactics of our early times, I will give, in detail, the whole progress of the preparations which were made for the expected attack, and, as nearly as I can, I will give the commands of Capt. Teter, our officer, in his own words.

In the first place he collected all our men together, and related the battles and skirmishes he had been in, and really they were not few in number. He was in Braddock's defeat, Grant's defeat, the taking of Fort Pitt, and nearly all the battles which took place between the English, and the French and Indians, from Braddock's defeat until the capture of that place by Gen. Forbes. He reminded us, "that in case the Indians should succeed, we need expect no mercy: that every man, woman and child, would be killed on the spot. They have been defeated at one fort, and now they are mad enough. If they should succeed in taking ours, all their vengeace will fall on our heads. We must fight for ourselves and one another, and for our wives and children, brothers and sisters. We must make the best preparations we can; a little after daybreak we shall hear the crack of their guns."

He then made a requisition of all the powder and lead in the fort. The ammunition was accurately divided amongst all the men, and the amount supposed to be fully sufficient. When this was done, "Now," says the captain, "when you run your bullets, cut off the necks very close, and scrape them, so as to make them a little less, and get patches one hundred finer than those you commonly use, and have them well oiled, for if a rifle happens to be choked in the time of battle, there is one gun and one man lost for the rest of the battle. You will have no time to unbritch a gun and get a plug to drive out a bullet. Have the locks well oiled and your flints sharp, so as not to miss fire."

Such were his orders to his men. He then said to the women, "These yellow fellows are very handy at setting fire to houses, and water is a very good thing to put out fire. You must fill every vessel with water. Our fort is not well stockaded, and these ugly fellows may rush into the middle of it, and attempt to set fire to our cabins in twenty places at once." They fell to work, and did as he had ordered.

The men having put their rifles in order, "Now," says he, "let every man gather in his axes, mattocks and hoes, and place them inside of his door; for the Indians may make a dash at them with their tomahawks to cut them down, and an axe in that case might hit, when a gun would miss fire."

Like a good commander, our captain, not content with giving orders, went from house to house to see that every thing was right.

The ladies of the present day will suppose that our women were frightened half to death with the near prospect of such an attack of the Indians. On the contrary, I do not know that I ever saw a merrier set of women in my life. They went on with their work of carrying water and cutting bullet patches for the men, apparently without the least emotion of fear; and I have every reason to believe that they would have been pleased with the crack of the guns in the morning.

During all this time we had no sentinels placed around the fort, so

confident was our captain that the attack would not be made before daybreak.

I was at that time thirteen or fourteen years of age, but ranked as a
fort soldier. After getting my gun and all things else in order, I went
up into the garret loft of my father's house, and laid down about the middle of the floor, with my shot pouch on and my gun by my side, expecting to be waked up by the report of the guns at daybreak, to take my
station at the port-hole assigned me, which was in the second story of
the house.

I did not awake till about sunrise, when the alarm was all over. The
family which we supposed had been killed, had come into the fort about
daybreak. Instead of the house being burnt, it was only a large old log,
on fire, near the house, which had been seen by our expresses. If they
had seen any thing like fire between that and the fort, it must have been
fox fire. Such is the creative power of imagination, when under the influence of fear.

———.0.———

CHAPTER XI.

COSHOCTON CAMPAIGN.

THIS campaign took place in the summer of 1780, and was directed
against the Indian villages at the forks of the Muskingum.

The place of rendezvous was Wheeling; the number of regulars and
militia about eight hundred. From Wheeling they made a rapid march,
by the nearest route to the place of their destination. When the army
reached the river a little below Salem, the lower Moravian town, Col.
Broadhead sent an express to the missionary of that place, the Rev. John
Heckewelder, informing him of his arrival in his neighborhood, with his
army, requesting a small supply of provisions, and a visit from him, in
his camp. When the missionary arrived at the camp, the general informed him of the object of the expedition he was engaged in, and inquired of him whether any of the christian Indians were hunting, or engaged
in business in the direction of his march. On being answered in the
negative, he stated that nothing would give him greater pain than to hear
that any of the Moravian Indians had been molested by the troops, as
these Indians had always, from the commencement of the war, conducted themselves in a manner that did them honor.

A part of the militia had resolved on going up the river to destroy the
Moravian villages, but were prevented from executing their project by
Gen. Broadhead and Col. Shepherd of Wheeling.

At White-eye's plain, a few miles from Coshocton, an Indian prisoner was taken. Soon afterwards two more Indians were discovered, one of whom was wounded, but both made their escape.

The commander, knowing that these two Indians would make the utmost dispatch in going to the town, to give notice of the approach of the army, ordered a rapid march, in the midst of a heavy fall of rain, to reach the town before them, and take it by surprise. The plan succeeded. The army reached the place in three divisions. The right and left wings approached the river a little above and below the town, while the centre marched directly upon it. The whole number of the Indians in the village, on the east side of the river, together with ten or twelve from a little village some distance above, were made prisoners without firing a single shot. The river having risen to a great height, owing to the recent fall of rain, the army could not cross it. Owing to this, the villages with their inhabitants on the west side of the river escaped destruction.

Among the prisoners, sixteen warriors were pointed out by Pekillon, a friendly Delaware chief, who was with the army of Broadhead.

A little after dark, a council of war was held to determine on the fate of the warriors in custody. They were doomed to death, and by the order of the commander were bound, taken a little distance below the town, and dispatched with tomahawks and spears, and scalped.

Early the next morning, an Indian presented himself on the opposite bank of the river and asked for the big captain. Broadhead presented himself, and asked the Indian what he wanted. To which he replied, "I want peace." "Send over some of your chiefs," said Broadhead. "May be you kill," said the Indian. He was answered, "They shall not be killed." One of the chiefs, a well looking man, came over the river and entered into conversation with the commander in the street; but while engaged in conversation, a man of the name of Wetzel came up behind him, with a tomahawk concealed in the bosom of his hunting shirt, and struck him on the back of his head. He fell and instantly expired.

About eleven or twelve o'clock, the army commenced its retreat from Coshocton. Gen. Broadhead committed the care of the prisoners to the militia. They were about twenty in number. After marching about half a mile, the men commenced killing them. In a short time they were all dispatched, except a few women and children, who were spared and taken to Fort Pitt, and after sometime exchanged for an equal number of their prisoners.

——:o:——

CHAPTER XII.

CAPTIVITY OF MRS. BROWN.

On the 27th day of March, 1789, about ten o'clock in the forenoon, as Mrs. Brown was spinning in her house, her black woman, who had stepped out to gather sugar water, screamed out, "Here are Indians."— She jumped up, ran to the window, and then to the door, where she was met by one of the Indians presenting his gun. She caught hold of the muzzle, and turning it aside, begged him not to kill her, but take her prisoner. The other Indian in the mean time caught the negro woman and her boy about four years old, and brought them into the house. They then opened a chest and took out a small box and some articles of clothing, and without doing any further damage, or setting fire to the house, set off with herself and son, about two years and a half old, the black woman and her two children, the oldest four years and the youngest one year old. After going about one and a half miles they halted and held a consultation, as she supposed, about killing the children. This she understood to be the subject by their gestures and frequently pointing at the children. To one of the Indians who could speak English, she held out her little boy and begged him not to kill him, as he would make a fine little Indian after awhile. The Indian made a motion to her to walk on with her child. The other Indian then struck the negro boy with the pipe end of his tomahawk, which knocked him down, and then dispatched him by a blow with the edge across the back of the neck and scalped him.

About four o'clock in the evening, they reached the river, about a mile above Wellsburg, and carried a canoe, which had been thrown up in some drift wood, into the river. They got into this canoe, and worked it down to the mouth of Brush run, a distance of about five miles. They pulled up the canoe into the mouth of the run, as far as they could, then went up the run about a mile, and encamped for the night. The Indians gave the prisoners all their own clothes for covering, and added one of their own blankets. Awhile before daylight, the Indians got up and put another blanket over them.

About sunrise they began their march up a very steep hill, and about two o'clock halted on Short creek, about twenty miles from the place whence they had set out in the morning. The place where they halted had been an encampment shortly before, as well as a place of deposit for the plunder which they had recently taken from the house of a Mr. Van-

.meter, whose family had been killed. The plunder was deposited in a sycamore tree. Here they kindled a fire and put on a brass kettle, with a turkey which they had killed on the way, to boil in sugar water.

Mr. Glass, the first husband of Mrs. Brown, was working with a hired man in a field, about a quarter of a mile from the house, when his wife and family were taken, but knew nothing of the event until two o'clock. After searching about the place, and going to several houses in quest of his family, he went to Mr. Wells's fort, collected ten men besides himself, and the same night lodged in a cabin on the bottom on which the town now stands.

Next morning they discovered the place from which the Indians had taken the canoe from the drift, and their tracks at the place of their embarkation. Mr. Glass could distinguish the track of his wife by the print of the high heel of her shoe. They crossed over the river and went down on the other side until they came near the mouth of Rush Run; but discovering no tracks of the Indians, most of the men concluded that they would go to the mouth of Muskingum, by water, and therefore wished to turn back. Mr. Glass begged of them to go as far as the mouth of Short creek, which was only two or three miles farther. To this they agreed. When they got to the mouth of Rush run, they found the canoe of the Indians. This was identified by a proof, which goes to shew the presence of mind of Mrs. Brown. While going down the river, one of the Indians threw into the water several papers, which he had taken out of Mr. Glass's trunk, some of which she picked up out of the water, and under pretence of giving them to the child, dropped them into the bottom of the canoe. These left no doubt. The trail of the Indians and their prisoners up the run to their camp, and then up the river hill, was soon discovered. The trail at the time, owing to the softness of the ground and the height of the weeds, was easily followed.

About an hour after the Indians had halted, Mr. Glass and his men came within sight of the smoke of their camp. The object then was to save the lives of the prisoners, by attacking the Indians so unexpectedly, as not to allow them time to kill them. With this view they crept as slyly as they could, till they got within something more than one hundred yards from the camp. Fortunately, Mrs. Brown's little son had gone to a sugar tree to get some water; but not being able to get it out of the bark trough, his mother had stepped out of the camp to get it for him. The negro woman was sitting some distance from the two Indians, who were looking attentively at a scarlet jacket which they had taken some time before. On a sudden they dropped the jacket, and turned their eyes towards the men, who supposing they were discovered, immediately discharged several guns, and rushed upon them, at full speed, with an Indian yell. One of the Indians, it was supposed, was wounded the first fire, as he fell and dropped his gun and shot pouch. After running about one hundred yards, a second shot was fired after him, by Major M'Guire, which brought him to his hands and knees; but there was no time for pursuit, as the Indians had informed Mrs. Brown that there was another encampment close by. They therefore returned home with all speed, and reached the Beach bottom fort that night.

The other Indian, at the first fire, ran a little distance beyond Mrs. Brown, so that she was in a right line between him and the white men. Here he halted for a little to put on his shot pouch, which Mr. Glass, for the moment, mistook for an attempt to kill his wife with a tomahawk.

This artful maneuver no doubt saved the life of the savage, as his pursuers durst not shoot at him without risking the life of Mrs. Brown.

---:o:---

CHAPTER XIII.

LEWIS WETZEL.

The following narrative goes to shew how much may be effected by the skill, bravery, and physical activity of a single individual, in the partisan warfare carried on against the Idians, on the western frontier.

Lewis Wetzel was the son of John Wetzel, a German, who settled on Big Wheeling, about fourteen miles from the river. He was amongst the first adventnrers into that part of the country. His education, like that of his cotemporaries, was that of the hunter and warrior. When a boy he adopted the practice of loading and firing his rifle as he ran. This was a means of making him so destructive to the Indians afterwards.

When about thirteen years old, he was taken prisoner by the Indians, together with his brother Jacob, about eleven years old. Before he was taken he received a slight wound in the breast from a bullet, which carried off a small piece of his breast bone. The second night after they were taken, the Indians encamped at the Big Lick, twenty miles from the river, on the waters of M'Mahan's creek. The boys were not confined. After the Indians had fallen asleep, Lewis whispered to his brother Jacob that he must get up and go back home with him. Jacob at first objected, but afterwards got up and went along with him. When they had got about one hundred yards from the camp, they sat down on a log. "Well," said Lewis, "we can't go home baretooted; I will go back and get a pair of moccasons for each of us;" and accordingly did so, and returned. After sitting a little longer, "Now," says he, "I will go back and get father's gun, and then we'll start." This he effected. They had not traveled far on the trail by which they came, before they heard the Indians coming after them. It was a moonlight night. When the Indians came pretty nigh them, they stepped aside into the bushes, let them pass, then fell into their rear and traveled on. On the return of the Indians they did the same. They were then pursued by two Indians on horseback, whom they dodged in the same way. The next day they reached Wheeling in safety, crossing from the Indian shore to Wheeling island.

on a raft of their own making. By this time Lewis had become almost spent from his wound.

In the year 1782, after Crawford's defeat, Lewis went with a Thomas Mills, who had been in the campaign, to get his horse, which he had left near the place where St. Clairsville now stands. At the Indian springs, two miles from St. Clairsville, on the Wheeling road, they were met by about forty Indians, who were in pursuit of the stragglers from the campaign. The Indians and white men discovered each other about the same moment. Lewis fired first and killed an Indian, while the Indians wounded Mills in the heel, who was soon overtaken and killed. Four of the Indians then singled out, dropped their guns, and pursued Wetzel. Wetzel loaded his rifle as he ran. After running about half a mile, one of the Indians having got within eight or ten steps of him, Wetzel wheeled round and shot him down, ran, and loaded his gun as before. After going about three quarters of a mile farther, a second Indian came so close to him, that when he turned to fire, the Indian caught the muzzle of the gun, and as he expressed it, "he and the Indian had a severe wring." He however succeeded in bringing the muzzle to the Indians breast, and killed him on the spot. By this time, he as well as the Indians were pretty well tired; yet the pursuit was continued by the two remaining Indians. Wetzel, as before, loaded his gun, and stopped several times during this latter chase: when he did so, the Indians treed themselves. After going something more than a mile, Wetzel took advantage of a little open piece of ground over which the Indians were passing, a short distance behind him, to make a sudden stop for the purpose of shooting the foremost, who got behind a little sapling, which was too small to cover his body. Wetzel shot and broke his thigh. The wound, in the issue, proved fatal. The last of the Indians then gave a little yell, and said, "No catch dat man, gun always loaded," and gave up the chase, glad no doubt to get off with his life.

It is said that Lewis Wetzel, in the course of the Indian wars in this part of the country, killed twenty-seven Indians, besides a number more along the frontier settlements of Kentucky.

—:o:—

CHAPTER XIV.

ADAM POE.

In the summer of 1782, a party of seven Wyandots made an incursion into a settlement some distance below Fort Pitt, and several miles from the Ohio river. Here finding an old man alone, in a cabin, they killed him, packed up what plunder they could find, and commenced their retreat. Amongst their party was a celebrated Wyandot chief, who, in addition to his fame as a warrior and counsellor, was, as to his size and strength, a real giant.

The news of the visit of the Indians soon spread through the neighborhood, and a party of eight good riflemen was collected in a few hours for the purpose of pursuing the Indians. In this party were two brothers of the names of Adam and Andrew Poe. They were both famous for courage, size and activity.

This little party commenced the pursuit of the Indians, with a determination, if possible, not to suffer them to escape, as they usually did on such occasions, by making a speedy flight to the river, crossing it, and then dividing into small parties, to a meet at a distant point in a given time.

The pursuit was continued the greater part of the night after the Indians had done the mischief. In the morning, the party found themselves on the trail of the Indians, which led to the river. When arrived within a little distance of the river, Adam Poe, fearing an ambuscade, left the party, who followed directly on the trail, to creep along the brink of the river bank, under cover of the weeds and bushes, to fall on the rear of the Indians, should he find them in ambuscade. He had not gone far before he saw the Indian rafts at the water's edge. Not seeing any Indians, he stepped softly down the bank with his rifle cocked. When about half way down, he discovered the large Wyandot chief and a small Indian within a few steps of him. They were standing with their guns cocked, and looking in the direction of our party, who by this time had gone some distance lower down the bottom. Poe took aim at the large chief, but his rifle missed fire. The Indians hearing the snap of the gunlock, instantly turned round and discovered Poe, who being too near them to retreat, dropped his gun and sprang from the bank upon them, and seizing the large Indian by the clothes on his breast, and at the same time embracing the neck of the small one, threw them both down on the ground, himself being uppermost. The small Indian soon extricated himself, ran to the raft, got his tomahawk, and attempted to dispatch

Poe; the large Indian holding him fast in his arms with all his might, the better to enable his fellow to effect his purpose. Poe, however, so well watched the motions of his assailant, that, when in the act of aiming his blow at his head, by a vigorous and well-directed kick with one of his feet, he staggered the savage, and knocked the tomahawk out of his hand. This failure, on the part of the small Indian, was reproved by an exclamation of contempt from the large one.

In a moment the Indian caught up his tomahawk again, approached more cautiously, brandishing his tomahawk, and making a number of feigned blows in defiance and derision. Poe, however, still on his guard, averted the real blow from his head, by throwing up his arm, and receiving it on his wrist in which he was severely wounded; but not so as to lose entirely the use of his hand.

In this perilous moment, Poe, by a violent effort, broke loose from the Indian, snatched up one of the Indian's guns, and shot the small Indian through the breast, as he ran up the third time to tomahawk him.

The large Indian was now on his feet, and grasping Poe by a shoulder and leg, threw him down on the bank. Poe instantly disengaged himself and got on his feet. The Indian then seized him again, and a new struggle ensued, which, owing to the slippery state of the bank, ended in the fall of both combatants into the water.

In this situation, it was the object of each to drown the other. Their efforts to effect their purpose were continued for some time with alternate success, sometimes one being under the water and sometimes the other. Poe at length seized the tuft of hair on the scalp of the Indian, with which he held his head under water, until he supposed him drowned.

Relaxing his hold too soon, Poe instantly found his gigantic antagonist on his feet again, and ready for another combat. In this they were carried into the water beyond their depth. In this situation they were compelled to loose their hold on each other and swim for mutual safety. Both sought the shore, to seize a gun and end the contest with bullets. The Indian being the best swimmer, reached the land first. Poe seeing this, immediately turned back into the water, to escape, if possible, being shot, by diving. Fortunately the Indian caught up the rifle with which Poe had killed the other warrior.

At this juncture, Andrew Poe, missing his brother from the party, and supposing from the report of the gun which he shot, that he was either killed or engaged in conflict with the Indians, hastened to the spot. On seeing him, Adam called out to him to "kill the big Indian on shore." But Andrew's gun, like that of the Indian's, was empty. The contest was now between the white man and the Indian, who should load and fire first. Very fortunately for Poe, the Indian, in loading, drew the ramrod from the thimbles of the stock of the gun with so much violence, that it slipped out of his hand and fell a little distance from him. He quickly caught it up, and rammed down his bullet. This little delay gave Poe the advantage. He shot the Indian as he was raising his gun to take aim at him.

As soon as Andrew had shot the Indian, he jumped into the river to assist his wounded brother to shore; but Adam, thinking more of the honor of carrying the scalp of the big Indian home as a trophy of victory than of his own safety, urged Andrew to go back and prevent the struggling savage from rolling himself into the river and escaping. Andrew's solicitude for the life of his brother prevented him from complying with this request.

In the mean time, the Indian, jealous of the honor of his scalp even in the agonies of death, succeeded in reaching the river and getting into the current, so that his body was never obtained.

An unfortunate occurrence took place during this conflict. Just as Andrew arrived at the top of the bank for the relief of his brother, one of the party who had followed close behind him, seeing Adam in the river, and mistaking him for a wounded Indian, shot at him and wounded him in the shoulder. He however recovered from his wounds.

During the contest between Adam Poe and the Indians, the party had overtaken the remaining six of them. A desperate conflict ensued, in which five of the Indians were killed. Our loss was three men killed and Adam Poe severely wounded.

Thus ended this Spartan conflict, with the loss of three valiant men on our part, and with that of the whole Indian party excepting one warrior. Never on any occasion was there a greater display of desperate bravery, and seldom did a conflict take place, which, in the issue, proved fatal to so great a proportion of those engaged in it.

The fatal result of this little campaign, on the side of the Indians, occasioned a universal mourning among the Wyandot nation. The big Indian and his four brothers, all of whom were killed at the same place, were amongst the most distinguished chiefs and warriors of their nation.

The big Indian was magnanimous as well as brave. He, more than any other individual, contributed, by his example and influence, to the good character of the Wyandots for lenity towards their prisoners. He would not suffer them to be killed or ill treated. This mercy to captives was an honorable distinction in the character of the Wyandots, and was well understood by our first settlers, who, in case of captivity, thought it a fortunate circumstance to fall into their hands.

It is consoling to the historian to find instances of those endowments of mind which constitute human greatness even among savages. The original stamina of those endowments, or what is called *genius*, are but thinly scattered over the earth, and there can be little doubt but that the lower grades of society possess their equal proportion of the bases of moral greatness, or in other words, that there is as much of *native genius*, in proportion to numbers, amongst savages, as there is amongst civilized people. The difference between these two extremes of society is merely the difference of education. This view of human nature, philosophically correct, is well calculated to increase the benevolence of even the good Samaritan himself, and encourage his endeavors for the instruction of the most ignorant, and the reformation of the most barbarous.

Had the aboriginals of our country been possessed of science to enable them to commit to the faithful page of history the events of their intercourse with us since the discovery and settlement of their native land by the Europeans, what would be the contents of this history! Not such as it is from the hands of our historians, who have presented nought but the worst features of the Indian character, as exhibited in the course of their wars against the invaders of their country, while the wrongs inflicted on them by civilized men have occupied but a very small portion of the record. Their sufferings, their private virtues, their bravery and magnanimity in war, together with their individual instances of greatness of mind, heroism, and clemency to captives in the midst of the cruelties of their barbarous warfare, must soon be buried with themselves in the tomb of their national existence.

----:0:----

CHAPTER XV.

THE JOHNSONS.

The following narrative goes to show that the long continuance of the Indian war had inspired even the young lads of our country not only with all the bravery but all the subtilty of the Indians themselves.

In the fall of the year 1793, two boys of the name of John and Henry Johnson, the first thirteen and the latter eleven years old, whose parents lived in Carpenter's station, a little distance above the mouth of Short creek, on the east side of the Ohio river, were sent out in the evening to hunt the cows. At the foot of a hill, at the back of the bottom, they sat down under a hickory tree to crack some nuts. They soon saw two men coming towards them, one of whom had a bridle in his hand. Being dressed like white men, they mistook them for their father and an uncle in search of horses. When they discovered their mistake and attempted to run off, the Indians, pointing their guns at them, told them to stop or they would kill them. They halted and were taken prisoners.

The Indians, being in pursuit of horses, conducted the boys by a circuitous route over the Short creek hills in search of them, until late in the evening, when they halted at a spring in a hollow place, about three miles from the fort. Here they kindled a small fire, cooked and ate some victuals, and prepared to repose for the night.

Henry, the youngest of the boys, during the ramble had affected the greatest satisfaction at having been taken prisoner. He said his father was a hard master, who kept him always at hard work, and allowed him no play; but that for his part he wished to live in the woods and be a hunter. This deportment soon brought him into intimacy with one of the Indians, who could speak very good English. The Indians frequently asked the boys if they knew of any good horses running in the woods. Sometime before they halted, one of the Indians gave the largest of the boys a little bag, which he supposed contained money, and made him carry it.

When night came on, the fire was covered up, the boys pinioned, and made to lie down together. The Indians then placed their hoppis straps over them, and laid down, one on each side of them, on the ends of the straps.

Pretty late in the night the Indians fell asleep; and one of them becoming cold, caught hold of John in his arms, and turned him over on the outside. In this situation, the boy, who had kept awake, found means to get his hands loose. He then whispered to his brother, made him get up, and untied his arms. This done, Henry thought of nothing but running off as fast as possible; but when about to start, John caught hold of him, saying, "We must kill these Indians before we go." After some hesitation, Henry agreed to make the attempt. John then took one of the rifles of the Indians, and placed it on a log with the muzzle close to the head of one of them. He then cocked the gun, and placed his little brother at the britch, with his finger on the trigger, with instructions to pull it as soon as he should strike the other Indian.

He then took one of the Indian's tomahawks, and standing astraddle of the other Indian, struck him with it. The blow, however, fell on the back of the neck and to one side, so as not to be fatal. The Indian then attempted to spring up; but the little fellow repeated his blows with such force and rapidity on the skull, that, as he expressed it, "the Indian laid still and began to quiver."

At the moment of the first stroke given by the elder brother with the tomahawk, the younger one pulled the trigger, and shot away a considerable portion of the Indian's lower jaw. This Indian, a moment after receiving the shot, began to flounce about and yell in the most frightful manner. The boys then made the best of their way to the fort, and reached it a little before daybreak. On getting near the fort they found the people all up and in great agitation on their account. On hearing a woman exclaim, "Poor little fellows, they are killed or taken prisoners!" the oldest one answered, "No mother, we are here yet."

Having brought nothing away with them from the Indian camp, their relation of what had taken place between them and the Indians was not fully credited. A small party was soon made up to go and ascertain the truth or falsehood of their report. This party the boys conducted to the spot by the shortest route. On arriving at the place, they found the Indian whom the oldest brother had tomahawked, lying dead in the camp; the other had crawled away, and taken his gun and shot-pouch with him. After scalping the Indian, the party returned to the fort, and the same day a larger party went out to look after the wounded Indian, who had crawled some distance from the camp and concealed himself in the top of a fallen tree, where, notwithstanding the severity of his wound, with a Spartan bravery he determined to sell his life as dearly as possible. Having fixed his gun for the purpose, on the approach of the men to a proper distance, he took aim at one of them, and pulled the trigger, but his gun missed fire. On hearing the snap of the lock, one of the men exclaimed, "I should not like to be killed by a dead Indian!" The party concluding that the Indian would die at any rate, thought best to retreat, and return and look for him after some time. On returning, however, he could not be found, having crawled away and concealed himself in some other place. His skeleton and gun were found sometime afterwards.

The Indians who were killed were great warriors and very wealthy. The bag, which was supposed to contain money, it was conjectured was got by one of the party, who went out first in the morning. On hearing the report of the boys, he slipped off by himself, and reached the place before the party arrived. For some time afterwards he appeared to have a greater plenty of money than his neighbors.

The Indians themselves did honor to the bravery of these two boys. After their treaty with Gen. Wayne, a friend of the Indians who were killed made inquiry of a man from Short creek, what had become of the boys who killed the Indians? He was answered that they lived at the same place with their parents. The Indian replied, "You have not done right: you should make kings of those boys."

———:o:———

CHAPTER XVI.

SETTLEMENT OF THE COUNTRY.

HAVING thus given to the reader, in the preceding pages, a connected history of the wars with the Indians, from the earliest settlement of the country until the treaty of peace made by Gen. Wayne in 1794, I will go back to the year 1772, and trace the various steps by which our settlements advanced to their present vigorous state of existence.

The settlements on this side of the mountains commenced along the Monongahela, and between that river and the Laurel ridge, in the year 1772. In the succeeding year they reached the Ohio river. The greater number of the first settlers came from the upper parts of the then colonies of Maryland and Virginia. Braddock's trail, as it was called, was the route by which the greater number of them crossed the mountains. A less number of them came by the way of Bedford and Fort Ligonier, the military road from Eastern Pennsylvania to Pittsburg. They effected their removals on horses furnished with pack-saddles. This was the more easily done, as but few of these early adventurers into the wilderness were encumbered with much baggage.

Land was the object which invited the greater number of these people to cross the mountain; for as the saying then was, "it was to be had here for taking up." That is, building a cabin and raising a crop of grain, however small, of any kind, entitled the occupant to four hundred acres of land, and a pre-emption right to one thousand acres more adjoining, to be secured by a land office warrant. This right was to take effect if there happened to be so much vacant land, or any part thereof, adjoining the tract secured by the settlement right.

At an early period the government of Virginia appointed three commissioners to give certificates of settlement rights. These certificates, together with the surveyor's plat, were sent to the land office of the state, where they laid six months, to await any caveat which might be offered. If none was offered the patent then issued.

There was, at an early period of our settlements, an inferior kind of land title, denominated a "tomahawk right," which was made by deadening a few trees near the head of a spring, and marking the bark of some one or more of them with the initials of the name of the person who made the improvement. I remember having seen a number of those "tomahawk rights" when a boy. For a long time many of them bore the names of those who made them. I have no knowledge of the efficacy of the tomahawk improvement, or whether it conferred any right whatever, unless followed by an actual settlement. These rights, however, were often bought and sold. Those who wished to make settlements on their favorite tracks of land, bought up the tomahawk improvements, rather than enter into quarrels with those who made them. Other improvers of the land with a view to actual settlement, and who happened to be stout veteran fellows, took a very different course from that of purchasing the tomahawk rights. When annoyed by the claimants under those rights, they deliberately cut a few good hickories, and gave them what was called in those days "a laced jacket," that is, a sound whipping.

Some of the early settlers took the precaution to come over the mountains in the spring (leaving their families behind), to raise a crop of corn, and then return and bring them out in the fall. This I should think was the better way. Others, especially those whose families were small, brought them with them in the spring. My father took the latter course. His family was but small, and he brought them all with him. The Indian meal which he brought over the mountain was expended six weeks too soon, so that for that length of time we had to live without bread. The lean venison and the breast of the wild turkeys we were taught to call bread, and the flesh of the bear was denominated meat. This artifice did not succeed very well; for after living in this way some time we became sickly, the stomach seeming to be always empty and tormented with a sense of hunger. I remember how narrowly the children watched the growth of the potatoe tops, pumpkin and squash vines, hoping from day to day to get something to answer in the place of bread. How delicious was the taste of the young potatoes when we got them! What a jubilee when we were permitted to pull the young corn for roasting ears! still more so when it had acquired sufficient hardness to be made into jonny-cakes by the aid of a tin grater! We then became healthy, vigorous, and contented with our situation, poor as it was.

My father, with a small number of his neighbors, made their settlements in the spring of 1773. Though they were in a poor and destitute

situation, they nevertheless lived in peace; but their tranquility was not
of long continuance. Those most atrocious murders of the peaceable inoffensive Indians at Captina and Yellow creek, brought on the war of
lord Dunmore in the spring of the year 1774. Our little settlement then
broke up. The women and children were removed to Morris's fort, in
Sandy creek glade, some distance to the east of Uniontown. The fort
consisted of an assemblage of small hovels, situated on the margin of a
large and noxious marsh, the effluvia of which gave most of the women
and children the fever and ague. The men were compelled by necessity
to return home, risking the tomahawk and scalping knife of the Indians,
to raise corn to keep their families from starvation the succeeding winter.
Those sufferings, dangers and losses, were the tribute we had to pay to
that thirst for blood which actuated those veteran murderers who brought
the war upon us! The memory of the sufferers in this war, as well as
that of their descendants, still looks back upon them with regret and ab-
horrence, and the page of history will consign their names to posterity
with the full weight of infamy they deserve.

A correct and detailed view of the origin of societies, and their progress from one condition or point of wealth, science and civilization, to
another, is always highly interesting, even when received through the
dusky medium of history, oftentimes but poorly and partially written ; but
when this retrospect of things past and gone is drawn from the recollec-
tions of experience, the impressions which it makes on the heart are of
the most vivid, deep and lasting kind.

The following history of the state of society, manners and customs of
our forefathers, is to be drawn from the latter source; and it is given to
the world with the recollection that many of my cotemporaries, still living, have, as well as myself, witnessed all the scenes and events herein
described, and whose memories would speedily detect and expose any
errors the work may contain.

The municipal, as well as ecclesiastical institutions of society, whether
good or bad, in consequence of their long continued use, give a corresponding cast to the public character of society whose conduct they direct,
and the more so because in the lapse of time the observance of them becomes a matter of conscience.

This observation applies in full force to that influence of our early land
laws which allowed four hundred acres and no more to a settlement right.
Many of our first settlers seemed to regard this amount of the surface of
the earth as the allotment of Divine Providence for one family, and believed that any attempt to get more would be sinful. Most of them,
therefore, contented themselves with that amount, although they might
have evaded the law, which allowed but one settlement right to any one
individual, by taking out the title papers in the names of others, to be
afterwards transferred to them, as if by purchase. Some few indeed pursued this practice, but it was held in detestation.

My father, like many others, believed, that having secured his legal
allotment, the rest of the country belonged of right to those who chose to
settle in it. There was a piece of vacant land adjoining his tract, amounting to about two hundred acres. To this tract of land he had the pre-

emption right, and accordingly secured it by warrant; but his conscience would not permit him to retain it in his family: he therefore gave it to an apprentice lad whom he had raised in his house. This lad sold it to an uncle of mine for a cow and calf, and a wool hat.

Owing to the equal distribution of real property directed by our land laws, and the sterling integrity of our forefathers in their observance of them, we have no districts of "sold land," as it is called, that is, large tracts of land in the hands of individuals or companies who neither sell nor improve them, as is the case in Lower Canada and the northwestern part of Pennsylvania. These unsettled tracts make huge blanks in the population of the country wherever they exist.

The division lines between those whose lands adjoined, were generally made in an amicable manner by the parties concerned, before any survey of them was made. In doing this they were guided mainly by the tops of ridges and water courses, but particularly the former. Hence the greater number of farms in the western parts of Pennsylvania and Virginia bear a striking resemblance to an amphitheater. The buildings occupy a low situation, and the tops of the surrounding hills are the boundaries of the tract to which the family mansion belongs.

Our forefathers were fond of farms of this description, because, as they said, they are attended with this convenience, "that every thing comes to the house down hill." In the hilly parts of the state of Ohio, the land having been laid off in an arbitrary manner, by straight parallel lines, without regard to hill or dale, the farms present a different aspect from those on the east side of the river opposite. There the buildings as frequently occupy the tops of the hills as any other situation.

Our people had become so accustomed to the mode of "getting land for taking it up," that for a long time it was generally believed that the land on the west side of the Ohio would ultimately be disposed of in that way.

Hence almost the whole tract of country between the Ohio and Muskingum was parceled out in tomahawk improvements; but these latter improvers did not content themselves with a single four hundred acre tract apiece. Many of them owned a great number of tracts of the best land, and thus, in imagination, were as "wealthy as a South Sea dream." Many of the land-jobbers of this class did not content themselves with marking the trees, at the usual height, with the initials of their names; but climbed up the large beech trees, and cut the letters in their bark, from twenty to forty feet from the ground. To enable them to identify those trees, at a future period, they made marks on other trees around them as references.

Most of the early settlers considered their land of little value, from an apprehension that after a few years' cultivation it would lose its fertility, at least for a long time. I have often heard them say that such a field would bear so many crops, and another so many more or less than that. The ground of this belief concerning the short-lived fertility of the land in this country, was, the poverty of a great proportion of the land in the lower parts of Maryland and Virginia, which, after producing a few crops, became unfit for use, and was thrown out into commons.

*c

In their unfavorable opinion of the nature of the soil of our country our forefathers were utterly mistaken. The native weeds were scarcely destroyed before the white clover and different kinds of grass made their appearance. These soon covered the ground, so as to afford pasture for the cattle by the time the wood range was eaten out, as well as protect the soil from being washed away by drenching rains, so often injurious in hilly countries.

Judging from Virgil's* test of fruitful and barren soils, the greater part of this country must possess every requisite for fertility. The test is this. Dig a hole of any reasonable dimensions and depth: if the earth which was taken out, when thrown lightly back into it does not fill up the hole, the soil is fruitful; but if it more than fill it up, the soil is barren.

Whoever chooses to try this experiment will find the result indicative of the richness of our soil. Even our graves, notwithstanding the size of the vault, are seldom finished with the earth thrown out of them, and they soon sink below the surrounding surface.

------·o·------

CHAPTER XVII.

HOUSE FURNITURE AND DIET.

THE settlement of a new country in the immediate neighborhood of an old one, is not attended with much difficulty, because supplies can be readily obtained from the latter; but the settlement of a country very remote from any cultivated region, is a very different thing; because at the outset, food, raiment, and the implements of husbandry, are obtained only in small supplies and with great difficulty. The task of making new establishments in a remote wilderness, in time of profound peace, is sufficiently difficult; but when, in addition to all the unavoidable hardships attendant on this business, those resulting from an extensive and furious warfare with savages are superadded; toil, privations and sufferings, are then carried to the full extent of the capacity of men to endure them.

---

*Ante locum capies oculis, alteque jubebis
In solido puteum demitti, omnemque repones
Rursus humum, et pedibus summas æquabis arenas.
Si deerunt: rarum, pecorique et vitibus almis
Aptius uber erit. Sin in sua posse negabunt
Ire loca, et scrobibus superabit terra repletis,
Spissus ager: glebas cunctantes crassaque terga
Expecta, et validis terram proscinde juvencis.
Vir. Geo. lib. 2, l. 230.

Such was the wretched condition of our forefathers in making their settlements here. To all their difficulties and privations, the Indian war was a weighty addition. This destructive warfare they were compelled to sustain almost single-handed, because the revolutionary contest with England gave full employment for the military strength and resources on the east side of the mountains.

The following history of the poverty, labors, sufferings, manners and customs, of our forefathers, will appear like a collection of "tales of olden times," without any garnish of language to spoil the original portraits, by giving them shades of coloring which they did not possess.

I shall follow the order of things as they occurred during the period of time embraced in these narratives, beginning with those rude accommodations with which our first adventurers into this country furnished themselves at the commencement of their establishments. It will be a homely narrative, yet valuable on the ground of its being real history.

If my reader, when viewing, through the medium which I here present, the sufferings of human nature in one of its most depressed and dangerous conditions, should drop an involuntary tear, let him not blame me for the sentiment of sympathy which he feels. On the contrary, if he should sometimes meet with a recital calculated to excite a smile or a laugh, I claim no credit for his enjoyment. It is the subject matter of the history, and not the historian, which makes those widely different impressions on the mind of the reader.

In this chapter it is my design to give a brief account of the household furniture and articles of diet which were used by the first inhabitants of our country. A description of their cabins and half-faced camps, and their manner of building them, will be found elsewhere.

The furniture for the table, for several years after the settlement of this country, consisted of a few pewter dishes, plates and spoons, but mostly of wooden bowls, trenchers and noggins. If these last were scarce, gourds and hard-shelled squashes made up the deficiency.

The iron pots, knives and forks, were brought from the east side of the mountains, along with the salt and iron, on pack-horses.

These articles of furniture correspond very well with the articles of diet on which they were employed. "Hog and hommony" were proverbial for the dish of which they were the component parts. Journeycake and pone were, at the outset of the settlements of the country, the only forms of bread in use for breakfast and dinner. At supper, milk and mush were the standard dish. When milk was not plenty, which was often the case, owing to the scarcity of cattle or the want of proper pasture for them, the substantial dish of hommony had to supply the place of them. Mush was frequently eaten with sweetened water, molasses, bear's oil, or the gravy of fried meat.

Every family, besides a little garden for the few vegetables which they cultivated, had another small inclosure containing from half an acre to an acre, which they called a "truck-patch," in which they raised corn for roasting-ears, pumpkins, squashes, beans and potatoes. These, in the latter part of the summer and fall, were cooked with their pork, venison and bear meat, for dinner, and made very wholesome and well tasted dishes. The standard dinner dish for every log-rolling, house-raising and harvest-day, was a pot-pie, or what in other countries is called "sea-pie." This, besides answering for dinner, served for a part of the supper also,—the remainder of it from dinner being eaten with milk in the evening, after the conclusion of the labor of the day.

In our whole display of furniture, the delf, china, and silver were unknown. It did not then, as now, require contributions from the four quarters of the globe to furnish the breakfast table, viz: the silver from Mexico, the coffee from the West Indies, the tea from China, and the de'f and porcelain from Europe or Asia. Yet our homely fare, and unsightly cabins and furniture, produced a hardy, veteran race, who planted the first footsteps of society and civilization in the immense regions of the west. Inured to hardihood, bravery and labor, from their early youth, they sustained with manly fortitude the fatigue of the chase, the campaign and scout, and with strong arms "turned the wilderness into fruitful fields," and have left to their descendants the rich inheritance of an immense empire blessed with peace and wealth.

I well recollect the first time I ever saw a tea-cup and saucer, and tasted coffee. My mother died when I was about six or seven years old, and my father then sent me to Maryland with a brother of my grandfather, Mr. Alexander Wells, to school.

At Col. Brown's, in the mountains, (at Stony creek glades,) I for the first time saw tame geese; and by bantering a pet gander, I got a severe biting by his bill, and beaten by his wings. I wondered very much that birds so large and strong should be so much tamer than the wild turkeys. At this place, however, all was right, excepting the large birds which they called geese. The cabin and its furniture were such as I had been accustomed to see in the backwoods, as my country was then called.

At Bedford every thing was changed. The tavern at which my uncle put up was a stone house, and to make the change more complete, it was plastered in the inside both as to the walls and ceiling. On going into the dining room, I was struck with astonishment at the appearance of the house. I had no idea that there was any house in the world which was not built of logs; but here I looked round the house and could see no logs, and above I could see no joists; whether such a thing had been made by the hands of man, or had grown so of itself, I could not conjecture. I had not the courage to inquire any thing about it.

When supper came on, "my confusion was worse confounded." A little cup stood in a bigger one, with some brownish looking stuff in it, which was neither milk, hommony nor broth. What to do with these little cups and the little spoon belonging to them, I could not tell; and I was afraid to ask any thing concerning the use of them.

It was in the time of the war, and the company were giving accounts of catching, whipping, and hanging the tories. The word *jail* frequently occurred. This word I had never heard before; but I soon discovered its meaning, was much terrified, and supposed that we were in danger of the fate of the tories; for I thought, as we had come from the backwoods, it was altogether likely that we must be tories too. For fear of being discovered I durst not utter a single word. I therefore watched attentively to see what the big folks would do with their little cups and spoons. I imitated them, and found the taste of the coffee nauseous beyond any thing I ever had tasted in my life; I continued to drink, as the rest of the company did, with the tears streaming from my eyes, but when it was to end I was at a loss to know, as the little cups were filled immediately after being emptied. This circumstance distressed me very much, as I durst not say I had enough. Looking attentively at the grown persons, I saw one man turn his little cup bottom upwards and put his little spoon across it; I observed that after this his cup was not filled again; I followed his example, and to my great satisfaction, the result as to my cup was the same.

The introduction of delf ware was considered by many of the backwoods people as a culpable innovation. It was too easily broken, and the plates of that ware dulled their scalping and clasp knives; tea ware was too small for men, but might do for women and children. Tea and coffee were only slops, which in the adage of the day, "did not stick by the ribs." The idea was, they were designed only for people of quality, who do not labor, or the sick. A genuine backwoodsman would have thought himself disgraced by showing a fondness for those slops. Indeed, many of them have to this day very little respect for them.

——:0:——

CHAPTER XVIII.

DRESS.

On the frontiers, and particularly amongst those who were much in the habit of hunting, and going on scouts and campaigns, the dress of the men was partly Indian and partly that of civilized nations.

The hunting shirt was universally worn. This was a kind of loose frock, reaching half way down the thighs, with large sleeves, open before, and so wide as to lap over a foot or more when belted. The cape was large, and sometimes handsomely fringed with a ravelled piece of cloth of a different color from that of the hunting shirt itself. The bosom of this dress served as a wallet to hold a chunk of bread, cakes, jerk, tow for wiping the barrel of the rifle, or any other necessary for the hunter or warrior. The belt, which was always tied behind, answered for several purposes besides that of holding the dress together. In cold weather the mittens, and sometimes the bullet-bag, occupied the front part of it; to the right side was suspended the tomahawk, and to the left the scalping knife in its leathern sheath. The hunting shirt was generally made of linsey, sometimes of coarse linen, and a few of dressed deer skins. These last were very cold and uncomfortable in wet weather.

The shirt and jacket were of the common fashion. A pair of drawers or breeches, and leggins, were the dress of the thighs and legs. A pair of moccasons answered for the feet much better than shoes. These were made of dressed deer skin. They were mostly made of a single piece, with a gathering seam along the top of the foot, and another from the bottom of the heel, with gaiters as high as the ankle joint or a little higher. Flaps were left on each side to reach some distance up the legs. These were nicely adapted to the ankles and lower part of the leg by thongs of deer skin, so that no dust, gravel or snow, could get within the moccason.

The moccasons in ordinary use cost but a few hours labor to make them. This was done by an instrument denominated a moccason awl, which was made of the back spring of an old clasp knife. This awl, with its buckhorn handle, was an appendage of every shot pouch strap, together with a roll of buckskin for mending the moccasons. This was the labor of almost every evening. They were sewed together and patched with deer skin thongs, or whangs as they were commonly called.

In cold weather the moccasons were well stuffed with deer's hair or dry leaves, so as to keep the feet comfortably warm; but in wet weather it was usually said that wearing them was "a decent way of going barefooted;" and such was the fact, owing to the spongy texture of the leather of which they were made.

Owing to this defective covering of the feet, more than to any other circumstance, the greater number of our hunters and warriors were afflicted with the rheumatism in their limbs. Of this disease they were all apprehensive in wet or cold weather, and therefore always slept with their feet to the fire to prevent or cure it as well as they could. This practice unquestionably had a very salutary effect, and prevented many of them from becoming confirmed cripples in early life.

In the latter years of the Indian war our young men became more enamored of the Indian dress throughout, with the exception of the match coat. The drawers were laid aside and the leggins made longer, so as to reach the upper part of the thigh. The Indian breech clout was adopted. This was a piece of linen or cloth nearly a yard long, and eight or nine inches broad. This passed under the belt before and behind, leaving the ends for flaps, hanging before and behind over the belt. These belts were sometimes ornamented with some coarse kind of embroidery work. To the same belts which secured the breech clout, strings which supported the long leggins were attached. When this belt, as was often the case, passed over the hunting shirt, the upper part of the thighs and part of the hips were naked.

The young warrior, instead of being abashed by this nudity, was proud of his Indian-like dress. In some few instances I have seen them go into places of public worship in this dress. Their appearance however did not add much to the devotion of the young ladies.

The linsey petticoat and bed gown, which were the universal dress of our women in early times, would make a strange figure in our days. A small home-made handkerchief, in point of elegance, would illy supply the place of that profusion of ruffles with which the necks of our ladies are now ornamented.

They went barefooted in warm weather, and in cold their feet were covered with moccasons, coarse shoes or shoe-packs, which would make but a sorry figure beside the elegant morocco slippers often embossed with bullion, which at present ornament the feet of their daughters and grand-daughters.

The coats and bed gowns of the women, as well as the hunting shirts of the men, were hung in full display on wooden pegs around the walls of their cabins, so that while they answered in some degree the place of paper-hangings or tapestry, they announced to the stranger as well as neighbor the wealth or poverty of the family in the articles of clothing. This prac-tice has not yet been wholly laid aside amongst the backwoods families.

The historian would say to the ladies of the present time, Our ances-tors of your sex knew nothing of the ruffles, leghorns, curls, combs, rings, and other jewels with which their fair daughters now decorate themselves. Such things were not then to be had. Many of the younger part of them were pretty well grown up before they ever saw the inside of a store room, or even knew there was such a thing in the world, unless by hear-say, and indeed scarcely that.

Instead of the toilet, they had to handle the distaff or shuttle, the sickle or weeding hoe, contented if they could obtain their linsey clothing and cover their heads with a sun bonnet made of six or seven hundred linen.

—:o:—

CHAPTER XIX.

THE FORT.

My reader will understand by this term, not only a place of defense, but the residence of a small number of families belonging to the same neigh-borhood. As the Indian mode of warfare was an indiscriminate slaugh-ter of all ages and both sexes, it was as requisite to provide for the safety of the women and children as for that of the men.

The fort consisted of cabins, block-houses and stockades. A range of cabins commonly formed one side at least of the fort. Divisions, or par-titions of logs, separated the cabins from each other. The walls on the outside were ten or twelve feet high, the slope of the roof being turned wholly inward. A very few of these cabins had puncheon floors: the greater part were earthen.

The block-houses were built at the angles of the fort. They projected about two feet beyond the outer walls of the cabins and stockades. Their upper stories were about eighteen inches every way larger in di-mension than the under one, leaving an opening at the commencement of the second story, to prevent the enemy from making a lodgment under their walls. In some forts, instead of block-houses, the angles of the fort were furnished with bastions. A large folding gate made of thick slabs, nearest the spring, closed the fort. The stockades, bastions, cabins and block-house walls, were furnished with port-holes at proper heights and distances. The whole of the outside was made completely bullet-proof.

It may be truly said that necessity is the mother of invention, for the whole of this work was made without the aid of a single nail or spike of iron, and for this reason, such things were not to be had.

In some places less exposed, a single block-house with a cabin or two constituted the whole fort.

Such places of refuge may appear very trifling to those who have been in the habit of seeing the formidable military garrisons of Europe and America; but they answered the purpose, as the Indians had no artillery. They seldom attacked, and scarcely ever took one of them.

The families belonging to these forts were so attached to their own cabins on their farms, that they seldom moved into the fort in the spring until compelled by some alarm, as they called it; that is, when it was announced by some murder that the Indians were in the settlement.

The fort to which my father belonged, was, during the first years of the war, three quarters of a mile from his farm; but when this fort went to decay, and became unfit for defense, a new one was built at his own house. I well remember that when a little boy the family were sometimes waked up in the dead of night by an express with a report that the Indians were at hand. The express came softly to the door or back window, and by a gentle tapping waked the family; this was easily done, as an habitual fear made us ever watchful and sensible to the slightest alarm. The whole family were instantly in motion: my father seized his gun and other implements of war; my step mother waked up and dressed the children as well as she could; and being myself the oldest of the children, I had to take my share of the burthens to be carried to the fort. There was no possibility of getting a horse in the night to aid us in removing to the fort; besides the little children, we caught up what articles of clothing and provision we could get hold of in the dark, for we durst not light a candle or even stir the fire. All this was done with the utmost dispatch and the silence of death; the greatest care was taken not to awaken the youngest child: to the rest it was enough to say *Indian*, and not a whimper was heard afterwards. Thus it often happened that the whole number of families belonging to a fort, who were in the evening at their homes, were all in their little fortress before the dawn of the next morning. In the course of the succeeding day, their household furniture was brought in by parties of the men under arms.

Some families belonging to each fort, were much less under the influence of fear than others, and who after an alarm had subsided, in spite of every remonstrance would remove home, while their more prudent neighbors remained in the fort. Such families were denominated "foolhardy," and gave no small amount of trouble by creating such frequent necessities of sending runners to warn them of their danger, and sometimes parties of our men to protect them during their removal.

—:0:—

CHAPTER XX.

CARAVANS.

THE acquisition of the indispensable articles of salt, iron, steel and castings, presented great difficulties to the first settlers of the western country. They had no stores of any kind, no salt, iron, nor iron works; nor had they money to make purchases where those articles were to be obtained. Peltry and furs were their only resources, before they had time to raise cattle and horses for sale in the Atlantic states.

Every family collected what peltry and fur they could obtain throughout the year for the purpose of sending them over the mountains for barter.

In the fall of the year, after seeding time, every family formed an association with some of their neighbors for starting the little caravan. A master driver was selected from among them, who was to be assisted by one or more young men, and sometimes a boy or two. The horses were fitted out with pack-saddles, to the hinder part of which was fastened a pair of hobbles made of hickory withs: a bell and collar ornamented his neck. The bags provided for the conveyance of the salt were filled with feed for the horses: on the journey a part of this feed was left at convenient stages on the way down, to support the return of the caravan. Large wallets, well filled with bread, jerk, boiled ham and cheese, furnished provision for the drivers. At night, after feeding, the horses, whether put in pasture or turned out into the woods, were hobbled, and the bells were opened. The barter for salt and iron was made first at Baltimore. Frederick, Hagerstown, Oldtown and Cumberland, in succession, became the place of exchange. Each horse carried two bushels of alumn salt, weighing eighty-four pounds the bushel. This, to be sure, was not a heavy load for the horses, but it was enough considering the scanty subsistence allowed them on the journey.

The common price of a bushel of alumn salt at an early period was a good cow and calf; and until weights were introduced, the salt was measured into the half bushel by hand as lightly as possible. No one was permitted to walk heavily over the floor while the operation was going on.

The following anecdote will serve to shew how little the native sons of the forest knew of the etiquet of the Atlantic cities.

A neighbor of my father, some years after the settlement of the country, had collected a small drove of cattle for the Baltimore market. Amongst the hands employed to drive them was one who had never seen any condition of society but that of woodsmen.

At one of their lodging places in the mountain, the landlord and his hired man, in the course of the night, stole two of the bells belonging to the drove, and hid them in a piece of woods.

The drove had not gone far in the morning before the bells were missed, and a detachment went back to recover the stolen bells. The men were found reaping in the field of the landlord; they were accused of the theft, but they denied the charge. The torture of sweating, according to the custom of that time, that is, of suspension by the arms pinioned behind their backs, brought a confession. The bells were procured and hung around the necks of the thieves: in this condition they were driven on foot before the detachment until they overtook the drove, which by this time had gone nine miles. A halt was called and a jury selected to try the culprits. They were condemned to receive a certain number of lashes on the bare back from the hand of each drover. The man above alluded to was the owner of one of the bells. When it came to his turn to use the hickory, "Now," says he to the thief, "you infernal scoundrel, I'll work your jacket nineteen to the dozen. Only think what a rascally figure I should make in the streets of Baltimore without a bell on my horse." The man was in earnest: having seen no horse used without bells, he thought they were requisite in every situation.

———:o:———

CHAPTER XXI.

HUNTING.

THIS was an important part of the employment of the early settlers of this country. For some years the woods supplied them with the greater amount of their subsistence, and with regard to some families in certain times, the whole of it; for it was no uncommon thing for families to live several months without a mouthful of bread. It frequently happened that there was no breakfast until it was obtained from the woods. Fur and peltry were the people's money; they had nothing else to give in exchange for rifles, salt and iron, on the other side of the mountains.

The fall and early part of the winter was the season for hunting the deer, and the whole of the winter, including part of the spring, for bears and fur skinned animals. It was a customary saying that fur is good during every month in the name of which the letter r occurs.

The class of hunters with whom I was best acquainted were those whose hunting ranges were on the western side of the river and at the distance of eight or nine miles from it. As soon as the leaves were pretty well down, and the weather became rainy accompanied with light snows, these men, after acting the part of husbandmen, so far as the state of warfare permitted them to do so, soon began to feel that they were hunters. They became uneasy at home; every thing about them became disagreeable; the house was too warm, the feather bed too soft, and even the good wife was not thought for the time being a proper companion; the mind of the hunter was wholly occupied with the camp and chase.

I have often seen them get up early in the morning at this season, walk hastily out and look anxiously to the woods, and snuff the autumnal winds with the highest rapture, then return into the house and cast a quick and attentive look at the rifle, which was always suspended to a joist by a couple of buck's horns or little forks; his hunting dog understanding the intentions of his master, would wag his tail, and by every blandishment in his power express his readiness to accompany him to the woods.

A day was soon appointed for the march of the little cavalcade to the camp. Two or three horses furnished with pack-saddles were loaded with flour, Indian meal, blankets, and every thing else requisite for the use of the hunter.

A hunting camp, or what was called a half-faced cabin, was of the following form: the back part of it was sometimes a large log: at the distance of eight or ten feet from this two stakes were set in the ground a few inches apart, and at the distance of eight or ten feet from these two more to receive the ends of the poles for the sides of the camp; the whole slope of the roof was from the front to the back; the covering was made of slabs, skins or blankets, or, if in the spring of the year, the bark of hickory or ash trees; the front was left entirely open; the fire was built directly before this opening; the cracks between the logs were filled with moss, and dry leaves served for a bed. It is thus that a couple of men in a few hours will construct for themselves a temporary but tolerably comfortable defense from the inclemencies of the weather; the beaver, otter, muskrat and squirrel are scarcely their equals in dispatch in fabricating for themselves a covert from the tempest!

A little more pains would have made a hunting camp a defense against the Indians. A cabin ten feet square, bullet proof and furnished with port holes, would have enabled two or three hunters to hold twenty Indians at bay for any length of time; but this precaution I believe was never attended to; hence the hunters were often surprised and killed in their camps.

The site for the camp was selected with all the sagacity of the woodsmen, so as to have it sheltered by the surrounding hills from every wind, but more especially from those of the north and west.

An uncle of mine, of the name of Samuel Teter, occupied the same camp for several years in succession. It was situated on one of the southern branches of Cross creek. Although I had lived many years not more than fifteen miles from the place, it was not till within a very few years that I discovered its situation, when it was shewn to me by a gentleman living in the neighborhood. Viewing the hills round about it, I soon perceived the sagacity of the hunter in the site for his camp. Not a wind could touch him, and unless by the report of his gun or the sound of his

axe, it would have been by mere accident if an Indian had discovered his
concealment.

Hunting was not a mere ramble in pursuit of game, in which there was
nothing of skill and calculation; on the contrary, the hunter before he set
out in the morning was informed by the state of the weather in what situation he might reasonably expect to meet with his game, whether on the
bottoms, sides or tops of the hills. In stormy weather the deer always
seek the most sheltered places and the leeward sides of the hills. In
rainy weather in which there is not much wind, they keep in the open
woods on the highest ground,

In every situation it was requisite for the hunter to ascertain the course
of the wind, so as to get to the leward of the game. This he effected by
putting his finger in his mouth and holding it there until it became warm;
then holding it above his head, the side which first becomes cold shews
which way the wind blows.

As it was requisite too for the hunter to know the cardinal points, he
had only to observe the trees to ascertain them. The bark of an aged
tree is thicker and much rougher on the north than on the south side.
The same thing may be said of the moss, it is thicker and stronger on the
north than on the south side of the trees,

The whole business of the hunter consists of a succession of intrigues.
From morning to night he was on the alert to *gain the wind* of his game,
and approach them without being discovered. If he succeeded in killing
a deer, he skinned it and hung it up out of the reach of the wolves, and
immediately resumed the chase till the close of the evening, when he bent
his course towards his camp; when arrived there, he kindled up his fire,
and together with his fellow hunter cooked his supper. The supper finished, the adventures of the day furnished the tales for the evening; the
spike buck, the two and three pronged buck, the doe and the barren doe,
figured through their anecdotes with great advantage, It should seem
that after hunting awhile on the same ground, the hunters became acquainted with nearly all the gangs of deer within their range, so as to
know each flock of them when they saw them. Often some old buck, by
the means of his superior sagacity and watchfulness, saved his little gang
from the hunter's skill, by giving timely notice of his approach. The
cunning of the hunter and that of the old buck were staked against each
other, and it frequently happened that at the conclusion of the hunting
season, the old fellow was left the free uninjured tenant of his forest; but
if his rival succeeded in bringing him down, the victory was followed by
no small amount of boasting on the part of the conqueror.

When the weather was not suitable for hunting, the skins and carcasses
of the game were brought in and disposed of.

Many of the hunters rested from their labors on the Sabbath day, some
from a motive of piety, others said that whenever they hunted on Sunday, they were sure to have bad luck all the rest of the week.

————·0·————

CHAPTER XXII.

THE WEDDING.

For a long time after the first settlement of this country the inhabitants in general married young. There was no distinction of rank, and very little of fortune. On these accounts the first impression of love resulted in marriage, and a family establishment cost but a little labor and nothing else.

A description of a wedding, from the beginning to the end, will serve to shew the manners of our forefathers, and mark the grade of civilization which has succeeded to their rude state of society in the course of a few years.

At an early period the practice of celebrating the marriage at the house of the bride began, and it should seem with great propriety. She also has the choice of the priest to perform the ceremony.

In the first years of the settlement of this country, a wedding engaged the attention of a whole neighborhood, and the frolick was anticipated by old and young with eager anticipation. This is not to be wondered at, when it is told that a wedding was almost the only gathering which was not accompanied with the labor of reaping, log-rolling, building a cabin, or planning some scout or campaign.

In the morning of the wedding day, the groom and his attendants assembled at the house of his father, for the purpose of reaching the mansion of his bride by noon, which was the usual time for celebrating the nuptials, which for certain must take place before dinner.

Let the reader imagine an assemblage of people, without a store, tailor or mantuamaker, within an hundred miles, and an assemblage of horses, without a blacksmith or saddler within an equal distance. The gentlemen dressed in shoe-packs, moccasons, leather breeches, leggins, and linsey hunting shirts, all home-made. The ladies dressed in linsey petticoats and linsey or linen bed gowns, coarse shoes, stockings, handkerchiefs, and buckskin gloves, if any; if there were any buckles, rings, buttons or ruffles, they were the relics of old times, family pieces from parents or grand-parents. The horses were caparisoned with old saddles, old bridles or halters, and pack-saddles, with a bag or blanket thrown over them: a rope or string as often constituted the girth as a piece of leather.

The march, in double file, was often interrupted by the narrowness and obstructions of our horse-paths, as they were called, for we had no roads; and these difficulties were often increased, sometimes by the good, and sometimes by the ill will of neighbors, by falling trees and tying grape wines across the way.   Sometimes an ambuscade was formed by the way side, and an unexpected discharge of several guns took place, so as to cover the wedding company with smoke.   Let the reader imagine the scene which followed this discharge, the sudden spring of the horses, the shrieks of the girls, and the chivalric bustle of their partners to save them from falling.   Sometimes, in spite of all that could be done to prevent it, some were thrown to the ground ; if a wrist, elbow or ankle happened to be sprained, it was tied with a handkerchief, and little more was thought or said about it.

Another ceremony took place before the party reached the house of the bride, after the practice of making whiskey began, which was at an early period.   When the party were about a mile from the place of their destination, two young men would single out to run for the bottle: the worse the path, the more logs, brush and deep hollows, the better, as these obstacles afforded an opportunity for the greater display of intrepidity and horsemanship.   The English fox chase, in point of danger to the riders and their horses, was nothing to this race for the bottle.   The start was announced by an Indian yell, when logs, brush, mud holes, hill and glen, were speedily passed by the rival ponies.   The bottle was always filled for the occasion, so that there was no use for judges; for the first who reached the door was presented with the prize, with which he returned in triumph to the company.   On approaching them he announced his victory over his rival by a shrill whoop.   At the head of the troop he gave the bottle to the groom and his attendants, and then to each pair in succession, to the rear of the line, giving each a dram; and then putting the bottle in the bosom of his hunting shirt, took his station in the company.

The ceremony of the marriage preceded the dinner, which was a substantial backwoods feast of beef, pork, fowls, and sometimes venison and bear meat, roasted and boiled, with plenty of potatoes, cabbage and other vegetables.   During the dinner the greatest hilarity always prevailed, although the table might be a large slab of timber, hewed out with a broad-axe, supported by four sticks set in auger holes, and the furniture some old pewter dishes and plates, the rest wooden bowls and trenchers.   A few pewter spoons, much battered about the edges, were to be seen at some tables; the rest were made of horns.   If knives were scarce, the deficiency was made up by the scalping knives, which were carried in sheaths suspended to the belt of the hunting shirt.

After dinner the dancing commenced, and generally lasted until the next morning.   The figures of the dances were three and four handed reels, or square sets and jigs.   The commencement was always a square four, which was followed by what was called jigging it off, that is, two of the four would single out for a jig, and were followed by the remaining couple.   The jigs were often accompanied with what was called cutting out, that is, when any of the parties became tired of the dance, on intimation, the place was supplied by some of the company, without any interruption of the dance; in this way a dance was often continued till the musician was heartily tired of his situation.   Toward the latter part of the night, if any of the company through weariness attempted to conceal themselves for the purpose of sleeping, they were hunted up, paraded on the floor, and the fiddler ordered to play "hang out till morning."

About nine or ten o'clock a deputation of young ladies stole off the bride and put her to bed. In doing this it frequently happened that they had to ascend a ladder instead of a pair of stairs, leading from the dining and ball room to the loft, the floor of which was made of clapboards lying loose and without nails. This ascent one might think would put the bride and her attendants to the blush; but as the foot of the ladder was commonly behind the door, which was purposely open for the occasion; and its rounds at the inner ends were well hung with hunting shirts, petticoats and other articles of clothing, the candles being on the opposite side of the house, the exit of the bride was noticed but by a few. This done, a deputation of young men in like manner stole off the groom and placed him snugly by the side of his bride. The dance still continued, and if seats happened to be scarce, which was often the case, every young man when not engaged in the dance was obliged to offer his lap as a seat for one of the girls, and the offer was sure to be accepted. In the midst of this hilarity the bride and groom were not forgotten. Pretty late in the night some one would remind the company that the new couple must stand in need of some refreshment; Black Betty, which was the name of the bottle, was called for and sent up the ladder. But sometimes Black Betty did not go alone. I have many times seen as much bread, beef, pork and cabbage, sent along with her, as would afford a good meal for half a dozen of hungry men. The young couple were compelled to eat more or less of whatever was offered them.

In the course of the festivity, if any wanted to help himself to a dram and the young couple to a toast, he would call out, "Where is Black Betty? I want to kiss her sweet lips." Black Betty was soon handed to him, when, holding her up in his right hand, he would say, "Here's health to the groom, not forgetting myself, and here's to the bride, thumping luck and big children!" This, so far from being taken amiss, was considered as an expression of a very proper and friendly wish; for big children, especially sons, were of great importance, as we were few in number and engaged in perpetual hostility with the Indians, the end of which no one could foresee. Indeed many of them seemed to suppose that war was the natural state of man, and therefore did not anticipate any conclusion of it; every big son was therefore considered as a young soldier.

But to return. It often happened that some neighbors or relations, not being asked to the wedding, took offense; and the mode of revenge adopted by them on such occasions, was that of cutting off the manes, foretops, and tails of the horses of the wedding company.

Another method of revenge which was adopted when the chastity of the bride was a little suspected, was that of setting up a pair of horns on poles or trees, on the route of the wedding company. This was a hint to the groom that he might expect to be complimented with a pair of horns himself.

On returning to the infare, the order of procession and the race for Black Betty was the same as before. The feasting and dancing often lasted several days, at the end of which the whole company were so exhausted with loss of sleep, that several days' rest were requisite to fit them to return to their ordinary labors.

Should I be asked why I have presented this unpleasant portrait of the rude manners of our forefathers? I in my turn would ask my reader, why are you pleased with the histories of the blood and carnage of battles? Why are you delighted with the fictions of poetry, the novel and romance? I have related truth, and only truth, strange as it may seem. I have depicted a state of society and manners which are fast vanishing from the memory of man, with a view to give the youth of our country a knowledge of the advantage of civilization, and to give contentment to the aged by preventing them from saying, "that former times were better than the present."

—:o:—

CHAPTER XXIII.

THE HOUSE WARMING.

I will proceed to state the usual manner of settling a young couple in the world.

A spot was selected on a piece of land of one of the parents for their habitation. A day was appointed shortly after their marriage for commencing the work of building their cabin. The fatigue party consisted of choppers, whose business it was to fall the trees and cut them off at proper lengths—a man with his team for hauling them to the place, and arranging them, properly assorted, at the sides and ends of the building —and a carpenter, if such he might be called, whose business it was to search the woods for a proper tree for making clapboards for the roof. The tree for this purpose must be straight-grained, and from three to four feet in diameter. The boards were split four feet long, with a large frow, and as wide as the timber would allow. They were used without planing or shaving. Another division were employed in getting puncheons for the floor of the cabin; this was done by splitting trees about eighteen inches in diameter, and hewing the faces of them with a broad-axe. They were half the length of the floor they were intended to make.

The materials for the cabin were mostly prepared on the first day, and sometimes the foundation laid in the evening; the second day was allotted for the raising.

In the morning of the next day the neighbors collected for the raising. The first thing to be done was the election of four corner-men, whose business it was to notch and place the logs, the rest of the company furnishing them with the timbers. In the mean time the boards and puncheons were collecting for the floor and roof, so that by the time the cabin was a few rounds high, the sleepers and floor began to be laid. The door was made by cutting or sawing the logs in one side so as to make an opening about three feet wide; this opening was secured by upright pieces of timber about three inches thick, through which holes were bored into the ends of the logs for the purpose of pinning them fast. A similar opening, but wider, was made at the end for the chimney. This was built of logs, and made large, to admit of a back and jambs of stone. At the square two end logs projected a foot or eighteen inches beyond the wall, to receive the butting poles as they were called, against which the ends of the first row of clapboards was supported. The roof was formed by making the end logs shorter until a single log formed the comb of the roof. On these logs the clapboards were placed, the ranges of them lapping some distance over those next below them, and kept in their places by logs placed at proper distances upon them.

The roof and sometimes the floor were finished on the same day of the raising; a third day was commonly spent by a few carpenters in leveling off the floor, making a clapboard door, and a table. This last was made of a split slab, and supported by four round legs set in auger holes; some three-legged stools were made in the same manner. Some pins, stuck in the logs at the back of the house, supported some clapboards which served for shelves for the table furniture. A single fork, placed with its lower end in a hole in the floor, and the upper end fastened to a joist, served for a bedstead, by placing a pole in the fork with one end through a crack between the logs in the wall. This front pole was crossed by a shorter one within the fork, with its outer end through another crack. From the front pole, through a crack between the logs of the end of the house, the boards were put on which formed the bottom of the bed. Sometimes other poles were pinned to the fork a little distance between these, for the purpose of supporting the front and foot of the bed, while the walls were the support of its back and head. A few pegs around the walls, for the display of the coats of the women and hunting shirts of the men, and two small forks or buck's horns to a joist for the rifle and shot pouch, completed the carpenter work.

In the mean time masons were at work. With the heart pieces of the timber of which the clapboards were made, they made billets for chunking up the cracks between the logs of the cabin and chimney. A large bed of mortar was made for daubing up these cracks; and a few stones formed the back and jambs of the chimney.

The cabin being finished, the ceremony of house warning took place, before the young couple were permitted to move into it. This was a dance of the whole night's continuance, made up of the relations of the bride and groom and their neighbors. On the day following, the young couple took possession of their new mansion.

——:0:——

CHAPTER XXIV.

WORKING.

Tʜᴇ necessary labors of the farms along the frontiers were performed with every danger and difficulty imaginable. The whole population of the frontiers, huddled together in their little forts, left the country with every appearance of a deserted region; and such would have been the opinion of a traveler concerning it, if he had not seen here and there some small fields of corn or other grain in a growing state.

It is easy to imagine what losses must have been sustained by our first settlers owing to this deserted state of their farms. It was not the full measure of their trouble that they risked their lives, and often lost them, in subduing the forest and turning it into fruitful fields; but compelled to leave them in a deserted state during the summer season, a great part of the fruits of their labors was lost by this untoward circumstance. The sheep and hogs were devoured by the wolves, panthers and bears. Horses and cattle were often let into their fields, through breaches made in their fences by the falling of trees, and frequently almost the whole of a little crop of corn was destroyed by squirrels and raccoons, so that many families, even after an hazardous and laborious spring and summer, had but little left for the comfort of the dreary winter.

The early settlers on the frontiers of this country were like Arabs of the desert of Africa, in at least two respects. Every man was a soldier, and from early in the spring till late in the fall was almost continually in arms. Their work was often carried on by parties, each one of whom had his rifle and every thing else belonging to his war dress. These were deposited in some central place in the field. A sentinel was stationed on the outside of the fence, so that on the least alarm the whole company repaired to their arms, and were ready for combat in a moment.

Here again the rashness of some families proved a source of difficulty. instead of joining the working parties, they went out and attended their farms by themselves, and in case of alarm, an express was sent for them, and sometimes a party of men to guard them to the fort. These families, in some instances, could boast that they had better crops, and were every way better provided for in the winter than their neighbors: in other instances their temerity cost them their lives.

In military affairs, when every one concerned is left to his own will, matters were sure to be badly managed. The whole frontiers of Pennsylvania and Virginia presented a succession of military camps or forts. We had military officers, that is to say, captains and colonels; but they in many respects were only nominally such. They could advise, but not command. Those who chose to follow their advice did so, to such an extent as suited their fancy or interest. Others were refractory and thereby gave much trouble. These officers would leave a scout or campaign, while those who thought proper to accompany them did so, and those who did not remained at home. Public odium was the only punishment for their laziness or cowardice. There was no compulsion to the performance of military duties, and no pecuniary reward when they were performed.

It is but doing justice to the first settlers of this country to say, that instances of disobedience of families and individuals to the advice of our officers, were by no means numerous. The greater number cheerfully submitted to their directions with a prompt and faithful obedience.

——:o:——

CHAPTER XXV.

MECHANIC ARTS.

In giving a history of the state of the mechanic arts, as they were exercised at an early period of the settlement of this country, I shall present a people, driven by necessity to perform works of mechanical skill, far beyond what a person enjoying all the advantages of civilization, would expect from a population placed in such destitute circumstances.

My reader will naturally ask where were their mills for grinding grain —where their tanners for making leather—where their smith shops for making and repairing their farming utensils? Who were their carpenters, tailors, cabinet workmen, shoemakers and weavers? The answer is, those manufacturers did not exist, nor had they any tradesmen who were professedly such. Every family were under the necessity of doing every thing for themselves as well as they could.

The hommony blocks and hand mills were in use in most of our houses. The first was made of a large block of wood about three feet long, with an excavation burned in one end, wide at the top and narrow at the bottom, so that the action of the pestle on the bottom threw the corn up to the sides towards the top of it, from whence it continually fell down into the centre. In consequence of this movement, the whole mass of the grain was pretty equally subjected to the strokes of the pestle. In the fall of the year, whilst the Indian corn was soft, the block and pestle did very well for making meal for journeycake and mush, but were rather slow when the corn became hard.

The sweep was sometimes used to lessen the toil of pounding grain into meal. This was a pole of some springy elastic wood, thirty feet long or more, the but end of which was placed under the side of a house or a large stump. This pole was supported by two forks, placed about one third of its length from its but end, so as to elevate the small end about fifteen feet from the ground. To this was attached, by a large mortise, a piece of sapling about five or six inches in diameter, and eight or ten feet long, the lower end of which was shaped so as to answer for a pestle, and a pin of wood was put through it at a proper height, so that two persons could work at the sweep at once. This simple machine very much lessened the labor and expedited the work.

I remember that when a boy I put up an excellent sweep at my father's. It was made of a sugar tree sapling, and was kept going almost constanly from morning till night by our neighbors for several weeks.

In the Greenbrier country, where they had a number of saltpetre caves, the first settlers made plenty of excellent gunpowder by means of these sweeps and mortars.

A machine still more simple than the mortar and pestle was used for making meal when the corn was too soft to be beaten. It was called a grater. This was a half circular piece of tin, perforated with a punch from the concave side, and nailed by its edges to a block of wood. The ears of corn were rubbed on the rough edges of the holes, while the meal fell through them on the board or block to which the grater was nailed, which being in a slanting direction, discharged the meal into a cloth or bowl placed for its reception. This, to be sure, was a slow way of making meal, but necessity has no law.

The hand mill was better than the mortar and grater. It was made of two circular stones, the lowest of which was called the bed stone, the upper one the runner. These were placed in a hoop, with a spout for discharging the meal. A staff was let into a hole in the upper surface of the runner, near the outer edge, and its upper end through a hole in a board fastened to a joist above, so that two persons could be employed in turning the mill at the same time. The grain was put into the opening in the runner by hand. These mills are still in use in Palestine, the ancient country of the Jews. To a mill of this sort our Savior alluded, when, with reference to the destruction of Jerusalem, he said, "Two women shall be grinding at a mill, the one shall be taken and other left."

This mill is much preferable to that used at present in upper Egypt for making the dhourra bread. It is a smooth stone, placed on an inclined plane, upon which the grain is spread, which is made into meal by rubbing another stone up and down upon it.

Our first water mills were of that description denominated tub mills. It consists of a perpendicular shaft, to the lower end of which a horizontal wheel of about four or five feet in diameter is attached: the upper end passes through the bed stone and carries the runner, after the manner of a trundlehead. These mills were built with very little expense, and many of them answered the purpose very well. Instead of bolting cloths, sifters were in general use. These were made of deer skins in the state of parchment, stretched over a hoop and perforated with a hot wire.

Our clothing was all of domestic manufacture. We had no other resource for clothing, and this indeed was a poor one. The crops of flax often failed, and the sheep were destroyed by the wolves. Linsey, which is made of flax and wool, the former the chain, and the latter the filling, was the warmest and most substantial cloth we could make. Almost every house contained a loom and almost every woman was a weaver.

Every family tanned their own leather. The tan vat was a large trough sunk to the upper end in the ground. A quantity of bark was easily obtained every spring in clearing and fencing land. This, after drying, was brought in, and in wet days was shaved and pounded on a block of wood with an axe or mallet. Ashes was used in place of lime for taking off the hair. Bear's oil, hog's lard and tallow, answered the place of fish oil. The leather, to be sure, was coarse; but it was substantially good. The operation of currying was performed by a drawing knife with its edge turned after the manner of a currying knife. The blacking for the leather was made of soot and hog's lard.

Almost every family contained its own tailors and shoemakers. Those who could not make shoes could make shoe-packs. These, like moccasons, were made of a single piece of leather, with the exception of a tongue piece on the top of the foot, which was about two inches broad and circular at the lower end, and to which the main piece of leather was sewed with a gathering stitch. The seam behind was like that of a moccason, and a sole was sometimes added. The women did the tailor work. They could all cut out and make hunting shirts, leggins and drawers.

The state of society which existed in our country at an early period of its settlement, was well calculated to call into action every native mechanical genius. There was in almost every neighborhood, some one whose natural ingenuity enabled him to do many things for himself and his neighbors, far above what could have been reasonably expected. With the very few tools which they brought with them into the country, they certainly performed wonders. Their plows, harrows with their wooden teeth, and sleds, were in many instances well made. Their cooper-ware, which comprehended every thing for holding milk and water, was generally pretty well executed. The cedar-ware, by having alternately a white and red stave, was then thought beautiful. Many of their puncheon floors were very neat, their joints close, and the top even and smooth. Their looms, although heavy, did very well. Those who could not exercise these mechanic arts were under the necessity of giving labor or barter to their neighbors in exchange for the use of them, so far as their necessities required.

An old man in my father's neighborhood had the art of turning bowls, from the knots of trees, particularly those of the ash. In what way he did it I do not know, or whether there was much mystery in his art. Be that as it may, the old man's skill was in great request, as well-turned wooden bowls were amongst our first-rate articles of household furniture.

My brothers and myself once undertook to procure a fine suit of these bowls made of the best wood, the ash. We gathered all we could find on our father's land, and took them to the artist, who was to give, as the saying was, one half for the other. He put the knots in a branch before the door, when a freshet came and swept them all away, not one of them being ever found. This was a dreadful misfortune. Our anticipation of an elegant display of new bowls was utterly blasted in a moment, as the poor old man was not able to repair our loss or any part of it.

My father possessed a mechanical genius of the highest order, and necessity, which is the mother of invention, occasioned the full exercise of his talents. His farming utensils were the best in the neighborhood. After making his loom he often used it as a weaver. All the shoes belonging to the family were made by himself. He always spun his own shoe-thread, saying that no woman could spin shoe-thread as well as he could. His cooper-ware was made by himself. I have seen him make a small, neat kind of wooden ware, called set work, in which the staves were all attached to the bottom of the vessel, by means of a groove cut in them by a strong clasp knife and a small chisel, before a single hoop was put on. He was sufficiently the carpenter to build the best kind of houses then in use, that is to say, first a cabin, and afterwards the hewed log house, with a shingled roof. In his latter years he became sickly, and not being able to labor, he amused himself with tolerably good imitations of cabinet work.

Not possessing sufficient health for service on the scouts and campaigns, his duty was that of repairing the rifles of his neighbors when they needed it. In this business he manifested a high degree of ingenuity. A small depression on the surface of a stump or log, and a wooden mallet, were his instruments for straightening the gun barrel when crooked. Without the aid of a bow string he could discover the smallest bend in a barrel, and with a bit of steel he could make a saw for deepening the furrows when requisite. A few shots determined whether the gun might be trusted.

Although he never had been more than six weeks at school, he was nevertheless a first rate penman and a good arithmetician. His penmanship was of great service to his neighbors in writing letters, bonds, deeds of conveyance, &c.

Young as I was, I was possessed of an art which was of great use, viz: that of weaving shot pouch straps, belts and garters. I could make my loom and weave a belt in less than one day. Having a piece of board about four feet long, an inch auger, spike gimlet, and a drawing knife, I needed no other tools or materials for making my loom.

It frequently happened that my weaving proved serviceable to the family, as I often sold a belt for a day's work, or making an hundred rails; so that although a boy, I could exchange my labor for that of a full grown person for an equal length of time.

——:o:——

CHAPTER XXVI.

MEDICINE.

This amongst a rude and illiterate people consisted mostly of specifics. As far as I can recollect them, they shall be enumerated, together with the diseases for which they were used.

The diseases of children were mostly ascribed to worms; for the expulsion of which a solution of common salt was given, and the dose was always large. I well remember having been compelled to take half a table spoonful when quite small. To the best of my recollection it generally answered the purpose.

Scrapings of pewter spoons was another remedy for the worms. This dose was also large, amounting, I should think, from twenty to forty grains. It was commonly given in sugar.

Sulphate of iron, or green copperas, was a third remedy for the worms. The dose of this was also larger than we should venture to give at this time.

For burns, a poultice of Indian meal was a common remedy. A poultice of scraped potatoes was also a favorite remedy with some people.—— Roasted turnips, made into a poultice, was used by others. Slippery elm bark was often used in the same way. I do not recollect that any internal remedy or bleeding was ever used for burns.

The croup, or what was then called the "bold hives," was a common disease among the children, many of whom died of it. For the cure of this, the juice of roasted onions or garlic was given in large doses.—— Wall ink was also a favorite remedy with many of the old ladies. For fevers, sweating was the general remedy. This was generally performed by means of a strong decoction of Virginia snake root. The dose was always very large. If a purge was used, it was about half a pint of a strong decoction of walnut bark. This, when intended for a purge, was peeled downwards; if for a vomit, it was peeled upwards. Indian physic, or bowman root, a species of ipecacuanha, was frequently used for a vomit, and sometimes the pocoon or blood root.

For the bite of a rattle or copper-snake, a great variety of specifics were used. I remember when a small boy to have seen a man, bitten by a rattle-snake, brought into the fort on a man's back. One of the company dragged the snake after him by a forked stick fastened in its head. The body of the snake was cut into pieces of about two inches in length, split open in succession, and laid on the wound to draw out the poison, as they expressed it. When this was over, a fire was kindled in the fort and the whole of the serpent burnt to ashes, by way of revenge for the injury he had done. After this process was over, a large quantity of chestnut leaves was collected and boiled in a pot. The whole of the wounded man's leg and part of his thigh were placed in a piece of chestnut bark, fresh from the tree; and the decoction was poured on the leg so as to run down into the pot again. After continuing this process for some time, a quantity of the boiled leaves were bound to the leg. This was repeated several times a day. The man got well; but whether owing to the treatment bestowed on his wound, is not so certain.

A number of native plants were used for the cure of snake bites.— Among them the white plantain held a high rank. This was boiled in milk, and the decoction given the patient in large quantities. A kind of fern, which, from its resemblance to the leaves of the walnut, was called walnut fern, was another remedy. A plant with fibrous roots, resembling the seneca snake root, of a black color, and a strong but not disagreeable smell, was considered and relied on as the Indian specific for the cure of the sting of a snake. A decoction of this root was also used for the cure for colds. Another plant, which very much resembles the one above mentioned, but which is violently poisonous, was sometimes mistaken for it and used in its place. I knew two young women, who, in consequence of being bitten by rattle-snakes, used the poisonous plant instead of the other, and nearly lost their lives by the mistake. The roots were applied to their legs in the form of a poultice. The violent burning and swelling occasioned by the inflammation discovered the mistake in time to prevent them from taking any of the decoction, which, had they done, would have been instantly fatal. It was with difficulty that the part to which the poultice was applied was saved from mortification, so that the remedy was worse than the disease.

Cupping, sucking the wound, and making deep incisions which were filled with salt and gun-power, were also amongst the remedies for snake bites.

It does not appear to me that any of the internal remedies, used by the Indians and the first settlers of this country, were well adapted for the cure of the disease occasioned by the bite of a snake. The poison of a snake, like that of a bee or a wasp, must consist of a highly concentrated and very poisonous acid, which instantly inflames the part to which it is applied. That any substance whatever can act as a specific for the decomposition of this poison, seems altogether doubtful. The cure of the fever occasioned by this animal poison, must be effected with reference to those general indications which are regarded in the cure of other fevers of equal force. The internal remedies alluded to, so far as I am acquainted with them, are possessed of little or no medical efficacy. They are not emetics, cathartics, or sudorifies. What then? They are harmless substances, which do wonders in all those cases in which there is nothing to be done.

The truth is, the bite of a rattle or copper-snake, in a fleshy or tendinous part, where the blood vessels are neither numerous or large, soon healed under any kind of treatment. But when the fangs of the serpent, which are hollow, and eject the poison through an orifice near the points, penetrate a blood vessel of any considerable size, a malignant and incu-

rable fever was generally the immediate consequence, and the patient
often expired in the first paroxysm.

The same observations apply to the effects of the bite of serpents when
inflicted on beasts. Horses were frequently killed by them, as they were
commonly bitten somewhere about the nose, in which the blood vessels
are numerous and large. I once saw a horse die of the bite of a rattle-
snake : the blood for some time before he expired exuded in great quantity through the pores of the skin.

Cattle were less frequently killed, because their noses are of a grisly
texture, and less furnished with blood vessels than those of a horse.—
Dogs were sometimes bitten, and being naturally physicians, they commonly scratched a hole in some damp place, and held the wounded part
in the ground till the inflammation abated. Hogs, when in tolerable order,
were never hurt by them, owing to the thick substratum of fat between the
skin, muscular flesh, and blood vessels. The hog generally took immediate revenge for the injury done him, by instantly tearing to pieces and
devouring the serpent which inflicted it.

The itch, which was a very common disease in early times, was commonly cured by an ointment made of brimstone and hog's lard.

Gun-shot and other wounds were treated with slippery elm bark, flax-
seed, and other such like poultices. Many lost their lives from wounds
which would now be considered trifling and easily cured. The use of
the lancet, and other means of depletion, in the treatment of wounds,
constituted no part of their cure in this country, in early times.

My mother died in early life of a wound from the tread of a horse,
which any person in the habit of letting blood might have cured by two
or three bleedings, without any other remedy. The wound was poul-
ticed with spikenard root, and soon terminated in an extensive mortification.

Most of the men of the early settlers of this country were affected with
the rheumatism. For relief from this disease, the hunters generally slept
with their feet to the fire. From this practice they certainly derived
much advantage. The oil of rattle-snakes, geese, wolves, bears, raccoons, ground-hogs and pole-cats, was applied to the swelled joints, and
bathed in before the fire.

The pleurisy was the only disease which was supposed to require blood
letting ; but in many cases a bleeder was not to be had.

Coughs and pulmonary consumptions were treated with a great variety
of syrups, the principal ingredients of which were spikenard and elecam-
pane. These syrups certainly gave but little relief.

Charms and incantations were in use for the cure of many diseases.—
I learned, when young, the incantation, in German, for the cure of burns,
stopping blood, tooth-ache, and the charm against bullets in battle ;
but for the want of faith in their efficacy, I never used any of them.

The erysipelas, or St. Anthony's fire, was circumscribed by the blood
of a black cat. Hence there was scarcely a black cat to be seen, whose
ears and tail had not been frequently cropped off for a contribution of
blood.

*Y

Whether the medical profession is productive of most good or harm, may still be a matter of dispute with some philosophers, who never saw any condition of society in which there were no physicians, and therefore could not be furnished with a proper test for deciding the question.— Had an unbeliever in the healing art been amongst the early inhabitants of this country, he would have been in a proper situation to witness the consequences of the want of the exercise of this art. For many years in succession there was no person who bore even the name of a doctor within a considerable distance of the residence of my father.

For the honor of the medical profession, I must give it as my opinion that many of our people perished for want of medical skill and attention.

The pleurisy was the only disease which was, in any considerable degree, understood by our people. A pain in the side called for the use of the lancet, if there was any to be had; but owing to its sparing use, the patient was apt to be left with a spitting of blood, which sometimes ended in consumption. A great number of children died of the croup. Remittent and intermittent fevers were treated with warm drinks for the purpose of sweating; and the patients were denied the use of cold water and fresh air; consequently many of them died. Of those who escaped, not a few died afterwards of the dropsy or consumption, or were left with paralytic limbs. Deaths in childbed were not unfrequent. Many, no doubt, died of the bite of serpents, in consequence of an improper reliance on specifics possessed of no medical virtue.

My father died of an hepatic complaint, at the age of about forty-six.— He had labored under it for thirteen years. The fever which accompanied it was called "the dumb ague," and the swelling in the region of the liver, "the ague cake." The abscess burst, and discharged a large quantity of matter, which put a period to his life in about thirty hours after the discharge.

Thus I for one may say, that in all human probability I lost both my parents for want of medical aid.

CHAPTER XXVII.

SPORTS.

THESE were such as might be expected among a people, who, owing to their circumstances as well as education, set a higher value on physical than on mental endowments, and on skill in hunting and bravery in war, than on any polite accomplishments or fine arts.

Amusements are, in many instances, either imitations of the business of life, or at least of some of its particular objects of pursuit. On the part of young men belonging to nations in a state of warfare, many amusements are regarded as preparations for the military character which they are expected to sustain in future life. Thus the war-dance of savages is a pantomime of their stratagems and horrid deeds of cruelty in war, and the exhibition prepares the minds of their young men for a participation in the bloody tragedies which they represent. Dancing, among civilised people, is regarded, not only as an amusement suited to the youthful period of human life, but as a means of inducing urbanity of manners and a good personal deportment in public. Horse racing is regarded by the statesman as a preparation, in various ways, for the equestrian department of warfare: it is said that the English government never possessed a good cavalry, until, by the encouragement given to public races, their breed of horses was improved. Games, in which there is a mixture of chance and skill, are said to improve the understanding in mathematical and other calculations.

Many of the sports of the early settlers of this country were imitative of the exercises and stratagems of hunting and war. Boys are taught the use of the bow and arrow at an early age; but although they acquired considerable adroitness in the use of them, so as to kill a bird or squirrel sometimes, yet it appears that in the hands of the white people, the bow and arrow could never be depended upon for warfare or hunting, unless made and managed in a different manner from any specimens of them which I ever saw.

In ancient times, the bow and arrow must have been deadly instruments in the hands of the barbarians of our country; but I much doubt whether any of the present tribes of Indians could make much use of the flint arrow heads, which must have been so generally used by their forefathers.

Fire arms, wherever they can be obtained, soon put an end to the use of the bow and arrow; but independently of this circumstance, military, as well as other arts, sometimes grow out of date and vanish from the world. Many centuries have elapsed since the world has witnessed the destructive accuracy of the Benjaminites in their use of the sling and stone; nor does it appear to me that a diminution, in the size and strength of the aboriginals of this country, has occasioned a decrease of accuracy and effect in their use of the bow and arrow. From all the ancient skeletons which have come under my notice, it does not appear that this section of the globe was ever inhabited by a larger race of human beings than that which possessed it at the time of its discovery by the Europeans.

One important pastime of our boys was that of imitating the noise of every bird and beast in the woods. This faculty was not merely a pastime, but a very necessary part of education, on account of its utility in certain circumstances. The imitations of the gobbling and other sounds of wild turkeys, often brought those keen eyed and ever watchful tenants of the forest within reach of the rifle. The bleating of the fawn brought its dam to her death in the same way. The hunter often collected a company of mopish owls to the trees about his camp; and while he amused himself with their hoarse screaming, his howl would raise and obtain responses from a pack of wolves, so as to inform him of their neighborhood, as well as guard him against their depredations.

This imitative faculty was sometimes requisite as a measure of precaution in war. The Indians, when scattered about in a neighborhood, often collect together, by imitating turkeys by day, and wolves or owls by night. In similar situations our people did the same. I have often witnessed the consternation of a whole neighborhood in consequence of a few screeches of owls. An early and correct use of this imitative faculty was considered as an indication that its possessor would become in due time a good hunter and a valiant warrior.

Throwing the tomahawk was another boyish sport, in which many acquired considerable skill. The tomahawk, with its handle of a certain length, will make a given number of turns in a given distance. Say at five steps, it will strike with the edge, the handle downwards; at the distance of seven and a half, it will strike with the edge, the handle upwards; and so on. A little experience enabled the boy to measure the distance with his eye, when walking through the woods, and strike a tree with his tomahawk in any way he chose.

The athletic sports of running, jumping and wrestling, were the pastime of boys, in common with the men.

A well grown boy, at the age of twelve or thirteen years, was furnished with a small rifle and shot pouch. He then became a fort soldier, and had his port hole assigned him. Hunting squirrels, turkeys and raccoons, soon made him expert in the use of his gun.

Dancing was the principal amusement of our young people of both sexes. Their dances, to be sure, were of the simplest forms—three and four handed reels and jigs. Country dances, cotilions and minuets, were unknown. I remember to have seen, once or twice, a dance which was called "the Irish trot:" but I have long since forgotten its figure.

Shooting at marks was a common diversion among the men, when their stock of ammunition would allow it, which, however, was far from being always the case. The present mode of shooting off-hand was not then in practice : it was not considered as any trial of the value of a gun, nor indeed as much of a test of the skill of a marksman. Their shooting was from a rest, and at as great a distance as the length and weight of the barrel of the gun would throw a ball on a horizontal level. Such was their regard to accuracy, in those sportive trials of their rifles, and of their own skill in the use of them, that they often put moss, or some other soft substance on the log or stump from which they shot, for fear of having the bullet thrown from the mark, by the spring of the barrel.— When the rifle was held to the side of a tree for a rest, it was pressed against it as lightly as possible for the same reason.

Rifles of former times were different from those of modern date : few of them carried more than forty-five bullets to the pound, and bullets of a less size were not thought sufficiently heavy for hunting or war.

Dramatic narrations, chiefly concerning Jack and the Giant, furnished our young people with another source of amusement during their leisure hours. Many of those tales were lengthy, and embraced a considerable range of incident. Jack, always the hero of the story, after encountering many difficulties, and performing many great achievements, came off conqueror of the Giant. Many of these stories were tales of knight-errantry, in which case some captive virgin was released from captivity and restored to her lover.

These dramatic narrations concerning Jack and the Giant bore a strong resemblance to the poems of Ossian, the story of the Cyclops and Ulysses in the Odyssey of Homer, and the tale of the Giant and Great-heart in the Pilgrim's Progress, and were so arranged as to the different incidents of the narration, that they were easily committed to memory. They certainly have been handed down, from generation to generation from time immemorial. Civilization has indeed banished the use of those ancient tales of romantic heroism ; but what then ? It has substituted in their place the novel and romance.

It is thus that in every state of society the imagination of man is eternally at war with reason and truth. That fiction should be acceptable to an unenlightened people is not to be wondered at, as the treasures of truth have never been unfolded to their mind ; but that a civilised people themselves should, in so many instances, like barbarians, prefer the fairy regions of fiction to the august treasures of truth, developed in the sciences of theology, history, natural and moral philosophy, is truly a sarcasm on human nature. It is as much as to say, that it is essential to our amusement, that, for the time being, we must suspend the exercise of reason, and submit to a voluntary deception.

Singing was another but not very common amusement among our first settlers. Their tunes were rude enough, to be sure. Robin Hood furnished a number of our songs ; the balance were mostly tragical, and were denominated "love songs about murder." As to cards, dice, backgammon, and other games of chance, we knew nothing about them.— These are amongst the blessed gifts of civilization.

————:o:————

CHAPTER XXVIII.

WITCHCRAFT.

I SHALL not be lengthy on this subject. The belief in witchcraft was prevalent amongst the early settlers of the western country. To the witch was ascribed the tremendous power of inflicting strange and incurable diseases, particularly on children—of destroying cattle by shooting them with hair balls, and a great variety of other means of destruction—of inflicting spells and curses on guns and other things—and lastly, of changing men into horses, and after bridling and saddling them, riding them in full speed over hill and dale to their frolics and other places of rendezvous. More ample powers of mischief than these cannot be imagined.

Wizards were men supposed to be possessed of the same mischievous power as the witches; but it was seldom exercised for bad purposes.— The power of the wizards was exercised almost exclusively for the purpose of counteracting the malevolent influence of the witches of the other sex. I have known several of those witch-masters, as they were called, who made a public profession of curing the diseases inflicted by the influence of witches; and I have known respectable physicians, who had no greater portion of business in the line of their profession, than many of those witch-masters had in theirs.

The means by which the witch was supposed to inflict diseases, curses, and spells, I never could learn. They were occult sciences, which no one was supposed to understand excepting the witch herself, and no wonder, as no such arts ever existed in any country.

The diseases of children, supposed to be inflicted by witchcraft, were those of the internal dropsy of the brain, and the rickts. The symptoms and cure of these destructive diseases were utterly unknown in former times in this country. Diseases which could neither be accounted for nor cured, were usually ascribed to some supernatural agency of a malignant kind.

For the cure of diseases inflicted by witchcraft, the picture of the supposed witch was drawn on a stump or piece of board, and shot at with a bullet containing a little bit of silver. This bullet transferred a painful and sometimes a mortal spell on that part of the witch corresponding with the part of the portrait struck by the bullet. Another method of cure was that of getting some of the child's water, which was closely corked up in a vial and hung up in a chimney. This complimented the witch with a stranguary, which lasted as long as the vial remained in the chimney. The witch had but one way of relieving herself from any spell inflicted on her in any way, which was that of borrowing something, no matter what, of the family to which the subject of the exercise of her witchcraft belonged.

I have known several poor old women much surprised at being refused requests which had usually been granted without hesitation, and almost heart broken when informed of the cause of the refusal.

When cattle or dogs were supposed to be under the influence of witchcraft, they were burnt in the forehead by a branding iron, or when dead, burned wholly to ashes. This inflicted a spell upon the witch which could only be removed by borrowing, as above stated.

Witches were often said to milk the cows of their neighbors. This they did by fixing a new pin in a new towel for each cow intended to be milked. This towel was hung over her own door, and by means of certain incantations, the milk was extracted from the fringes of the towel after the manner of milking a cow. This happened when the cows were too poor to give much milk.

The first German glass-blowers in this country drove the witches out of their furnaces by throwing living puppies into them.

The greater or less amount of belief in witchcraft, necromancy and astrology, serves to show the relative amount of philosophical science in any country. Ignorance is always associated with superstition, which, presenting an endless variety of sources of hope and fear, with regard to the good or bad fortunes of life, keep the benighted mind continually harassed with groundless and delusive, but strong and often deeply distressing impressions of a false faith. For this disease of the mind there is no cure but that of philosophy. This science shows to the enlightened reason of man, that no effect whatever can be produced in the physical world without a corresponding cause. This science announces that the death bell is but a momentary morbid motion of the nerves of the ear, and the death watch the noise of a bug in the wall, and that the howling of the dog, and the croaking of the raven, are but the natural languages of the beast and fowl, and no way prophetic of the death of the sick.— The comet, which used to shake pestilence and war from its fiery train, is now viewed with as little emotion as the movements of Jupiter and Saturn in their respective orbits.

An eclipse of the sun, and an unusual freshet of the Tiber, shortly after the assassination of Julius Cæsar by Cassius and Brutus, threw the whole of the Roman empire into consternation. It was supposed that all the gods of heaven and earth were enraged, and about to take revenge for the murder of the emperor; but since the science of astronomy foretells in the calendar the time and the extent of the eclipse, the phenomenon is not viewed as a miraculous and portentous, but as a common and natural event.

That the pythoness and wizard of the Hebrews, the monthly soothsayers, astrologers and prognosticators of the Chaldeans, and the sybils of the Greeks and Romans, were mercenary impostors, there can be no doubt.

To say that the pythoness, and all others of her class, were aided in their operations by the entervention of familiar spirits, does not mend the matter; for spirits, whether good or bad, possess not the power of life and death, health and disease, with regard to man and beast. Prescience is an incommunicable attribute of God, and therefore spirits cannot foretell future events.

The afflictions of Job, through the intervention of Satan, were miraculous. The possessions mentioned in the New Testament, in all human probabilty, were maniacal diseases, and if, at their cures, the supposed evil spirit spoke with an audible voice, these events were also miraculous, and effected for a special purpose. But from miracles, no general conclusion can be drawn with regard to the divine government of the world.

The conclusion is, that the powers professed to be exercised by the occult science of necromancy and other arts of divination, were neither more nor less than impostures.

Amongst the Hebrews, the profession of arts of divination was thought deserving of capital punishment, because the profession was of Pagan origin, and of course incompatible with the profession of theism, and a theocratic form of government. These jugglers perpetrated a debasing superstition among the people. They were also swindlers, who divested their neighbors of large sums of money and valuable presents without an equivalent.

On the ground then of fraud alone, according to the genius of the criminal codes of the ancient governments, the offense deserved capital punishment.

But is the present time better than the past with regard to a superstitious belief in occult influences? Do no traces of the polytheism of our forefathers remain among their christian descendants? This inquiry must be answered in the affirmative. Should an almanac-maker venture to give out the christian calendar without the column containing the signs of the zodiac, the calendar would be condemned as totally deficient, and the whole impression would remain on his hands.

But what are those signs? They are the constellations of the zodiac, that is, clusters of stars, twelve in number, within and including the tropics of Cancer and Capricorn. These constellations resemble the animals after which they are named. But what influence do these clusters of stars exert on the animal and the plant? Certainly none at all; and yet we have been taught that the northern constellations govern the divisions of living bodies alternately from the head to the reins, and in like manner the southern from the reins to the feet. The sign then makes a skip from the feet to Aries, who again assumes the government of the head, and so on.

About half these constellations are friendly divinities, and exert a salutary influence on the animal and the plant. The others are malignant in their temper, and govern only for evil purposes. They blast during their reign the seed sown in the earth, and render medicine and the operations of surgery unsuccessful.

We have read of the Hebrews worshipping the hosts of heaven whenever they relapsed into idolatry; and these same constellations were the hosts of heaven which they worshipped. We, it is true, make no offering to these hosts of heaven, but we give them our faith and confidence.—— We hope for physical benefits from those of them whose dominion is friendly to our interests, while the reign of the malignant ones is an object of dread and painful apprehension.

Let us not boast very much of our science, civilization, or even christianity, while this column of the relics of paganism still disgraces the christian calendar.

I have made these observations with a view to discredit the remnants of superstition still existing among us. While dreams, the howling of the dog, and the croaking of the raven, are prophetic of future events, we are not good christians. While we are dismayed at the signs of heaven, we are for the time being pagans. Life has real evils enough to contend with, without imaginary ones.

:0:

CHAPTER XXIX.

MORALS.

In the section of the country where my father lived, there was, for many years after the settlement of the country, "neither law nor gospel." Our want of legal government was owing to the uncertainty whether we belonged to the state of Virginia or Pennsylvania. The line which at present divides the two states, was not run until some time after the conclusion of the revolutionary war. Thus it happened, that during a long period of time we knew nothing of courts, lawyers, magistrates, sheriffs or constables. Every one was therefore at liberty "to do whatsoever was right in his own eyes."

As this is a state of society which few of my readers have ever witnessed, I shall describe it as minutely as I can, and give in detail those moral maxims which in a great degree answered the important purposes of municipal jurisprudence.

In the first place, let it be observed that in a sparse population, where all the members of the community are well known to each other, and especially in a time of war, where every man capable of bearing arms is considered highly valuable as a defender of his country, public opinion has its full effect, and answers the purposes of legal government better - than it would in a dense population in time of peace.

Such was the situation of our people along the frontiers of our settlements. They had no civil, military or ecclesiastical laws, at least none that were enforced; and yet "they were a law unto themselves," as

*Q

to all the leading obligations of our nature in all the relations in which
they stood to each other. The turpitude of vice and the majesty of moral virtue were then as apparent as they are now, and they were then regarded with the same sentiments of aversion or respect which they in-
spire at the present time. Industry in working and hunting, bravery in
war, candor, honesty, hospitality, and steadiness of deportment, received
their full reward of public honor and public confidence among our rude
forefathers, as well as among their better instructed and more polished
descendants. The punishments which they inflicted upon offenders by
the imperial court of public opinion, were well adapted for the reformation of the culprit, or his expulsion from the community.

The punishment for idleness, lying, dishonesty, and ill fame generally,
was that of "hating the offender out," as they expressed it. This mode
of chastisement was like the *atimia* of the Greeks. It was a public expression, in various ways, of a general sentiment of indignation against
such as transgressed the moral maxims of the community to which they
belonged, and commonly resulted either in the reformation or banishment
of the person against whom it was directed.

At house-raisings, log-rollings, and harvest-parties, every one was expected to do his duty faithfully. A person who did not perform his share
of labor on these occasions, was designated by the epithet of "Lawrence,"
or some other title still more opprobrious; and when it came to his turn
to require the like aid from his neighbors, the idler felt his punishment
in their refusal to attend to his calls.

Although there was no legal compulsion to the performance of military
duty; yet every man of full age and size was expected to do his full
share of public service. If he did not do so, he was "hated out as a
coward." Even the want of any article of war equipments, such as ammunition, a sharp flint, a priming wire, a scalping knife, or tomahawk,
was thought highly disgraceful. A man, who without a reasonable excuse failed to go on a scout or campaign when it came to his turn, met
with an expression of indignation in the countenances of all his neighbors,
and epithets of dishonor were fastened upon him without mercy.

Debts, which make such an uproar in civilised life, were but little
known among our forefathers at an early settlement of this country.—
After the depreciation of the continental paper, they had no money of
any kind; every thing purchased was paid for in produce or labor. A
good cow and calf was often the price of a bushel of alum salt. If a
contract was not faithfully fulfilled, the credit of the delinquent was at an
end.

Any petty theft was punished with all the infamy that could be heaped
on the offender. A man on a campaign stole from his comrade a cake
out of the ashes in which it was baking. He was immediately named 'the
Bread rounds.' This epithet of reproach was bandied about in this way.
When he came in sight of a group of men, one of them would call, 'Who
comes there?' Another would answer, 'The Bread-rounds.' If any
one meant to be more serious about the matter, he would call out, 'Who
stole a cake out of the ashes?' Another replied by giving the name of
the man in full. To this a third would give confirmation by exclaiming,

'That is true and no lie.' This kind of 'tongue-lashing' he was doomed to bear for the rest of the campaign, as well as for years after his return home.

If a theft was detected in any of the frontier settlements, a summary mode of punishment was always resorted to. The first settlers, as far as I knew of them, had a kind of innate or hereditary detestation of the crime of theft, in any shape or degree, and their maxim was that 'a thief must be whipped.' If the theft was something of some value, a kind of jury of the neighborhood, after hearing the testimony, would condemn the culprit to Moses's law, that is, to forty stripes save one. If the theft was of some small article, the offender was doomed to carry on his back the flag of the United States, which then consisted of thirteen stripes. In either case, some able hands were selected to execute the sentence, so that the stripes were sure to be well laid on.

This punishment was followed by a sentence of exile. He then was informed that he must decamp in so many days and be seen there no more on penalty of having the number of his stripes doubled.

For many years after the law was put in operation in the western part of Virginia, the magistrates themselves were in the habit of giving those who were brought before them on charges of small thefts, the liberty of being sent to jail or taking a whipping. The latter was commonly chosen, and was immediately inflicted, after which the thief was ordered to clear out.

In some instances stripes were inflicted; not for the punishment of an offense, but for the purpose of extorting a confession from suspected persons. This was the torture of our early times, and no doubt sometimes very unjustly inflicted.

If a woman was given to tattling and slandering her neighbors, she was furnished by common consent with a kind of patent right to say whatever she pleased, without being believed. Her tongue was then said to be harmless, or to be no scandal.

With all their rudeness, these people were given to hospitality, and freely divided their rough fare with a neighbor or stranger, and would have been offended at the offer of pay. In their settlements and forts, they lived, they worked, they fought and feasted, or suffered together, in cordial harmony. They were warm and constant in their friendships. On the other hand they were revengeful in their resentments; and the point of honor sometimes led to personal combats. If one man called another a liar, he was considered as having given a challenge which the person who received it must accept, or be deemed a coward, and the charge was generally answered on the spot with a blow. If the injured person was decidedly unable to fight the aggressor, he might get a friend to do it for him. The same thing took place on a charge of cowardice, or any other dishonorable action. A battle must follow, and the person who made the charge must fight either the person against whom he made it, or any champion who chose to espouse his cause. Thus circumstanced, our people in early times were much more cautious of speaking evil of their neighbors than they are at present.

Sometimes pitched battles occurred, in which time, place, and seconds were appointed beforehand. I remember having seen one of these pitched battles in my father's fort, when a boy. One of the young men knew very well beforehand that he should get the worst of the battle, and no doubt repented the engagement to fight; but there was no getting over it. The point of honor demanded the risk of battle. He got his whipping; they then shook hands, and were good friends afterwards.

The mode of single combat in those days was dangerous in the extreme. Although no weapons were used, fists, teeth and feet were employed at will; but above all, the detestable practice of gouging, by which eyes were sometimes put out, rendered this mode of fighting frightful indeed. It was not, however, so destructive as the stiletto of an Italian, the knife of a Spaniard, the small sword of the Frenchman, or the pistol of the American or English duelist.

Instances of seduction and bastardy did not frequently happen in our early times. I remember one instance of the former, in which the life of the man was put in jeopardy by the resentment of the family to which the girl belonged. Indeed, considering the chivalrous temper of our people, this crime could not then take place without great personal danger from the brothers or other relations of the victims of seduction, family honor being then estimated at a high rate.

I do not recollect that profane language was much more prevalent in our early times than at present.

Among the people with whom I was conversant, there was no other vestige of the christian religion than a faint observance of Sunday, and that merely as a day of rest for the aged and play-day for the young.

The first christian service I ever heard was in the Garrison church in Baltimore county, in Maryland, where my father had sent me to school. I was then obout ten years old. The appearance of the church, the windows of which were Gothic, the white surplice of the minister, and the responses in the service, overwhelmed me with surprise. Among my school-fellows in that place, it was a matter of reproach to me that I was not baptized, and why? Because, as they said, I had no name. Such was their notion of the efficacy of baptism.

—:0:—

CHAPTER XXX.

THE REVOLUTION.

The American revolution was the commencement of a new era in the history of the world. The issue of that eventful contest snatched the sceptre from the hands of the monarch, and placed it, where it ought to be, in the hands of the people.

On the sacred altar of liberty it consecrated the rights of man, surrendered to him the right and power of governing himself, and placed in his hands the resources of his country, as munitions of war for his defense.— The experiment was indeed bold and hazardous ; but success has hitherto more than justified the most sanguine anticipations of those who made it. The world has witnessed, with astonishment, the rapid growth and confirmation of our noble fabric of freedom. From our distant horizon, we have reflected a strong and steady blaze of light on ill fated Europe, from time immemorial involved in the fetters and gloom of slavery.— Our history has excited a general and ardent spirit of inquiry into the nature of our civil institutions, and a strong wish on the part of the PEOPLE in distant countries, to participate in our blessings.

But will an example, so portentous of evil to the chiefs of despotic institutions, be viewed with indifference by those who now sway the sceptre with unlimited power, over the many millions of their vassals ?— Will they adopt no measures of defense against the influence of that freedom, so widely diffused and so rapidly gaining strength throughout their empires ? Will they make no effort to remove from the world those free governments, whose example gives them such annoyance? The measures of defense will be adopted, the effort will be made ; for power is never surrendered without a struggle.

Already nations, which, from the the earliest period of their history, have constantly crimsoned the earth with each other's blood, have become a band of brothers for the destruction of every germ of human liberty. Every year witnesses an association of the monarchs of those nations, in unhallowed conclave, for the purpose of concerting measures for effecting their dark designs. Hitherto the execution of those measures has been, alas! too fatally successful.

It would be impolitic and unwise in us to calculate on escaping the hostile notice of the despots of continental Europe. Already we hear, like distant thunder, their expressions of indignation and threats of vengeance. We ought to anticipate the gathering storm without dismay, but not with indifference. In viewing the dark side of the prospect before us, one source of consolation, of mubh magnitude, presents itself.—

It is confidently expected, that the brave and potent nation, with whom we have common origin, will not risk the loss of that portion of liberty, which at the expense of so much blood and treasure, they have secured for themselves, by an unnatural association with despots, for the unholy purpose of making war on the few nations of the earth, which possess any considerable portion of that invaluable blessing; on the contrary, it is hoped by us that they will, if necessity should require, employ the bravery of their people, their immense resources, and the trident of the ocean, in defense of their own liberties, and by consequence those of others.

Legislators, fathers of our country! lose no time, spare no expense in hastening on the requisite means of defense, for meeting with safety and with victory the impending storm, which sooner or later must fall upon us.

———·o·———

CHAPTER XXXI.

CIVILIZATION.

The causes which led to the present state of civilization in the western country, are subjects which deserve some consideration.

The state of society and manners of the early settlers, as presented in these notes, shews very clearly that their grade of civilization was indeed low enough. The descendants of the English cavaliers from Maryland and Virginia, who settled mostly along the rivers, and the descendants of the Irish, who settled in the interior parts of the country, were neither remarkable for science or urbanity of manners. The former were mostly illiterate, rough in their manners, and addicted to the rude diversions of horse racing, wrestling, shooting, dancing, &c. These diversions were often accompanied with personal combats, which consisted of blows, kicks, biting, and gouging. This mode of fighting was what they called *rough and tumble.* Sometimes a previous stipulation was made to use the fists only. Yet these people were industrious, enterprising, generous in their hospitality, and brave in the defense of their country.

These people, for the most part, formed the cordon along the Ohio river, on the frontiers of Pennsylvania, Virginia and Kentucky, which defended the country against the attacks of the Indians during the revolutionary war. They were the janizaries of the country, that is, they were soldiers when they chose to be so, and when they chose laid down their arms. Their military service was voluntary, and of course received no pay.

With the descendants of the Irish I had but little acquaintance, although I lived near them. At an early period they were comprehended in the Presbyterian church, and were more reserved in their deportment than their frontier neighbors, and from their situation being less exposed to the Indian warfare, took less part in that war.

The patriot of the western region finds his love of country and national pride augmented to the highest grade, when he compares the political, moral, and religious character of his people, with that of the inhabitants of many large divisions of the old world. In Asia and Africa, generation after generation passes without any change in the moral and religious character or physical condition of the people.

On the Barbary coast, the traveler, if a river lies in his way and happens to be too high, must either swim it or wait until it subsides. If the traveler is a christian, he must have a firman and a guard. Yet this was once the country of the famous Cathagenians.

In Upper Egypt, the people grind meal for their dhoura bread, by rubbing it between two flat stones. This is done by women.

In Palestine, the grinding of grain is still performed by an ill-constructed hand mill, as in the days of our Savior. The roads to the famous city of Jerusalem are still almost in the rude state of nature.

In Asiatic Turkey, merchandise is still carried on by caravans, which are attended with a military guard; and the naked walls of the caravansera is their fortress and place of repose at night, instead of a place of entertainment. The streets of Constantinople, instead of being paved, are in many places almost impassable from mud, filth, and the carcasses of dead beasts. Yet this is the metropolis of a great empire.

Throughout the whole of the extensive regions of Asia and Africa, man, from his cradle to his grave, sees no change in the aspect of any thing around him, unless from the desolations of war. His dress, his ordinary salutations of his neighbors, his diet and his mode of eating it, are prescribed by his religious institutions; and his rank in society, as well as his occupation, are determined by his birth. Steady and unvarying as the lapse of time in every department of life, generation after generation beats the dull monotonous round. The Hindoo would sooner die a martyr at the stake, than sit on a chair or eat with a knife and fork.

The descendant of Ishmael is still "a wild men." Hungry, thirsty and half naked, beneath a burning sun, he traverses the immense and inhospitable desert of Zahara, apparently without any object, because his forefathers did so before him. Throughout life he subsists on camel's milk and flesh, while his only covering from the inclemency of the weather is a flimsy tent of camel's hair. His single, solitary virtue, is that of hospitality to strangers: in every other respect he is a thief and a robber.

The Chinese still retain their alphabet of thirty-six thousand *hieroglyphics*. They must never exchange it for one of twenty letters, which would answer an infinitely better purpose.

Had we pursued the course of the greater number of the nations of the earth, we should have been this day treading in the footsteps of our forefathers, from whose example in any respect we should have thought it criminal to depart in the slightest degree.

Instead of a blind or superstitious imitation of the manners and customs of our forefathers, we have thought and acted for ourselves, and we have changed ourselves and every thing around us.

The linsey and coarse linen of the first settlers of the country, have been exchanged for the substantial and fine fabrics of Europe and Asia—the hunting shirt for the fashionable coat of broad cloth—and the moccason for boots and shoes of tanned leather. The dresses of our ladies are equal in beauty, fineness and fashion, to those of the cities and countries of Europe and Atlantic America.

It is not enough that persevering industry has enabled us to purchase the "purple and fine linen" from foreigners, and to use their porcelain and glass-ware, whether plain, engraved or gilt; we have nobly dared to fabricate those elegant, comfortable, and valuable productions of art for ourselves.

A well founded prospect of large gains from useful arts and honest labor has drawn to our country a large number of the best artisans of other countries. Their mechanic arts, immensely improved by American genius, have hitherto realised the hopeful prospect which induced their emigration to our infant country.

The horse paths, along which our forefathers made their laborious journeys over the mountains for salt and iron, were soon succeeded by wagon roads, and those again by substantial turnpikes, which, as if by magic enchantment, have brought the distant region, not many years ago denominated *"the backwoods,"* into a close and lucrative connection with our great Atlantic cities. The journey over the mountains, formerly considered so long, so expensive, and even perilous, is now made in a very few days, and with accommodations not displeasing to the epicure himself. Those giants of North America, the different mountains composing the great chain of the Allegany, formerly so frightful in their aspect, and presenting so many difficulties in their passage, are now scarcely noticed by the traveler, in his journey along the gradurated highways by which they are crossed.

The rude sports of former times have been discontinued. Athletic trials of muscular strength and activity, in which there certainly is not much of merit, have given way to the more noble ambition for mental endowments and skill in useful arts. To the rude and often indecent songs, but roughly and unskillfully sung, have succeeded the psalm, the hymn, and swelling anthem. To the clamorous boast, the provoking banter, the biting sarcasm, the horrid oath and imprecation, have succeeded urbanity of manners, and a course of conversation enlightened by science and chastened by mental attention and respect.

Above all, the direful spirit of revenge, the exercise of which so much approximated the character of many of the first settlers of our country to that of the worst of savages, is now unknown. The Indian might pass in safety among those, whose remembrance still bleeds at the recollection of the loss of their relatives, who have perished under the tomahawk and scalping knife of the savages.

The Moravian brethren may dwell in safety on the sites of the villages desolated, and over the bones of their brethren and forefathers murdered, by the more than savage ferocity of the whites. Nor let it be supposed that the return of peace produced this salutary change of feeling towards the tawney sons of the forest. The thirst for revenge was not wholly allayed by the balm of peace : several Indians fell victims to the private vengeance of those who had recently lost their relations in the war, for some years after it had ceased.

If the state of society and manners, from the commencement of the settlements in this country, during the lapse of many years, owing to the sanguinary character of the Indian mode of warfare and other circumstances, was in a state of retrogression, as was evidently the case—if ignorance is more easily induced than science—if society more speedily deteriorates than improves—if it be much easier for the civilised man to become wild, than for the wild man to become civilised ;—I ask, what means have arrested the progress of the early inhabitants of the western region toward barbarism ?—What agents have directed their influence in favor of science, morals, and piety ?

The early introduction of commerce was among the first means of changing, in some degree, the existing aspect of the population of the country, and giving a new current to public feeling and individual pursuit.

The huntsman and warrior, when he had exchanged his hunter's dress for that of civilised man, soon lost sight of his former occupation, and assumed a new character and a new line of life,—like the soldier, who, when he receives his discharge and lays aside his regimentals, soon loses the feeling of a soldier, and even forgets in some degree his manual exercise.

Had not commerce furnished the means of changing the dresses of our people and the furniture of their house—had the hunting shirt, moccason, and leggins, continued to be the dress of our men—had the three-legged stool, the noggin, the trencher and wooden bowl, continued to be the furniture of our houses,—our progress towards science and civilization would have been much slower.

It may seem strange that so much importance is attached to the influence of dress in giving the moral and intellectual character of society.

In all the institutions of despotic governments we discover evident traces of the highest grade of human sagacity and foresight. It must have been the object of the founders of those governments to repress the genius of man, divest the mind of every sentiment of ambition, and prevent the cognizance of any rule of life, excepting that of a blind obedience to the despot and his established institutions of religion and government : hence the canonical laws of religion, in all governments despotic in principle, have prescribed the costume of each class of society, their diet and their manner of eating it ; and even their household furniture is in like manner prescribed by law. In all these departments, no deviation from the law or custom is permitted or even thought of. The whole science of human nature, under such governments, is that of a knowledge of the duties of the station of life prescribed by parentage, and the whole duty of man that of a rigid performance of them ; while reason, having nothing

H

to do with either the one or the other, is never cultivated.

Even among christians, those founders of religious societies have succeeded best who have prescribed a professional costume for their followers, because every time the disciple looks at his dress he is put in mind of his obligations to the society to which he belongs, and he is therefore the less liable to wander into strange pastures.

The English government could never subdue the *esprit du cour* of the north of Scotland, until, after the rebellion of '45, the prohibition of wearing the tartan plaid, the kilt and the bonnet amongst the Highlanders, broke down the spirit of the clans.

I have seen several of the Moravian Indians, and wondered that they were permitted to wear the Indian dress. Their conduct, when among the white people, soon convinced me that the conversion of those whom I saw was far from being complete.

There can be little doubt but that, if permission should be given by the supreme power of the Mussulman faith, for a change, at the will of each individual, in dress, household furniture, and in eating and drinking, the whole Mohammedan system would be overthrown in a few years. With a similar permission, the Hindoo superstition would share the same fate.

We have yet some districts of country where the costume, cabins, and in some measure the household furniture of their ancestors, are still in use. The people of these districts are far behind their neighbors in every valuable endowment of human nature. Among them the virtues of chastity, temperance, and industry, bear no great value, and schools and places of worship are but little regarded. In general, every one "does what is right in his own eyes."

In short, why have we so soon forgotten our forefathers, and everything belonging to our former state? The reason is, everything belonging to our former state has vanished from our view, and we meet with nothing in remembrance of them. The recent date of the settlement of our country is no longer a subject of reflection. Its immense improvements present to the imagination the results of the labors of several centuries, instead of the work of a few years; and we do not often take the trouble to correct the false impression.

The introduction of the mechanic arts has certainly contributed not a little to the morals and scientific improvement of the country.

The carpenter, the joiner and mason, have displaced the rude, unsightly and uncomfortable cabins of our forefathers, by comfortable, and in many instances elegant mansions of stone, brick, hewn and sawn timbers.

The ultimate objects of civilization are the moral and physical happiness of man. To the latter, the commodious mansion house, with its furniture, contributes essentially. The family mansions of the nations of the earth furnish the criteria of the different grades of their moral and mental condition. The savavages universally live in tents, wigwams, or lodges covered with earth. Barbarians, next to these, may indeed have habitations something better, but of no value and indifferently furnished. Such are the habitations of the Russian Tartar and Turkish peasantry.

Such is the effect of a large, elegant, and well furnished house, on the feelings and deportment of a family, that if you were to build·one for a family of savages, by the occupancy of it they would lose their savage character; or if they did not choose to make the exchange of that character for that of civilization, they would forsake it for the wigwam and the woods.

This was done by many of the early stock of backwoodsmen, even after they built comfortable houses for themselves. They no longer had the chance of "a fall hunt;" the woods pasture was eaten up; they wanted "elbow room." They therefore sold out, and fled to the forest of the frontier settlements, choosing rather to encounter the toil of turning the wilderness into fruitful fields a second time, and even risk an Indian war, than endure the inconveniences of a crowded settlement. Kentucky first offered a resting place for those pioneers, then Indiana, and now the Missouri; and it cannot be long before the Pacific ocean will put a final stop to the westward march of those lovers ·of the wilderness.

Substantial buildings have the effect of giving value to the soil and creating an attachment for the family residence. Those who have been accustomed to poetry, ancient or modern, need not be told how finely and how impressively the household gods, the blazing hearth, the plentiful board, and the social fireside figure in poetical imagery. And this is not "tying up nonsense for a song." They are realities of life in its most polished states: they are among its best and most rational enjoyments: they associate the little family community in parental and filial affection and duty, in which even the well clothed child feels its importance, claims and duties.

The amount of attachment to the family mansion furnishes the criterion of the relative amount of virtue in the members of a family. If the head of a family should wander from the path of paternal duty, and become addicted to vicious habits, in proportion as his virtue suffers a declension, his love of his home and family abates, until, any place, however base and corrupting it may be, is more agreeable to him than the once *dulce domum*. If a similar declension in virtue happens on the part of the maternal chief of the family mansion, the first effect of her deviation from the path of maternal virtue is, that "her feet abideth not in her own house." The same observations apply to children. When the young man or woman, instead of manifesting a strong attachment to the family mansion, is "given to outgoing," to places of licentious resort, their moral ruin may be said to be at no great distance.

Architecture is of use even in the important province of religion.— Those who build no houses for themselves, build no temples for the service of God, and of course derive the less benefit from the institutions of religion. While our people lived in cabins, their places of worship were tents, as they were called, their seats logs, their communion tables rough slabs of hewn timber, and the covering of the worshippers the leaves of the forest trees.

Churches have succeeded to tents with their rude accommodations for public worship. The very aspect of those sacred edifices fills the mind

of the beholder with a religious awe, and as to the most believing and
sincere, it serves to increase the fervor of devotion. Patriotism is augmented by the sight of the majestic forum of justice, the substantial
public highway, and the bridge with its long succession of ponderous
arches.

Rome and Greece would no doubt have fallen much sooner, had it not
been for the patriotism inspired by their magnificent public edifices.—
But for these, their histories would have been less complete and lasting
than they have been.

Emigration has brought to the western regions the wealth, science
and arts of our eastern brethren, and even of Europe. These we hope
have suffered no deterioration in the western country. They have contributed much to the change which has been effected in the moral and
scientific character of our country.

The ministry of the gospel has contributed no doubt immensely to the
happy change which has been effected in the state of our western society.
At an early period of our settlements three Presbyterian clergymen commenced their clerical labors in our infant settlements,—the Rev. Joseph
Smith, the Rev. John M'Millan, and the Rev. Mr. Bowers, the two
latter of whom are still living. They were pious, patient, laborious men,
who collected their people into regular congregations, and did all for
them which their circumstances would allow. It was no disparagement
to them that their first churches were the shady grove, and their first
pulpits a kind of tent, constructed of a few rough slabs, and covered with
clapboards. "He who dwelleth not exclusively in temples made with
hands," was propitious to their devotions.

From the outset they prudently resolved to create a ministry in the
country, and accordingly established little grammar schools at their own
houses or in their immediate neighborhoods. The course of education
which they gave their pupils, was indeed not extensive; but the piety
of those who entered into the ministry more than made up the deficiency.
They formed societies, most of which are now large and respectable, and
in point of education their ministry has much improved.

About the year 1792, an academy was established at Canonsburg, in
Washington county, in the western part of Pennsylvania, which was
afterwards incorporated under the name of Jefferson College.

The means possessed by the society for the undertaking were indeed
but small; but they not only erected a tolerable edifice for the academy,
but created a fund for the education of such pious young men as were
desirous of entering into the ministry, but were unable to defray the
expenses of their education. This institution has been remarkably successful in its operations. It has produced a large number of good
scholars in all the literary professions, and added immensely to the science of the country.

Next to this, Washington College, situated in the county town of the
county of that name, has been the means of diffusing much of the light
of science through the western country.

Too much praise cannot be bestowed on those good men who opened
these fruitful sources of instruction for our infant country, at so early a

period of its settlement. They have immensely improved the depart-ments of theology, law, medicine and legislation, in the western regions.

At a later period the Methodist society began their labors in the west-ern parts of Virginia and Pennsylvania. Their progress at first was slow, but their zeal and perseverance at length overcame every obstacle, so that they are now one of the most numerous and respectable societies in this country. The itinerant plan of their ministry is well calculated to convey the gospel throughout a thinly scattered population. Accordingly their ministry has kept pace with the extension of our settlements. The little cabin was scarcely built, and the little field fenced in, before these evangelical teachers made their appearance amongst them, collected them into societies, and taught them the worship of God.

Had it not been for the labors of these indefatigable men, our country, as to a great extent of its settlements, would have been at this day a semi-barbaric region. How many thousands and tens of thousands of the most ignorant and licentious of our population have they instructed – and reclaimed from the error of their ways! They have restored to so-ciety even the most worthless, and made them valuable and respectable as citizens, and useful in all the relations of life. Their numerous and zealous ministry bids fair to carry on the good work to any extent which our settlements and population may require.

With the Catholics I have but little acquaintance, but have every rea-son to believe, that in proportion to the extent of their flocks, they have done well. In this country they have received the episcopal visitations of their bishops. In Kentucky they have a cathedral, a college and a bishop. In Indiana they have a monastery of the order of St. Trap, which is also a college, and a bishop.

Their clergy, with apostolic zeal, but in an unostentatious manner, have sought out and ministered to their scattered flocks throughout the country, and as far as I know, with good success.

The societies of Friends in the western country are numerous, and their establishments in good order. Although they are not much in fa-vor of a classical education, they are nevertheless in the habit of giving their people a substantial English education. Their habits of industry and attention to useful arts and improvments are highly honorable to themselves and worthy of imitation.

The Baptists in the state of Kentucky took the lead in the ministry, and with great success. Their establishments are, as I have been in-formed, at present numerous and respectable in that state. A great and salutary revolution has taken place in this community of people. Their ministry was formerly quite illiterate; but they have turned their attention to science, and have already erected some very respectable literary es-tablishments in different parts of America.

The German Reformed and Lutheran churches in our country, as far as I know of them, are doing well. The number of the Lutheran con-gregations is said to be at least one hundred; that of the Reformed, it is presumed, is about the same amount.

It is remarkable that throughout the whole extent of the United States, the Germans, in proportion to their wealth, have the best churches, organs and grave-yards. It is a fortunate circumstance that those of our citizens who labor under the disadvantage of speaking a foreign language, are blessed with a ministry so evangelical as that of these very numerous and respectable communities.

The Episcopalian church, which ought to have been foremost in gathering their scattered flocks, have been the last, and done the least of any christian community in the evangelical work. Taking the western country in its whole extent, at least one half of its population was originally of Episcopalian parentage; but for want of a ministry of their own they have associated with other communities. They had no alternative but that of changing their profession or living and dying without the ordinances of religion. It can be no subject of regret that those ordinances were placed within their reach by other hands, whilst they were withheld by those, by whom, as a matter of right and duty, they ought to have been given. One single *ohorea episcopus*, or suffragan bishop, of a faithful spirit, who, twenty years ago, should have "ordained them elders in every place" where they were needed, would have been the instrument of forming Episcopal congregations over a great extent of country, and which by this time would have become large, numerous and respectable; but the opportunity was neglected, and the consequent loss to this church is irreparable.

So total a neglect of the spiritual interests of so many valuable people, for so great a length of time, by a ministry so near at hand, is a singular and unprecedented fact in ecclesiastical history, the like of which never occurred before.

It seems to me, that if the twentieth part of their number of christian people, of any other community, had been placed in Siberia, and dependent on any other ecclesiastical authority in this country, that that authority would have reached them many years ago with the ministration of the gospel. With the earliest and most numerous Episcopacy in America, not one of the eastern bishops has yet crossed the Allegany mountains, although the dioceses of two of them comprehended large tracts of country on the western side of the mountains. It is hoped that the future diligence of this community will make up, in some degree, for the negligence of the past.

There is still an immense void in this country which it is their duty to fill up. From their respectability, on the ground of antiquity among the reformed churches, the science of their patriarchs, who have been the lights of the world—from their number and great resources, even in America—she ought to hasten to fulfil the just expectations of her own people, as well as those of other communities, in contributing her full share to the science, piety, and civilization of our country.

From the whole of our ecclesiastical history, it appears, that, with the exception of the Episcopal church, all our religious communities have done well for their country.

The author begs that it may be understood, that with the distinguishing tenets of our religious societies he has nothing to do, nor yet with the excellencies nor defects of their ecclesiastical institutions. They are noticed on no other ground than that of their respective contributions to the science and civilization of the country.

The last, but not the least of the means of our present civilization, are our excellent forms of government and the administration of the laws.

In vain, as means of general information, are schools, colleges, and a ministry of the gospel of the best order. A land of liberty is a land of crime, as well as of virtue.

It is often mentioned, as a matter of reproach to England, that, in proportion to her population, they have more convictions, executions, and transportaions, than any other country in Europe. Should it be asked, what is the reason of the prevalence of crime in England? Is it, that human nature is worse there than elsewhere? We answer, no.—There is more liberty there than elsewhere in Europe, and that is the true and only solution of the matter in question. Where a people are at liberty to learn what they choose, to think and act as they please, and adopt any profession for a living or a fortune, they are much more liable to fall into the commission of crimes, than a people who from their infancy have been accustomed to the dull, monotonous march of despotism, which chains each individual to the rank and profession of his forefathers, and does not permit him to wander into strange and devious paths of hazardous experiments.

In America, should a stranger read awhile our numerous publications of a religious nature, the reports of missionary and Bible societies, at first blush he would look upon the Americans as a nation of saints; let him lay these aside, and read the daily newspapers, he will change his opinion, and for the time being consider them as a nation abounding in crimes of the most atrocious dye. Both portraits are true.

The greater the amount of freedom, the greater the necessity of a steady and faithful administration of justice, but more especially of criminal justice; because a general diffusion of science, while it produces the most salutary effects, on a general scale, produces also the worst of crimes, by creating the greater capacity for their commission. There is scarcely any art or science, which is not in some hands and under certain circumstances made an instrument of the most atrocious vices.—The arts of navigation and gunnery, so necessary for the wealth and defense of a nation, have often degenerated into the crime of piracy. The beautiful art of engraving, and the more useful art of writing, have been used by the fraudulent for counterfeiting all kinds of public and private documents of credit. Were it not for science and freedom, the important professions of theology and physic would not be so frequently assumed by the pseudo priest and the quack without previous acquirements, without right, and for purposes wholly base and unwarrantable.

The truth is, the western country is the region of adventure. If we have derived some advantage from the importation of science, arts and wealth; we have on the other hand been much annoyed and endangered, as to our moral and political state, by an immense importation of vice, associated with a high grade of science and the most consummate art in the pursuit of wealth by every description of unlawful means. The steady administration of justice has been our only safety from destruction, by the pestilential influence of so great an amount of moral depravity in our infant country.

Still it may be asked whether facts warrant the beleif that the scale is fairly turned in favor of science, piety and civilization—whether in regard to these important endowments of our nature, the present time is better than the past—whether we may safely consider our political institutions so matured and settled that our personal liberty, property and sacred honor, are not only secured to us for the present, but likely to remain the inheritance of our children for generations yet to come. Society, in its best state, resembles the sleepping volcano, as to the amount of latent moral evil which it always contains. It is enough for public safety, and all that can reasonably be expected, that the good predominate over the evil. The moral and political means, which have been so successfully employed for preventing a revolutionary explosion, have, as we trust, procrastinated the danger of such an event for a long time to come. If we have criminals, they are speedily pursued and brought to justice.

The places of our country, which still remain in their native state of wilderness, do not, as in many other countries, afford notorious lodgments for thieves. Our hills are not, as in the wilderness of Judea, "hills of robbers." The ministry of the holy gospel is enlightening the minds of our people with the best of all sciences, that of God himself, his divine government and man's future state.

Let it not be thought hard that our forums of justice are so numerous, the style of their architecture so imposing, and the business which occupies them so multifarious; they are the price which freedom must pay for its protection. Commerce, circulating through its million channels, will create an endless variety of litigated claims. Crimes of the deepest dye, springing from science and liberty themselves, require constantly the vigilance and coercion of criminal justice. Even the poorest of our people are solicitous for the education of their children. Thus the great supports of our moral and political state, resting on their firmest bases, public opinion and attachment to our government and laws, promise stability for generations yet to come.

APPENDIX.

APPENDIX.

——:o:——

THE author of the History of the Valley had intended to postpone the subject of the following pages, and give the subject matter thereof in a second edition; but at the request of a highly respectable subscriber, and on consulting the printer, it is found that this addition to his work will not greatly increase the expense of the present volume. It is therefore deemed expedient to gratify public curiosity by giving the following sketches. If any one should be found incredulous enough to doubt the correctness of his statements, he can only say to such individuals, that they can have occular proof of the truth of each by taking the trouble to examine for themselves.

I.

FACE OF THE COUNTRY.

That portion of the Valley lying between the Blue Ridge and Little North Mountain, is generally about an average of twenty-five miles wide, commencing at the Cohongoraton (Potomac,) and running from thence a southerly course to the commencement of the northern termination of Powell's Fort mountains, a distance of about forty-five miles.

This region, it has already been stated in a preceding chapter, when the country was first known to the white people, was one entire and beautiful prairie, with the exception of narrow fringes of timber immediately bordering on the water courses. The Opequon, (pronounced Opeckon) heads at the eastern base of the Little North Mountain, and thence passing through a fine tract of limestone country seven or eight miles, enters into a region of slate. This tract of slate country commences at the northern termination of Powell's Fort mountains, and is six or eight miles in width east and west, and continues to the Potomac a distance of about forty-five miles. The Opequon continues its serpentine course through the slate region, and empties into the Potomac about fifteen or sixteen miles above Harpers-Ferry. It is thought by some individuals that this water course is susceptible of navigation for small craft, twenty-four or twenty-five miles from its mouth. This slate region of country is comparatively poor, unproductive land; yet in the hands of industrious and skilful farmers, many very valuable and beautiful farms are to be seen in it. About twenty years ago a scientific Frenchman suggested to the author the opinion "that this region of slate country was, at some remote period of the world, covered with a mountain, an abrasion of which had taken place by some great convulsion of nature.—— This he inferred from an examination of the base of the Fort Mountain—— the stratum of the slate at the foot of which being precisely similar to that of the slate at the edges of the region of this slate country." The author will not venture an opinion of his own on this subject, but has given that of an individual who it was said at the time was a man of considerable philosophical and scientific acquirements.

East of this slate country commences another region of fine limestone land, averaging ten or twelve miles in width, and for its extent certainly unsurpassed in point of natural beauty, fertility and value, by any section of country in Virginia.

Powell's Fort presents to the eye much gradeur and sublimity.   Tradition informs us that an Englishman by the name of Powell, at the early settlement of our country, discovered silver ore in the West Fort Mountain, and commenced the business of money coining; and when any attempts were made to arrest him, he would escape into the mountain and conceal himself.   From this circumstance it acquired the name of Powell's Fort.   The late Capt. Isaac Bowman, about thirty years ago, pointed out to the author the site of Powell's shop, where it was said he wrought his metal, the ruins of which were then to be seen.   Capt. Bowman also informed the author that several crucibles and other instruments, which he had frequently seen, had been found about the ruins of this shop, so that there is no doubt of the truth of the tradition that this man Powell was in the practice of melting down some sort of metal, if he did not actually counterfeit money.

The grandeur and sublimity of this extraordinary work of nature consist in its tremendous height and singular formation.   On entering the mouth of the Fort, we are struck with the awful height of the mountains on each side, probably not less than a thousand feet.   Through a very narrow passage, a bold and beautiful stream of water rushes, called Passage creek, which a short distance below works several fine merchant mills.—— After travelling two or three miles, the valley gradually widens, and for upwards of twenty miles furnishes arable land, and affords settlements for eighty or ninety families, several of whom own very valuable farms.—— The two mountains run parallel about twenty-four or twenty-five miles, and are called the East and West Fort mountains, and then are merged into one, anciently called Masinetto, now Masinutton mountain.   The Masinutton mountain continues its course about thirty-five or thirty-six miles southerly, and abruptly terminates nearly opposite Keisletown, in the county of Rockingham.   This range of mountains divides the two great branches of the Shenandoah river, called the South and North forks. This mountain, upon the whole, presents to the eye something of the shape of the letter Y, or perhaps more the shape of the houns and tongue of a wagon.

The turnpike road from New-Market, crossing Masinutton and Blue Ridge into the county of Culpeper, is held as private property.   The dwelling-house where the toll is received stands on the summit of Masinutton, from which each of the valleys of the North and South rivers presents to the delighted vision of the traveler a most enchanting view of the country for a vast distance. The little thrifty village of New-Market, with a great number of farms and their various improvements, are seen in full relief. On the east side of the mountain, on the South river and Hawksbill creek, are to be seen a number fine farms, many of them studden with handsome brick buildings. Upon the whole, the traveler is amply rewarded, by this gratifying sight, for his labor and fatigue in ascending the mountain, which is said to be two miles from its base to its summit. There is a considerable depression where the road crosses at this place, called Masinutton gap.

From the East Fort mountain, at a point nearly opposite Woodstock, the South river presents to the eye precisely the appearance of three distinct streams of water crossing the valley from the western base of the Blue Ridge to the foot of the Fort mountain. At the northern end of the West Fort mountain, from an eminence, Winchester can be distinctly seen, at a distance of not less than sixteen miles, air measure, and a great portion of the county of Frederick can be overlooked from this elevated point.— There is also an elevated point about five miles south of Front Royal, on the road leading from thence to Luray, from which there is a most ravishing view of the eastern section of the county of Frederick, and the tops of the mountains bordering on the north side of the Cohongoruton.

After leaving this eminence, and proceeding southerly towards Luray, from the undulating form of the country between the South river and Blue Ridge, for a distance of fourteen or fifteen miles, it appears constantly to the traveler as if he were nearly approaching the foot of a considerable mountain, and yet there is none to cross his way. The South river, for seventy or eighty miles on each side, affords large proportions of fine alluvial lands—in many parts of it first-rate high lands, which are generally finely improved, and owned by many wealthy and highly respectable proprietors. The new county of Page, for its extent, contains as much intrinsic wealth as any county west of the Blue Ridge, with the exception of Jefferson.

The valley of the North river, from the West Fort mountain to the eastern base of the Little North mountain, is generally fine limestone land, undulating, and finely watered. It is also highly improved, with a density of population perhaps unequaled by any section of Virginia; and it is believed there is more cash in the hands of its citizens than in any part of the state for the same extent.

It is hardly necessary to state that the three counties of Jefferson, Berkeley and Frederick, contain a greater proportion of fertile lands than any other section of the state; but unfortunately, it may with truth be affirmed that it is a badly watered country. There are many neighborhoods in which nothing like a spring of water is to be seen. It is however true, that there are many fine large limestone springs, remarkable for the great quantity of water which is discharged from them. But nature appears to have distributed her favors in this respect unequally.

The counties of Morgan, Hampshire and Hardy, are remarkable for their mountains and fine freestone water. From the mountainous character of this section, it is but sparsely inhabited in many parts of it. The

South and North branches of the Cohongoruton (Potomac) afford considerable quantities of as fine fertile alluvial land as any part of the U. S. Patterson's creek also furnishes a considerable body of fine land.   Capon river, Lost river, and Back creek, furnish much fine land, and are all thickly populated.

The western part of Frederick, Berkeley and Shenandoah, include considerable portions of mountainous country.   The Little North mountain commences near the Cohongoruton, having Back creek valley on the west, which extends about thirty-five miles into the interior, to the head waters of the creek.   This mountain runs a southerly course, parallel with the Great North mountain, passing through the three counties just mentioned.   This tract of mountain land is comparatively poor and unproductive.   It is, however, pretty thickly populated, by a hardy race of people.   In our mountains generally, wherever spots of arable land are to be found, (which are chiefly in the glens,) there scattered settlers are to be found also.

East of the Shenandoah river the Blue Ridge is thickly populated, and many fine productive farms are to be seen.   The vast quantity of loose stone thickly scattered over the surface of this mountain, one would be ready to believe, would deter individuals from attempting its cultivation; but it is a common saying among those people, that if they can only obtain as much earth as will cover their seed grain, they are always sure of good crops.

The public road crosses the Blue Ridge, from the South river valley into the county of Madison.   From the western base of the mountain to to the summit, it is said to be five miles.   On the top of the mountain, at this place, there is a large body of level land, covered almost exclusively with large chestnut timber, having the appearance of an extensive swamp, and producing great quantities of the skunk cabbage.   But little of it has been reclaimed and brought into cultivation.   It produces fine crops of grass, rye, oats, potatoes and turnips; but it is said to be entirely too moist for the production of wheat, and too cool for the growth of Indian corn.   The people in its neighborhood say that there is not a week throughout the spring, summer and autumn, without plentiful falls of rain, and abundant snows in the winter.   In the time of long droughts on each side of the mountain, this elevated tract of country is abundantly supplied with rains.   It is also said, that from this great height nearly the whole county of Madison can be seen, presenting to the eye a most fascinating and delightful view.

On the summit of the West Fort mountain, about fifteen miles south of Woodstock, there is also a small tract of land, remarkable for its depth of fine rich soil, but inaccessible to the approach of man with implements of husbandry.   This tract produces immense quantities of the finest chestnut, though from the great difficulty of ascending the mountain, but little benefit is derived from it to the neighboring people.

In our western mountains small bodies of limestone lands are to be met with, one of the most remarkable of which is what is called the "Sugar Hills," pretty high up the Cedar creek valley.   This tract is said to contain four or five hundred acres, and lies at the eastern base of Paddy's mountain. It derives its name from two causes: first, when discovered it was covered chiefly with the sugar maple; and secondly, several of its knobs resemble in shape the sugar loaf. Its soil is peculiarly adapted to the production of wheat of the finest quality, of which, let the seasons be as they may, the land never fails to produce great crops, which generally commands seven or eight cents per bushel more than any other wheat grown in its neighborhood. The Hessian fly has not yet been known to injure the crops while growing.

Paddy's mountain is a branch of the Great North mountain, and is about eighteen or twenty miles long. It takes its name from an Irishman, whose name was Patrick Black, who first settled at what is now called Paddy's gap in this mountain. This fact was communicated to the author by Moses Russell, Esq.

II.

NATURAL CURIOSITIES.

It would require perhaps several volumes to give a minute description of all the natural and interesting curiosities of our country. The inquisitive individual can scarcely travel more than a mile or two in any direction among our mountains, but some sublime and grand work of nature presents itself to the eye, which excites his wonder and admiration.— The author must therefore content himself with a brief description of comparatively a few of the most remarkable. He will commence his narrative with Harpers-Ferry. This wonderful work of nature has been so accurately described by Mr. Jefferson, that it is deemed unnecessary to give a detailed description of it. Suffice it to say, that no stranger can look at the passage of the waters of the Potomac and Shenandoah, rushing through the yawning gap of the mountain, without feeling awe at the grandeur and sublimity of the scene, and ready to prostrate himself in adoration before that omnipotent God whose almighty arm hath made all things according to his own wisdom and power.

It is much to be regretted that a Captain Henry, during the administration of the elder Adams in 1799, when what was called the provisional army was raising, and a part of which was stationed at Harpers-Ferry, greatly injured one of the most interesting curiosities of this place. A rock of extraordinary shape and of considerable size stands on the brink of a high hill, on the south side of the tung or point of land immediately in the fork of the river. The apex of this rock was a broad flat table, supported on a pivot, on which Mr. Jefferson, during his visit to this place, inscribed his name, from which it took the name of Jefferson's rock.

The years 1798 and 1799 were a period of extraordinary political excitement. The two great political parties, federal and democratic, of our country, were at this period completely organised, and an interesting struggle for which party should have the ascendancy was carried on.— This same Capt. Henry, whether actuated by the same motive which impelled the Macedonian youth to murder Philip his king, or whether he hoped to acquire popularity with his party, (he calling himself a federalist,) or whether from motives purely hostile towards Mr. Jefferson and all the democratic party, placed himself at the head of a band of soldiers, and with the aid of his myrmidons, hurled off the apex of this rock, thus wantonly, and to say the least, unwisely destroying the greatest beauty of this extraordinary work of nature. By this illiberal and unwise act, Capt. Henry has "condemned his name to everlasting fame."

CAVES IN THE COUNTY OF JEFFERSON.

About seven or eight miles above Harpers-Ferry, on the west side of the Shenandoah, nearly opposite the Shannondale springs, from a quarter to a half mile from the river, a limestone cave has been discovered, which contains several beautiful incrustations or stalactites formed from the filtration of the water.

Near Mecklenburg, (Shepherdstown,) another cave has been found, out of which considerable quantities of hydraulic limestone is taken, and when calcined or reduced to lime, is found to make a cement little if any inferior to plaster of paris. Out of this cave a concreted limestone was taken, which the author saw in the possession of Dr. Boteler of Shepherdstown, which at first view presents to the eye, in shape, a striking resemblance to that of a fish of considerable size. A smaller one was found at the some time, which has a strong resemblance to a mink.—— Several intelligent individuals were induced to believe they were genuine petrifactions.

CAVES IN THE COUNTY OF FREDERICK.

In the county of Frederick are to be seen five or six of those caves.—— Zane's cave, now on the lands owned by the heirs of the late Maj. James Bean, is the one described by the late Mr. Jefferson, in his "Notes on Virginia." This cave the author partially explored about eighteen months ago, but found it too fatiguing to pursue his examination to any extent. The natural beauty of this place has of late years been greatly injured from the smoke of the numerous pine torches used to light it.—— All the incrustations and spars are greatly darkened, giving the cave a somber and dull appearance. The author was informed, on his visit to this place, that Maj. Bean, shortly before his death, cut out several of the spars, reduced them to lime, sprinkled it over some of his growing crops, and found that it produced all the effects of gypsum.

On the lands late the residence of Captain Edward McGuire, dec'd, is another cave of some considerable extent; but its incrustations and spars are of a muddy yellowish color, and not considered a very interesting curiosity.

Adjoining the lands of Mr. James Way, the former residence of the late Col. C. M. Thruston, an extensive cave of very singular and curious formation was discovered many years ago. On exploring it with the aid of a pocket compass, the needle was found running to every part of it.

On the east side of the Shenandoah river, some two or three miles below Berry's Ferry, at the base of the Blue Ridge, a cave of considerable extent has been discovered, containing several curiosities. About two miles below this cave on the same side of the river, is to be seen what was anciently called Redman's fishery. At the base of a rock a large subterraneous stream of water is discharged into the river. At the approach of winter myriads of fish make their way into this subterraneous stream, and take up their winter quarters. In the spring they return into the river. By placing a fish-basket in the mouth of the cavern, great quantities of fine fresh-water fish are taken, both in the autumn and spring of the year. The author recollects being at this place upwards of fifty years ago, just after Mr. Redman had taken up his fish-basket, and can safely affirm, that he drew out of the water from two to three bushels of fish at a single haul.

On Crooked run, near Bethel meeting house, on the lands now owned by Mr. Stephen Grubb, is a limestone cave, which the author has more than once been in. It does not exceed one hundred yards in length, and is remarkable only for its production of saltpetre, and preserving fresh meats in hot weather.

The Panther cave, on the north bank of Cedar creek, owned by Major Isaac Hite, about a half or three-fourths of a mile west of the great highway from Winchester to Staunton, is a remarkable curiosity. Nature has here formed a most beautiful and solid upright wall of gray limestone rock, of about one hundred yards in length, near the west end of which is to be seen an elegant arch, of about sixty feet in front, ten or twelve feet high in the center, and extending twenty-five or thirty feet under the body of the wall. There are two circular apertures running into the body of the rock from the arch, one about twelve inches in diameter, the other somewhat smaller. Whether these openings do or do not lead into large apartments or caverns in the body of the rock, is not and probably never will be known. Tradition relates that at the early settlement of the country this place was known to be the haunt and habitation of the panther, from which it derives its name.

We have two natural wells in this county; one at what is called the Dry marsh, a drain of the Opequon, about two miles east of the creek, not more than a quarter of a mile north of the road leading from Winchester to Berryville. This natural well in dry seasons furnishes several contiguous families with water. It is formed by a natural circular opening in an apparently solid limestone rock. Its walls are undulating, and in times of dry seasons the water sinks some sixteen or eighteen feet below the surface, but at all times furnishes abundant supplies. In the winter, no matter how great the degree of cold, small fish are frequently drawn up with the water from the well. In times of freshets, the water rises above the surface, and discharges a most beautiful current for several weeks at a time. Tradition relates that this well was discovered at the first settlement of the neighborhood.

The other natural well is the one described by Mr. Jefferson. This natural curiosity first made its appearance on the breaking up of the hard winter of 1789–80. All the old people of our country doubtless recollect the great falls of snow and severity of this remarkable winter. The author was born, and lived with his father's family until he was about thir-

teen years of age, within one and a half miles of this natural well.——
The land at that period was owned by the late Feilding Lewis, of
Fredericksburg, Va., but is now the property of the heirs of the late
Mr. Thomas Castleman, in the neighborhood of Berryville. Nature had
here formed a circular sink of a depth of some fourteen or fifteen feet,
and fifty or sixty feet in diameter at the surface.   In the spring of the
year 1780, the earth at the bottom of this sink suddenly gave way and
fell into the cavity below, forming a circular aperture about the ordinary
circumference of a common artificial well.   It was soon discovered that
a subterraneous stream of water passed under the bottom.   There being
no artificial or natural means to prevent the earth immediately about the
well from falling in, the aperature is greatly enlarged, forming a sloping
bank, by which a man on foot can easily descend within eight of ten feet
of the water. The current of water is quite perceptible to the eye.   The
whole depth of the cavity is thirty or thirty-five feet.

CAVES IN THE COUNTY OF SHENANDOAH.

Within two or three miles of Woodstock, on the lands of the late
William Payne, Esq., is an extensive cavern, which it is said has never
yet been explored to its termination.   It contains many curious incrustations, stalactites, &c.   From the mouth of this cave a constant current
of cold air is discharged, and the cavern is used by its owners as a place
to preserve their fresh meats in the hottest seasons of the year.

On the east side of the South fork of the Shenandoah river, three or four
miles south of Front Royal, there are two caves but a short distance
apart, which, like all other caves, contain beautiful curiosities.   One of
them many years ago was visited and explored by the late celebrated
John Randolph of Roanoke; but the author has never been able to learn
whether he committed to writing his observations upon it.   One of its
greatest curiosities is an excellent representation of the hatter's kettle.

Within about three miles north-west of Mt. Jackson, Shaffer's cave is
situated.   It has been explored about half a mile.   It is not very remarkable for its production of natural curiosities.   Tradition relates an
amusing story in connection with it.   A very large human skeleton was
many years ago found in this cavern, the skull bone of which a neighboring man had the curiosity to take to his dwelling house.   This aroused
the ghost of the dead man, who, not being pleased with the removal of
his head, very soon appeared to the depredator and harassed him until he
became glad to return the skull to its former habitation.   The ghost
then became appeased and ceased his visits.   It is said that there are
many persons to this day in the neighborhood, who most religiously believe that the ghost did really and truly compel the offender to return his
skull.   The author saw in the possession of Dr. Wetherall, of Mt. Jackson, one of the arm bones of this skeleton, that part extending from the
shoulder to the elbow, which was remarkable for its thickness, but was
not of very uncommon length.   At that time he had not been visited by
the ghost to demand his arm; but perhaps he was not so tenacious of it
as he was of his head.

In the county of Page, within about three miles of Luray, a cave, but little inferior to Weyer's cave, was some years ago discovered, a graphic description of which was written by W. A. Harris, Esq., and published in the Woodstock Sentinel of the Valley, and copied pretty generally throughout the Union.

EBBING AND FLOWING SPRINGS.

Pretty high up Cedar creek there is a beautiful spring of clear mountain water, issuing from the western side of the Little North mountain, in a glen, which ebbs and flows twice in every twenty-four hours. It rises at ten o'clock in the morning, and ebbs at four in the evening. It is in a perfect state of nature, has considerable fall immediately from its mouth, so that it cannot conveniently be ascertained precisely what is its greatest rise and fall. When the author saw it it was down, and he could not conveniently spare the time to wait to see it rise. But the author's informant (Mr. J. Bond) went with him to the spring, and assured him that he has repeatedly seen it rise. The author is also informed that there is a salt sulphur spring, on the land late the property of Mr. John Lee, but a short distance from where the Staunton stage road crosses Cedar creek, which has a dairy erected over it. The respectable widow of Mr. Lee informed the author that this spring ebbs and flows twice in every twenty-four hours, and that if care is not particularly taken at every flow, its current is so strong as to overset the vessels of milk placed in the water.

FALLING RUN.

Some thirteen or fourteen miles south-west of Winchester, and within about two miles of the residence of Moses Russell, Esq., in the county of Frederick, is to be seen what is called the Falling run. Between what the neighboring people call Falling ridge (the commencement of Paddy's mountain) and the Great North mountain, pretty near the summit, on the east side of the mountain, a fine large spring rises, forming a beautiful lively stream of sufficient force to work a grist mill. This stream pursues its serpentine course thro' a glen several hundred yards in width, of gradual descent, between the mountain and Falling ridge. Pursuing its course in a northerly direction from its fountain, for about one and a half miles, it makes a pretty sudden turn to the east, and shoots over a solid granite rock probably not less than one hundred feet high. The first eighteen or twenty feet of the rock over which the water passes is a little sloping, over which the water spreads and covers a surface of fifteen or sixteen feet, from whence the fall is entirely perpendicular, and strikes on a mass of solid rock; it then forms an angle of about forty-five degress, rushing and foaming over an undulating surface of about ninety or one hundred feet; from thence is a third fall of about the same length, and then pitches into a hole of considerable depth; from thence it escapes down a more gradual descent, and suddenly becomes a gentle, smooth, placid current, as if it is pleased to rest from the violent agitations and turmoils through which it had just passed. At the first base reached by the water, a perpetual mist arises, which, viewed on a clear sunshiny day, presents to the eye a most interesting and beautiful sight. The whole fall is little if any less than three hundred feet.

A short distance to the south of this place, at the junction of the Falling ridge with the North mountain, is to be seen what the neighboring people call "the Pinnacle." The apex of this pinnacle is a flat, broad table, supported on a pivot, and can be set in motion by the hands of a man, and will continue to vibrate for several minutes. There are several small caverns in this rock, and it is known to be the abode of the turkey buzzards in the winter, where they remain in a state of torpitude. Mr. Russell informed the author that he once took out a torpid buzzard in the winter, laid it on the sunny side of the rock, and it very soon regained life and motion.

TROUT POND.

In the county of Hardy, about eight or nine miles south of the late residence of James Sterrett, Esq. deceased, and a little east of Thornbottom, is situated a most beautiful miniature lake, called the Trout pond. A large spring rises near the summit of the Great North mountain, descending on the west side into a deep glen, between the mountain and a very high ridge immediately east of Thornbottom, in which glen nature has formed a receptacle of unknown depth for this stream of water. This stream forms an area of about one and a half acres, nearly an oblong square. Nature never presented to the eye a more perfectly beautiful sheet of water. It is as transparent as crystal, and abounds with fine trout fish.

The late Col. Taverner Beale, upwards of forty years ago, described this place to the author, and stated that he could safely affirm that he believed he had seen ten thousand trout at a single view in this pond. Col. Beale also informed the author that himself and a friend of his once made a raft, pus floated to the centre of the pond, where they let down a plumb and line, (the author does not now recollect the length of the line, though, it was certainly not less than forty feet,) but did not succeed in reaching the bottom. A Mr. Gochenour, who resides near this place, informed the author that he had heard it was fathomed many years ago, and was found to be sixty feet deep, but did not know the certainty or truth of this report. The water is discharged at the north-east corner of the pond, and after descending about two miles, works a saw mill, and thirty or forty yards from the mill falls into a sink and entirely disappears. This sink is in the edge of Thornbottom, a pretty narrow strip of limestone land, which affords between the mountains a residence for four or five families, each of whom has a fine spring of water, all which, after running a short distance, also disappear. The stream of water from the pond, doubtless considerably increased by the waters of Thornbottom, again appears at the northern termination of a very high ridge called "the Devil's garden." It bursts out in one of the finest and largest springs the author has ever seen. It is said that this subterranean passage of the water is fully eight miles in length. This spring is within about one quarter of a mile from Mr. Sterrett's dwelling house, and forms a beautiful stream of water called Trout run, which is a valuble tributary of the Capon river.

"The devil's garden" is truly a wonderful work of nature. Between two lofty ridges of the Sandy ridge and North mountain a strip of ground, about a mile in width, commences rising gently from the head of Trout run, and pursues its regular ascent for three miles, when it abruptly terminates, at its southern extremity, in a vast pile of granite rocks, having a perpendicular height of some four or five hundred feet. This immense pile is entirely separated from and independent of its neighboring mountains, having a vast chasm on its two sides and southern termination. At its south end it is covered with nearly level rocks, forming a floor of about an acre. This floor is curiously marked with fissures on the surface of various distances apart. On the eastern side stands a statue, or perhaps it may more appropriately be called a bust, about seven feet high : the head, neck and shoulders bear a strong resemblance to those of a man, and from the breast downwards it gradually enlarges in size from two and a half to three feet in diameter. It is without arms.— It stands on a level table of rock, is of a dark color, and presents to the eye a frowning, terrific appearance. When this singular curiosity was first discovered, some superstitious people concluded it was the image of the Devil; and hence the name of "The Devil's garden." Near his satanic majesty anciently stood a four-square stone pillar, of about two and a half feet diameter, and ten or twelve feet high. This pillar is broken off at its base, crosses a chasm, and reclines, something in the form of an arch, against the opposite rock.

About one hundred feet below the stand of the statue, a door lets into numerous caverns in the rock, the first of which forms a handsome room of moderate size, the floors above and below being tolerably smooth and level. From this room there is a handsome flight of stone steps ascending into a room of larger size, until twelve different apartments are passed through, and then reaches the top of the rocks. The late Mr. Sterrett, in riding with the author to view this extraordinary work of nature, said that it was difficult for an old man to get access to the inlet, of course I did not attempt it. Mr. Babb, who resides in its neighborhood, informed the author that he had frequently explored the cavern; and the young people of the neighborhood, male and female, frequently, in parties of pleasure, visit and pass through its various apartments.

LOST RIVER.

Here again the eye is presented with another evidence of the all-powerful arm of God! This river heads in several small springs, on a high ridge of land near Brock's gap, which divides the waters of the North fork of the Shenandoah from the waters of the Lost river. This water course meanders through a beautiful valley of fine alluvial land, a distance of about twenty-five miles. On its west side, some ten or twelve miles below its head springs, is a cavern at the eastern base of "Lost river mountain," which has been explored about one hundred yards (some say more) from its mouth. Over the inlet is a handsomely turned arch twelve or fourteen feet wide, and six or seven high. From this cavern is discharged a stream of beautiful water, remarkable for its degree of coldness. It is called "the cold spring cave." The mouth of this cave effectually preserves fresh meats of every kind from injury in the hottest seasons.— This cave exhibits but few curiosities.

Some ten or twelve miles further down, the river comes in contact with Lost river mountain, (which is of considerable magnitude,) has cut its way through the mountain, and about two miles further down has to encounter a second mountain called Timber ridge, through which it has forced its way, and one and a half or two miles further has to contend with Sandy ridge, a mountain of considerable height and width. Here the water and mountain appear to have a mighty struggle for the ascendency. In flood times, Mrs. River, despising all obstructions, forces her way through a yawning, frowning chasm. But at times of low water, when her ladyship is less powerful, his giantship, the mountain, defies all her power to remove a huge mass of adamantine rocks, which obstructs her passage in the gap; but to remedy this evil, Mrs. River has adroitly and cunningly undermined the mountain, formed for herself a subterraneous passage, and generously supplied her sister Capon with all the water she has to spare. It is impossible for the inquisitive eye to view this mighty work of nature without being struck with the idea of the great obstruction and mighty difficulty this water had to contend with in forcing a passage through this huge mountain. The author viewed this place with intense interest and curiosty. At the western base of the mountain, the water has found various apertures, one of which is under the point of a rock, of seven or eight feet wide, which appears to be the largest inlet. For the distance of about a quarter of a mile from the sink, not a drop of water is to be seen in times of drought. There are several large springs which issue from the mountain in the gap, forming a small stream, which always runs through it. The water of the river has a subterraneous passage of full three miles, and is discharged in several very large springs at the eastern base of the mountain. These several springs form the great fountain head of Capon river.

An old man and his son, (their names not recollected,) whose dwelling is very near the sink, related a very singular occurrence which they represented as having happened a few days before the author's visit to this place. They stated that several dogs were in pursuit of a deer on the mountain—that the deer ran to the brink of a rock, at least one hundred feet high, which is very near the sink, and the poor animal being pretty closely pursued, leaped from the rock, and falling on a very rough, stony surface, was terribly crushed and bruised by the fall, and instantly expired. They immediately ran to it and opened the large veins in the neck, but little blood was discharged. They took off the skin and cut up the flesh; but most parts of it were so much bruised and mangled as to be unfit for use.

Capon river exhibits several great natural curiosities. Near its head waters is a rock called "the Alum rock," from which exudes native alum, and forms a beautiful incrustation on its face, which the neighboring people collect in small quantities, but often sufficient for their domestic purposes of staining their cloths.

About two miles above the forks of this river is situated "Caudy's castle," a most stupendous work of nature. It is said by tradition that in the time of the wars between the white and red people, a man by the name of James Caudy, more than once took shelter on the rock from the pursuit of the Indians, from whence its name. It consists of a fragment of the mountain, separated from and independent of the neighboring mountains, forming, as it were, a half cone, and surrounded with a yawning chasm. Its eastern base, washed by the Capon river, rises to the majestic height of four hundred and fifty or five hundred feet, while its eastern side is a solid mass of granite, directly perpendicular. A line drawn round its base probably would not exceed one thousand on twelve hundred yards. From its western side it may be ascended by a man on foot to within about ninety or one hundred feet of its summit. From thence the rock suddenly shoots up something in the form of a comb, which is about ninety or one hundred feet in length, eight or ten feet in thickness, and runs about north and south. On the eastern face of the rock, from where the comb is approached, a very narrow undulating path is formed, by pursuing which, active persons can ascend to its summit. The author called on Mr. John Largent, (from whom he received much kindness and attention,) and requested Mr. L. to be his pilot, which request was readily acceded to. Mr. L.'s residence is less than half a mile from the spot. In his company the author undertook to ascend this awful precipice. Along the path a few laurel shrubs have grown out of the fissures of the rock. With the aid of the shrubbery, the author succeeded in following Mr. Largent until they reached within twenty or twenty-five feet of the summit, where they found a flat table, four or five feet square, on which a pine tree of five or six inches diameter has grown some ten or twelve feet high. This afforded a convenient resting place. By supporting myself with one arm around the body of the tree, and a cane in the other hand, I ventured several times to look down the precipice, but it produced a disagreeable giddiness and painful sensation of the eyes.— From this elevated situation an extensive view of what is called the white mountain presents itself for a considerable distance, on the east side of Capon river. The beautiful whiteness of this mountain is produced by a considerable intermixture of fine white sand with the rocks, which almost exclusively form the west side of Capon mountain for several miles.

Nine or ten miles below this place, in a deep rugged glen three or four miles east of Capon, on the west side of the mountain, the "Tea table" is to be seen, than which nature in her most sportive mood has seldom performed a more beautiful work. This table presents the form of a man's hat, with the crown turned downwards. The stem (if it may be so termed) is about four feet diameter and about four feet high. An oval brim, some seven or eight feet in diameter, and seven or eight inches thick, is formed around the top of the stem, through which a circular tube arises, twelve or fourteen inches in diameter. Through this tube a beautiful stream of transparent water arises, and regularly flows over the whole surface of this large brim, presenting to the eye one of the most beautiful fountains in nature's works.

ICE MOUNTAIN.

This most extraordinary and wonderful work of God's creation certainly deserves the highest rank in the history of the natural curiosities of our country. This mountain is washed at its western base by the North river, a branch of the Capon. It is not more than one quarter of a mile north of the residence of Christopher Heiskell, Esq., at North river mills, in the county of Hampshire, twenty-six miles north-west of Winchester. The west side of this mountain, for about one mile, is covered with loose stone of various size, many of which are of a diamond shape. It is probably six or seven hundred feet high, very steep, and presents to the eye a most grand and sublime spectacle.

At the base of the mountain, on the western side, for a distance of about one hundred yards, and ascending some twenty-five or thirty feet, on removing the loose stone, which is easily done with a small prise, the most perfectly pure and crystal looking ice, at all seasons of the year, is to be found, in blocks of from one or two pounds to fifteen or twenty in weight.* At the base of this bed of ice a beautiful spring of pure water is discharged, which is by many degrees colder than any natural spring water the author has ever seen. It is believed that its natural temperature is not many degrees above the freezing point. Very near this spring the owner of the property has removed the stone, and erected a small log dairy, for the preservation of his milk, butter, and fresh meats. When the author saw this little building, which was late in the month of April, the openings between the logs, (on the side next the cavity from which the stone had been taken out,) for eighteen inches or two feet from the floor was completely filled with ice, and above one half the floor was covered with ice several inches thick. This is the more remarkable from its being a known fact that the sun shines with all its force from eight or nine o'clock in the morning until late in the evening, on the surface covering the ice, but the latter defies its power. Mr. Deevers, who is the owner of the property, informed the author that milk, butter, or fresh meats of every kind, are perfectly safe from injury for almost any length of time in the hottest weather. If a fly venture in, he is immediately stiffened with the cold and becomes torpid. If a snake in his rambles happens to pass over the rocks covering the ice, he soon loses all motion, and dies. Christopher Heiskell, Esq. informed the author that several instances had occurred of the snakes being found dead among the rocks covering the ice. An intelligent young lady at the same time stated that

---

*The neighboring people assert, that at the setting in of the winter season, the ice commences melting, and soon disappears, not a particle of which is to be found while the winter remains. If this be true, it renders this place still more remarkable and extraordinary. The order of nature, in this immediate locality, seems to be reversed: for, when it is summer all around this singular spot, here it is covered with the ice of winter, and *vice versa*. We cannot account for this effect, except the cause be some chemical laboratory under the surface, operating from the influence of the external atmosphere, but in opposition to it.

she had seen instances of this character. In truth, it was upon her first suggesting the fact, that the author was led to make inquiry of Mr. Heiskell. Mr. Devers stated that he had several times removed torpid flies from his dairy into a more temperate atmosphere, when they soon recovered life and motion and flew off.

Nature certainly never formed a better situation for a fine dairy establishment. But it will probably be asked by some persons, where is the milk to come from to furnish it? The time will probably come, and perhaps is not very distant, when our mountains will be turned to good account. Their sources of wealth are not yet known; but the spirit of enterprise and industry is abroad, and the present generation will hardly pass away before the most astonishing changes will be seen in every part of our happy country.

THE HANGING ROCKS.

These, or, as they are sometimes called, "Blue's Rocks," are another wonderful work of nature. They are situated on the Wappatomaka, about four miles north of Romney, the seat of justice for the county of Hampshire. The author has several times viewed this place with excited feelings and admiration. The river has cut its way through a mountain probably not less than five hundred feet high. By what extraordinary agency it has been able to do this, it is impossible conceive, unless we look to that almighty power whose arm effects all his great objects at pleasure. On the east side of the river is a huge mass of rocks which forms a perpendicular wall several hundred yards in length, and not less than three hundred feet high. The opposite point of the mountain is more sloping, and may be ascended by a man on foot. On the top of the mountain is a level bench of land, pretty clear of stone, and fine rich soil, upwards of one hundred yards in width; but, from the difficulty of approaching it, it remains in a state of nature. It would, if it could be brought into cultivation, doubtless well reward the husbandman for his labors.

The public road, leading from Romney into the great western highway, passes between the margin of the river and the great natural wall formed by the rocks. The center of the rocks for about eighty or one hundred yards, is composed of fine gray limestone, while on each side are the common granite mountain stone.

The reader will recollect that this is the place where a most bloody battle was fought between contending parties of the Catawba and Delaware Indians, noticed in a preceding chapter of this volume.

One other natural curiosity remains to be noticed, and that is, what is called the "Butterfly rocks." These rocks are to be seen in Fry's gap, on Cedar creek, in the county of Frederick. The whole mass of rocks are intermixed with petrified flies, of various sizes. The entire shape of the wings, body, legs, head, and even the eyes of the flies, are distinctly to be discovered. The rocks are of deep brown color, and of the slate species.

The author will conclude this section with a brief notice of an avalan-

*x

che or mountain slide, which he has omitted to notice in its proper place. In the month of June, in the remarkable wet spring and summer of the year 1804, during a most tremendous and awful flood of rain, near the summit of the Little North mountain, a vast column of water suddenly gushed from the eastern side, and rapidly descending, with its tremendous current, tore away every tree, of whatever size, rocks of eight or ten tons weight, hurling them into the level lands below, and threatening desolation and destruction to everything which was within the limits of its vortex. In its passage down the mountain it opened a chasm from ten to fifty yards in width, and from eight or ten to twelve or fifteen feet in depth. The farm of Mr. David Funkhouser, which the flood took in its course, was greatly injured, and a beautiful meadow covered over with the wood, stone, and other rubbish. The flood ran into the lower floor of his dwelling house, the foundation of which is elevated at least three feet above the surface of the ground. This rent in the side of the mountain, at the distance of five or six miles, presented for many years the appearance of a very wide road. It is now grown up thickly with young pine timber, and so crowded that there is scarcely room for a man to pass between them.

III.

MEDICINAL SPRINGS—WATERING PLACES.

OUR country abounds in medical waters. Numerous sulphur springs exist, particularly in the slate lands and mountains. Springs, of various qualities of water, are also to be seen, several of which are remarkable for their superior virtues in the cure of the various disorders of the human body.

It is not within the plan of this work to notice all the medical springs which the author has seen and heard of. He will content himself with a brief account of those deemed most valuable, beginning with BATH, in the county of Morgan.

This is doubtless the most ancient watering place in the valley. Tradition relates that those springs were known to the Indians as possessing valuable medical properties, and were much frequented by them. They were anciently called the "Berkeley Warm Springs," and have always kept their character for their medical virtues. They are much resorted to not only for their value as medicinal waters, but as a place (in the season) of recreation and pleasure. Bath has become a considerable village, is the seat of justice for Morgan county, and has several stores and boarding houses. It is too publicly known to require further notice in this work.

SHANNONDALE.

It is not more than twelve or fourteen years since this spring was first resorted to as a watering place, though it was known for some years before to possess some peculiar medicinal qualities. A few extraordinary cures were effected by the use of the water, of obstinate scorbutic complaints, and it suddenly acquired a high reputation. A company of gentlemen in its neighborhood joined and purchased the site, and forthwtth erected a large brick boarding house, and ten or twelve small buildings for the accommodation of visitors. For several years it held a high rank among our watering places.

SALUS SPRINGS, COMMONLY CALLED BOND'S SPRINGS.

These are situated between the Little North mountain and Paddy's mountain, forming the head fountain of Cedar creek, and about twenty-eight or thirty miles south-west of Winchester, and seven or eight miles north-west of Woodstock. These springs are acquiring a high character for their valuable medical qualities, though it is only four or five years since they have been resorted to. It is well ascertained that the water from at least one of them has the powerful quality of expelling the bots from the horse.

Another of the springs is called "the Poison spring," and it is asserted by the people of the neighborhood that by drinking the water freely, and bathing the part wounded, it will immediately cure the bite of any poisonous snake.

There are five or six beautiful transparent springs within a circumference of one hundred and fifty or two hundred yards, several of which are yet unimproved. Nature has seldom done more for an advantageous watering place than she has exhibited at these springs. No place the author has ever seen presents more conveniences for the construction of baths.— One of the springs is discharged from an elevated point of a ridge, and has fall and water enough to construct any reasonable number of shower baths. It is asserted by those who attend the springs, that several great cures of obstinate scorbutic complaints have been made by the use of the water. One remarkable instance was related to the author. A little boy, of eight or nine years of age, had become dreadfully disordered by eruptions all over his body, which formed large running ulcers. The complaint baffled all the efforts of the most skillful phisicians in the neighborhood, and continued for about twelve months, when the child's life was despaired of. An uncle of the child, who was acquainted with the valuable quality of these waters, took him to the springs, and by repeatedly washing his body with the water of the poison spring, and also his freely drinking it, in ten or twelve days the child was perfectly cured, and has ever since remained in fine health. Within one and a quarter miles from this place there is a fine white sulphur spring, which is said to possess very active cathartic qualities. It is also said that the water has a sweetish taste, and is by some called the sweet sulphur spring. The water has a pure crystal look, and is discharged from a spring at the base of Paddy's mountain. Plunging baths may be multiplied at pleasure.— The waters are pretty cool; a handsome bath house is erected, and the visitors use it freely.

Sixteen neat looking dwelling houses have been erected by as many proprietors within the last four or five years; but unfortunately there is no regular boarding house established, which has heretofore prevented much resort to this place. In the hands of a man of capital and enterprise, it doubtless might be made one of the most charming rural summer retreats west of the Blue ridge. It has the advantage of a most beautiful summer road much the greater part of the whole route from Winchester; what is called Frye's gap, within twelve miles of Winchester, being by far the worst part of it; and an excellent road can be made at inconsiderable expense across the Little North mountain. Travelers passing up or down the valley, would in the summer season find this a delightful resting place, if it was put in a proper state of improvement for their accommodation, nor is it more than seven or eight miles out of the direct road. The present buildings are arranged so as to leave in the center a beautiful grove of young oak and other timber, which affords a lovely shade in hot weather. Near Capt. J. Bond's dwelling house, within three hundred yards of the mineral springs, there ir a fine large limestone spring.

ORKNEY SPRINGS, COMMONLY CALLED YELLOW SPRINGS.

These springs are near the head waters of Stony creek, about seventeen or eighteen miles south-west of Woodstock. The waters are composed of several lively springs, are strong chalybeate, and probably impregnated with some other mineral besides iron. Every thing the water passes through or over is beautifully lined with a bright yellow fringe or moss. The use of this water is found very beneficial for the cure of several complaints. There are ten or twelve small buildings erected by the neighboring people for their private accommodation.

The author visited this watering place about four years ago. A Mr. Kaufman had brought with him, the day preceding, the materials for a small framed dwelling house. He reached the place early in the day, raised his house, had the shingles and weatherboarding nailed on, the floor laid, and doors hung, and ate his dinner in it the next day at one o'clock. The author had the pleasure of dining with the old gentleman and lady, when they both communicated the foregoing statement of facts to him. A free use of this water acts as a most powerful cathartic, as does also a small quantity of the fringe or moss mixed with any other kind of water.

CAPON SPRINGS, MORE PROPERLY FRYE'S SPRINGS.

The late Henry Frye, of Capon, upwards of forty years ago, informed the author that he was the first discoverer of the valuable properties of this celebated watering place. He stated that he was hunting, and killed a large bear on the side of the mountain near the springs, and becoming dry, he descended the glen in search of water, where he found a large spring, but it was thickly covered with moss and other rubbage; on removing which, he drank of the water, and found it disagreeably warm. It at once occurred to him that it possessed some valuable medical qualities. The next summer his wife got into bad health, and was afflicted with rheumatic and probably other debilitating disorders. He went and cleared out the springs, erected a small cabin, removed his wife there, and remained four or five weeks, when the use of the waters had restored his wife to a state of fine health. From this occurrence it took the name of "Frye's springs," and was called by that name for many years. By what whim or caprice the name was changed to that of "Capon," the author cannot explain. It is situated four miles east of Capon river, and with what propriety it has taken the name of that river, the reader can as readily determine as the author. This place is too publicly known to require a minute description in this work; suffice it to say, that it is located in a deep narrow glen, on the west side of the Great North mountain.—— The road across the mountain is rugged and disagreeable to travel, but money is now raising by lottery to improve it. The trustees for several years past have imposed a pretty heavy tax upon visitors for the use of the waters. This tax is intended to raise funds for keeping the baths, &c. in repair. There are seventeen or eighteen houses erected without much regard to regularity, and a boarding establishment capable of accommodating fifty or sixty visitors, which is kept in excellent style.

The waters at this place are a few degrees cooler than the waters of Bath; but it is believed by many that they possess some qualities far more powerful. There is no fact better known, than that an exclusive use of the water for five or six days, (like the waters at Salus,) will expel the bots from horses. This place is twenty-two miles south-west of Winchester.

WHITE SULPHUR SPRING, HOWARD'S LICK.

This fine white sulphur spring lies about four miles west of Lost river, in a most romantic retired glen in the mountains. It is almost wholly in a state of nature, the nearest dwelling house to it being about two miles, and is but little known and resorted to as a watering place. The spring has been cleaned out, and a small circular wall placed around it, and a beautiful lively stream of water discharged. It would probably require a tube of one and a half or two inches diameter to vent the water. Every thing the water passes over or touches is pretty thickly incrusted with pure white sulphur. The water is so highly impregnated as to be quite unpleasant to the taste, and can be smelled thirty or forty feet from the spring. The use of the water is found very efficacious in several complaints, particularly in autumnal bilious fevers. The people in the neighborhood say, that persons attached with bilious complaints, by a single dose of Epsom salts, worked off with this water, in three or four days are entirely relieved and restored to heath. The author cannot pretend to express his own opinion of the valuable properties of this water, merely having seen it as a transient passenger. But he has no hesitation in saying that it presents to the eye the appearance of by far the most valuable sulphur water he has ever yet seen. There is level land enough around it for the erection of buildings sufficient for the accommodation of a great many visitors. A fine and convenient road can be had to it from Lost river, a gap in the mountain leading to it being generally quite level, and wide enough for the purpose. It is probably twenty-three or twen-four miles south-west of Capon springs.

PADDY'S GAP, OR MAURER'S WHITE SULPHUR SPRING.

This is a small pure white sulphur spring, and is said to possess some valuable medicinal qualities. It lies in Paddy's gap, about half way between Capon and Salus springs.

PEMBROKE SPRINGS.

These are situated about one mile south of the residence of Moses Russell, Esq., seventeen miles north-west of Winchester. The waters are considered too cold to bathe in. A bath house has been erected, but it is little used. The waters are pure and salubrious, discharged from the base of the North mountain, and if good accommodations were kept, it would doubtless become a resting place for travelers in the season for visiting the Capon springs. Mr. George Ritenour has lately erected a tannery at this place, and it will probably become a place of business.

WILLIAMS'S WHITE SULPHUR SPRINGS, FORMERLY DUVALL'S.

These are situated about six miles north-east of Winchester. A commodious boarding house has been erected by Mr. Williams, who is going on yearly with additional improvements, to meet the increasing popularity of the establishment.

There are three or four other sulphur springs which were formerly places of considerable resort, but they have fallen into disrepute. The author therefore considers it unnecessary to give them any particular notice in this work. Many chalybeate springs are to be met with in our mountains, but it is not deemed necessary to describe them.

GRAY EARTH.

The author will conclude with a brief notice of a light gray earth of singular texture, and probably containing some highly valuable properties. A considerable bank of this earth or clay is to be seen about two miles below Salus springs. When dissolved in water it makes a beautiful whitewash, and is said to be more adhesive than lime. It is remarkably soft, being easily cut with a knife, has an unctuous or rather soapy feel when pressed between the fingers, and when mixed with a small quantity of water, forms a tough adhesive consistence, very much resembling dough made of wheat flour.

The author, when he first heard of this bank of earth, concluded it was probably fuller's earth, so highly prized by the manufacturers of cloth, &c. in England; but upon an examination of it, it does not appear to answer the description given by chemists of that earth. It is highly probable that it would be found a most valuable manure, and in all likelihood would on trial make a beautiful ware of the pottery kind for domestic use. It would, in the opinion of the writer, be well worth while for manufacturers and others to visit this place and examine for themselves. The author has no pretensions to a knowledge of chemistry, and therefore cannot give anything like an analytical description of this singular and curious kind of earth.

————:o:————

IV.

Description of Weyer's Cave.

BY R. L. COOKE, A. M.

WEYER'S CAVE is situated near the northern extremity of Augusta county, Va., seventeen miles north-east of Staunton, on the eastern side of the ridge running nearly N. and E. parallel to the Blue Ridge, and somewhat more than two miles distant from it.

The western declivity of this ridge is very gradual, and the visitor, as he approaches from that direction, little imagines from its appearance that it embowels one of Nature's masterpieces. The eastern declivity, however, is quite precipitous and difficult of ascent.

The Guide's house is situated on the northern extremity of this ridge, and is distant eight hundred yards from the entrance of the Cave. In going from the house to the Cave, you pass the entrance of Madison's Cave, which is two hundred and twenty yards from the other. Madison's Cave was known and visited as a curiosity, long before the discovery of Weyer's, but it is now passed by and neglected, as unworthy of notice, compared with its more imposing rival, although it has had the pen of a Jefferson to describe its beauties.

Let me remark here, that the incurious visitor, who goes because others go, and is but slightly interested in the mysteries of Nature, may retain his usual dress when he enters the Cave which I am attempting to describe ;—but if he is desirous of prying into every recess,—climbing every accessible precipice,—and seeing all the beauties of this subterranean wonder, I would advise him to provide himself with such habiliments as will withstand craggy projections, or receive no detriment from a generous coating of mud.

The ascent from the bottom of the hill to the mouth of the Cave is steep, but is rendered less fatiguing, by the zigzag course of the path, which is one hundred and twenty yards in length.

Before entering the Cave, let us rest ourselves on the benches before the door, that we may become perfectly cool, while the Guide unlocks the door, strikes a light and tells the story of its first discovery.

It seems that about the year 1804, one Bernard Weyer ranged these hills as a hunter. While pursuing his daily vocation, he found his match in a lawless Ground Hog, which not only eluded all his efforts, but eventually succeeded in carrying off the traps which had been set for his capture. Enraged at the loss of his traps he made an assault upon the domicil of the depredator, with spade and mattock.

A few moments labor brought him to the ante-chamber of this stupendous Cavern, where he found his traps safely deposited.

The entrance originally was small and difficult of access; but the enterprise of the Proprietor has obviated these inconveniences: it is now enclosed by a wooden wall, having a door in the centre, which admits you to the ANTE-CHAMBER.

At first it is about eight feet in height, but after proceeding a few yards, in a S. W. direction, it becomes contracted to the space of three or four feet square.

At the distance of twenty-four feet from the entrance,—descending at an angle of nineteen degrees,—you reach the DRAGON'S ROOM, so called from a stalactitic concretion, which the Nomenclator undoubtedly supposed to resemble that nondescript animal..

Above the Dragon's room there is an opening of considerable beauty, but of small size, called the Devil's Gallery.

Leaving this room, which is not very interesting, you proceed in a more southerly direction, to the entrance of SOLOMON'S TEMPLE, through a high but narrow passage, sixty-six feet in length, which is by no means difficult of access. Here you make a perpendicular descent of thirteen feet, by means of an artificial bank of earth and rock, and you find yourself in one of the finest rooms in the whole Cave. It is irregular in shape, being thirty feet long, and forty-five broad—runing nearly at right angles to the main course of the Cave. As you raise your eyes, after descending the bank before mentioned, they rest upon an elevated seat, surrounded by sparry incrustations, which sparkle beautifully in the light of your candles.

This is not unaptly styled Solomon's Throne. Every thing in this room, receives its name from the Wise Man; immediately to the left of the steps, as you descend, you will find his Meat-house; and at the eastern extremity of the room, is a beautiful pillar of white stalactite, somewhat defaced by the smoke of candles, called by his name. With strange inconsistency, an incrustation resembling falling water, at the right of the steps, has obtained the name of the Falls of Niagara.

Passing Solomon's Pillar, you enter another room, more irregular than the first, but still more beautiful. It would be impossible adequately to describe the magnificence of this room. I shall therefore merely observe, that it is thickly studded with beautiful stalactites, resembling, in form and color, the roots of radishes, which have given the appellation of RADISH ROOM to this delightful place.

I cannot refrain from reprobating here, the vandal spirit of some visitors, who regardless of all prohibitions, will persist in breaking off and defacing, these splendid specimens of Nature's workmanship, forgetting that a single blow may destroy the work of centuries.

The main passage to the rest of the Cavern is immediutely opposite to the entrance to Solomon's Temple, and you reach it by an ascent of twelve feet, to what is called The Porter's Lodge. From this place, pursuing the same course, you pass along a passage varying from ten to thirty feet in height—from ten to fifteen in breadth—and fifty-eight in length, until you reach BARNEY's HALL, which receives its name from the fancied resemblance of a prostate stalactite, at the base of one that is upright, to old Com. Barney, and the cannon that he used at the "Bladensburgh races."

Near the centre of the room, which is small and scarcey deserves the name, an upright board points out to the visitor the main path of the Cave, which runs to the right. Two passages run off to the left—the first one to a large, irregular room, called the LAWYER's OFFICE, in which is a fine spring, or rather a reservoir where the droppings from the ceiling have collected;—the other, through a passage to what is called THE ARMORY, from an incrustation that has received the name of Ajax's Sheild. Between the Lawyer's Office and the Armory, and communicating with both, is another large, irregular apartment, which is named WEYER's HALL, after the original discoverer of the Cave, who together with his dog, stands immortalised in one corner.

Before we get bewildered and lost in this part of the Cave, which is more intricate than any other, let us return to the guide board in Barney's Hall, and pursue the route usually taken by visitors. Following the right hand opening mentioned above, which is rather low, being not more than five feet high, you pass into the TWIN ROOM, taking heed lest you fall into the Devil's Bake Oven, which yawns close by your feet.—This room is small, and communicates directly with the BANNISTER ROOM, which is fifty-nine feet from the guide board. The arch here suddenly expands, and becomes elevated to the height of thirty feet, and by dint of hard climbing you may return to the Porter's Lodge, through a passage directly over the one which you have just passed.

A descent of thirty-nine feet due west from the Twin Room, brings you to the TANYARD, which contains many beauties. The floor is irregular; in some places sinking into holes somewhat resembling tan vats, which together with several hanging stalactites resembling hides, have given a name to this immense apartment. On the S. E. side of the room, immediately to the left of the main path, is a large opening, which admits you at once into the Armory.

It may be well to remark here, that a notice of many beautiful appearances in the different rooms has been omitted, because they are noted upon the Map of the Cave, lately published by the author of this sketch.

Changing your course to the N. W. you leave the Tanyard by a rough but not difficult ascent of twenty feet, at an angle of eighteen degrees, into what may be considered an elevated continuation of the same room, but which has been deservedly dignified with a distinct appellation.

To your right, as you step upon level ground, you will observe a perpendicular wall of rock, rising with great regularity; if you strike upon it with your hand, it sends forth a deep, mellow sound, strongly resembling the tones of a Bass Drum, whence the room has received the name of the DRUM ROOM. Upon a closer examination, this apparent wall will be found to be only a thin stalactitic partition, extending from the ceiling to the floor.

*L

You leave the Drum Room by a flight of natural steps, seven feet in perpendicular height.   A large opening now presents itself, which expands to an extensive apartment, to reach which it is necessary to make a nearly perpendicular descent of ten feet, by means of substantial stone steps.   This apartment is the far-famed BALL ROOM.   It is one hundred feet long, 36 wide, and about twenty-five high, running at right angles to the path by which you entered it.   The general course of this room is from N. to S.—but at the northern extremity, there is a gradual ascent, bearing round to the east, until you reach a precipice of twenty or thirty feet, from which you can look down into the Tanyard.

Near the center of the Ball Room, is a large calcareous deposit, that has received the name of Paganini's Statue, from the circumstance that it furnishes a good position for the music, whenever balls are given in these submundane regions.   The floor is sufficiently level to admit of dancing upon it, and it was formerly common to have balls here.   The ladies are accommodated with a convenient Dressing Room, the only opening to which communicates directly with the Ball Room.

You leave this room by a gradual ascent of forty-two feet at the southern extremity.   This acclivity is called The Frenchman's Hill, from the following circumstance :—Some years since, a French gentleman visited the Cave, accompanied only by the Guide; they had safely gone through, and returning, had reached this hill, when by some accident both their lights were extinguished, and they were left in Egyptian darkness, without the means of relighting them.   Fortunately, the Guide, from his accurate knowledge of localities, conducted him safely to the entrance—a distance of more than five hundred feet.

Another gentleman by the name of Patterson, has immortalised his name by attempting the same feat, although it was a complete failure.— Hearing of the Frenchman's adventure, he sent his company ahead, and undertook to find his way back without a light, from the Ball Room to the entrance.   He succeeded in ascending the steps, but had proceeded only a few paces farther, when his feet slipped from under him, and he was laid prostrate in an aperture, where he lay unhurt until his companions, alarmed at his protracted absence, returned for him.   His resting place is called Patterson's Grave, to this day.

From the French Hill, a long, irregular passage extends, in a N. W. direction, which is denominated the Narrow Passage.   This passage is fifty-two feet long—from three to five feet wide—and from four to eight high.   It leads you to the brink of a precipice twelve feet high.

Natural indentations in the face of this precipice, afford a convenient means of descent, and these natural steps have received the name of Jacob's Ladder.   To correspond with this name, as in Solomon's Temple, everything is named after the Patriarch; a flat rock opposite to the end of the Narrow Passage, is Jacob's Tea Table! and a deep, inaccessible perforation in the rock by its side, is Jacob's Ice house! !   Descending the Ladder, you turn to the left, and pass through a narrow opening, still continuing to descend though less perpendicularly, to the centre of a small apartment called the DUNGEON.

This room communicates immediately with the SENATE CHAMBER,

over nearly half of which stretches a thin flat rock, at the height of six or eight feet from the the the floor, forming a sort of gallery, which probably suggested the name which has been given to the room.

The Senate Chamber communicates by a high, broad opening, with a much larger apartment, called Congress Hall,—an appellation bestowed rather on account of its proximity to the last mentioned room than from any thing particularly appropriate in the room itself. It is long, and like the Ball Room runs at right angles to the main path, which winds to the left, as you enter. Its course is nearly N. & S. and a wall, perforated in many places, runs through its whole length. Instead of pursuing the customary route, we will turn to the right and explore the dark recess that presents itself.

The floor of Congress Hall is very uneven, and at the northern extremity rises somewhat abruptly. If you climb this ascent, and pass through one of the perforations in the wall above mentioned, you can see through the whole extent of the other half of the room,—but cannot traverse it, on account of two or three deep pits that occupy the whole space between the western side of the room and the wall.

Turning to the right of the opening through which you just passed, your eye vainly attempts to penetrate the deep, dark abyss that is presented to view, and you hesitate to descend. Its name—The Infernal Regions!—does not offer many inducements to enter it: in addition to this, the suspicion that it contained fixed air, for many years deterred the curious from visiting it, and consequently it has not until recently, been thoroughly explored.

In the spring of 1833, I determined at all hazards to explore this room—for I doubt the existence of any bad air, as I had never detected any in the course of extensive researches in almost every part of the Cave. My brother and the guide accompanied me, each carrying two candles, and thus prepared we descended twenty feet before we reached a landing place. Here our candles burned dimly, and great care was necessary to prevent them from going out entirely; yet we experienced no difficulty of breathing, or any other indication of the presence of this much dreaded gas. The floor is not horizontal, but inclined at an angle of fifteen or twenty degrees, and when we emerged from the pit into which we had first entered, our candles shone brightly, and displayed to our view a room more extensive than any that I have yet described. Its greatest length was from W. to E. and it seemed to run nearly parallel to the path over which we have just travelled. From its length we are induced to believe that it approached very near the Ball room with which it might communicate, by some yet undiscovered passage. So strongly were we impressed with this idea, that we determined, if practicable, to ascertain how far we were correct. For this purpose I set my watch exactly with my brother's, and requested him to go to the Ball room and pursue as far as possible, a low passage that leads to the right, from the foot of the Frenchman's hill, while I went to the eastern extremity of this immense apartment. At an appointed moment I fired a pistol—but the only answer was the deafening reverberations of the sound rolling like thunder along the lofty arches. I shouted—but no return met my ear save the hollow echo of my own voice, and

I began to think we had been hasty in our opinion. At this moment a beautiful stalactite sparkled in the light of the candle, and I forgot my desire to discover an unknown passage, in my anxiety to secure this prize. Taking the butt of the pistol, I hammered gently upon it to disengage it from the rock where it hung. I was surprised to hear the taps distinctly answered apparently from the centre of the solid rock, and a repetition of the blow brought a repetition of the answer. After comparing our impressions, we were satisfied there could be but little space between the two rooms.

We have lingered so long in these Infernal Regions,* that we must hasten back to the spot whence we diverged in the centre of Congress Hall. Our course now lies to the S. W. up a perpendicular ascent of seventeen feet to what is called the Lobby. From this place, an expert climber may pass through secret passages and bye rooms to the end of the Cave, without once entering the main path. You have ascended to the Lobby only to descend again on the other side, when you reach the most magnificent apartment in the whole Cave.

This is WASHINGTONS' HALL, so called in token of respect for the memory of our Country's Father, and is worthy of bearing the name.—— Its length is two hundred and fifty-seven feet—its breadth from ten to twenty—its height thirty-three, and it is remarkably level and straight through the whole length. Not far from the centre of this room, is an immense deposite of calcareous matter rising to the height of six or seven feet, which strikingly resembles a statue clothed in drapery. This is Washington's Statue, and few can look upon it as seen by the dim light of two or three candles which rather stimulate than repress the imagination, without experiencing a sensation of solemnity and awe, as if they were actually in the presence of the mighty dead.

By ascending a bank, near the entrance, of five or six feet perpendicular height, you enter another room called the THEATRE, from the fact that different parts of it correspond to the stage, gallery and pit. I notice this room, which is otherwise uninteresting, for the purpose of mentioning a circumstance, related to me by Mr. Bryan a former guide, which confirms an opinion that I have long entertained, that the whole Cave is thoroughly ventilated by some unknown communication with the upper air. About six years since, during a heavy and protracted rain which raised the waters of the South River that flows at the bottom of the cave-hill, to an unprecedented height, Mr. B. conducted a company through the Cave. As he ascended the stairs that lead to the Lobby, he heard the rush of water; fearing that the Cave was flooding, he directed the visitors to remain in Congress Hall, while he investigated the cause of the unusual and alarming noise. Cautiously descending into Washington's Hall, he followed the sound until he arrived opposite to the entrance of the Theatre, in which he saw a column of water pouring from the ceiling into the pit, and losing itself in the numerous crevices that abound. When the rain ceased, the flood was stayed, and it has never been repeated; but even at the present time, small pebbles and gravel,

---

*For an account of some recent interesting discoveries in this room, see note on page 296.

resembling that found on the top of the hill, may be seen in the Theatre. No aperture is visible from within, neither has any perforation been discovered on the surface of the hill—yet beyond a doubt, some communication with the exterior does exist.

I have said that the breadth of Washington's Hall is from ten to twenty feet; this must be understood as applying to the lower part of the room, for the arch stretches over a rock twenty feet high, which forms the left wall, and embraces another room called Lady Washington's room. The entrance to this apartment is opposite to the Statue, and is on a level with the Hall. The wall that separates the two rooms, is ten feet thick, and is named The Rock of Gibraltar. One or two candles placed upon this rock, produce a fine effect, particularly if every other light is extinguished; for it shows you the arch, spreading out with beautiful regularity, until it is lost in the surrounding darkness, and imagination, supplying the deficiency of vision, peoples the dark recesses with hosts of matterless phantoms. You leave this splendid apartment at the S. W. extremity, by a rough and narrow, but high passage, running at the foot of the Pyramids of Egypt and Cleopatra's Needle! At the end of this passage, in a recess to the right is another spring or reservoir, similar to the one in the Lawyer's Office. A descent of eight or ten feet brings you into the Diamond Room, which may be considered as forming a part of The Church, a long, irregular room more lofty than any that we have yet entered. Its length is one hundred and fifty-two feet—its breadth from ten to fifteen—and its height fifty! At the farthest extremity, a beautiful white spire shoots up to a considerable height, which is appropriately styled The Steeple, and has no doubt, suggested the name of the room. Nearly opposite to the centre of the Church, is a recess of considerable extent and elevation, which forms a very good Gallery; in the rear of the Gallery, and in full view from below, is a great number of pendant stalactites several feet long and of various sizes, ranged like the pipes of an organ, and bearing a striking resemblance to them. If these stalactites are struck by any hard substance, they send forth sounds of various pitches, according to their sizes, and if a stick be rapidly run along several of them at once, a pleasing variety of notes is produced. This formation is called the Organ.

Passing under the Steeple, which rests on an arch elevated not more than ten feet, you enter the Dining Room. This room is named from a long natural table, that stands on the left, and is not quite as large as the Church, though its height is sixty. feet. But for the sort of wall which the Steeple makes, it might be considered as a continuation of the Church. A little to the left of the table, you will see a small uninviting opening; if you are not deterred by its unpromising appearance, we will enter and see whither it will lead us. Proceeding only a few paces you will suddenly find yourself in an immense apartment, parallel to the Dining room, extending to the Gallery in the Church, with which it communicates. This is Jackson's Room, and is rather uninteresting on account of its irregularity, but it leads to one that deserves notice. Directly opposite to the little passage which conducted you hither, is a large opening; passing this, the walls contract until only a narrow pass a few feet long, is left, which conducts you, if not to the most magnificent, at least to one of the most beautiful and interesting portions of the whole Cavern. There is but one apartment, and that is small, but the GARDEN OF EDEN, for so it is called, derives its beauty from the singular arrangement of the immense stalactites, that hang from the roof, and unite with the stalagmites which have ascended from the floor to meet them: or in few words, it seems as if at some former period, a sheet of water had poured down from the roof and by some wonderful operation of Nature had become suddenly petrified. This sheet is not continuous, but strongly resembles the folds of heavy drapery, and you may pass among its windings as through the mazes of a labyrinth, and the light of a candle shines distinctly through any part of it. A portion of the floor of this room is composed of beautiful fine yellow sand; the floor of most, if not all other portions of the Cave, is a stiff clay, with very few indications of sand.

We must now retrace our steps to the Dining Room, for there is no other place of egress; but as we return, let us make a short digression to the left, into a small passage that does not appear to extend very far. Be careful!—there is a deep hole just before you!—now hold your candle above your head and look through the opening, which is large enough to admit the body of a man; you will see a deep unexplored abyss,

"*Where the footstep of mortal has never trod.*"

No man has yet ever ventured into this forbidding place, for it can be entered only by means of a rope ladder, but it is my intention if my courage does not fail me, to attempt at no distant period, to explore the hidden mysteries of the apartment.

Once more in the Dining Room, let us hasten to the completion of our task. The main path pursues the same course from this room, that it has done ever since you entered Washington's Hall; but your way now lies up a sort of hill, in the side of which, is the opening through which you are to pass. If you are adventurous, you will follow me above the opening, up the nearly perpendicular face of the rock, to the height of fifty feet, where a ledge of rock extends itself, forming the left side of the Dining Room. From this eminence, called the Giant's Causeway, you can look down into the Dining Room, on one side, and Jackson's Room on the other.

Great caution is necessary in climbing this height, lest too much confidence be reposed in the projecting stalagmites, that offer a convenient and seemingly a secure foot hold to the incautious adventurer. It must be remembered that they are formed by droppings from the roof, and are generally based on the mud. By cautiously descending the ledge a few feet on the opposite side to that which we ascended, we shall be enabled to reach with ease, the room which has already been attained by the rest of the company, who have been less adventurous than ourselves and passed through the opening already pointed out, in ascending the Causeway.

This room, or perhaps it should be called passage, is denominated THE WILDERNESS, from the roughness of the path-way, and is only ten feet wide, but it rises to the immense height of ninety or one hundred feet! As we come along the Causeway, and look down upon our right, we shall see our company forty or fifty feet below us, while our eyes can scarcely penetrate through the darkness, to the ceiling above our heads. Upon the very verge of the rock on which we are standing, are several beautiful white stalagmites, or rather columns, grouped together, among which one stands pre-eminent. This is Bonaparte with his body-guard, crossing the Alps! The effect is peculiarly fine when viewed from below.

Without descending from our dangerous elevation, we will go on our way a little further. Proceeding only a few paces from the Emperor, you find yourself upon an arch under which your company is passing, which is very appropriately called The Natural Bridge; but it should be crossed with great caution—if at all—for foot hold is insecure, and there is danger of being precipitated to the floor beneath. Retracing our steps nearly to Bonaparte's statue, we will descend an inclined plane on the left, and by a jump of six feet, rejoin our friends at the end of the Wilderness.

You are now upon the lowest level of the Cave, and at the entrance of the farthest room. This is Jefferson's Hall—an extensive and level but not very elevated apartment. Before I describe this room, we must diverge a little and visit one or two rooms that branch off from the main path. Directly to your right, as you emerge from the Wilderness, there rises an immense mass, apparantly of solid stalagmite, thirty-six feet long —thirty feet broad—and thirty feet high; this mass is beautiful beyond description; very much resembling successive stories, and is called the Tower of Babel! The most magnificent portion of the Tower is on the back or northern part, but it is difficult of access, for it is necessary to climb up the surface of the rock to the height of fifteen or twenty feet ; the view however amply repays you for the labor. For a few moments, you can scarcely convince yourself that an immense body of water is not pouring over the precipice, in a foaming torrent—so white, so dazzling is the effulgence of the rock, and when this impression is effaced, the words of the pious Bard rush into the mind, where he describes the awful effects that will follow the consummation of all things;

> 'The Cataract, that like a Giant wroth,
> 'Rushed down impetuously, as seized at once
> 'By sudden frost, with all his hoary locks,
> 'Stood still!!'

One might almost imagine that Pollock had visited this wonder, and caught the idea so forcibly expressed above, from viewing this magnificent scene.

We have already so much exceeded our intended limits, that we can only look into the large apartment that occupies the space behind the Tower, which is called Sir Walter Scott's Room, and then hasten back to the main path.

Jefferson's room, that we left some time since, is very irregular in shape, and is two hundred and thirty-five feet long, following the various windings. What is commonly called the end of the Cave, is distinguished by two singular, thin, lamellar rocks, five or six feet in diameter, united at their bases, but spreading out so that the outer edges are several feet apart; this is called the Fly Trap! To the left of the Fly Trap, is a large recess, where you will fiind a fine spring of water, at which the weary visitor is glad to slake his thirst, after the fatigues of his arduous undertaking.

Very many visitors have their curiosity satisfied long before they have gone over the ground that we have, but I am writing for those only, who like me, are not satisfied until everything is seen that is worthy of notice. Such would not excuse me, did I not mention one more curiosity, that few are inclined to visit. A few yards beyond the Fly-trap, there is an opening in the solid wall, at the height of about twelve feet, through which you are admitted by a temporary ladder. By hard climbing, you soon penetrate to the end of the recess, where you find the source of the Nile! This is a beautiful, limpid spring, covered over with a thin pellicle of stalagmite, yet sufficiently strong to bear your weight;—in this crust, there is a perforation that gives you access to the water beneath.

I have thus very cursorily described, as far as it is practicable, this wonderful cavern, but I feel convinced that no pen can adequately describe an object so extensive, so magnificent, and so varied in tis beauties. I shall only add a few remarks in explanation of the motives that induced me to prepare this sketch, and some general facts that could not, with propriety, have been stated in the description of individual portions of the Cave. To settle a dispute relative to its depth, I was induced to make a full and accurate survey of the whole Cavern, which I found had never been done. This was undertaken solely for my own gratification, but the solicitations of the Proprietor, and others, have induced me to construct a sort of Map, which is now before the public. This Description therefore, may be depended upon, as being as accurate as possible, for the distances, heights, elevations, &c. are given from actual measurement. The dotted line in the map, represents what has so often been called the "main path," and if we measure this line the length of the Cave is one thousand six hundred and fifty feet. By following its windings, the distance may be more than doubled.

At all times, the air of the Cave is damp, but the dampness of the floor depends much upon the seasons; if you except a moist place near the Fly-trap, there is no standing water in all the Cave. The temperature remains invariably at fifty-six degrees, in all parts, from which it follows that the air feels quite warm, to a visitor in winter, and directly the reverse in summer, and it is therefore important that in the summer he should become perfectly cool before he enters, and in winter, before he leaves it. The spring and fall are the best seasons fos visiting the Cave, for then the atmosphere without, is nearly of the same temperature with that within, and it is more dry at these times.

The question is often asked—which of the two great curiosities of Virginia is the greatest, Weyer's Cave or the Natural Bridge? This is not a fair question, neither can it be easily answered; for they are totally different in themselves, and in their effects upon observers. You visit the Natural Bridge in the full blaze of noon-day, and when you reach the object of your curiosity, it bursts at once upon your view, in all its magnifi cence and grandeur, you comprehend at once the magnitude of the scene, and you turn away, overpowered with a sense of the majesty of Him who has spanned that gulf, and thrown His arch across it. Visit it as often as you please, this feeling returns upon you with unabated force—but no new impressions are made—you have seen the whole.

You visit the Cave by the dim light of a few candles; of course no impression will at first be produced, or if any, an unfavorable one. As successive portions of the Cavern are presented to view, they produce successive and varied emotions. Now you are filled with delight at the beauty of the sparkling ceilings;—again, this feeling is mingled with admiration, as some object of more than ordinary beauty presents itself;—and anon you are filled with awe at the magnitude of the immense chambers, the hollow reverberations of the lofty arches, and the profuse display of the operations of an omnipotent hand. Indistinctness of vision, allows free scope to the imagination, and consequently greatly enhances your pleasure.

Many persons go away from the Cave disappointed; they hear of rooms and ceilings, and if they do not expect to see them plaistered and white washed, they think at least that they will be mathematically regular in form, and that they will be able to walk in them with as much ease and see as many wonders as they would in a visit to Aladin's palace! A visit to the Cave is not unattended with fatigue, but the pleasure you derive from it, is ample compensation.

[The author of this pamphlet has omitted to notice what I consider one of the greatest and most beautiful of nature's curiosities in this grand work of nature, i. e., what is called the rising moon. In a dark recess, on the Eastern side of the cave, this curiosity appears in full relief. It is a very natural representation of the moon in her last quarter, rising in the morning.]

(NOTE A.)

Since the publication of the first edition of this Description, a discovery of great interest has been made in the Infernal Regions, which deserves notice, on account of its extraordinary richness and rarity. The floor of this apartment, until recently, has been supposed to be solid rock, but it isn ow ascertained to be a rich mine of calcareous deposites, surpassing in beauty anything ever yet discovered in this or any other Cavern. By perforating the floor with a crow bar, it was found to consist of successive layers of brilliant white crystals, to the depth of three feet—the layers being often interrupted, and varying in width.

The crystals are usually pendent from the lower surfaces of the layers, though very many of them serve as pillars to support the superincumbent mass. After penetrating through the layers, a large geode or hollow space was discovered, extending many yards horizontally, but only three feet deep, which was half full of very limpid water. In this cavity the crystals assume the form of well-defined dog-tooth spar, and are unrivalled in brilliancy and beauty. In the course of extensive and minute explorations in different Caves in this and other States, I have never met with a

*M

similar formation, or with crystals of such transcendent beauty. By the kindness of the Proprietor, I have been enabled to make a choice collection of specimens, embracing almost every variety. For one of these I have refused $100.

(NOTE B.)

Much has been said of late, of another Cave that has been discovered within two years, in the immediate vicinity of Weyer's. A few words respecting it may not be uninteresting. You gain admittance by a long flight of steps, and immediately find yourself in a large apartment, the first veiw of which, (under the circumstances in which I first saw it—by the light of several hundred candles,) is very imposing.

Pillars and enormous pendent stalactites impart an air of wildness and irregularity to the scene, that is not observable in the other Cave. There are few narrow passages;—the cavern seems to be comprised in one immense room, its floor however being so uneven and rugged, and the view so much curtailed by pillars and stalactites that extend nearly to the floor, that the effect which otherwise would be produced by its vastness, is very sensibly diminished. I have not space to describe this Cave more minutely, but will briefly give my impressions of the comparative merits of these rival claimants of our admiration. We are immediately struck with astonishment and pleasure, at the general view that is presented to us in Weast's Cave, as long as we look at it at a little distance—but our emotions are not very varied; and when we examine closely the objects of our admiration, our emotions subside, for their beauty is gone.

As we enter Weyer's Cave, we are not transported with those violent yet agreeable emotions, but as we proceed, new and richer beauties rise successively before us, and our feelings rise with them, until they reach an almost painful degree of intenseness, nor is the effect lessened by the most minute examination of the objects of our admiration. Weast's Cave richly deserves a visit from all who love to contemplate the works of Nature, but in variety, in beauty, and in general effect, it must yield the palm to Weyer's.

V.

——:o:——

ACCOUNT OF THE MEDICAL PROPERTIES
OF THE
GREY SULPHUR SPRINGS.

————

THE great reputation which the Mineral Springs of Virginia have of late years acquired, causes them to be resorted to, in great numbers, not only by invalids from every section of the U. S. and foreign parts, but also by individuals of leisure and fashion, whose principal object is, to pass the summer in an agreeable manner. The properties of the Warm, Hot, Sweet, White Sulphur, Salt Sulphur, and Red Sulphur Springs, are generally known. Those of the Grey Sulphur having been ascertained only within the two last years, have yet to be made public, and in order to do so, we are induced to give, in this form, an account of the situation and medical properties, together with a statement of some of the cases benefited by the use of the waters.

The Grey Sulphur Springs are situated near the line, dividing the counties of Giles and Monroe, Va., on the main road leading from the court-house of the one to that of the other. They are 3-4 of a mile from Peterstown, nine miles from the Red Sulphur, and by the county road, twenty and a quarter miles from the Salt Sulphur Spring. In traveling to the Virginia Springs, by either the main Tennessee or Goodspur Gap road, and crossing the country from Newbern, by the stage road to the Sulphur Springs, the Grey Sulphur are the first arrived at. They are thirty miles distant from Newbern. The location is such as to admit of many and varied improvements, which when completed, will render this spot an elegant and desirable resort during the summer months, independent of the high medicinal properties of the Mineral Waters.

The present improvements consist of a brick Hotel ninety feet long and thirty-two wide; two ranges of cabins one hundred and sixty-two feet long each, which, with other buildings in connexion, afford accommodation for from ninety to one hundred visitors.

There are two springs at this establishment, situated within five feet of each other and inclosed in one building. Although rising so near to each other, yet they differ most materially in their action on the system. Both appear to be peculiarly serviceable in dyspeptic cases, and in such as orig-inate in a disordered state of the stomach—the one in those, in which in-flammation exists, the other in such as proceed from torpidity. They have hitherto been known as Large and Small Springs; but having succeeded towards the close of the last season in procuring a much larger supply of water at the Small Spring, than is afforded by the Large, a change of names became necessary. The large will hereafter be known as the Anti-Dyspeptic, and the Small as the Aperient, which names will serve to point out their peculiar characteristics.

These Springs have been classed by Professor Shepard, as *"Alkaline Sulphurous,"* a variety so rarely met with, that another is not known in the United States. The waters are beautifully clear, and highly charged with gas, which render them light and extremely pleasant, especially that of the Anti-Dyspeptic Spring, which produces none of those unpleasant sensations so frequently felt on the first drinking of Mineral Waters.

When first purchased some of the water was submitted to a chemist for analysis; the quantity, however, was too small for him to ascertain all its ingredients. A more recent examination has been made by Professor C. U. Shepard, who has furnished us with the following abstract of an article which appears in the April Number (1836) of Professor Silliman's Journal of Science and arts.

"The following is the most satisfactory view which my experiments enable me to present of the condition of these Waters.

Specific gravity, 1,003.

SOLUBLE INGREDIENTS.

Nitrogen,
Hydro-Sulphuric acid,
Bi-Carbonate of Soda,*
A Super Carbonate of Lime,
Chloride of Calcium,
Chloride of Sodium,
Sulphate of Soda,
An Alkaline or earthy Crenate, or both,
Silicic acid.

INSOLUBLE INGREDIENTS.

Sulphuret of Iron,
Crenate of Per Oxide of Iron,
Silicic acid,
Alumina,
Silicate of Iron.

My experiments do not permit me to point out the differences between the two Springs with precision. The new Spring appears to give rise to a greater amount of hydro-sulphuric acid, as well as of iron and silicic acid. Probably it may differ in still other respects. I have not examined it for Iodine or Bromine."

As no regular analysis was attempted, the quantities in which these several ingrdients exist, still remain undetermined. That they are in different proportions in the two Springs, is evident not only from their deposites, but also from their action on the system. The action of the Anti-Dyspeptic Spring is diuretic and gently aperient, tending to restore the

---

*It cannot be determined whether free carbonic acid exists in these waters without going into a quantitative analysis.—C. U. S.

healthy performance of the functions, and reduce or diffuse the local irritation of disease. The Aperient Spring while it possesses all the alkaline properties of the other, has an aperient and alterative action. Possessing more iron, (of which the other has but a trace,) it acts more powerfully as a tonic, whilst its other ingredients cause it to act *in some cases* as a very powerful aperient.

As these Springs have been visited by invalids, only during the two last seasons, it is reasonable to suppose that all their properties have not yet been discovered, nor all the cases ascertained in which they can be beneficially used. In fact, owing to the small quantity of water furnished hitherto by the Aperient Spring, its qualities have been but little tested, and there can be no doubt, (judging from its constituents) that it will be found equally salubrious as the Anti-Dyspeptic Spring, only better adapted to another class of cases. To give a general idea of the properties of these waters, we might say that they are peculiarly serviceable in those diseases which originate in a disordered state of the stomach and bowels, and also in hepatic affections. It is proper, however, to enter more into details, and we therefore, submit the following synopsis of the medical properties of the *Anti-Dyspeptic* Spring.

MEDICAL PROPERTIES.

1. It relieves nausia and headaches, arising from disordered stomachs.

2. Neutralizes acidity, and if taken at meals, or immediately after, it has a tendency to prevent those unpleasant sensations so often experienced by invalids, from indiscretion in dieting.

3. Is an excellent tonic, exciting appetite and imparting strength to digestion.

4. Quiets irritation of the alimentary canal.

5. Controls and lessens the force of the circulation when unnaturally excited by disease, and often in this way, is remedial in internal inflammation of the organs.

6. It tranquilizes nervous irritability.

7. Is a mild and certain expectorant, often allaying dyspnœa, and promoting recovery from chronic ailments of the chest or wind pipe.

8. It alters the action of the liver, where this has been previously deranged, in a manner peculiar to itself, and under circumstances in which the ordinary alteratives are forbidden by reason of their excitive or otherwise irrelevant properties.

9. It is also sudorific or diaphoretic; and

10. When taken at bedtime, often proves itself soporific; apparently stifling that indescribable, but too well understood inquietude which so frequently and unhappily interrupts or prevents the repose of the invalid, and especially of the dyspeptic.

Having thus briefly stated the properties of this Spring, we submit the following statement of cases, treated at the Gray Sulphur, illustrative of the effect of the waters, and in corroboration of what has been advanced. Except those which are noticed in their proper places, all are either directly from the pen of the sufferers themselves, or were immediately dictated by them in the form in which they appear in the notes. The originals are in our possession, signed by the individuals whose cases are referred to.

No. 1.

Dear Sir,—I take pleasure in stating that the waters of the Grey Sulphur have proved quite beneficial, during a visit of ten days, both to Mrs. S. and myself. We have both been suffering with that distressing malady, Dyspepsia, for a long time, and in my case with a general nervous debility, a weak and torpid state of the stomach and the bowels, and at times great distress of the head and mind, and nervous excitement, *even to spasms*. After drinking freely of the *Anti-Dyspeptic* Spring, *even at meals*, the water produced a fine glow and perspiration, suspended the nervous irritation and distress, and acting as a tonic for the stomach, created a strong appetite and enabled me to partake, with impunity, of any or *all* the solid and delicate dishes with which your table abounded. The water of the *Anti-Dyspeptic* Spring, corrected and prevented acidity of the stomach, and seemed to give activity and strength to that organ—but we required a free use of the *Aperient* Spring, in the mornings, to prevent a constipation of the bowels, which the *Anti-Dyspeptic* Spring seemed to produce.* A glass or two of the *Anti-Dyspeptic* Spring, on retiring, produced a glow, allayed nervous irritation, and induced a fine night's sleep; and we have, as well as our servant woman, who was in a debilitated state of health, experienced more benefit here than from any of the Waters we have as yet visited.

Respectfully yours, &c.

No. 2.

Dear Sir,—It gives me great pleasure to inform you of the general effects of your Anti-Dyspeptic Spring, in my case. During the three day's trial of the waters, I am convined of its diuretic ahd diaphoretic qualities, and in one instance it acted as an alterative on my liver, producing a free discharge of billious matter. My general health has improved, the symptoms of my disease (Neuralgia) have mitigated, my appetite increased, my pulse has become more tranquil and regular, and my sleep more continued and refreshing. I have also gained strength and weight, (three pounds in three days,) during my short sojourn with you.

Yours respectfully,

No. 3.

On the 6th of August, 1835, I arrived at the Gray Sulphur Springs, in a state of much depression, accompanied by a fever and a rapid pulse—both arising from a complication of disorders belonging to the throat, the stomach and bowels. In the afternoon I drank of the Anti-Dyspeptic Spring, and its immediate effect was to produce a gentle moisture of the skin, and to reduce the pulse from an *hundred beats in a minute* to about

---

*In a few instances this effect was complained of, but we found it was only in those cases where habitual costiveness existed, and this was easily remedied by making use of the Aperient Spring before breakfast.

eighty. In the evening, my system generally was relieved. On going to bed I drank of the same spring, and on the following morning felt a continuance of the same agreeable influence, and an improved appetite. In the afternoon there was a further reduction of pulse, and my fever entirely subsided, but partially returned in the night, with quickness of pulse, but by no means accelerated as it was when I came. In the course of the *second* day, the pulse beat *sixty per minute*, but quickened again. The first twenty-four or thirty-six hours experience was followed by similar effects, the two following days, one of which I confined myself to the Aperient Spring, and perceived no difference. Neither of them had the effect to move my bowels, but on the contrary to constipate them. I am much inclined to believe, that a continuance of these waters might have a salutary influence upon my very *singular*, very troublesome, and very obstinate case, if I can judge of their agreeable effect upon my skin, my spirits and system generally, in so short a time as *three days*. There was a continued reduction of the pulse from an accelerated action, produced at the————Sulphur Spring, by drinking its waters; but it varied, being considerably quickened in the evening and during the night. The appetite was much improved and continued uniform. I regret that I could not remain long enough at the Grey Sulphur to test its effects upon my chronic complaints.

No. 4.

Mr. H————had had frequent hemorrhages, accompanied with a pain in the chest—his cough was slight, but he suffered much from phlegm. Twenty-four hours after being at the Grey Sulphur, on examining his pulse, it was found to be about one hondred. Made use of the Anti-Dyspeptic Spring, taking about three tumblers per diem. Three days after, (about the same hour of the day,) his pulse was again examined and found to be reduced to seventy-six beats per minute, and he felt much better. Having left home for ————Spring, he thought it his duty to go there. About a month after, he returned. He had gradually improved in health, and looked much better; and was evidently so. His pulse, however, was much too frequent, and he could not get it lowered. After leaving the Grey Sulphur, it had risen up, to from eighty-five to ninety, and in the afternoon was frequently at one hundred. In the afternoon of the day he arrived, his pulse was counted, and found to be one hundred. After remaining five days, he again left for the ————Spring, his pulse varied, during his stay at the Grey, from seventy-five to ninety, but never reached so high as one hundred. His complexion became clearer, his spirits better, and his cough entirely left him. It had been gradually lessening at the————Spring, but he could not get rid of it altogether, and was, moreover, very annoying to him early in the mornings. In reply to an enquiry, he stated, after a little reflection, "that he had not coughed once, that he could recollect, since his (recent) arrival at the Grey, and expectorated with more ease the phlegm which collected in his throat."

NOTE.—The above is extracted from notes we kept of a few cases during last summer. Not intending, at first, to publish them; we did not ask the consent of Mr. H;, and we hope he will pardon the liberty we have taken.

The three following cases, which occurred in 1834, we give from notes made soon after, and whilst the circumstances were fresh in our memory, and for the correctness of which we hold ourselves responsible.

No. 5.

Mr. A. W. of Baltimore, arrived at the Grey Sulphur, in August, 1834. His health had been feeble for some time, though in appearance he looked but little like an invalid. On the morning of the second day after his arrival at the Grey Sulphur, he had, whilst standing at the Spring house, a considerable hemorrhage—a half pint of blood, at least, was spit up in a very short time. A little common salt was administered, which had the effect of stopping it. It being deemed improper for him to move immediately, he was induced to lie down on one of the benches. About half an hour after this occurrence, his pulse was felt for the first time. It then beat one hundred and eighteen per minute; nor did it vary for the next half hour. He was persuaded to take some of the water of the Anti-Dyspeptic Spring, which he was loth at first to do, lest a recurrence of the hemorrhage should take place. He took about a half pint of water, in small quantities at a time, with intervals of from fifteen to twenty minutes between each. In about an hour from the drinking of the first portion of the water, the pulse was reduced to ninety-eight beats per minute. Soon after, he was assisted up to his room and put to bed. His pulse was not again examined until about 4 o'clock in the afternoon, (the hemorrhage had occurred about 10 o'clock, A. M.) it was then found to have fallen to eighty-six. In the course of the day, he had taken about a pint of water, in quantities of about a half tumbler at a time. The next morning his pulse was again examined, and found to have fallen to eighty-four beats per minute. In the course of the day, he left his bed and came down stairs, and the day following, he left the Grey for the Red Sulphur, to obtain Medical advice. His pulse was not examined after he left his bed.

No. 6.

Mr. M., of South-Carolina, had been long a dyspeptic, and had suffered, for many years, from *Chronic Diarrhœa*. Early in the season of 1834, he visited the Saratoga Springs—the water proved injurious to him.— From thence he visited the White Sulphur, Salt Sulphur, and Red Sulphur Springs, without experiencing material benefit. When he arrived at the Grey Sulphur Springs, he was exceedingly feeble and had to be assisted about, and for several days scarce ever left his chamber, except at meal times. His passages were very frequent, from eight to ten during the night, and about the same number during the day. He had entirely lost the power of secreting urine, and all liquids which he drank passed through his bowels mixed up with undigested food. His passages were thin and of a whitish clay color, apparantly made up of water and undigested food, the latter so little changed as to be easily recognised. In three days, his passages were reduced to from two to three each night, and about the same number during the day, the consistency and color also changed. In a week's time, this change was still greater. The number of passages were about the same, but they became of a bright yellow color, and similar to a child's in consistency. He moreover secreted urine freely, and on one occasion he informed us, that he had passed a large quantity of "pure bile." His bowels remained nearly in this state, during the time he remained at the Spring, (about a fortnight,) but he improved greatly in bodily health, walked out, was cheerful, and in every respect appeared better. The intended stoppage of the stage hurried him off earlier than he wished. He left the Grey Sulphur with the belief that he had derived considerable benefit from the use of the Waters. It is proper to remark, that his appetite was enormous, and that he did not restrict himself in his diet.

NOTE.—There were several other cases of Diarrhœa at the Grey Sulpher, in 1834; all were materially benefited by the use of the Anti-Dyspeptic Spring.

No. 7.

Mr. L—— arrived at the Grey Sulphur Springs about 4 o'clock in the afternoon. He had been for some time in a delicate state of health and had suffered much during the day. Early in the morning he had been seized with nausea, which brought on vomiting. The irritation increased during the day, and the vomiting became frequent and easily excited—all food was immediately rejected, and so irritable became the stomach, that two mouthfuls of water, taken a short time before reaching the Grey Sulphur, were thrown up before he could recline back in his carriage. He was very much exhausted when he arrived, but without sitting down, requested to be shown to the Spring. We accompanied him down. He took a glass of the Anti-Dyspeptic Spring, paused for a few seconds, then took another. A minute or two elapsed, and he then drank several in quick succession. The precise properties of the water had not then been ascertained, and we felt bound to caution him against making such free use of an untried water, although we then knew nothing of his case. He laid down the glass and walked up to the house with us.—On the way, he mentioned the particulars already given—in continuation, he stated, that on drinking the first tumbler of water, he experienced a slight nausea, as the first of it reached the coat of the stomach, but that this wore off almost instantaneously. Being much exhausted and exceedingly thirsty, he determined to venture a second, although he firmly believed that both would be thrown up. Not the slightest nausea was experienced on drinking the second tumbler of water. Surprised at this effect, he determined to ascertain what would be the effect of taking it in larger quantities, and for this purpose he drank about four tumblers more, when he was prevented from proceeding further by our remarks. The great quantity he had taken, not only produced no unpleasant sensations, but on the contrary, removed those he had previously experienced, and served to revive him. In the course of the afternoon, he took two or three glasses more of the water. About 7 o'clock, supper was served, of which he partook freely, making choice of substantial food, such as boil-ed chicken, bread, rice, &c. Not the slightest nausea was produced.—Fearing a recurrence the next morning, he was advised to take some of the water before he left his bed. We were informed, that a slight nausea was felt, but it immediately wore off on drinking a glass of water.—In similar attacks, which this gentleman had previously had, each was succeeded by such costiveness that medicine had to be resorted to. In the present one, there was no occasion for medicine; the evacuations were large and the bowels continued regular during the time he remained; nor did he at any time thereafter, experience any nausea, with which we were made acquainted.

No. 8.

Extract of a letter, dated New York, Jan. 21, 1836.

"It gives me great pleasure to inform you, that I fully realized all the benefit I had been led to anticipate from the use of the Waters of the Grey Sulphur (Anti-Dyspeptic) Spring, with which you so kindly provided me. On Monday morning, I was very *sea sick*, so that I could not leave my berth without vomiting, but on taking half a tumbler of the water, I was sensibly relieved. I continued to use it agreeably to your directions, taking half a tumbler at intervals of fifteen minutes, till the bottle was exhausted. By that time, I had so far recovered as to be able to go about the deck with great comfort, and took a hearty meal, both at dinner and supper. The next morning, however, the weather having become more boisterous, and the sea running high, I was again very sick, but my resource had failed me, and I had only to yield myself quietly to the influence of that most distressing affection. From the result of the experiment, I am satisfied that it is the best remedy for *sea sickness* that I have ever heard of, and that, had not the supply of water failed, I should not have lost one meal during the voyage.

The following note which has been kindly furnished us, refers to the same subject:—

Dear Sir,—The following is an extract of a letter received by me, from Mr. J. H., who went passenger by the Steam Boat Wm. Gibbons, in January last, showing the very beneficial effects of the Grey Sulphur Water, in relieving him from sea sickness.

"The effects of the water on me, were most beneficial, and while the supply lasted, relieved me entirely of nausea, so that I was enabled to eat heartily."

Having been at sea with Mr. H., I bear testimony that he is a complete victim to sea sickness, and I do not know any one on whom the effects of that water could be better tested.

No. 9.

Sir,—It affords me pleasure to bear testimony to the efficacy of the waters of the Grey Sulphur Spring in my case. I have been suffering from Dyspepsia, for at least fifteen years, during which time it has made fearful inroads on a naturally delicate constitution. The disease had progressed so far (a few years ago) that the slight stimulus of food, produced an immediate evacuation after every meal. This state of things could not last, and a most violent inflammation of the bowels ensued, which brought me to the borders of the grave, and eventuated in the formation of a *fistula in anno.* The sinusses spread so far, and became so numerous, that I was forced to have some of them laid open, but having a predisposition to pulmonary affections, it was not deemed prudent to operate on all of them. My digestive organs had not recovered their strength, and the irritation of undigested food, (though I had lived extremely low) kept up the inflammation, and this at last extended to the neck of the bladder, and became extremely distressing. To remove the inflammation and obtain relief, I had recourse to mustard poultices and opiates, but the relief was very temporary. Whilst suffering much from this cause, I was induced to set off for the Virginia Springs. At that time, my bodily health was so much impaired, that I was almost incapable of transacting business: all employmennt, (even reading) was irksome to me. My digestion was so bad that I scarce knew what to live on; every thing, however plain, appeared to disagree with me, and I was at times truly wearied of life, for I looked forward only to a life of pain and suffering. Such was my situation, when in 1834, I left my home for the Springs. On my journey, I did not improve in health, but on the contrary, had a slight attack of diarrhœa. The irritation around the bladder continued, or rather increased, so that I was obliged to make use of opiates daily, and sometimes, two or three times in the course of the day. The first Spring I arrived at, was the Grey Sulphur. This I consider fortunate, as I found, on trial, that all of the others were too stimulating for me, with the exception of the Red Sulphur, and from that, I am not aware of experiencing any material benefit. Be this as it may, it enabled me satisfactorily to ascertain that the waters of the Grey Sulphur Spring, were decidedly beneficial in my case. I can scarcely describe my situation when I arrived at your Spring. I was weak, feverish, and laboring under a kind of nervous excitement, whilst the inflammation had evidently increased, and I suffered much from it, especially towards evening. I have been thus particular, that the action of the water may be more distinctly understood. The first day of my arrival, I drank freely of the Anti-Dyspeptic Spring. I took no note of the quantity, but drank whenever I felt thirsty, or had an inclination, and I must confess, with but little expectation of finding relief, or at least, not immediate, for your Spring had not then obtained that celebrity, which I am glad to find it has since acquired. Judge, then, of my very agreeable surprise, at finding in the evening, (the time when the paroxisms of pain were usually the most violent,) that they were so slight that I had no need of medicine. I retired to rest and slept soundly. The next day I was not at all annoyed, and at the usual time, I scarcely perceived that there was any irritation at all.— The third day I was entirely relieved, and had no return during my stay at the Spring, nor had I occasion once to use any medicine.

Other changes not less important, also took place. The diarrhœa ceased on the second day, and in the course of the week the evacuations, from being thin and of a whitish clay colour, became of an orange colour, and acquired considerable firmness, and in a short time afterwards, acquired all the characteristics of healthy passages. It is needless to say that my digestion had improved. One thing is worthy of remark, and that is, that I found myself able to digest, not only plain food, but also the richer kinds, and even desserts; and this without suffering, and even without experiencing any unpleasant feeling after meals. I should here state, however, that I invariably took from one to two tumblers of the water after *each* meal, and I found this peculiarly serviceable after breakfast, when the tea (or coffee) became (almost invariably at first) acid. During my sojourn with you, I improved in every respect, and even the discharge from the fistulas ceased nearly altogether, and I returned home in (comparatively) excellent health, which I enjoyed, until unfortunately I was attacked with the influenza during the last winter. From that time I began to retrograde, and when summer arrived, I was in almost as bad condition as the year previous. The inflammation and irritation were quite as violent, and my digestion had again become disordered. I had experienced too much relief at the Grey Sulphur, to hesitate long as to the course proper to be pursued, and I again had the pleasure of visiting them the last season. I have only to say, that the same happy effects were produced, the only difference I observed was, that these were not so immediate as the year previous, but I amply compensated for this by their permanency. And I have now the pleasure of stating to you, that I have enjoyed, and am now enjoying (February 12th) better health than I have known for the last ten or twelve years, and most happy am I to state to you, that I have not had the slightest indication of inflammation in those regions where I had suffered so much.

I remain, Dear Sir, yours, &c.

No. 10.

Mr. B. has had a bronchial affection for many years, which at times, was so distressing as to compel him to remain propped up in a sitting posture, in bed, the whole night, and in this mode obtain some sleep.—To obtain relief from this affection, he now travelled. When he first arrived at the Grey Sulphur, the cough was very troublesome. Made use of the Anti-Dyspeptic Spring, which had the effect of producing a gentle perspiration, especially at night, and which effect was continued whenever the water was taken, during the whole time of his stay. The cough gradually diminished, until it almost disappeared altogether. At first there was considerable difficulty in getting up the phlegm, but after drinking the water a short time, it was expectorated with ease. During the time he was at the Grey Sulphur, he slept well—had an excellent appetite, and could easily digest whatever he partook of.   B.

The above statement of cases, was submitted to Professors James Moultrie, jun., and S. Henry Dickson, of the Medical College of the State of South-Carolina. The following letters will show the opinion entertained by these gentlemen relative to the medical properties of these waters.

Charleston, February 11th, 1836.

Dear Sir,—I have overlooked your intended publication, together he accompanying documents. I think the statements furnished by the latter, fully authorise you to put forth what you propose. The amount of experience with the waters is very small, to be sure, but such as it is, it is calculated to excite *strong presumption* in their favor. Indeed, considering their analysis, jointly with the facts furnished in your documents, I have confident expectations that they will prove among the most useful discoveries of that sort, yet made in our country. All thus early known of them, encourages us to look for future corroboration of the impression you have imbibed respecting their virtues. Considering their elements, they cannot be nugatory, and must, therefore, be productive of benefit or mischief. Reasoning from what we already know, the evidence appears to be altogether in favor of a salutary result.

Very truly, yours,
JAMES MOULTRIE, Jun. M. D.

J. D. Legare, Esq.

February 11th, 1836.

Dear Sir,—I have perused with attention and interest the papers sent me, containing reports of cases in which the Waters of your Virginia Spring have been tried; and do not hesitate to express the opinion, that they fully justify the statements made in your proposed publication. Professor Shepard's analysis exhibits a singular combination of ingredients, and prepare us to anticipate striking and gratifying results from the use of Waters containing remedies of such obvious efficiency. I confess, I am led to entertain sanguine expectations of benefit to a large class of patients, from these fountains, and shall be much disappointed if the "Grey Sulphur Springs" do not soon attain a high rank among the summer resorts of invalids, and of the fashionable world.

With great regard, I remain, Dear Sir, yours, faithfully,
S. HENRY DICKSON, M. D.

J. D. Legare, Esq.

We here close for the present, our account of the Medical Properties of the Grey Sulphur Springs. The report of cases might have been more extended, had we applied to all of the individuals, who have been benefited by the use of these Waters. It was not deemed necessary to do so. Invalids, with strongly marked cases, will in all probability, visit these Springs, during the next and succeeding seasons, and it is our intention to preserve a record of such as may be communicated to us.

JOHN D. LEGARE.

VI.

——:o:——

WINCHESTER.

THE reader will doubtless recollect that this flourishing town was established by law in the year 1752. In 1738, there were but two cabins erected near the run. It is now a very wealthy corporate town—has its own court of justice—is the seat of justice for the county of Frederick—is the place where the supreme courts of chancery and law are held for the county—the residence of many distinguished lawyers and physicians —has a flourishing academy and numerous classical and English schools —many mechanical establishments of first order—some thirty or forty retail stores—a number of taverns kept in best style—several confectionary shops—several merchant tailors, and almost every variety of business done in our seaport cities. Its buildings are many of brick of superior order. Taylor's Hotel is conspicuous for its great size and elegance of structure. Its front on Loudon street is ninety feet and runs its wings one hundred and thirty back—contains seventy rooms—is calculated to entertain numerous companies of visitors and boarders, and is kept in superb style. This building is three stories; the basement story is divided into cellars and several rooms furnished in the neatest manner; the attic is divided into lodging rooms, which are also furnished in neat style. It commands an immense business.

Within the last five or six years a rail-road has been constructed from Winchester to Harper's Ferry, on the Baltimore highway; six or seven spacious warehouses erected at the commencement of the road, and is the place of deposit of vast quantities of merchandise and produce of every variety. It now contains upwards of 4,000 inhabitants, and is a place of great business. Several gentlemen, descended from German ancestors, who have accumutated considerable wealth, are among them. It has two Presbyterian edifices, handsomely built, as places of public worship; one Catholic chapel; two Methodist meeting houses, and a splendid Episcocal church lately erected; the Baptists have a meeting house, as also the German Lutherans; and the Friends have a neat brick building. The people are divided into various religious sects, and it is believed much piety prevails. It is doubtless one of the finest watered towns in the valley, and a place of general good health. Fine water is conveyed through iron pipes to almost every part of the town; there are many hydrants erected in the streets; and many of the citizens have the water conveyed into their yards. This water is taken from a fine limestone spring about half a mile west of the town. There is a regular organised Fire company, remarkable for their excellent discipline and activity. But few houses have ever been destroyed by fire. The author recollects seeing an old house on Loudon street destroyed by fire upwards of thirty years ago; the wind blew a strong gale from the N. W., and notwithstanding the opposite side of the street was closely built with wooden houses, such was the activity of the fire company and other citizens, that every building was saved except the one which first took fire. Several years afterwards, a fire broke out in a wooden building at the N. end of the town, and the flames spread with great rapidity. It was said that twenty-two buildings took fire at the same time, and but two small buildings consumed; those two belonged to an old gentleman by the name of Benjamin Rutherford, and stood about one hundred and fifty yards apart. The astonishing exertions and activity of the fire company, together with the aid of every citizen, and even ladies, saved twenty out of the twenty-two buildings on fire at the same time; and what was remarkable, but little damage was done the buildings were saned. A few years ago, there were three old wooden buildings on Loudon street burnt down, but the flames were so kept under, that no other dameges were which done.— About sixty years ago, a framed building on Loudon street, which was called the "Long Ordinary," was destroyed by fire, and an old building on the west side of the town, called " The Brewery," was destroyed by fire.— The author recollects seeing this building on fire. It is believed that the foregoing statement contains a true account of all the houses destroyed by fire for the last sixty or seventy years. So that it may truly be said, that Winchester has heretofore been very fortunate.

STAUNTON.

This town may with truth be said to be classical ground. In the war of the Revolution, the Legislature had assembled at Richmond—the enemy advanced to the seat of government, and the Assembly adjourned and met at Charlottesville—Tarlton pursued them thither, and they again adjourned and met at Staunton—here they finished their session. Tarlton did not dare to interrupt them there, for the best of all reasons : the people of Augusta and adjoining counties were a brave, hardy, and active race, well acquainted with the use of the rifle; and if Tarlton had ventured to pursue them to Staunton, he would in all probability have met with another "Cowpen defeat." The citizens turned out manfully, well armed, and determined to contest his march to that place, and protect their legislators in their deliberations.

Staunton, like Winchester, has incorporated privileges, its own court o. justice, is the seat of justice for Augusta county, and the place for holding the Superior courts of law and chancery for the county,—is the residence of several distinguished lawyers and physicians, and is the site of a Lunatic Hospital of great reputation. It has several beautiful edifices erected for public worship, and fifteen or twenty retail stores, with four or five taverns kept in good style. It is surrounded by many valuable farms, and a considerable number of elegant brick dwelling houses, has several turnpike roads leading to East and West, North and South, from which it derives great advantages, and of course is a place of extensive business. In all human probability, it is destined at some future day to become the site of our State government. Its central situation—the fine health of the country—its contiguity to the numerous mineral springs—

its safety from danger of invasion from a foreign enemy in time of war, present most cogent arguments in its favor; and whenever our western counties shall be filled with population, we will have a considerable majority of the free white population west of the Blue Ridge, and it appears to the mind of the author, that the people of the west will not rest satisfied with their seat of government in its present situation.

Staunton has become conspicuous in the history of our State for other important reasons. It is the place where two large conventions of citizens were held some years ago, for deliberating on the great question of reforming our State Constitution. The last of which conventions was held in the month of July, 1825. In this convention upwards of one hundred members attended. Their proceedings were characterized by great temperance, but much energy. A most solemn appeal was made to the Legislature on this vital question, and at the ensuing session, an act passed submitting this question to the lawful voters of the State, which resulted in a majority of the citizens in favor of the necessity of calling a convention for the purpose of revising and amending the organic law of our State. This body was elected in the spring of 1826, and assembled at the capital in the city of Richmond, the ensuing autumn, and drew up certain amendments to the original constitution, which were submitted to the people for their final ratification or rejection. There were many of our ablest statesmen opposed to its ratification, but a majority of our citizens voted for its adoption.

LEWISBURG.

This is a thriving village in the county of Greenbrier, west of the Allegany mountains. It is yet but a small village, but the seat of justice for the county. There is a superior court of law and chancery and a court of appeals. It has become conspicuous in the history of the State, from the circumstance that a convention was lately held there of the citizens of the western part of the commonwealth, by which resolutions were passed, recommending a further amendment of the State Constitution, so as to give a more equal representation of the two great divisions of the State in the General Assembly. Neither is it undeserving of celebrity on account of its several religious edifices, among which the Presbyterian deserves first to be named from its size and commodious internal arrangement. The Methodists and Baptists respectively, have also chaste and convenient houses for public worship. There are several elegant brick dwelling houses in the village; from six to seven retail stores; and two public hotels, under excellent management. From the locality of the village, situated in the midst of a productive country, steadily increasing in population and wealth, it is destined to become a place of considerable business and importance. The face of the country contiguous to and surrounding the village, is beautifully diversified by hills and vallies, woods and fertile fields; and the town, with the whole of the circumjacent region, is remarkable for the salubrity and healthiness of its climate.

THE FINE ARTS.

From the youth of our commonwealth, and the character of our people, devoted almost exclusively, as they have been, to agriculture and its collateral pursuits, we cannot as yet, nor is it yet expected that we can, produce before the world, any Masters in the fine arts comparable with the old Masters of Europe. Yet, notwithstanding the fact that we have as yet no representitive in sculpture to stand by the side of Canova, nor in painting, a champion to compete with a Titian, a Guido, or a Stuart, yet we have not been wholly denied the genius of the pencil. Some ten years since, in the county of Berkeley, a young man of the name of —— M'Cautry, with the intuitive perception only exhibited by true genius, commenced, first in playful sketches, and shortly after in more serious efforts, the divine art of painting. Encouraged by his rapid advancement, he subsequently took a trip to the hallowed ground of Italy, there to perfect himself in the business of his choice. He promised much from improvement; but shortly after his return to his native country, he died, and with him the hopes of his friends.

Six years ago, a Mr. Henry Bowen, of Frederick county, a self-taught artist, commenced the business of a portrait painter, and such was his proficiency in the art that it may be almost said of him he was accomplished in it from the outset. He has since devoted himself assiduously to his employment, and has earned thereby, from the striking fidelity of his sketches to truth and to nature, a well-merited reputation. The author can bear the safest testimony to this character, from the specimens of Mr. Bowen's work which he has seen.

CULTURE OF SILK.

The excellent lady of Mr. Amos Lupton, residing within two and a half miles west of Winchester, has met with very encouraging success in her efforts at producing silk from the cultivation of the trees and the domestication of the worm. She exhibited to the author several pair of hose she had manufactured from this silk, and stated her intention of having the residue of the raw material spun, and woven into articles of wearing apparel. A hired woman, meantime, was employed in spinning the silk from the cocoons upon the common flax-wheel, and really made considerable headway in her delicate task. We hope that Mrs. Lupton will persevere in the enterprise: for we cannot but believe that our soil and climate are both well adapted for the culture of silk. Mr. L. has been completely successful in the raising of the Morus Multicaulis—the plants having grown very thriftily.

HYBRIDOUS.

An animal was begotten between the buck and a young cow about twenty years ago. This extraordinary and beautiful animal was produced in the neighborhood of Zane's Old Furnace. The owner intended selling it to a butcher to make a veal of it; but the late Maj. Bean purchased it, and intended to raise it by hand. He kept it several weeks, but it died, and with it the hopes of Mr. Bean and many of the neighbors. Mr. Bean flattered himself with high expectations of having in his possession one of the most rare, beautiful, and extraordinary curiosities in na-

*o

ture's works. The author did not get the opportunity of seeing this singular creature, but several of his neighbors visited Mr. Bean for the express purpose of viewing it, who reported the facts to the writer of this narrative. It was said to exhibit the head, neck, sholders and forelegs of its sire, and hinder parts that of the dam, and promised to grow to pretty good size. It was a male.

The author saw the skin of a double calf in the nighborhood of Luray. The hide was carefully taken off and stuffed. It had a double body, two distinct heads, and two tails, four perfect eyes, and but four legs. This singular extra natural production was in possession of Capt. John Gatewood, jr.

A COW WITH SIX LEGS.

Fifteen or sixteen years ago the late Samuel G. Sydnor owned a cow with six perfectly formed legs, which the author frequently saw. It had two extra legs formed on its shoulders, and when it walked these legs made regular motions. They hung over on each side, and were much smaller than the other legs.

SPLENDID IMPROVED FARM.

Bushrod B. Washington, Esq., a few years ago erected a very large brick dwelling house, in the neihborhood of Charlestown, Jefferson county, with all the necessary offices. This building with other improvements cost upwards of thirty thousand dollars.

The building was finished in the most tasteful style of modern architecture; but unfortunately, some two or three years ago, it accidentally took fire; and all the interior works were consumed. But the writer is informed Mr. W. has lately rebuilt it. The author obtained a sketch of its dimensions, but has unfortunately mislaid the memorandum. Suffice it to say, it is one of the largest and most elegant edifices in our country.

Judge Henry St. G. Tucker has erected in the neighborhood of Leetown a most splendid stone building—rough cast, finished in beautiful style—three stories high; but the writer does not recollect the exact size of the edifice, but it is a very large building. Jefferson county contains a great number of fine large dwelling houses, with other capital improvements. Berkeley county has many fine buildings and highly improved farms. In the county of Clarke, David H. Allen, Esq., has lately erected a brick dwelling on a beautiful eminence, from which there is a most enchanting view of the Blue Ridge and adjacent country. It is sixty-six feet by fifty, with a splendid portico, supported by a beautiful colonade twenty-five feet high, of solid pine pillars.

In front of the house is an extended lawn, partly covered with a sheet of transparent water, which adds greatly to the novelty and beauty of the scenery. Mr. Allen informed the writer, that some years ago the water course contained much dark alluvian mud, on each side, very miry and difficult to cross. He hauled out six thousand wagon loads of the mud upon the adjoining high lands, which so increased the fertility, that, for several years it was too rich for the production of wheat.

Mr. Allen is pretty extensively engaged in the stock way. A few years ago, he at one time owned one hundred and twenty head of horses, and a large stock of improved black cattle, sheep and hogs. Mr. Allen was bred to the law, but having married the daughter of the late Col. Griffin Taylor, got this fine estate by her; and his father being also wealthy, he soon abandoned the practice, and lived a retired and private life ever since.

Edward Jaquline Smith, Esq., has built a fine brick dwelling house, large and tastefully finished, on an extensive farm in the same neighborhood. He is a most judicious and successful farmer.

Col. J. W. Ware has erected a fine large brick building near Mr. Smith's, is also a successful farmer—is remarkable for breeding the very finest cattle; and his stable has been the stand, for several years, of the very finest horses which have been imported into our country.

Col. Joseph Tuly, in the county of Clarke, has built a most splendid and expensive mansion on his beautiful farm in the neighborhood of Millwood, which he has named "Tulyries." To give a detailed account of this fine building would be tedious, and perhaps tiresome to the reader. It is sufficient to say that this edifice is sixty feet by forty, of the best of brick—finished from the base to the attick in the most elegant style of modern architecture, and is covered with tin. A spacious portico, supported underneath with massive marble slabs, with pillars of solid pine, twenty-eight feet high, supporting the roof—forming a most beautiful colonade, based on square marble blocks; the porch floor laid with white marble, and marble steps; a spacious entry; a spiral stair-way running from the passage to the summit, on which there is a handsome cupola with a large brass ball erected; the fire places decorated with the finest marble mantles; his doors and windows of the best mahogany; with a green house in which there is sheltered a great variety of the richest exotic plants and flowers; the yard decorated with a great variety of native and imported trees and shrubbery, with several orange trees which bear fruit handsomely. Adjoining the yard, an extensive park is enclosed in the forest, within which enclosure there are a number of native elks and deer. The old buck elk will not suffer any stranger to intrude on his premises. Col. Tuly's father was born and raised in the state of Jersey, learned the trade of a tanner, came to Virginia a young man, commenced business on a small capital, and amassed a very considerable estate, the greater part of which he devised to his only son Joseph. The Col. carries on the tanning business extensively, and has added considerably to the estate left him by his father. He farms extensively and successfully, —and largely in the stock way.

Mr. John Kerfoot, twenty-five or thirty years ago, built a large, comfortable brick dwelling, finished in plain style, with most of his offices and all his slaves' houses of the same material. In approaching his residence it strikes the eye of the stranger as a sprightly village. Mr Kerfoot is beyond question one of the most enterprising, judicious, and successful farmers in our section of country. He has acquired more wealth by his agricultural pursuits, than any individual within the author's knowledge; has raised a large family of sons and daughters, and provided handsomely for them all; has given each of his sons fine farms and every necessary to commence business. His daughters as they have married and left him have each of them been handsomely portioned off. **Mr.** Kerfoot is, and has been for many years a member of the Baptist church—a liberal, consistent and most worthy member. He is rigidly punctual in his pecuniary engagements; it is said of him that he was never known to fail in a single instance to pay or fulfill any engagement he has entered into. Thus coming up to the golden Gospel rule of "doing to others as he would they should do unto him."

Mr. John Richardson is now the owner of the fine tract of land formerly owned by, and the residence of, the late Col. Warner Washington, called "Fairfield", on which he has established an extensive distillery. The still house is built of brick, attached to which a large yard is enclosed and nicely floored with the same material, for the purpose of raising and fattening pork. About every two months he sends off to the Baltimore market from eighty to one hundred head of finely fattened hogs. **Mr.** Richardson is a man of great industry and enterprise—farms extensively, and raises a fine stock of improved cattle. He, like many of our citizens, is the builder of his own fortune, having commenced on a very small capital.

The Rev. Thomas Kennerly has lately erected a beautiful, plain, extensive brick mansion at "Greenway court," the ancient residence of the late Lord Fairfax, now in the county of Clarke near the White Post village. James Madison Hite, Esq., resides in an elegant brick mansion, contiguous to the stone bridge.

Doct. James Hay has lately built in the same neighborhood a truly splendid edifice of considerable size and finished in the most elegant manner.

Doctor Berkeley, previous to his death, was engaged in erecting a brick house near the Shenandoah, of very extensive dimensions, but before he had finished it he was most cruelly murdered by his slaves, and his body consumed in a tremendous fire. He was robbed of a large sum of money by them, which they scattered about amongst their confederates—part of which was found; but it was said at the time, that a considerable part of it was lost. John Rust, Esq., has lately purchased a part of Doctor Berkeley's estate, including this fine building, which he has had finished in plain neat style.

Doctor Berkeley was killed in 1818. Three of his slaves, one female and two males, were tried and convicted for the murder, in Frederick court, and all three executed at Winchester, in the month of July, 1818. The representatives of the Doctor obtained an act of assembly, authorising them to sell off a number of the slaves who were suspected with being concerned in the murder, and they were sent to the South and sold. This estate now lies in the county of Warren.

Capt. Robert C. Burwell, just before the late war, had erected an elegant brick mansion in the neighborhood of Millwood. At the commencement of the war he commanded a company of the militia, and marched at the head of his company, and joined the standard of his country at Norfolk. He fell a sacrifice to that unhealthy climate and died.

Previously to leaving home, he provided his last will, in which he devised his fine estate to Philip Nelson, Esq., who married his sister, and now owns this elegant property.

The late Col. Charles Magill commenced, shortly before his death, on his fine farm about five miles S. of Winchester, a very large brick dwelling, but died before it was finished. Since his death it has been finished, and now is the residence of John S. Magill, Esq., one of his sons.

Mr. William A. Carter is now erecting a splendid brick dwelling, about two miles W. of Newtown Stephensburg, on a beautiful eminence which commands a most fascinating view of this village, the adjacent country and mountains east and west, for a vast distance. It is covered with English slate.

Joseph Neill, Esq., has erected a beautiful brick dwelling at the north end of N. T. Stephensburg, plastered and neatly whitened on the outside. His neat little farm on which the buildings are erected adjoins the village.

Mr. Isaac Hollingsworth has erected a splendid brick dwelling near Winchester, contiguous to his fine mills—his yard and curtilages handsomely enclosed with first rate stone walls.

There a number of other brick dwelling houses in the several counties named, exclusive of those particularly mentioned; and there are a considerable number of fine large stone buildings.

The residence of George H. Burwell, Esq., is most splendidly improved with stone buildings. It adjoins the village of Millwood, called "Carter Hall." The main building is sixty-six feet by thirty, three stories; with a wing at each end twenty-one feet long, two stories high; the whole building finished in the most tasteful style of modern architecture. This was the former residence of the late Col. Nathaniel Burwell, a gentleman of great wealth. The buildings stand on a beautiful eminence, and command a delightful view of the Blue Ridge and the adjacent neighborhood. The water is conveyed by force pumps from a fine spring to the dwelling house, yards, and stables, at a distance of about three hundred yards. This fine farm may with truth be said to be among the most elegantly improved estates west of the Blue Ridge.

Maj. Seth Mason has lately built a spacious stone dwelling, stone barn and stable, on the waters of Crooked Run, in the county of Frederick. The buildings are erected on a beautiful eminence, and command a fine view of the Blue Ridge a vast distance. From the Major's yard about one hundred farms are to be seen in full relief on the west side of the mountain.

Capt. Phenias Bowen has lately erected a stone dwelling, three stories high, near the Opequon, in Clarke county. The writer never obtained the exact dimensions of this building; but it is very large, and covered with tin. It is not finished.

The late Maj. Isaac Hite, on his fine large farm, about the year 1792, built a stone dwelling, near the great highway from Winchester to Staunton; a most spacious and elegant building, in the county of Frederick. At that period it was doubtless the most splendid building west of the Blue Ridge. In point of taste, and beauty of symmetry, it is certainly not exceeded by any country building the author has ever seen. It still stands to be admired by every beholder.

In the county of Shenandoah, the late Messrs. Isaac Bowman, Joseph Stover and Anthony Spengler, severally built large brick dwellings, but a short distance from Strasburg, each on a fine large farm. It is hardly deemed necessary for the author to proceed with a further detail of particular dwelling houses. It would require a large volume to contain an account of all the fine buildings in our valley. It is presumed that a sufficient number has been described to enable the reader to form an estimate of the vast improvement of our country within the last forty or fifty years. It is sufficient to say that many counties in the valley are equally well improved.

The great number of first rate merchant mills and factories deserve some particular notice, but it would swell this publication far beyond all reasonable limits to attempt a detail. The author will therefore content himself, and he hopes the reader will be content to have a brief description of Mr. Valentine Rhodes' mill on Cedar creek, the dividing line between Frederick and Shenandoah counties. The author is induced to give a passing notice to this building from the extraordinary and unparalleled labor performed by Rhodes, with the assistance of one of his sons, a youth of about twelve or fourteen years of age, in its construction and erection. Mr. Rhodes informed the author, that when he had purchased and paid for the site, including a small tract of land, for which he paid in advance, he had no more than ten dollars left. Mr. Rhodes is an ingenious mechanic and first rate mill-wright. He determined however, on building his mill; to enable himself to go on with it, that he would undertake every job at his trade that he could engage, and if he earned eighty or one hundred dollars, he would proceed with his own building until his money gave out; he would then engage in work as opportunity afforded until he could gather one or two hundred dollars more, and so proceeded on, until he got his mill to running. It was six years from the time he commenced until he got it to grinding.

But the most extraordinary, and the writer may truly say, wonderful circumstance attending this building, is the immense weight of stone and timbers used in its construction. The first story is built of stone of enormous size and weight, several of which are seven or eight feet long and fifteen or eighteen inches thick, doubtless weighing several tons each—all which Mr. Rhodes worked into the walls with his own personal labor. The only machine he used was the mill screw. The wall on the west side is at least five feet thick, and no part less than three. The first part of the mill-house was twenty-eight feet square, or perhaps thirty, to which he added another building fifty feet in length and thirty in width, stretching across the entire stream, except a small arm of the water course forming a small island, on which the first building is erected. The south end of the building juts against a solid perpendilar limestone rock twenty-five or thirty feet high, which forms one of the walls; nature has formed niches in this, which receive the ends of timbers fifty feet long and from ten to twelve inches square, which Mr. Rhodes raised and put in place with the aid of his son and mill screw—one end resting on the wall of the first

building and the other inserted ·in the natural niches in the stone wall.—
These powerful timbers are elevated about ten feet above the water. He
receives his customers' grain at each end of his mill: so it may be said it
stands in the two counties. It is doubtful whether a similar instance of
extraordinary exertion, enterprise and successful perseverance can be
found in our country.

Mr. Rhodes certainly deserves a premium for his wonderful diligence
and successful enterprise and perseverance in the construction of this extraordinary building. There have been several floods in the creek since
the mill was erected; but the immense strength of the dam and walls has
heretofore resisted the force of the waters, and the mill sustained no injury.

CHURCHES.

The Episcopal society have within a few years past erected several
beautiful houses of worship; one at Berryville, one at Millwood, one in
Winchester, (the latter a truly splendid building, with a first rate organ,)
and another at Middletown, which is also a beautiful and chaste structure,
and is truly creditable to the society. The writer heard a minister of the
gospel express the opinion, that it presented to the eye precisely what a
church edifice ought to exhibit, i. e., a ray of truth. The Roman Catholic society have erected chapels in several places. They have built a
superb edifice at Harper's Ferry, with a beautiful pulpit, with the image
of the Virgin Mary with the infant Jesus in her lap.

HARPER'S FERRY.

It is scarcely necessary to inform the reader that this is the location
of the U. S. armory, and in the several shops are generally employed
about three hundred first rate mechanics, engaged in the manufactory of
arms for the purposes of war. There are annually made about six or sev-
en thousand muskets, two or three thousand rifles, beside an immense
number of swords, pistols, and other side arms. The government em-
ploys at this establishment a superintendent ganeral, a paymaster and a
number of clerks. The quantity of iron, steel, brass and other materials
annually wrought up, is immense. A vast number of strangers annually
visit this place to gratify their curiosity in seeing and inspecting the pub-
tic works and great mechanical operations, so extensively carried on.—
The machinery of the musket factory is wrought by the waters of the Potomac, and that of the rifle factory by the waters of the Shenandoah.

This site for the public works it is said was first marked out or recommended by the immortal Washington, and is certainly evidence of his superior skill and judgment in all military matters.

A rail-road from Winchester to Harper's Ferry has been lately constructed, which has rendered Winchester a place of deposit for the vast pro-
ducts of our valley, but little inferior to some of our seaport towns. A
turnpike road from Winchester to Parkersburg on the Ohio river, a distance of about two hundred and eighty miles, has lately been finished;
and another McAdamized turnpike road from Winchester to Staunton,
has just been put in operation, and it is almost inconceivable what vast

quantities of produce, now find a ready way to Baltimore from the increased facilities of our improved roads to that market.

An improved road from Staunton across the Allegany mountains, is now going on to Parkersburg, which will still add great facilities to valley trade and greatly enhance the value of real estate in Western Virginia.— There is also a turnpike from Harrisonburg by way of the Warm Springs, Hot Springs, and White Sulphur, across the Allegany to Guyandot, by way of Kanawha. Those several turnpikes are passable at all seasons of the year, and greatly expedite the passenger's journey from east to west. These several turnpikes have been made at vast expense to the State and stockholders, notwithstanding which, improvements are still going on. A few years more and Western Virginia will vie with our northern and sister States with her vast improvements. Our valley is making great improvement in every agricultural pursuit. Copying after our great and good countryman, Washington, immense improvements have already been made, and are still making, in the rearing of fine animals of every variety. Stage coaches travelall our turnpike roads, drawn by the most splendid horses; and most of our substantial farmers rear the finest cattle, sheep, and hogs, and are greatly improving the fertility of their lands. Our valley furnishes the several markets with vast quanntities of superior beef, pork, mutton, butter, and the finest of breadstuffs. The quantities of oats annually raised for market are incalculable. Immense crops of the finest timothy, clover, and orchard grass hay, and corn fodder are annually consumed by our farmers' stock; and, notwithstanding the vast quantities raised, once in a while there are seasons of great scarcity of provender for sustaining the vast stock of animals kept on hand.

Our winters are frequently of great length and extremely severe. The author will here notice one winter which was remarkable for its long and excessive severity. When a youth, he frequently met with individuals who well recollected the hard winter of 1740. It was said that that remarkable winter produced the greatest depth of snow ever known in our climate. The snow fell to such an immense depth as to smother vast numbers of horned cattle, sheep, hogs, deer, and many other wild animals.

The author believes it will not be uninteresting to the reader to have a brief description of several remarkable works of nature in our valley, to gether with a notice of some elegant buildings and improvements on the farms of private individuals. He will begin with

JEFFERSON COUNTY.

WASHINGTON'S MASONIC CAVE.—About two and a half miles south east of Charlestown in this county is to be seen this cavern. Tradition informs us that Gen. Washington and a number of other gentlemen formed themselves into a Masonic Society and held their lodges in this cavern. The writer saw and partially explored it. It is not an extensive cavern, and is more remarkable from the fact of its having been used as a lodge room by Washington and others. It however has several different depart----- The author was not able to get into the lodge room. The entrance to which is quite low and narrow. The proprietor (Mr. Clark) informed the author that Washington's name, with the names of the several members of the lodge, is inscribed in the face of the rocks in the lodge room. A rock of very hard stone, which lies near a very fine lime spring convenient to the cave, has several inscriptions on it. The letters are the plain Roman character; but the author could not explain the meaning. They probably are masonic enigmas.

Having introduced the name "Washington," though a digression from the general subject, it will be well enough to notice several important anecdotes in the history of that great, heaven-protected man, which the writer has heard from respectable authority.

* The late Maj. Lawrance Lewis, a favorite nephew of Washington's, and who resided with him at "Mount Vernon" for several years, related the following remarkable anecdote of his uncle. In the battle fought between Braddock and the Indians, it is well known, Washington acted as one of Braddock's aids. After the battle, Daniel Craig—then of Winchester, but afterwards settled in Alexandria—became acquainted with Redhawk, a distinguished young Indian warrior. In a conversation with the Doct., Redhawk inquired what young officer (who was mounted on a very fine horse) it was, who rode with great rapidity from post to post, during the action. The Doct. replied, Col. Washington. Redhawk immediately stated, "I fired eleven deliberate shots at that man, but could not touch him. I gave over any further attempt, believing he was protected by the great Spirit, and could not be killed by a bullet." Redhawk further added, that his gun was never known to miss its aim before.

We have another tradition in this neighborhood in relation to this great man. It is stated that when he was retreating before the British army in Jersey, he once expressed to some of his officers his determination, if he was still pursued, and unable to make a stand, to continue his retreat until he reached Powell's Fort, which he would fortify and defy all their forces.* This tradition was communicated to the author by a highly respectable gentleman of this vicinity.

There was another tradition related to the author by an old lady, (Mrs. Elizabeth Madson,) on Roanoke river, of great respectability. She stated the following fact: Several old Indian chiefs had offered considerable premiums to any warrior or set of warriors, who would bring out Washington's scalp. Seven Indians who were living in the neighborhood of Roanoke, got to hear that Washington was on his way out to inspect the fort very near the Roanoke river. There were two roads leading to the fort; one across the point of the mountain, and the other on level land. The

---

*Powell's Fort is in fact a natural fortress. The mountains on each side are of immense height, and covered with loose stone; at the entrance, they come so close together that a few hundred men placed on the heights could destroy ten times their number, by hurling stone down on the enemy. If the enemy had attempted by a counter route to enter the fort, a few hundred active and brave riflemen, from the mountainous character of the country, could have cut to pieces an army of almost any force.

*P

one across the mountain was the shorter way; the other on the level land the better. The seven Indians placed themselves in ambush close to the side of the level road, and lay concealed two days and nights; but Washington did not pass. They grew impatient, and their chief, the third day, stated that he would go to the other road and ascertain whether Washington had not taken that route to the fort—the two roads being only one mile apart. He gave his men positive orders not to fire at any person that might pass in his absence. While he was gone, Col. Washington, Col. Lewis and Col. Preston, all three passed close by the enemy without being molested.

Another tradition informs us that Lord Fairfax appointed Washington one of his surveyors. He boarded with Capt. Charles Smith, within half a mile of Battletown. He kept his office in an upper room in the spring house. This small log building is on the farm owned by John B. Taylor, Esq.,—the only son of the late Col. Griffin Taylor, now in Clarke county.

THE INDIAN CHURCH.

This is said to be a most grand work of nature. It is a spacious and beautiful cavern, in a high rock, about four miles west of Watkins' Ferry, on the Virginia side of the Cohongoruton, (Potomac.) It is a circular dome of considerable height, with a most extraordinary spiral opening in the arch, resembling the steeple of a church. Seats are formed all around the interior; the inlet is by a large door. Tradition informs us that the Indians, when in possession of the country, used to assemble in considerable numbers in this place. For what particular object is not known; but it is probable they used it as a place of worship, or for holding their councils.

PROSPECT ROCK.

This splendid work of nature is in the county of Morgan, about three miles S. W. of Bath, immediately on the bank of Capon river. It is certainly not less than one thousand feet perpendicular height. Capon river viewed from this immense height presents to the eye a most curious and interesting sight. The river running a considerable distance to the west, makes a gradual turn around a point of level land—thence returning an easterly course to the base of the mountain, enclosing some two or three hundred acres of fine, fertile, alluvial land, constituting a most valuable farm. The river viewed from this rock appears to the eye not to exceed fifteen or twenty feet in width, and forms, as it were, the shape of a horse shoe. It is at this place, not less than fifty or sixty yards in width. The two points of the water are but a few poles apart at the base of the mountain. There is an extensive view of the valley up the river; some say fifteen miles. The top of the Allegany mountain can be distinctly seen from it.

NEW CREEK GAP.

This is seen in the county of Hardy, about twenty miles S. W. of Romend is too, a most tremendous work of nature. The author viewed this place with considerable awe and trepidation. The passage is quite narrow, between two mountains of stupendous height, probably from fifteen hundred to two thousand feet high. The points of the mountains are covered with numerous rocks, and appear to be hanging over the traveller's head. Through this passage is a fine, lively stream of water, which, after leaving the mountain, forms Patterson's Creek. At the west side of the mountain there are two streams—one from the south and the other from the north—which meet at the gap and unite their waters, and run through the gap directly an east course. About midway the gap is seen what is called "the spouting spring." This spring, it is said, is formed by a stream of water which runs to the northern base of the mountain, and has formed a subteraneous passway under the mountain, and bursts out in a lage spring in the gap. Near the eastern termination of the gap, nature has formed a natural dam of solid rock, quite across the cavity, twenty-five or thirty feet high. By the aid of this dam, Messrs. Harness and Turley convey the water to their iron works on Patterson's Creek.

A LARGE CAVE IN BERKELEY COUNTY.

Near the mouth of the Opequon, in the county of Berkeley, exists a large cave. In the year 1813, a man named ———, called in the evening at old Mrs. Furman's, staid till next morning, and after breakfast, told the old lady he would go into the cave and examine it, in order to ascertain whether he could or not obtain Saltpetre clay, for the making of powder. The old lady furnished him with candles, and he left her house alone, promising to return in the evening. He entered the cave, and was not seen or heard of that day. The second day passed over, and no tidings were heard of him. The old lady grew uneasy, apprehending he had lost himself in the cave, and would perhaps perish. The third day his absence continued, and the old lady proposed to two of her grown sons and another young man who happened to be at her house, to go in search of him. They at first objected, suggesting it was probable he had gone down the Potomac in some of the trading boats to Georgetown. She declared if they would not go, she would herself go and make the search. The young men then agreed to go, furnished themselves with sufficient lights, and forthwith proceeded to make search. They had not proceeded far into the cave before they found the poor fellow's hat, which satisfied them that he was in the cave. They continued the search, and at length found him in a most perilous and distressed condition. He stated to them, that he had not proceeded far into the cave before his candle by accident became extinguished, and he was left in mo.e than "Egyptian darkness." The second day he became distressed with thirst, but could find no water. He continued scrambling in the cave, in the hope of getting out, but instead of finding the entrance, got farther from it. At length he heard the dropping of water, and groping his way, he found the water was dropping into a deep cavern. He contrived to get into the cavity, and after reaching the bottom, the only chance he had to get the water into his mouth, was by laying himself down on his back, and letting the water drop into it. But after his thirst was assuaged, he could not get out of this sink, and he had given out all hope of relief, and reconciled himself to his fate—expecting to die in a very little time.

The young men, in searching for him, frequently called aloud; he could hear them, but was so exhausted and weakened, that he could not make himself heard by them until they approached very near his place of seclusion. They succeeded in raising him out of his confinement; he soon recovered his strength, and lived some fifteen or eighteen years after this perilous experiment.

There is an amusing tradition related in connexion with this cavern.— An old German, by the name of Bidinger, had ascertained that by building a fire in the mouth of the cave, the smoke would ascend and pass out at a small aperture in the rocks on the top of the hill, about three hundred yards from the entrance. This shrewd old man persuaded several young men that he could raise old Nick out of the cave, and invited them in the morning to go with him, and see his experiment. He directed a negro man to go to the mouth of the cave and raise a large pine fire. The old gentleman had ascertained about what time it would take for the smoke to show at the top of the hill; they assembled near the aperture, and he engaged in many incantations and juglings whilst watching for the smoke to appear. The young men waited with trepidation and fear. When the smoke burst out, the old man exclaimed "See, there he comes! see his smoke!" It was enough for the young men; they saw the devil's smoke, and precipitately took to flight, leaving the old gentleman to make the best terms that he could with his satanic majesty.

There is a most extraordinary cave a short distance from Shepherdstown. The Rev. Mr. Hill informed the author, that he once explored this cavern about one mile; it passes under the Potomac river, and reaching into the state of Maryland, contains a great variety of stalactite formations and beautiful curiosities.

HOUSE CAVE.

This cavern is on Apple ridge in the county of ———. It is remarkable for its vast depth, and has a pretty good room near its entrance. It is said this cave is not less than six hundred feet deep. At its termination a most delightful stream of cold water runs across its bottom. The author, several years ago, visited this place, and partially explored it; descending about one hundred feet into it. Two young men descended about one hundred feet below where the author stopped.

In the county of Frederick exists a cave on the land now owned by Doct. Walker M. Hite, near the waters of Cedar Creek. It is not so remarkable for its size as for its production of natural curiosities. Several years ago the author explored this cavern, but had abundant cause to regret his undertaking. He became so excessively fatigued that it was with great difficulty he was enabled to get out. He was reminded of an anecdote of a Dutch woman: Two men in the county of Shenandoah had missed their way in the night and got into the enclosure of a farmer, found the house, and asked the way out. The woman of the house replied, "So you come in so you got out acain." There are several other caves the author has heard of, but has not seen. There is cne on the land of Geo. F.

Hupp, Esq., the former residence of Mr. Joseph Stover, near Strasburg. This is said to be pretty extensive, and contains much stalactite matter.

On the land of Mr. Israel Allen, in the county of Shenandoah, exists a most valuable cavity, forming one of the finest dairies the author has ever seen. At the early settlement of the country, it was discovered that a small cavity in the rocks, on a pretty high hill, led to a charming stream of delightful water. But it was attended with some difficulty to descend and ascend the aperture to get the water. Mr. Allen built a handsome brick dwelling near the mouth of the cavity, then dug a well so as to strike the stream of water. At the depth of thirty-two feet below the surface, he came upon a bed of black alluvian mud, in removing which he found a very large human skeleton, which was greatly above the common size of the human frame. Mr. Allen himself was rather upwards of six feet high; he stated that he placed one of the leg bones and measured it by his own leg. It was between two and three inches longer than his own leg. From this data, it is probable the individual owner of this skeleton was little under, if not full eight feet high. Mr. Allen opened and improved the mouth of the cavern, and constructed one among the most valuable places for preserving milk, butter and fresh meats, in our country. The aperture from the milk house to the water is still open, and in warm weather discharges a constant current of cool air into the dairy, and keeps it perfectly cool. In winter the current of air is tepid and protects every thing in the dairy from freezing.

HARRISON'S CAVE.

In the county of Rockingham, on the land of Mr. ———— Harrison, on the Turnpike road leading from Winchester to Staunton, is to be seen a most beautiful cave, seven miles north of Harrisonburg, the seat of justice for the county. Mr. Harrison has improved the entrance into the cave with steps, so that it is very convenient to enter it. This cave (which the author explored,) presents several most interesting works of nature. Near the centre, a splendid column of about twenty-five feet high—a stalactite formation—stands as if designed to support the arch. Pretty near this column is setting the bust of a very large old woman, covered over with beautiful white drapery, in numerous folds—the walls generally covered with stalactite formations, several of which have a strong resemblance to the pipes of an organ. The whole length does not exceed three hundred yards. The floor is pretty level, and convenient to walk upon. It is generally above twenty-five feet high from the floor to the arch, and thirty-five or forty wide. The author heard of several other caves in Rockingham, but did not visit them.

At the head of the South Branch a man by the name of Ruthledge, was shot through the body by an Indian; the ball penetrated the left breast and passed out within an inch of the spine. This man recovered and lived many years after. There were two female children, daughters of John Moore, taken by the Indians and grew up with them. The elder had two children by a white trader; the younger became the wife of the distinguished war chief Blue Jacket. She left an Indian son with his father, was enceint, when brought home, and brought forth a daughter, who grew up and married a man by the name of John Stuart. Her father, Blue Jacket, secured her a tract of land on the waters of Lake Erie, to which Stuart removed and settled.

Two of John Cartmell's daughters were taken by the Indians and remained with them several years. Their brother went to the Indian country, obtained their release and brought them home.

James Stuart was shot while crossing the Greenbrier river, reached the opposite shore, and died immediately. Several others were killed the same summer, whose names are not recollected.

A few years ago, there was found on the banks of Greenbrier river, in the cavity of a rock, a very large human skeleton, his bow and arrows, mat, and tomahawk, and a deerskin was deposited with the body at the time of its burial; it was about ten feet below the surface.

Human skeletons have been frequently discovered on the margin of the water courses. About thirty years ago, Samuel McDonald discovered a human skull in the bank of the Cowpasture river. It was remarkable for its great size and thickness—had a visible mark of a tomahawk wound on it—supposed to be the head of a giant-like warrior. A walnut tree of immense size, which grew on the bank of the Cowpasture river, was blown down in a violent gale of wind, and a number of human bones were discovered in the cavity. The author was informed that the body of this tree was not less than six or seven feet in diameter. If so, as it must have grown over the bodies after they were buried, it was probably several hundred years old.

But to return from this digression. Mrs. Sarah Erskine, in her eighty-fourth year, was first married to John Pauly—they were removing to Kentucky, and on the 23d of Sept. 1779, on the east branch of New river, they were attacked by a party of five Shawnee Indians and a white man by the name of Morgan. Mr. Pauly was killed, and his little child, about two years old, had its brains dashed out against a tree and left a prey to wild beasts. This venerable and highly intelligent lady was once while a prisoner threatened with the most horrid destruction. An old chief who had a favorite son killed in a battle in Kentucky, had determined to revenge his son's death on her little son, who was born a few months after her captivity, and two young prisoners, Calway and Hoy. The old savage monster had determined to enclose them all in Mrs. Erskine's house and set fire to it. But Col. McKee, the British agent, successfully interposed; he called on Mrs. Erskine and told her not to be alarmed; that if he found that he could not restrain the violence of the old monster, he would immediately convey her off to Detroit: but from the friendly interposition of Mr. McKee, a majority of the Indians became opposed to the violent and vindictive revenge of the old savage. She was upwards of three years a prisoner. Her son, young Pauly, she brought home with her; he grew up, went to the west, became secretary to the great Missouri Fur Company, and was killed while engaged in that business. Mr. John Higgins came out to the Shawnee towns and redeemed and aided her in getting home to her friends.

There was a brother of Mr. John Pauly, also a married man, with his 'd one child, on his way to Kentucky. He was killed at the same time, his infant killed and his wife taken prisoner. She was taken to the Shawnee town, was claimed by two squaws, and taken to Detroit and sold, from whence she escaped, but never got home to her friends.

Mrs. Erskine stated to the author, that she did work for the men, making their garments—that on one particular occasion a warrior called on her to make him a calico shirt; the fellow informed her that he had lately returned from a trip to the neighborhood of the Sweet springs, in quest of a box of red paint.* He obtained his paint, and returning, he passed the house of a farmer, who had left his shot-pouch and powder horn hanging to the corner of his corn house. The Indian took off the pouch and horn, and left his own Buffalo horn, with a little powder, in place of it.— He observed to Mrs. Erskine that "it was an even exchange, no robbery." But if the owner had happened to discover the exchange at the moment, it is highly probable the fellow might have paid for his even exchange with his life.

Mrs. Erskine said that the Shawnee women, from the number of white persons taken among them, had greatly improved in their domestic arrangements, and several of them had become pretty good housekeepers.

Mrs. Erskine resides in Greenbrier county, near Lewisburg. The author met with her at her son's in Lewisburg, who is a highly respectable merchant of that place.

Tradition relates that the Sweet Springs were discovered by a man who was passing near the spring. A colt, which was following the horse he was riding, was bitten by a rattlesnake, when it immediately ran into the spring, where it continued for some time, nor could it be induced to come out until it had been entirely relieved from the pain occasioned by the wound.† The man examined the water and found that it possessed some valuable medicinal quality.

A man by the name of Robert Armstrong, in those troublesome times, had removed his family across the mountain to a place of safety. He was on a visit to his family, accompanied by a young man. Seven Indians approached his house, and were in the yard before discovered. Armstrong told the young man to jump into bed, and he threw a blanket over him. The Indians pushed into the house, and Armstrong went to the bed, raised the blanket, and asked the man if he was better. He replied in the negative. An Indian immediately asked "Man very sick?" "Yes, small pox very bad." They cried "wough" and ran off, crying as they ran, "small pox! small pox!" as far as they could be heard. It is said the Indians are dreadfully afraid of this disorder. Armstrong, by this stratagem, saved himself and property from being touched by the enemy.

In the year 1774, in the month of June, there were four white families settled on the head waters of Greenbrier, and apprehensive of danger, re-

*It was stated to the author, when in that section of country, that there is a considerable bank of beautiful red paint in Peters's mountain, five or six miles from the spring.

†Dr. Lewis, the present proprietor, informed the author that he had had a favorite dog bitten by a rattlesnake; he immersed him in the spring, and it entirely cured him of the bite.

moved their families into the settlement where they were safe. A man by the name of John Johnston came in, and stated he had seen fresh signs of Indians. The late Col. John Dickinson, a brave and active Indian fighter, raised a party of twenty-seven men, and marched out; but it was too or three days before they found any traces of Indians. They went to Jacob Riffle's house, found the beds totally cut open, and the feathers scattered to the winds. The Indians had kept themselves so completely concealed, that they could not be disocvered; yet they coutrived to kill one of Dickinson's men, named Malone, and wounded Robert McClay. Col. Dickinson was himself pretty severely wounded at the battle of the Point, in the year 1774, under Col. Lewis. The ball penetrated high up his shoulder and came out very near his spine. Yet he soon recovered, suffering but little from the wound. The Indians, after a few days lurking about, and discovering Dickinson's party to be too strong for them, fled. It is said there were only three Indians in the party.

The warrant of Mr Joseph Maye's land was issued in 1743, surveyed in 1746,—patent or grant issued in 1761. Joseph Maye, Esq., at about twelve years of age, was taken prisoner by a party of Indians; but was rescued by his friends after five days captivity, and brought safely home. This venerable and intelligent man was wounded at the battle of the Point. He was at the time preparing to shoot the Indian that wounded him, who was standing behind a tree that was rather small to protect him. It had a crook in the body, below which Mr. Maye attempted to fire at him—for which purpose he bent his right knee and stooped a little; but the fellow was too quick for him, fired at him and struck him very near the cap of his knee. The ball ranged down the bones of his leg, shivering them pretty much. He was not able to walk for three years afterwards. He however so far recovered as to be able to use his leg a-bout twenty years or upwards; but it frequently would inflame and break out, and he was finally compelled to have it amputated above his knee.— When the author saw this highly respectable old gentleman, he was eighty-four years of age, and appeared to enjoy fine heatth.

A story was told to the writer, of rather singular and extraordinary character. Seven Indians were lurking about one of the forts. A young woman had walked out, perhaps in search of wild fruit. The seven Indians seized her and took her off. They proceeded a few miles, and halted for the purpose of terrifying and tormenting the unfortunate girl.— They stripped her, tied her hands above her head to a sapling, and threw their tomahawks at her, trying how near they could pass their instruments by her body without wounding her. A bold and enterprising hunter happened to be within hearing of her screams, and ran to see what produced the poor girl's terrors. As he approached he discovered the scene, and with his rifle killed one of the party; the other six fled, and the hunter ran to the relief of the unfortunate sufferer, instantly cut the bandage from her hands, threw his hunting shirt around her, and directed her to run to the fort, and he instantly reloaded his rifle and followed her.— The remaining Indians, discovering there was but one man, gave chase. The hunter discovering this, slackened his pace, and as they approached r him, brought another down. He was master of the art of loading as he ran. The remaining five continued the chase until this brave and skillful marksman brought another down. The others continued the pursuit until the whole number was killed. The author can not vouch for the truth of this story, but has given it as he heard it related by several respectable individuals; the reader can take it for what it is worth.

George Keneade was killed, and his wife and four children taken off. An old Indian, soon after her arrival at the village, proposed to marry her, but she promptly refused the offer. The savage monster threatened to burn her. A Frenchman told her if she would consent to marry him, he would take her off. She consented to his offer, and he soon took her to Redstone, and married her. This Frenchman kept a little store in the Indian village. Paul Leash was the name of this Frenchman.

There were a number of people killed and taken prisoners by the same Indians, at the big bend of Jackson river. But Mr. Byrd, my informant, could not recollect the precise number or name of the sufferers.

There is an Indian grave near Man's Mills, on Jackson river, thirty yards or more in diameter, and perfectly round.* The author will here remark, that in all his excursions through that country, he never saw an Indian grave,† and heard of but two—the one just spoken of, and another on Peter's mountain. This is said to be in circular form, and covered entirely with stone.

During the troublesome times with the Indians, a party of them attacked the dwelling of Maj. Graham, on Greenbrier river, killed some of his children and took off a young daughter. She remained a prisoner for several years, and grew up with the savages; a short interval of peace took place with the tribes, and her father went out to the Indian country and found his daughter, whom he had for a long time believed was entirely lost to him, and brought her home. She soon manifested great uneasiness, and expressed a desire to return to the Indians.

A small party of Indians came into the neighborhood of Muddy creek, and killed a man near her father's residence, and as soon as she heard of the occurrence, made an attempt to run off to the Indians, but was prevented from doing so by the family. She after a while became better reconciled to remain with her connections, and married a worthy man, raised a respectable family of children, and was living, in the year 1836, in the county of Monroe. This is another among the many instances of white children, taken while quite young, growing up with the savages, and becoming so much attached to the manners and habits of the people in a state of nature, as to leave them with the greatest possible reluctance.

In the autumn of 1797, the author travelled through the State of Ohio. At Chilicothe he saw a young man named Williamson, who was on his way to his residence at the three Islands of the Ohio; he was returning

---

*Now entirely plowed down.

†There is a pretty considerable mound about two miles south of Frankfort, in Pendleton county, noticed in the first edition of this work.

*Q

with two of his brothers, one fourteen, the other about twelve years of age, who had been taken about three years before. He found them near the lakes, with different tribes, about sixty miles apart. The young man stated that it was with considerable difficulty he could prevail on the little fellows to leave the Indians; and even after he had started with them, they made several attempts to run off and get back to the Indians. He was at length compelled to obtain a canoe and descend the Allegany river with them, and by this means, and vigilant watching, he prevented their making their escape from him.

It is remarkable, that those children should have so soon lost their affection for their parents and brothers and sisters, as to prefer remaining with their savage captors. The author has been informed by persons who have been prisoners, that natives never apply the scourge to children, but treat them with the greatest indulgence. It is probably owing to this cause that white children become so much pleased with them.

The author attempted to converse with the boys, but immediately discovered that they had acquired all that coyness and diffidence so commonly manifested by the native Indians. They would scarcely answer a question; and before they answered yes or no, they would look at their elder brother, and at each other, and pause before either would reply; and that reply was only Yes, or No.

In the year 1774, there were four families,—Ash, Bumgardner, Croft, and Hupp,—who settled at a place called Tea Garden, at Ten Mile Creek, on Monongalia river. They had entered into a contract with the Indians for permission to occupy a certain quantity of land, and the privilege of hunting on the lands, for which they agreed to pay a small annual rent. When Dunmore's war commenced, a messenger was sent to them, warning them of their danger, and advising them to remove immediately into the fort at Redstone. The messenger stated to them, that if they remained they would all be killed. Several Indians were present, and their chief replied to the bearer of the message: "Tell your king he is a d— liar—the Indians will not kill them." And the people remained at their residence during the continuance of the war, without being disturbed by the enemy.

REGURGITARY SPRING.

This is a most singular and curious work of nature. The writer did not see it, but it was described by several intelligent, respectable gentlemen who had repeatedly examined it. On the summit of a high mountain, in the county of Hardy, five or six miles from Petersburg, a small village on the main fork of the South branch of the Wappatomaca, this spring makes its appearance. It ebbs and flows every two hours. When rising, it emits a gurgling noise, similar to the gurgling of any liquid running out at the bung-hole of a hogshead—runs freely two hours, and then ebbs, and the water entirely disappears. At every flow, sand and small pebbles are forced out with the water.

Samuel McDonald was wounded at the battle of the Point, under Col Lewis. He belonged to the company commanded by Capt. Dickinson. The ball passed through both his thighs, but neither was broken.

He recovered from his wounds, but continued a little lame as long as he lived. Mrs. Ellen McDonald, his widow, (eighty-three years of age, and still living,) informed the author that she once had two sisters taken by the Indians—one ten years of age and the other seven. They were prisoners seven years, lost their mother tongue, and spoke the Indian language perfectly. Two of Mr. McDonald's sisters were taken by the Cherokees.

In the year 1764, the Indians killed, at the house of James Clanahan, Edward Sampson and Joseph Mayes. They killed and took prisoners all the families, except three individuals. A woman seventy years of age had left the house, but returned and took a small trunk, in which she kept her caps and money, and carried it off, while the Indians were killing a number of persons around her; and finally made her escape.— There were but two other persons who escaped.

The Indians then passing up the cowpasture river, stopped at the house of William Fitzgerald. Thomas Thompson was there at the time. They barricaded the door, so that the Indians could not force it open.— The savages immediately set fire to the house, and Fitzgerald and Thompson were burnt to death. A little girl of Fitzgerald's was cruelly burnt. They killed its mother the next day, and took the child off. It was rescued by the whites and brought part of the way home; but died at Marlow's ford, Greenbrier river. Mrs. Sampson and her daughters were taken off by the Indians, and when they found they would be overtaken by the whites, a young warrior shot Mrs. Simpson through the body. She was found in a languishing condition, and brought part of the way home, but died on the way. Her daughters were never more heard of.

In 1779 a man by the name of McKeever was killed, and Thomas Grening and George Smith were fired at by the party who killed McKeever, but made their escape.. Both their wives and children were taken off as prisoners. Mrs. Smith made her escape from the savages, and on her way homeward was met by Col. John Hill, now of Pochahontas county, and conveyed to her friends in N. Carolina. ,

John Day's Fort, now Price's old Fort, formerly Keckley's Fort.— About 1772 John McNeil settled in the Little Levels; at that period there were very few settlers in that neighborhood. Mrs. Sarah Brown, the mother of Col. Brown in this neighborhood, at the age of ninety-one years, was able to walk about the neighborhood, and rode by herself to visit some of her children, who lived ten or fifteen miles off. Col. Brown stated to the author that a sugar tree of immense size, (at least six feet in diameter,) stood in one of his fields, and that it yielded him at least fifty pounds of sugar yearly. The Indians did no mischief after the war of 1763, until the year 1774. There were some Buffalo and Elk to be seen in the country at this period.

William Meeks, his wife, six children, and his mother, were taken off four or five years after the battle of the Point. Capt. Woods of the present county of Monroe, raised a party of seventeen men, pursued the enemy, and after several days march, overtook them late in the evening. The Indians had halted and been encamped three or four days. Capt. Woods and his party approached within a short distance of them without being discovered. Early the next morning, it being very foggy, the whites rushed in among the enemy. Capt. Woods and the Indian Capt. fired at each other, the muzzles of their guns almost touching ; but each of them springing to one side, neither shot took effect. Woods knocked the Indian down with his gun, and pursued the flying enemy. The fellow knocked down soon recovered and ran off.

Not one of the Indians was killed, but the prisoners were all rescued, and returned to their homes with the plunder all retaken, and the Indians losing all their own property.

COOK'S FORT, INDIAN CREEK.

In the year 1774, about the time of the attack on Donnally's fort, there were about three hundred people sheltered in this fortress. It was an oblong, and covered one and a half acres of ground. A Mrs. Bradsburn was killed.

Shortly before Wm. Meeks was taken, Steel Lafferty was killed at the mouth of Indian Creek, three miles off from the fort. Meeks heard the report of his death, immediately mounted his horse, and rode with all speed to his house, to the relief of two women ; as he approached the house, he called to them to open the door, which was immediately done, when he rushed into it, sprang to a port hole, saw two Indians running across a small field, near the house, fired at them, when one of them dropped his blanket and gun, increased his speed and got off; but it was believed he was shot through the body ; he never could be found, however.

In 1771, Mr. James Ellison removed from the State of Jersey, with his father, at which time he was about fifteen years of age. On the 19th of October, 1780, a party of seven or eight Indians attacked him, wounded him in the shoulder; the ball passing under his shoulderblade and out very near his spine ; he was tied and taken off a prisoner. The next day, when they had travelled about fifteen miles with him, while passing through a thicket, he suddenly escaped from them, and was pursued, but outran them and got off. This old and intelligent man, was afterwards in the battle of the Point, under Col. Lewis. The author saw him and conversed with him; he was then about eighty years of age.

Mr. Ellison has been a great and successful hunter. There were but very few buffalo and elk remaining in the country, but abundance of bears, deers, panthers, wolves, wild cats, and a vast number of turkies and other small game. Mr. Ellison stated that he might safely affirm that he had killed more than one thousand deer, three or four hundred bears, a great many panthers wolves, &c. The wild game was the chief dependence of the first settlers, for subsistence. There were a great many beavers, otters, and other fured animals taken by hunters.

Mr. John Lybrook,—born in Pennsylvania, aged seventy-three,—was too young to recollect when his father moved and settled on New river, at the mouth of Sinking creek, (this was in 1772,) now living in Giles county.

In the year 1774 the Indians commenced their outrages in this neighborhood. The first act of murder was perpetrated by four Indians near his father's house. Mr. Lybrook was then about ten or eleven years old.

About the first of July, my informant and several of his brothers and sisters, and several of Mr. Snydow's children, were at play on the edge of the river. They discovered the Indians approaching. John went to the shore and ran some distance along the margin of the water; but he discovered that an Indian on the bank had got ahead of him. The bank at that place was so precipitous that there was but one point that could be ascended. The Indian stooped to fire at two lads swimming the river, and John took this opportunity to ascend the bank by a narrow channel, worn in it by the feet of wild animals when they used it as a passage to and from the water. He darted by the Indian, who instantly pursued him. After running about one hundred yards, he leaped across a gulley worn by a small stream of water in the bank of the river. It was at least twelve feet wide. At this place the Indian halted, but would not try the leap, but threw a buffalo tug at the boy, which he felt strike his head and back; but the little fellow made his escape, and got safely to the fort at his father's house. Mr. Lybrook stated this fact to the author, and most solemnly declared it was true. Three of the Indians entered the canoe, and killed and scalped five of the children. A sister of my informant, a girl about thirteen years of age, had the presence of mind to turn the canoe (which she was in, with the other children,) stern foremost, whilst the Indians were engaged in killing and scalping their victims, and jumped out and ran. She was pursued by an Indian; her screams attracted the attention of a remarkably fierce dog, which immediately ran with the utmost speed to her relief. The Indian had got so near her, that he extended his arm to seize her; but the dog had approached near enough to save her. He ran so close to her that he threw her down; then seized the Indian by one of his thighs just above his knee, gave a violent jerk, and threw the fellow to the ground. The girl escaped; the dog hung on, tearing at him for a little time; but letting go his hold, he sprang at the fellow's throat. The Indian struck him a violent blow with a war club, and knocked him down. The dog then ran to the canoe and guarded the dead children until the people took them away for burial. The dog refused to follow them, immediately ran off, and raised a most piteous howl. Some of the party went to see what produced the distress of the dog, and found a little boy about six years old, who had been violently struck on the head with a war club, his skull severely fractured, and his brains oozing out and his head scalped. He was brother to my informant. The little fellow breathed about twenty-four hours, and then expired.—The author will take some further notice of Mrs. Lybrook in his next chapter.

Mrs. Margaret Hall—sixty-nine years of age—when ten years old, with a younger sister, and a little daughter of Richard Esty, were taken by a party of Shawnee Indians, on New river. Her mother, three sisters and brother, were killed at the time, and the prisoners taken to the Shawnee towns. The same morning Philip Kavanah was killed, and a young lad fifteen or sixteen years of age taken, named Francis Deny. Mrs. Hall was eighteen years with the Indians, and never returned home until after Gen. Wayne defeated them. Mrs. Hall was transferred by the Shawnees to the Delaware tribe. She was adopted by the Indian chief

Koothumpun, and her sister Elizabeth into the family of Petasue, commonly called Snake. The Indians had a few cattle, and used some milk and butter. Their bread was commonly made of pounded corn meal.— The English however, frequently furnished them with flour, which they usually baked in the ashes. The bread ate very well when fresh. They also made fritters and pancakes. The Shawnee women were far better housekeepers than the Delawares. The Shawnees lived better and more plentifully than the Delawares. A few years before Mrs. Hall returned home, a young Indian chief made love to her, and vehemently urged her to consent to marry him, which she peremptorily refused. He threatened her life if she would not consent. He continued his visits to her, and her foster mother urged her to consent to the match. The young squaws frequently congratulated her on her fine offer. She at length, by continued solicitations of the young chief, became so annoyed that she determined on taking flight to another village, seventy miles off, to which her foster sister and brother had removed. Early one morning she secured a very fine horse, mounted him, and pushed off. She travelled briskly, and reached her destination about sunset; traveling the seventy miles through a trackless wilderness. She found her foster sister, but her brother was out on a hunting excursion. She complained to her foster sister of the treatment she had received, who replied, "I will defend you with my life." The young warrior determined not to be defeated in this way, without another effort to secure her to himself, or take her life. He pursued her immediately, and reached the village to which she had fled, the next day in the afternoon. He soon found where she was, and called on her and told her if she did not immediately consent to become his wife, he would kill her. (Her foster sister stood by her.) She raised her hands and protested that she never would. He made a lunge at her with a long knife, but her sister threw herself between them, and received a slight wound in her side, the point of the knife striking a rib. The girl instantly seized the knife, and wrenching it from his hand, broke the blade and threw it away. They quickly commenced a furious fight, whilst she sat petrified, as it were, with fear. Her sister told her to run and hide herself, exclaiming, "He will kill me and then kill you." She then ran and concealed herself. But the young woman proved too stout for the fellow, gave him a severe drubbing, and drove him off. Her foster brother returned in about a fortnight, from his hunting expedition. She complained to him. He told her not to be uneasy; called him a dog, (the worst epithet they could apply to each other,) and said that if he ever made any farther attempts upon her, he would immediately kill him.— The fellow, however, never annoyed her again. He was some time after killed in Wayne's battle with the Indians. Mrs. Hall's residence is in Giles county, about four miles from the Grey Sulphur springs.

FIRE HUNTING.

. Mr. John Lybrook has been a most enterprising and successful hunter. He stated to the author that he had probably killed three thousand deers, five or six hundred bears, hundreds of panthers, wolves and wild cats; and an innumerable number of turkeys and small game.—

When he was about thirteen years of age, his father's dog treed a panther of enormous size. He came to the house and took down a rifle. His mother asked nim what he was going to do with the gun. He replied that he was going to see what the dog had treed. She remarked that it was probably a panther, and charged him, if it was, not to shoot at it, but to get his father to shoot it; adding, if he wounded it and did not kill it, it would tear him to pieces. He soon discoversd that it was a huge panther, standing at full length on a large limb of the tree, about twenty feet from the ground. He knew himself to be a sure marksman, and would not forego the temptation of firing at so fine a mark. Disobeying his mother's injunction, he took deliberate aim at his side a little behind the shoulder; and the ball passed through the animal's heart, and it fell dead. His mother was near scourging him for disobeying her orders; but he acquired great credit from his father and the neighborhood generally, for his bravery and firmness. It was the largest animal of the kind ever known to be killed in that part of the country. It measured upwards of fourteen feet from the end of the nose to the end of the tail.*

The author had frequently heard that the western people, in early times, practiced what they called "fire hunting," but never knew exactly what it meant, until Mr. Lybrook explained it to him. The hunters made stone hearths in one end of their canoes, on which they would raise large pine lights in the night, and set their canoes to floating down the stream. The deers usually collected in considerable numbers in the rivers, in order to feed on the moss which grew in them. As the light approached near the deer, it would would raise its head, and stare at it; and its eyes would shine as bright as diamonds. When the shining of the eye was seen, the hunter would consider himself near enough to shoot. Thousands and thousands of deer were killed in this way.

In 1778, grain grew scarce at the fort. Old Mr. Lybrook and the Snydows had several parcels of wheat standing in the stack, at their respective farms. Ten men were sent to thresh out the wheat. Mr. Lybrook, about fifteen years of age, was directed to take charge of the pack horses, to convey the wheat to the fort. (Preston's fort, about fifteen miles distant.) Two men were sent with him. When they reached the wheat yard, the threshers had left, and gone to his father's house or fort, and they (Mr. L. and the other two,) went there also. Mr. L. discovered a party of Indians on a high hill, who also discovered Mr. L. and his companions, and attempted to intercept them. They had to use great ingenuity and caution to elude the enemy, but got safe to the fort and gave information of the Indians skulking in the woods.

A brave and active man by the name of Scott, went out and killed one of the Indians, and the others immediately took to flight.

In the year 1775, peaceable times were had with the Indians. But in 1776, they recommenced their warfare, and continued with unabated fu-

---

* The author would not have ventured to state this fact, lest it might be suspected that he is disposed to deal in the relation of marvellous stories. But he related this story to Col. Welton, on the South branch, in Hardy county, who stated that he had himself killed one of enormous size.

ry until 1780. The white people had extended their settlements considerably to the west of New river; this afforded some protection to the settlers in this section; but the enemy would once in a while sculk into the neighborhood, commit murders and robberies, and steal horses, and then push off. This state of things continued for several years after the year 1780.

Mr. Lybrook, after his well managed trip for the conveyance of the wheat to the fort, was almost every year appointed * an Indian spy, and after he grew to manhood, he served regularly for three years in that capacity. His brother Philip and a Mr. Philips generally served with him. It was an arduous and dangerous service, but they were fortunate enough never to get hurt by the enemy.

The last time the hostile Indians were known to be in Greenbrier county, was in the summer of 1793. Three Indians came into the settlement, stole several horses, and attempted to make their escape.†

Matthew Farly, an intrepid hunter, raised ten men and pursued them. He came in sight of their encampment late in the evening, halted and remained until early next morning. Farly divided his men into two parties, and directed that each should fire separately at an Indian. Two of them had risen, and setting quietly; the third was lying down. When the whites approached near enough to fire, each party singled their object, fired, and the two Indians were killed; the third sprang to his feet, and ran up the side of the hill. Farley having reserved his fire, seeing the fellow endeavoring to make his escape, fired at him, and broke his thigh. He fell, rolled down the hill, and cried out "Enough, I give up." Farly was desirous of saving his life, but Charles Clay and others, whose friends had been massacred by the Indians, rushed upon him and dispatched him.

The Executive of Virginia rewarded this little company of men by paying for their tour of service.

The author was informed that in the year 1795, there was an outrage committed on the property of a farmer in Greenbrier county—charged to the Indians. The dwelling house, (in the absence of the family,) and a new wagon which was drawn up close to the house, were both set on fire and consumed together. But it is more probable that it was the work of incendiaries, who had first robbed the house, and then fired it with a view to conceal their villainy. Every Indian warrior was called home in the spring of 1794, when it was known that Gen. Wayne was preparing to invade their country with a powerful army. The Indians concentrated all their forces for their own defence, and after their decisive defeat by Wayne, immediately entered into a treaty, which put a final end to further hostilities by the savages in Western Virginia.

Col. Stuart, the clerk of Greenbrier court, expressed this opinion to the writer.

During the period of Indian hostilities, four Indians came into the settlement on the head of the Wappatommaca. They were said to belong to

---

* Near the mouth of Indian Creek, a branch of Greenbrier.
† The Indians were overtaken on the meshes of Cole rivet.

a tribe then at peace with the whites. One of them objected to traveling down the South branch fork, saying they would be in danger. The other three laughed at him. He separated from them, and took down the North fork. The three were pursued by white men, and killed on Mill Creek; the fourth was seen by a negro man belonging to Cunningham, and pursued seven or eight miles. As he was crossing the river, the negro fired at him. He fell into the water, but immediately sprang up and made his escape. His blanket was folded up, and placed on his back; the ball struck the blanket, and penetrated through several folds, but remained in it. When the Indian reached his tribe, he unfolded his blanket, and the bullet was found in it.

The men who committed the murder were apprehended and ordered to jail, but their neighbors raised a party of men, and rescued the prisoners, and set them at liberty. They were never brought to trial for the offense. The father of my informant was one of the party who effected the rescue.

APP'S VALLEY.

This valley is situated in the county of Tazewell, and took its name from Absalom Looney, a hunter, who is supposed to have been the first white man that explored it. It is about ten miles long, and generally about fifty rods wide. There is no stream of water running along it, nor across it. The branches that come down the mountain hollows, and the springs, all sink at the edge of the flat land and rise in a large spring at the lower end of the valley. When first visited by the white man, it was overgrown with the crab-apple, plum, and thorn, and covered with the most luxuriant herbage; affording the finest range for stock, and abounding with game.

In the autumn of 1775, Capt. James Moore removed with his family from Rockbridge county to this valley, having cleared some land the preceding spring, and raised a crop of corn. A short time afterwards, his brother-in-law, Robert Poage, settled near to him in the same valley.— The place was exceedingly secluded, and these two families were ten or twelve miles from any other settlement of whites. As this had been a favorite hunting ground of the Indians, they often visited it. Indeed, there was scarcely a year in which these families were not compelled to leave the valley and take shelter in a fort in the Bluestone settlement.

In the spring of 1782, the Indians attacked the house of Robert Poage at night. They burst the door open, but finding that there were several men in the house, (there happened to be three besides Mr. Poage,) they did not attempt to enter the house, but after watching it for some time, went off; and the next morning killed a young man by the name of Richards, who had been living for some time at Capt. Moore's. He had gone out early in the morning to put some deerskins to soak in a pond about a quarter of a mile from the house; and whilst engaged at the pond, he was shot and immediately scalped. At this time the families forted again in the Bluestone settlement; and soon afterwards Mr. Poage removed to Georgia.

*R

In Sept. 1784, the Indians again excited great alarm. The first that was known of their being in that part of the country, was the capture of James, one of Mr. Moore's sons. After breakfast, his father sent him to bring a horse from a waste plantation about two miles from where he lived. Accustomed to go about alone, and being out often after night, he was a fearless lad. But on this occasion, he had scarcely got out of sight of his father's house, before a most distressing panic came over him. At one time he determined to return, but feared his father's displeasure. When he got near the field where the horses were, three Indians sprang out from behind a log near his path and captured him at once. They then endeavored to catch some of the horses, but failing in this, they started with their captive to the Shawnee towns, situated on the head waters of Mad river, in Ohio.. This journey occupied about twenty days. Soon after reaching the towns, James was sold by the Indians who had captured him, to his sister, for an old horse. By her he was sent with a party of the tribe on a winter hunt, in which he suffered great hardships from hunger and exposure. In the following spring, at a great dance held at a town near to the one in which he lives, he was purchased by a French trader for fifty dollars, paid in goods.. The Frenchman was induced to purchase him, from seeing in the captive lad a striking likeness to one of his own sons. By Mr. Ariome and his wife James was treated as a son. At the time when he was sold by the Indians, James got an opportunity to communicate to his father, through a trader from Kentucky, intelligence of his release from the Indians, and that he had gone to the neighborhood of Detroit. This intelligence gave rise to hopes of seeing him again—hopes which but two of the family realised. And when they met him, it was at a place and in circumstances very different from what they had anticipated.

In 1785, the valley was again visited by the Indians. On the morning of the 14th of July, a party of between thirty and forty, led to the place by one of those who had captured James, attacked and destroyed Mr. Moore's family. At the time when it was broken up, Capt. Moore's family consisted of his wife, (who before marriage was a Miss Poage, of Rockbridge county,) seven children, an old English servant by the name of Simpson, Martha Evans, who was assisting Mrs. Moore, and two men hired as laborers. On that morning these men had gone out to reap wheat; and Mr. Moore was engaged about breakfast time in salting some horses that had come up from the range, and was some distance from the house. The Indians who had been watching in a grain-field about two hundred yards from the house, raised the war whoop, and rushed on. Capt. Moore ran towards the house, but seeing that the door was closed, and that the Indians would reach it as soon as he could, he ran across the small lot in which the house stood, but when he got on the fence he stopped, and was shot with seven balls. He then ran about fifty yards and fell. The Indians told one of the captives afterwards, that he might have escaped if he had not halted on the fence. Mrs. Moore and Martha Evans barred the door on the first alarm. The old Englishman, Simpson, was also in the house, and there were five or six rifles.— Martha Evans took three of them up stairs to Simpson, and called to him to shoot. He was in a bed; and on lifting the clothes, she saw that he had been shot in the side of the head, and was dying. There were two large fierce dogs that fought the Indians at the door until they were shot down. The door was soon cut down with the tomahawk. Three children were killed before the house was forced—two at the place where Mr. Moore was salting the horses, and one in the yard near the house. The prisoners were Mrs. Moore, John, Polly, Jane and an infant, and Martha Evans. Whilst the Indians were cutting down the door, Martha and Polly lifted a loose plank in the floor and got under it, taking the infant with them. It however began to cry, and Polly unwilling to set it out alone, went out with it. Martha remained concealed until after the house had been plundered and set on fire, and whilst the attention of the Indians was taken up in dividing the spoil, she slipped out at a back way and secreted herself under a log which lay across a branch not far from the house. A short time before they left the place, a stragling Indian seated himself on the log and began to work with the lock of his gun. She supposing that he saw her, and was going to shoot her, came out and gave herself up.

After plundering the house of everything that they chose to take, and setting all the buildings on fire, the Indians started for their towns, which stood near the place on which the town of Chilicothe now stands. John was sick and unable to travel, and was killed with the tomahawk on the first day; and the infant becoming fretful, was killed on the second or third day.

The men who were in the harvest field at the time when the Indians attacked the house, immediatdly took to flight and went with all speed to the Bluestone settlement; and in the evening a party of seven or eight men came to the place: but seeing the indications of a large party of Indians— after burying the three children and making a little search for the body of Capt. Moore, but without success, they returned, and an express was sent to Col. Cloyd of Montgomery county, a distance of sixty or seventy miles. He reached the place with a company of thirty-five or forty men, on the fourth day after the disaster. They made no attempt to follow the Indians. After searching for some time they found the body of Capt. Moore, and wrapping it in a saddle blanket, they buried it at the spot where he fell. His death was much regretted. He was a christian, a patriot, and a brave man. In the memorable battle of Guilford, he commanded one of the companies of the Virginia riflemen with great credit.

A short time after the Indians reached their towns with the captives, a war party of Cherokees halted there on their return from an attack on some of the settlements in Pennsylvania, in which they had been unsuccessful, and had lost some of their party. They laid a plan to avenge their loss, by murdering these captives. To accomplish this, they commenced a drunken frolic, taking care to get the Shawnees dead drunk, but to keep in some measure sober themselves. They then accomplished their purpose, when those to whom the captives belonged were unable to protecct them. Mrs. Moore and Jane were massacred. Polly Moore and Martha Evans escaped through the timely care of the squaws belonging to the families into which they had been adopted. When the drinking commenced they suspected the design; and secretly got these two off, and carefully secreted them in a thicket, two or three miles from the towns, until the Cherokees were gone. When they.were brought back, Polly was shown, in a pile of ashes, the half burnt bones of her mother and sister. Whether they had been put to the torture, or whether they had been tomahawked, and then burnt, she never ascertained certainly. The former is the more probable. With an Indian hoe she dug a hole, and gathered the bones out of the ashes as well as she could; and having covered them, rolled a stone over them. She was at the time in the tenth year of her age, an orphan, and an orphan amongst savages. Her comforts were her fellow captive and a copy of the New Testament which she had.— Her parents were pious. They had taught her to love and value the Bible. When the Indians were setting fire to the furniture which they had taken from her father's house, and which they had gathered into a pile in the yard, she saw her copy of the New Testament in it, and stepped up to the pile and took it, and put it under her arm. This she carefully preserved, and the old chief into whose family she had been adopted, often called her to him to read, although he could not understand a word of what he heard. He was kind to her.

In the latter part of the following autumn, a detachment of American troops attacked and destroyed the Indian towns; and burning up their whole stock of winter provisions, reduced them to a state of extreme want. As soon as they could, the Indians set off for Detroit. In the journey they encountered great hardships. The country was an unbroken wilderness, the snow often knee deep, the weather cold, and the game very scarce. Their principal food was the harkberry. They cut the trees down, gathered the berries, and after breaking them in their mortars, made broth of them. In the hardships of this journey, the captives had their full share. Sometime about the middle of the winter,.they reached Detroit; and early in March, Martha was sold, and about the same time Polly was sold, in a drinking spell, for a keg of rum, to a man by the name of Stogwell—an American by birth, but an unprincipled man—a tory, and an unfeeling wretch. Whilst living with him, her sufferings were greater than whilst with the Indians.

In one of Mr. Ariome's trading excursions, James who was with him, met with a Shawnee Indian whom he had known whilst a captive, who informed him of the ruin of his father's family; and late in the winter after Polly had been purchased by Stogwell, he learned where she was.— The following spring Stogwell removed to the neighborhood in which Mr. Ariome lived; and James and his sister met. The writer of this narrative, when he was a lad, has often heard them talk over the scenes of that meeting. What their feelings were, the reader must conjecture.— James lodged a complaint against Stogwell for the cruel treatment of his sister, with Col. M'Kee, the Indian agent at Detroit; and endeavored to obtain her release. In this he was unsuccessful, but it was decided that as soon as an opportunity should offer for her return to Virginia, she should be given up without any ransom; and Stogwell, from motives of policy, became less severe in his treatment. Martha Evans was also living in the same neighborhood, with a kind, independent farmer. These three were often together; and the subject of returning to their friends was often talked over. But serious difficulties were in the way. In the mean-time, the God whose providence had protected them thus far, was pre-paring the way for them.

The father of Martha Evans lived in the Walker's creek settlement, in the county of Giles. After the peace which followed Wayne's expedi-tion, Thomas Evans, his son, determined to find and release his sister, or perish in the attempt. He was an active, athletic young man—a first rate woodsman, cool, fearless and generous. He prepared for his expe-dition by furnishing himself with a good rifle, a full supply of ammuni-tion, a suit of buckskin, and a sufficient sum of money in specie; and set out to seek his sister amongst the savages of the western wilderness. The enterprise was full of hazard, but nothing daunted him. After various perils and unsuccessful attempts to get any tidings of her, he at length heard that she was near Detroit, and made his way thither. In the early part of October, 1797, he set out on his return to Virginia with his sister and James and Polly Moore. The two Moores got a passage in a trading boat down the lakes, about two hundred miles, to the Moravian towns.— There Mr. Evans and his sister met them with three horses. Fortunate-ly for them, a party of these friendly Indians were just starting on a winter hunt. With them they traversed the hunting ground of several tribes less friendly, and were protected in some situations which seemed full of dan-ger. They reached the neighborhood of Pittsburg in the beginning of winter, and remained with an uncle of Thomas Evans until spring. In the early part of spring they reached Rockbridge county, where the Moores met with their younger brother, Joseph, who at the time of the breaking up of his father's family was in Rockbridge, at his grandfather Poage's.

After some years, the Evans family moved to the west. James Moore resides on the tract of land owned by his father, Joseph resides in the same neighborhood. Each of them has raised a large family, and each has been for many years a professing Christian. Polly became a member of the church at an early period, and in 1798 was married to the Rev. Samuel Brown, for many years pastor of New Providence church. Few have lived more generally beloven by a large circle of acquaintances.— She closed her eventful life in the month of April, 1824, in the joyful triumphs of christian faith. Her remains rest beside those of her husband in the grave-yard of New Providence church. She became the mother of elev-en children; of these, one died in infancy and one in early youth. The nine who survive are all professors of religion. Of her seven sons, five are ministers of the gospel in the Presbyterian church; one is a farmer, and the youngest at this time (1837) is at college.—[Prepared for Ker-cheval's Hist. of the Val. by J. M. Brown.]

The author heard from Poage of Rockbridge county, a connection of the young prisoner, some additional circumstances in relation to the in-tended cruel treatment of the prisoner, by the savages. Soon after reach-ing their village, they held a council, and determined that James should run the gauntlet. They, as was their usual practice, placed themselves in two lines, with their scourges, and ordered the prisoner to run between them. James started, and when the first one struck him, he wheeled a-

round and made furious battle on the fellow. All of the Indians immediately gathered around him, patting and caressing him, and pronounced
him a good warrior.

The Rev. Mr. Brown, the author of the foregoing narrative, stated to
the author that he has no recollection of hearing this anecdote; but as
Mr. Poage is a much older man than Mr. Brown, and a man of a highly
respectable character, and could certainly have no motive to induce him
to misrepresent any of the facts connected with this interesting story, the
author has thought proper to give it to the reader, without holding himself
responsible for its truth.

WEYER'S CAVE, IN AUGUSTA COUNTY.

The reader will find a particular description of this grand work of nature in the appendix, written by a gentleman of scientific acquirements,
and is a most graphic account of it. The author of it resides in Staunton. The writer saw and explored this cave in the year 1836.

NATURAL BRIDGE, IN ROCKBRIDGE COUNTY.

Mr. Jefferson has given a most graphical and beautiful description of
this stupendous work of nature.* The author deems it hardly necessary
to attempt any additional description, except in one or two instances.—
The author saw this place for the first time in the month of June, 1819.
He again called to see it in the month of August, 1836. When he first
saw it, he was alone, and had crossed it before he knew he was near it.
He inquired at a house very near to it, and was informed by one of the
inmates that he had just crossed it, who then directed me the way to get
to it. Descending into a deep glen, I had to dismount my horse and
walk up the margin of a fine stream of beautiful clear water, until I approached within seventy or eighty yards of the arch, the view being obstructed by a point of rocks, until within that distance. Passing the
rocks, the most grand, sublime, and I may add, awful sight that I had
ever looked upon, burst suddenly in full view. It was a very clear day,
the sun rather past meridian, and not a speck of cloud or anything to obstruct the sight. The author was so struck with the grandeur and majesty of the scene, as to become for several minutes, terrified and nailed to
the spot, and incapable to move forward. After recovering in some degree from this, I may truly say, agonising mental state of excitement,
the author approached the arch with trembling and trepidation.

After some moments, he became more composed, and wrote the following lines:

> O! thou eternal architect Divine,
> All beautiful thy works do shine!
> Permit me thus to sing:
> Who can this towering arch explore,
> And not thy soverign power adore,
>   Eternal King?

---

* See Jefferson's notes on Virginia, pages 21 and 22, second edition.

A'wed at first sight, my blood was chill'd,
My trembling limbs and nerves all thrill'd
  Beneath this splendid pile.
My mind, howe'er, was soon on flame
To adore the great builder's name,
  Viewing the heavenly smile.*

Did'st thou, O God! this arch uprear,
To make us trembling mortals stare,
  And humbly own thy name?
Or did'st thou build it for thy pleasure,
To prove thy power without measure,
  And spread eternal fame?

Whate'er the motive or the plan,
It far exceeds the art of man;
  The grandeur of the scheme
Shows that the builder lives on high,
Beyond that blue, ethereal sky,
  And wields a hand supreme.

At the author's second visit to this place, he discovered on viewing the arch attentively, the image of a very large eagle, as if it was in full flight, with the image of a lion in chase of it. This sight is near the eastern edge of the arch. The author, however, had heard of those images before he saw them.

There is a story told in the neighborhood, in connection with this most wonderful work of nature, of a very extraordinary performance of one of the young students of Lexington college. Some years ago, several of the students rode out to view the bridge. One of them seeing the name of Washington inscribed in the face of the rock, observed to his companions that he would place his name above Washington's. He ascended the rock, and effected his object; when, looking at the yawning gulf beneath, he was afraid to attempt the descent, and requested his friends not to speak to him; then commenced climbing up the wall.—Some of the young men ran round on the bridge, and placed themselves in a posture to assist him, if he should get within their reach. The young man actually succeeded in getting so near them, that they seized him and drew him up;† but the moment he was on the bridge, from the great bodily exertion, and extreme mental excitement, he fainted, and lay some moments before he recovered.

This individual, in the year 1836, was residing in the village at Wythe court hourse. The author intended to visit him and converse with him on the subject, but was told by a friend that he conversed on the subject with great reluctance. Of course, the author declined his intended visit.

* The view through the arch.
† From the base to the the top of the arch, is two hundred feet perpendicular height.

SALT POND, IN GILES COUNTY.

This is a most beautiful work of nature. There are three mountains* of considerable magnitude, which meet at this place—the several mountains at their terminations forming a considerable chasm ; this affords a receptacle for the water. It presents to the beholder the appearance of a miniature lake of pure transparent water, and is about one mile in length, and generally from one quarter to half a mile in width. From its head to its termination, it lies nearly a north-east course. It is obstructed at its termination with vast piles of huge rock, over which it is discharged.— When this place was first known, the water found passage through the fissures of the rocks. In the year 1804, the remarkable wet spring and summer, which is doubtless recollected by every elderly person, it is supposed the vast quantity of leaves and other rubbish that washed into it, closed up the fissures in the rocks ; immediately after which it commenced rising. An elderly gentleman residing, in 1836, on New river, a few miles from it, (Col. Snydow,) informed the author that it had risen fully twenty-five feet since the year 1804. It is said to produce but few fish, there having been a few fine trout caught in it ; but vast numbers of the water lizard exist in it. Col. Snydow informed the writer that when this place was first known to the white people, vast numbers of buffaloes, elks and deers resorted to it, and drank freely of its waters ; from which circumstance it acquired the name of "Salt Pond." The author tasted the water, but could not discover that it had any saltish flavor.

Col. Snydow also informed the writer, that previous to the rising of the water, a very large spring raised at the head, and supplied the lake with water ; but since its rise, that spring has disappeared, and it is now fed by numerous small springs around its head.

The author recollects seeing, (in a description of this place, published in a northern Magazine, some years ago,) the opinion expressed that this wonderful work of nature had been formed within the memory of man ; but this is doubtless a mistake. Messrs. Snydow and Lybrook both stated to the writer that it existed when the country was first discovered. Col. Snydow particularly, stated that he could recollect it upwards of sixty years, and that it had not increased in length within that period, but had risen as above described.

Near this pool of water stands a wild cherry, which those gentlemen described to be ninety feet high to the first limb, perfectly straight, and not less than five feet in diameter.

THE ROYAL OAK.

This grand and majestic tree is within about one mile of Union, a very sprightly village, the seat of justice for Monroe county. It is of vast height, and is said to be eight feet in diameter. It has acquired the name from its immense size : towering over every other tree in the forest in that section of country.

---

*Peter's mountain, the Salt Pond mountain, and Baldknob mountain.

SOPIS KNOBS.

This is a part of the mountain contiguous to the village, Union; snd is the residence of Alexander Calder, Esq., who has erected a splendid brick dwelling house near the summit of the mountain. It is two miles from the village to Mr. Calder's house, a continued ascent from the village to his house, and considerably steep in places. Of course Mr. Calder's house stands on most elevated ground. Mr. Calder is a resident of Charleston, South Carolina, and has improved this place for his summer residence. The author rode to Mr. Calder's house for the purpose of viewing the splendid works of nature and art combined at this extraordinary place.

Col. Andrew Beirne, the representative in Congress, resides near Union, in Montgomery county, is said to be a man of great wealth, and has erected a splendid brick dwelling house and other fine improvements, on an extensive farm.

Col. Beirne informed the author that a tract of country for more than one hundred miles between Greenbrier county and the Kenawha, was inhabited; that it is very mountainous, but contains a large proportion of fertile lands.

This gentleman also expressed the opinion that it is one of the healthiest regions, both for man and beast, in all North America.

VALUABLE MINERALS.

Our mountains abound in valuable minerals. We have three manganese mines within about twenty miles of Winchester. The price of the article is, however, so much reduced of late years, that there is but little of it taken to market. The author is informed that a rich copper mine has lately been discovered, and a company formed for working it. It is said it yields well. Several lead mines are said to have been discovered, but as yet, they have not been very productive. There have been several coal mines opened, of the anthracite kind, one of which yields well. It is probable that on further research, sufficient quantities may be found to supply this section of country.

The people of our Valley have abundant cause to be humbly thankful to the Great Author of our existence for the blessings he has in his wisdom and benevolence provided for their happiness.

THE END.

INDEX.

Printed in the USA
CPSIA information can be obtained
at www.ICGtesting.com
LVHW012146261223
767492LV00005B/46